# UQ HOLDER!

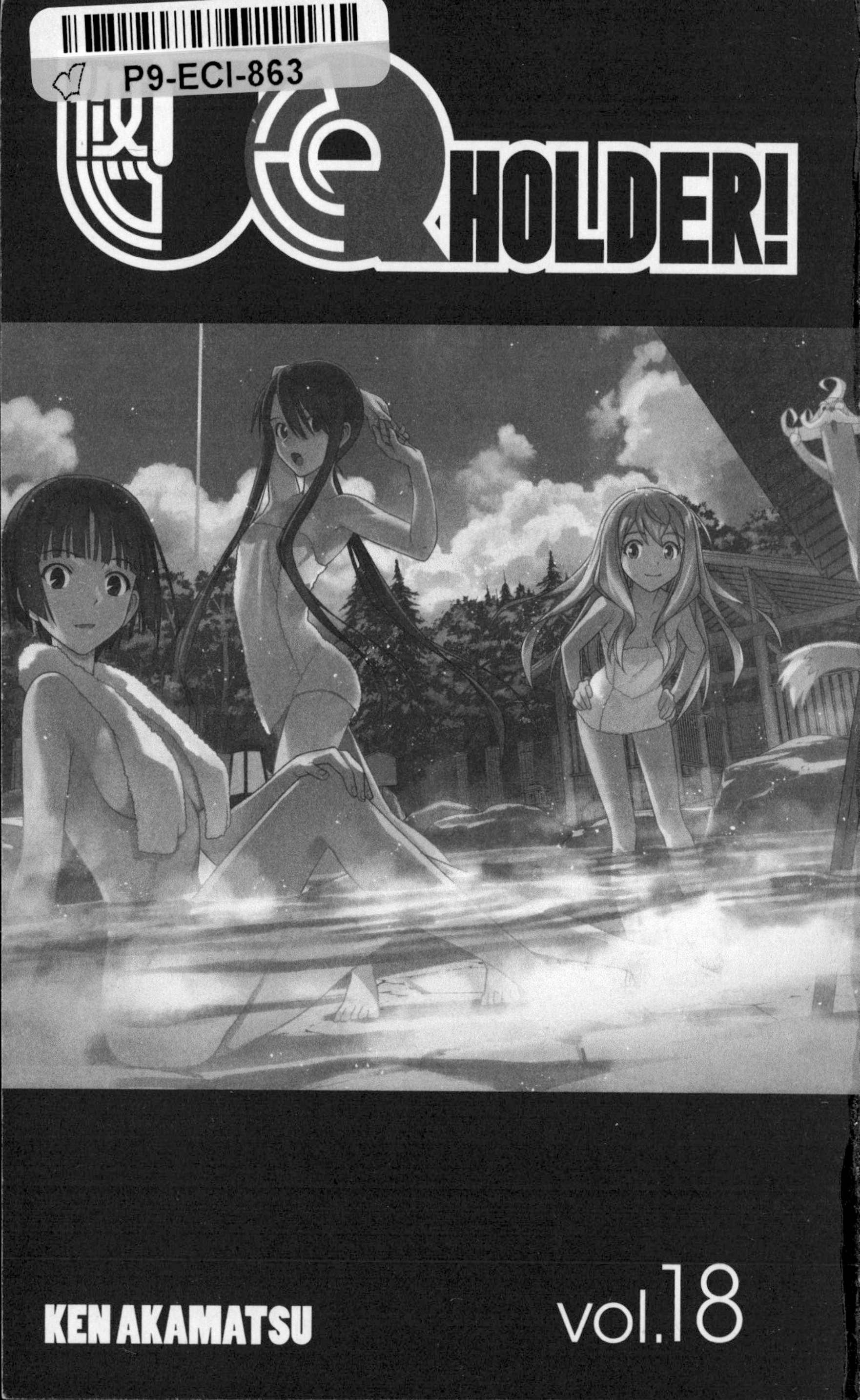

KEN AKAMATSU

vol.18

# CHARACTERS

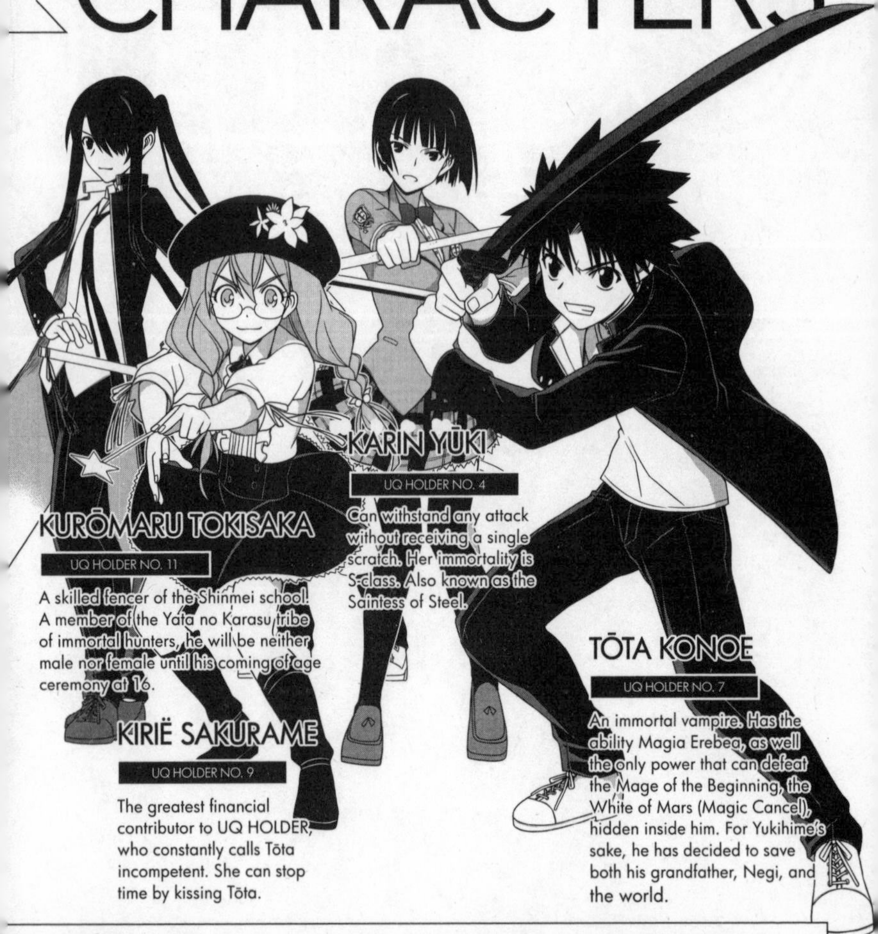

## KURŌMARU TOKISAKA

UQ HOLDER NO. 11

A skilled fencer of the Shinmei school. A member of the Yata no Karasu tribe of immortal hunters, he will be neither male nor female until his coming of age ceremony at 16.

## KIRIË SAKURAME

UQ HOLDER NO. 9

The greatest financial contributor to UQ HOLDER, who constantly calls Tōta incompetent. She can stop time by kissing Tōta.

## KARIN YŪKI

UQ HOLDER NO. 4

Can withstand any attack without receiving a single scratch. Her immortality is S-class. Also known as the Saintess of Steel.

## TŌTA KONOE

UQ HOLDER NO. 7

An immortal vampire. Has the ability Magia Erebea, as well the only power that can defeat the Mage of the Beginning, the White of Mars (Magic Cancel), hidden inside him. For Yukihime's sake, he has decided to save both his grandfather, Negi, and the world.

# UQ HOLDER IMMORTAL NUMBERS

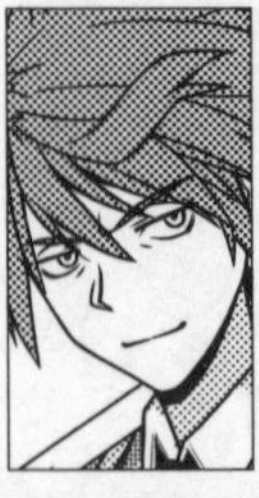

## JINBEI SHISHIDO

UQ HOLDER NO. 2

UQ HOLDER's oldest member. Became an immortal in the middle ages, when he ate mermaid flesh in the Muromachi Period. Has the "Switcheroo" skill that switches the locations of physical objects.

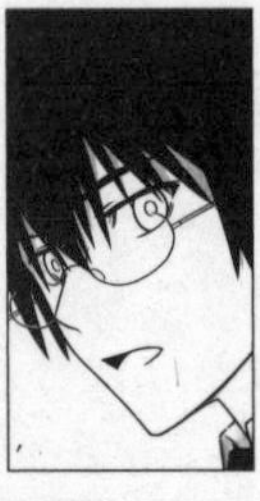

## GENGORŌ MAKABE

UQ HOLDER NO. 6

Manages the business side of UQ HOLDER's hideout and inn. He has a skill known as "Multiple Lives," so when he dies, another Gengorō appears.

# UQ HOLDER!

Ken Akamatsu Presents

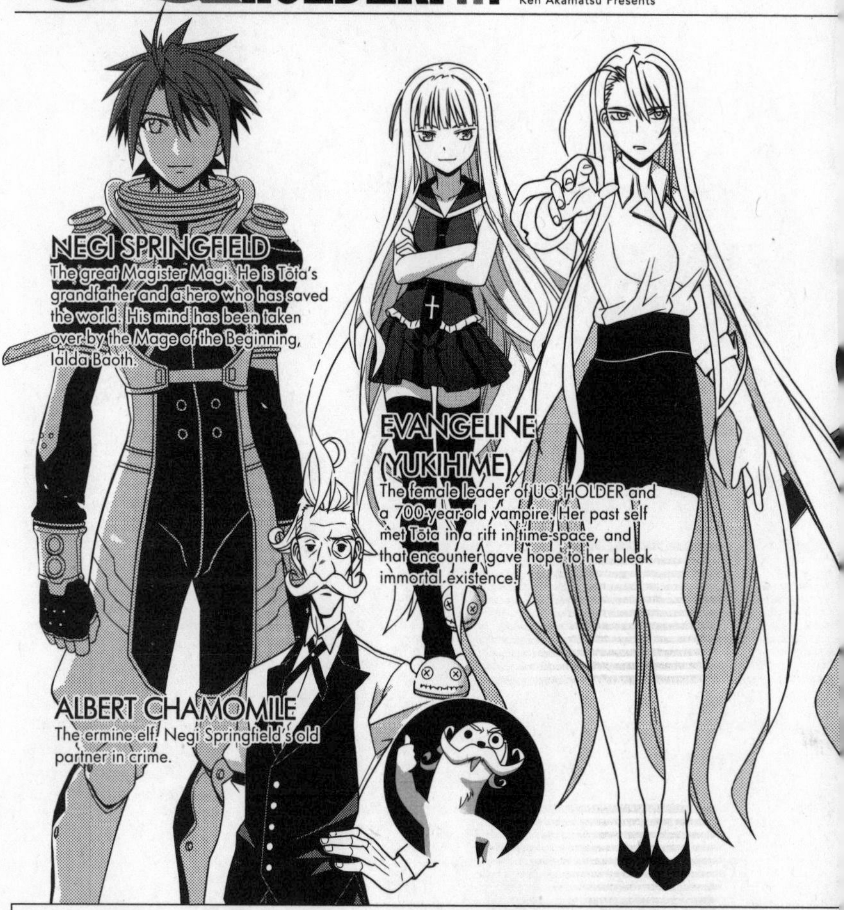

**NEGI SPRINGFIELD**

The great Magister Magi. He is Tōta's grandfather and a hero who has saved the world. His mind has been taken over by the Mage of the Beginning, Ialda Baoth.

**EVANGELINE (YUKIHIME)**

The female leader of UQ HOLDER and a 700-year-old vampire. Her past self met Tōta in a rift in time-space, and that encounter gave hope to her bleak immortal existence.

**ALBERT CHAMOMILE**

The ermine elf. Negi Springfield's old partner in crime.

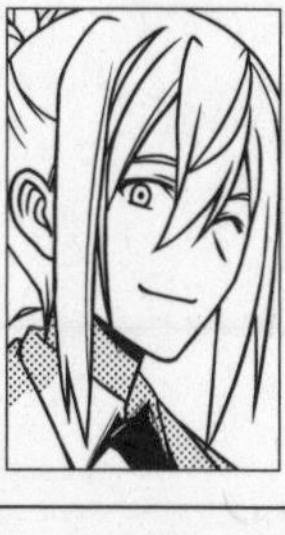

## IKKŪ AMEYA

UQ HOLDER NO. 10

After falling into a coma at age 13 and lying in a hospital bed for 72 years, he became a full-body cyborg at age 85. He's very good with his hands. ♡

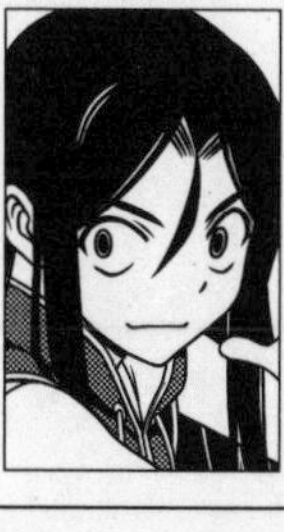

## SANTA SASAKI

UQ HOLDER NO. 12

A revenant brought back to life through necromancy. He has multiple abilities, including flight, intangibility, possession, telekinesis, etc.

# THE STORY SO FAR

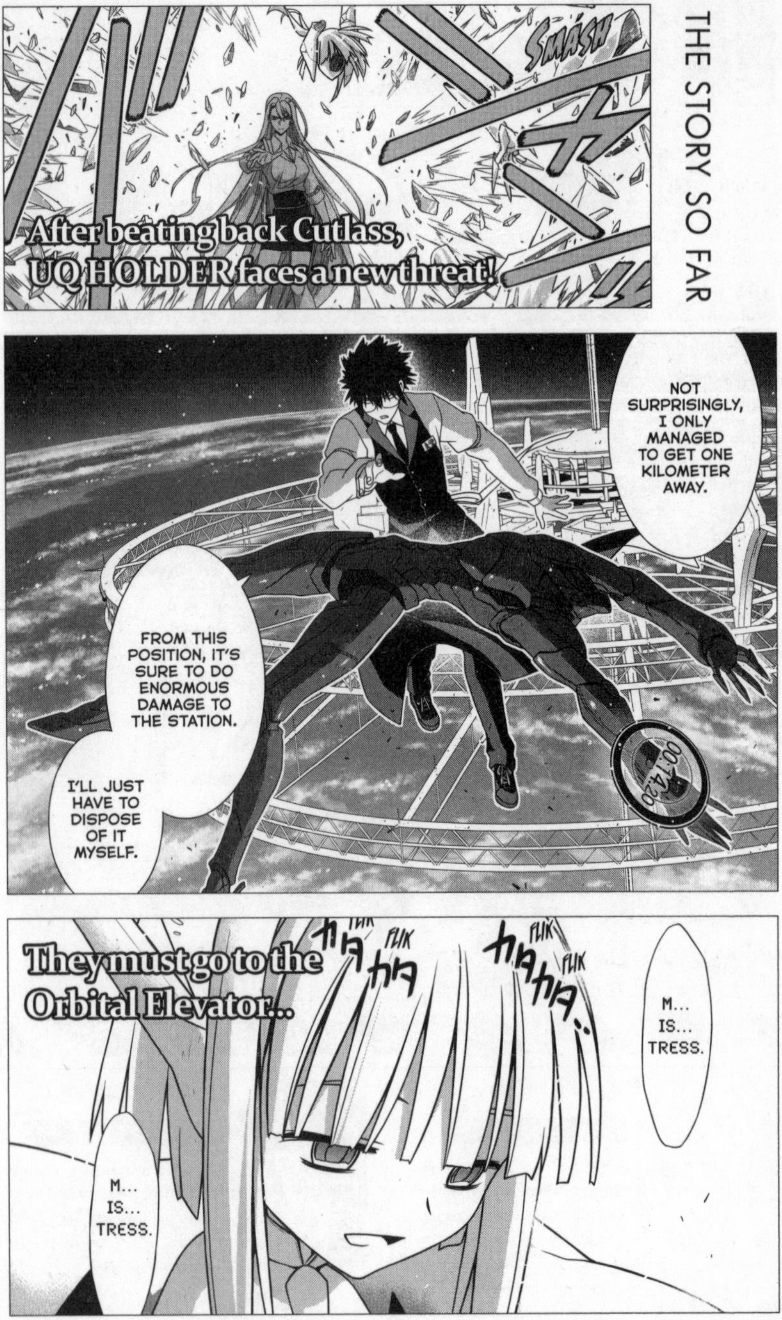
SMASH
After beating back Cutlass, UQ HOLDER faces a new threat!
NOT SURPRISINGLY, I ONLY MANAGED TO GET ONE KILOMETER AWAY.
FROM THIS POSITION, IT'S SURE TO DO ENORMOUS DAMAGE TO THE STATION.
I'LL JUST HAVE TO DISPOSE OF IT MYSELF.
00:14:20
M... IS... TRESS.
FLIK
FLIK
FLIK
FLIK
They must go to the Orbital Elevator...
M... IS... TRESS.

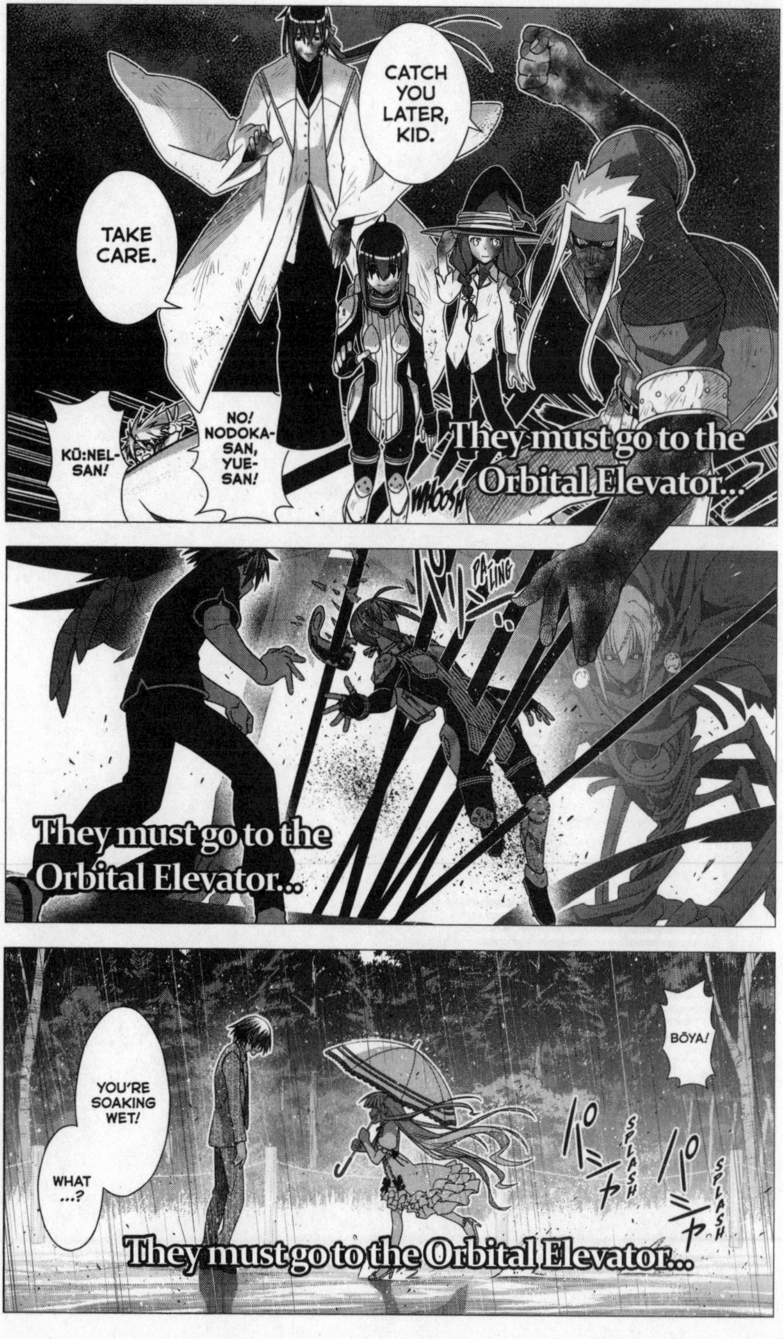

CATCH YOU LATER, KID.
TAKE CARE.
They must go to the Orbital Elevator...
NO! NODOKA-SAN, YUE-SAN!
KŪ:NEL-SAN!
WHOOSH
PA-LING
They must go to the Orbital Elevator...
BŌYA!
パシャ
SPLASH
パシャ
SPLASH
YOU'RE SOAKING WET!
WHAT ...?
They must go to the Orbital Elevator...

# CONTENTS

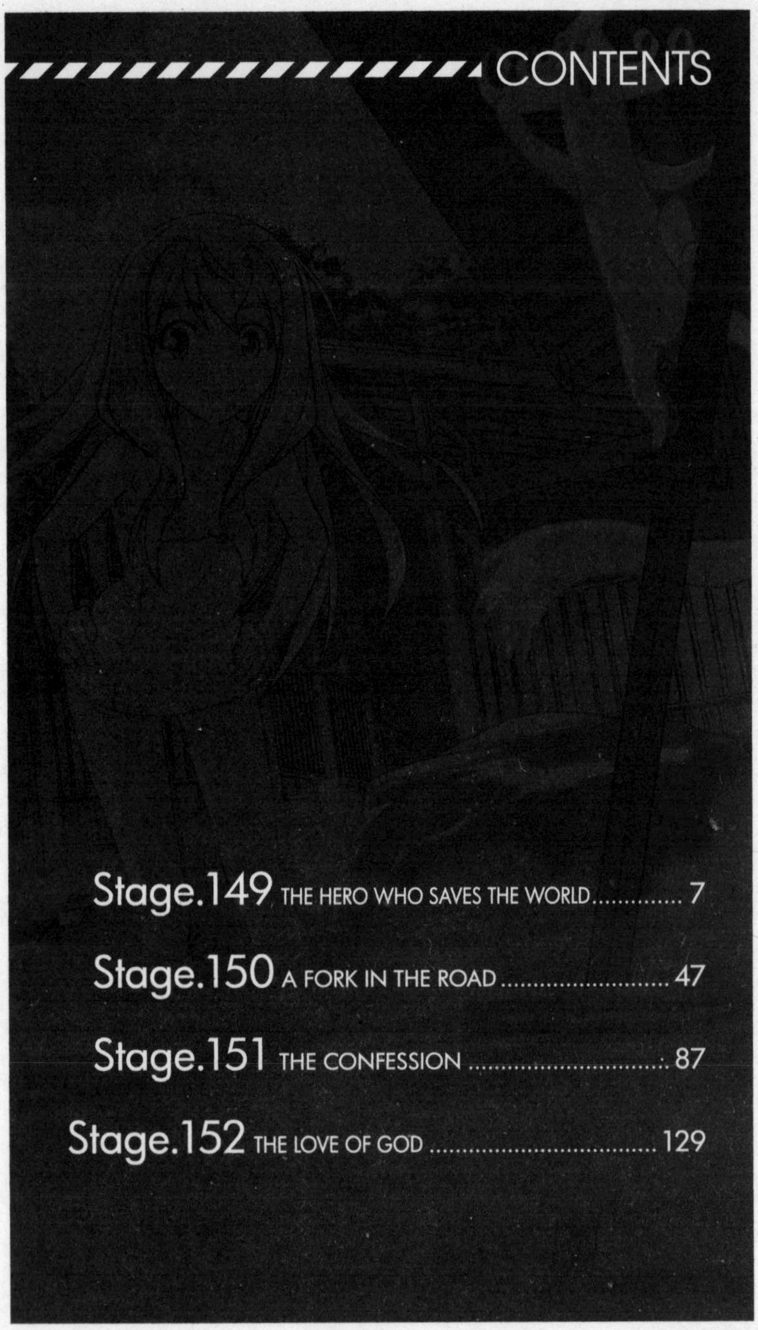

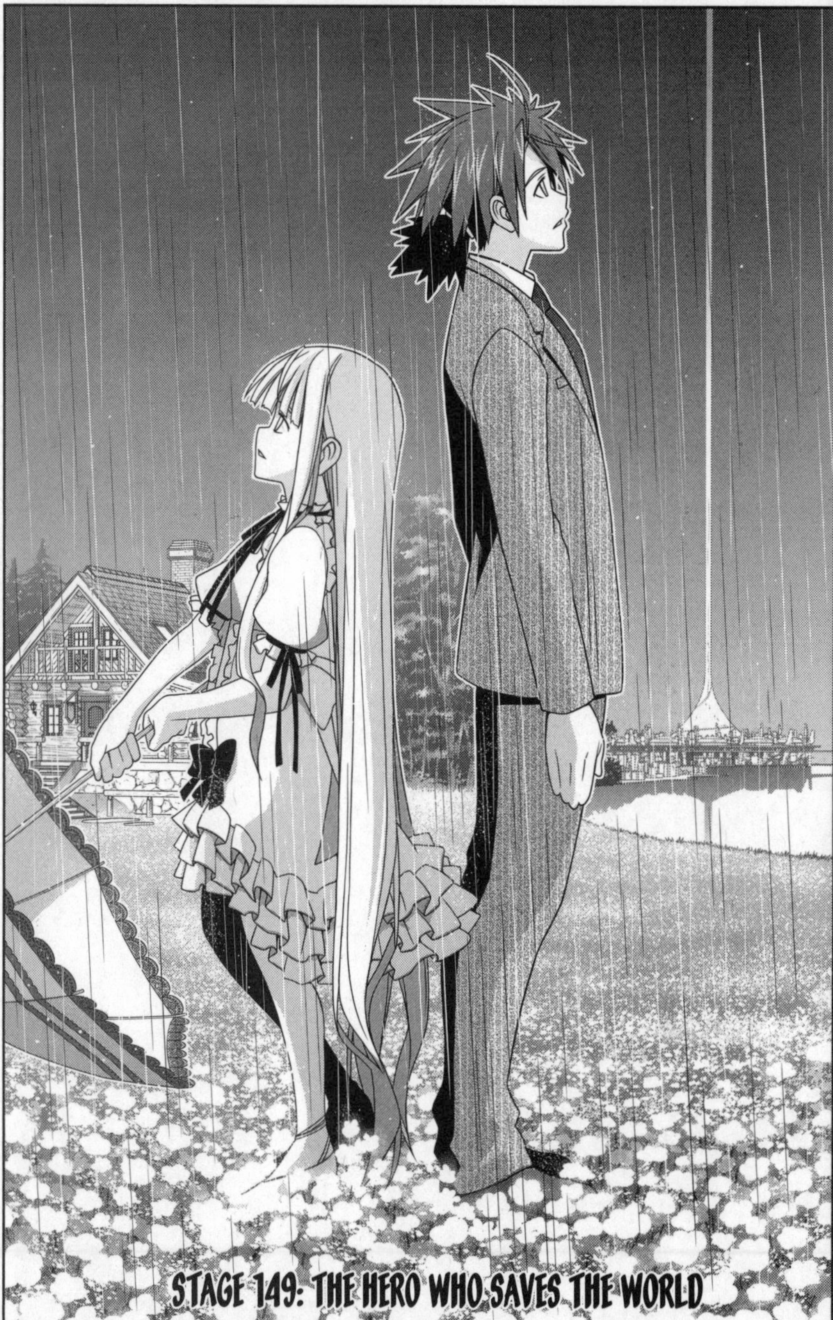
STAGE 149: THE HERO WHO SAVES THE WORLD

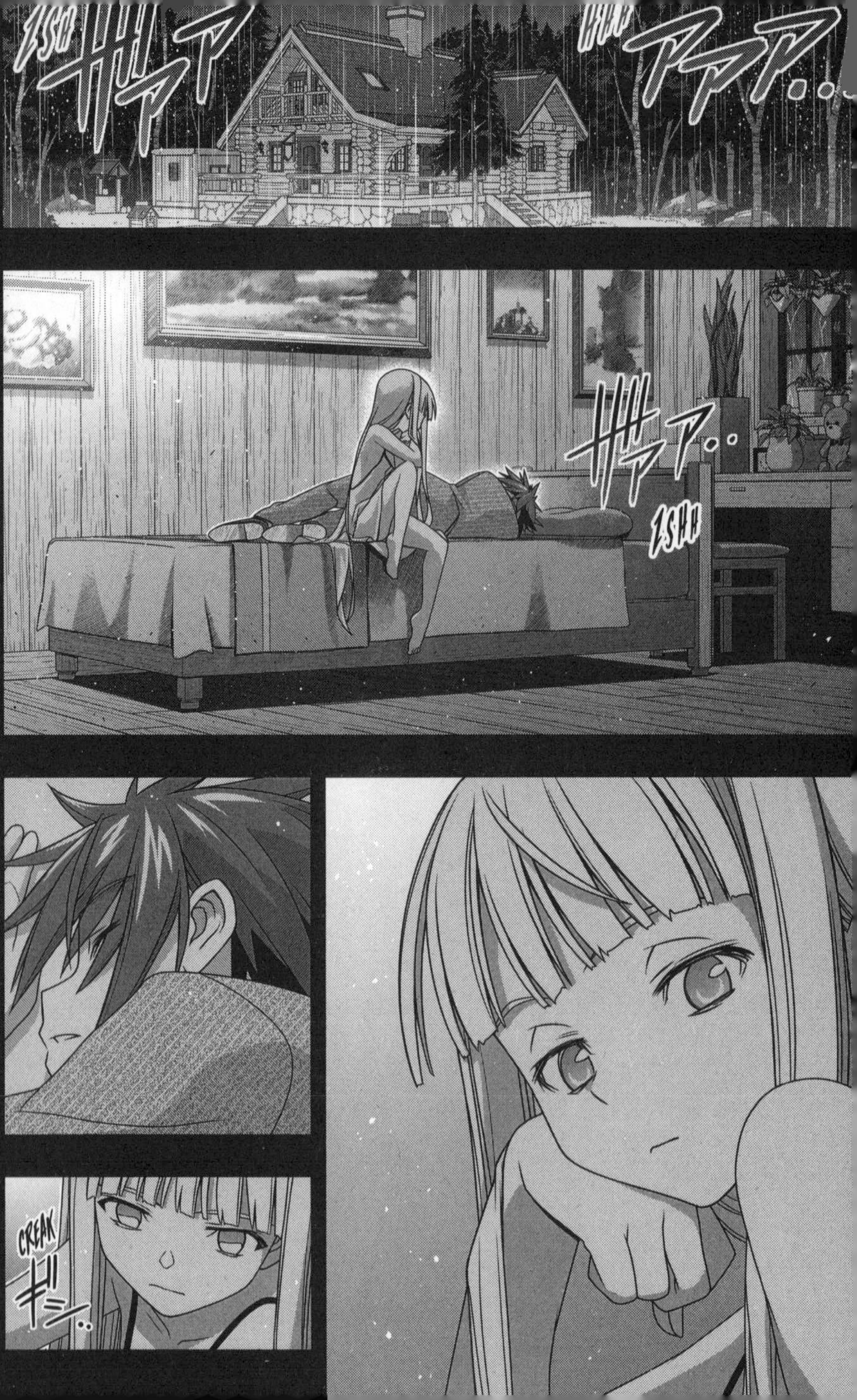
ZSH
ザァア
HHH
アアア...
ザァア..
ZSHH
CREAK
ギシ..

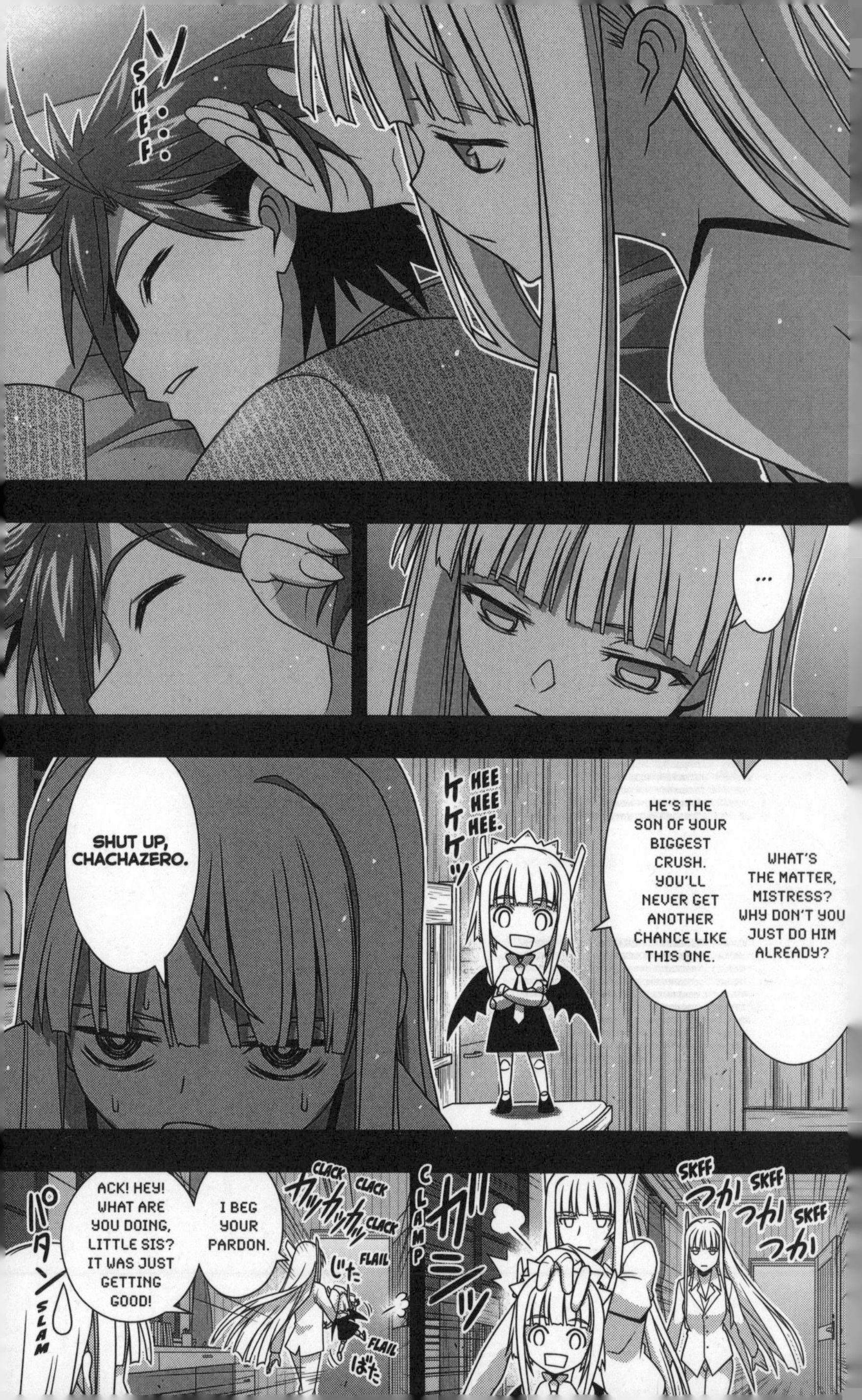
SHFF
...
HEE HEE HEE.
WHAT'S THE MATTER, MISTRESS? WHY DON'T YOU JUST DO HIM ALREADY?
HE'S THE SON OF YOUR BIGGEST CRUSH. YOU'LL NEVER GET ANOTHER CHANCE LIKE THIS ONE.
SHUT UP, CHACHAZERO.
SKFF
SKFF
SKFF
CLAMP
I BEG YOUR PARDON.
CLACK
CLACK
CLACK
FLAIL
FLAIL
ACK! HEY! WHAT ARE YOU DOING, LITTLE SIS? IT WAS JUST GETTING GOOD!
SLAM

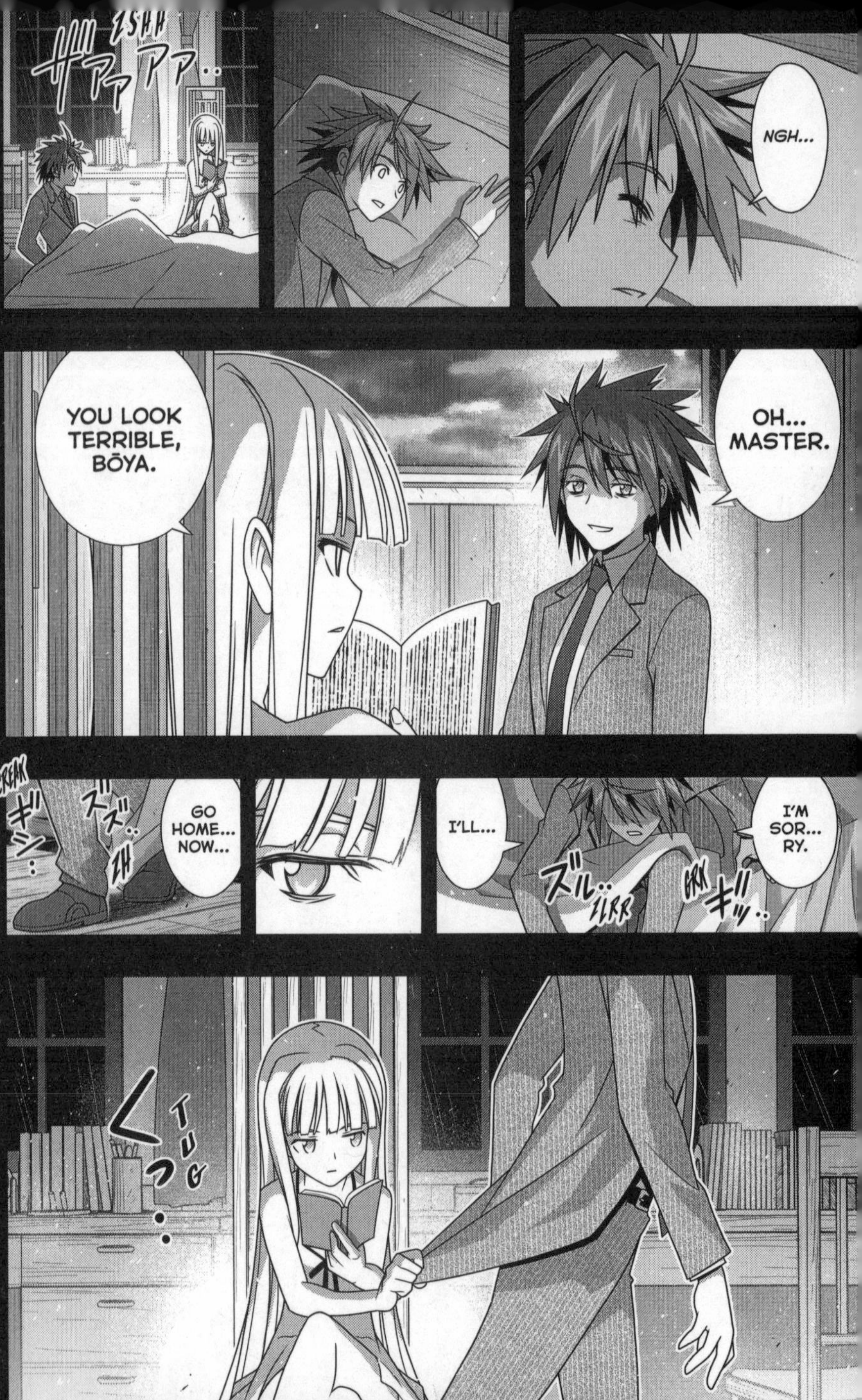
NGH...
ザァァア..
FSHH
OH... MASTER.
YOU LOOK TERRIBLE, BŌYA.
I'M SOR... RY.
ギッ..
GRK
ズル..
ZLRR
I'LL...
GO HOME... NOW...
ズズ..
ZH
ギシ..
CREAK
くっ..
TUG

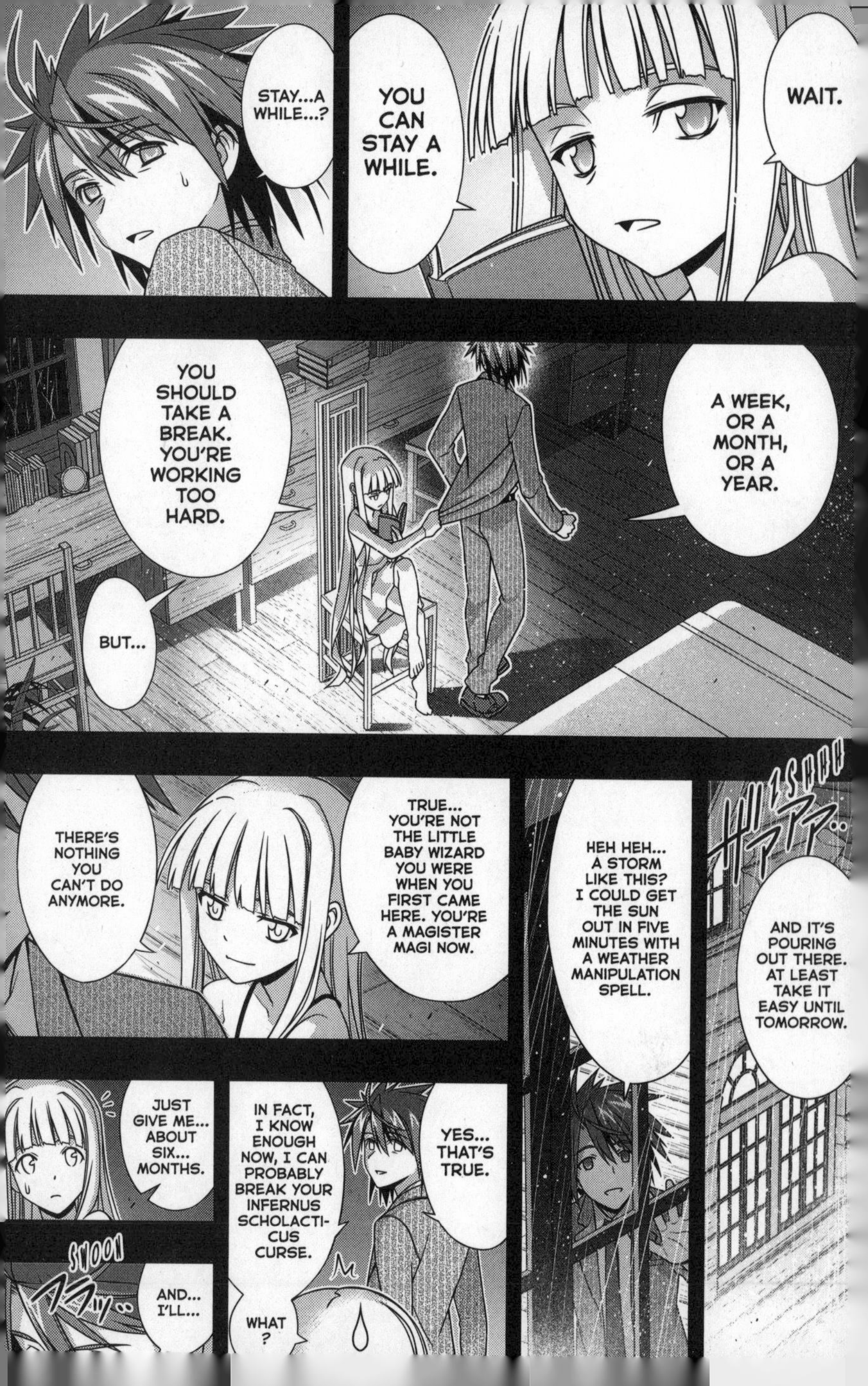
WAIT.
YOU CAN STAY A WHILE.
STAY...A WHILE...?
A WEEK, OR A MONTH, OR A YEAR.
YOU SHOULD TAKE A BREAK. YOU'RE WORKING TOO HARD.
BUT...
ZSHHH
AND IT'S POURING OUT THERE. AT LEAST TAKE IT EASY UNTIL TOMORROW.
HEH HEH... A STORM LIKE THIS? I COULD GET THE SUN OUT IN FIVE MINUTES WITH A WEATHER MANIPULATION SPELL.
TRUE... YOU'RE NOT THE LITTLE BABY WIZARD YOU WERE WHEN YOU FIRST CAME HERE. YOU'RE A MAGISTER MAGI NOW.
THERE'S NOTHING YOU CAN'T DO ANYMORE.
YES... THAT'S TRUE.
IN FACT, I KNOW ENOUGH NOW, I CAN PROBABLY BREAK YOUR INFERNUS SCHOLACTICUS CURSE.
WHAT?
JUST GIVE ME... ABOUT SIX... MONTHS.
SWOON
AND... I'LL...

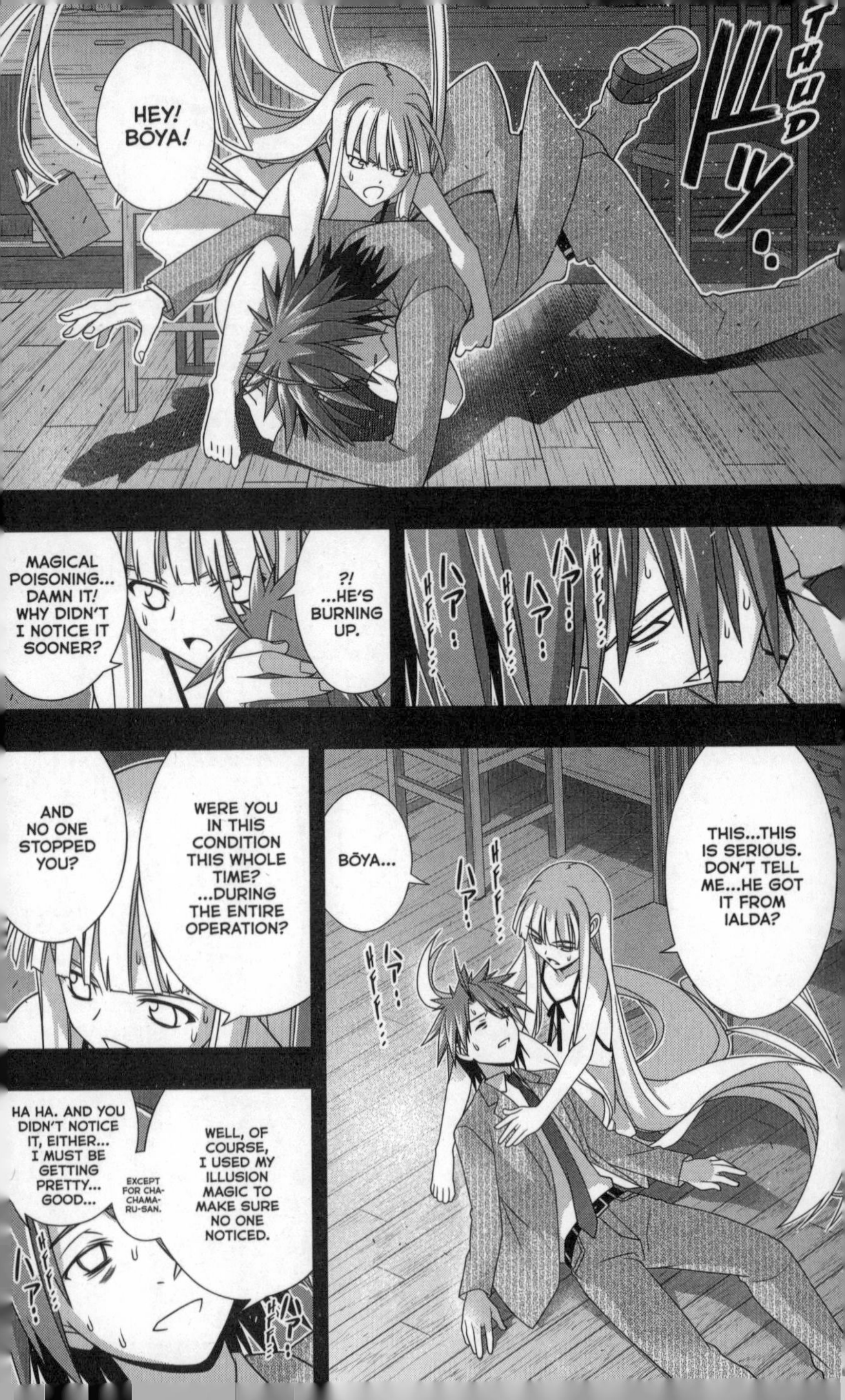
ドッ
THUD
HEY! BŌYA!
ハア・・ HFF...
ハア・・ HFF...
?! ...HE'S BURNING UP.
MAGICAL POISONING... DAMN IT! WHY DIDN'T I NOTICE IT SOONER?
THIS...THIS IS SERIOUS. DON'T TELL ME...HE GOT IT FROM IALDA?
BŌYA...
ハア・・ HFF...
ハア・・ HFF...
WERE YOU IN THIS CONDITION THIS WHOLE TIME? ...DURING THE ENTIRE OPERATION?
AND NO ONE STOPPED YOU?
WELL, OF COURSE, I USED MY ILLUSION MAGIC TO MAKE SURE NO ONE NOTICED.
EXCEPT FOR CHA-CHAMA-RU-SAN.
HA HA. AND YOU DIDN'T NOTICE IT, EITHER... I MUST BE GETTING PRETTY... GOOD...
ハア・・ HFF...
ハア・・ HFF...

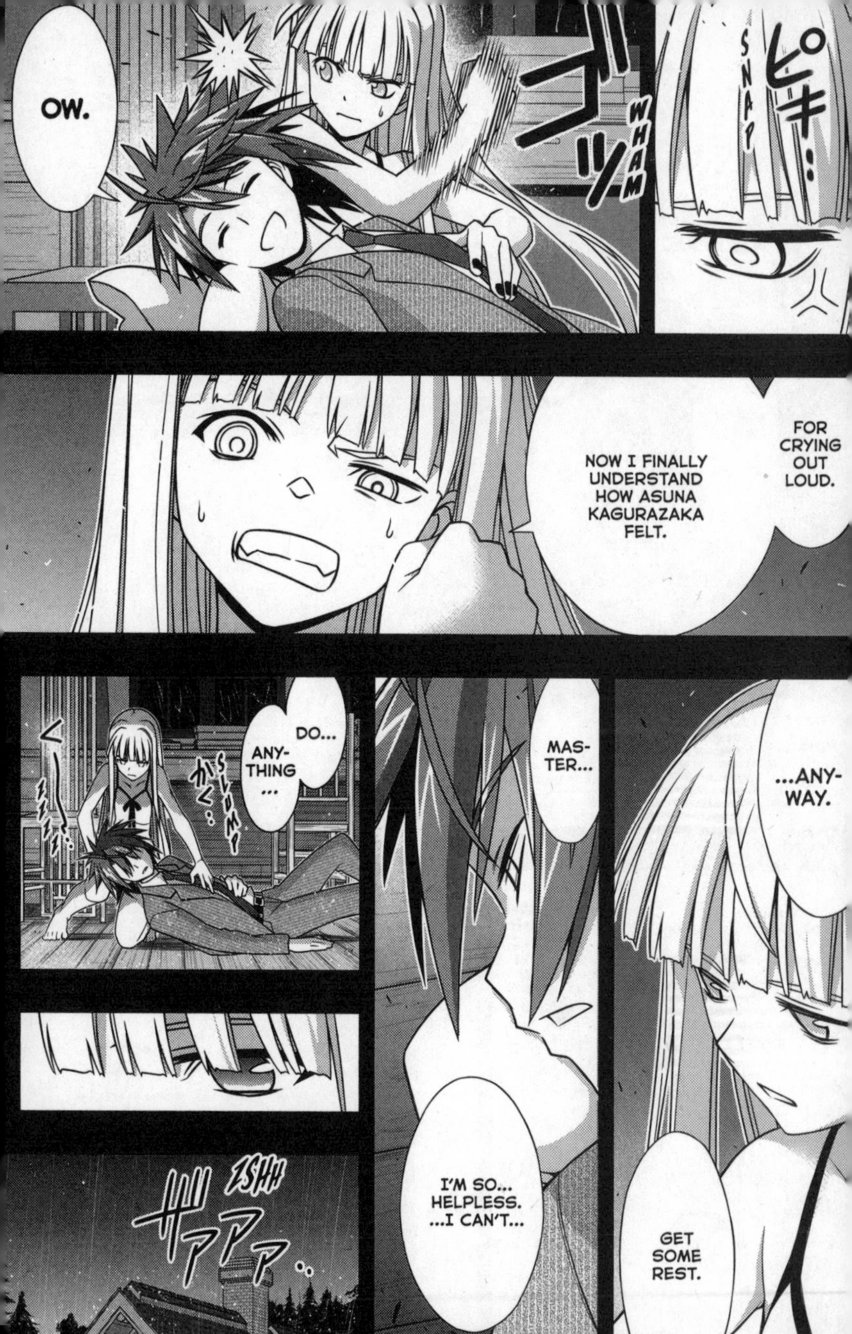
ピキ…
SNAP
ゴッ
WHAM
OW.
FOR CRYING OUT LOUD.
NOW I FINALLY UNDERSTAND HOW ASUNA KAGURAZAKA FELT.
...ANY-WAY.
GET SOME REST.
MAS-TER...
I'M SO... HELPLESS. ...I CAN'T...
DO... ANY-THING...
かくっ..
SLUMP
ザァァァ..
ZSHH

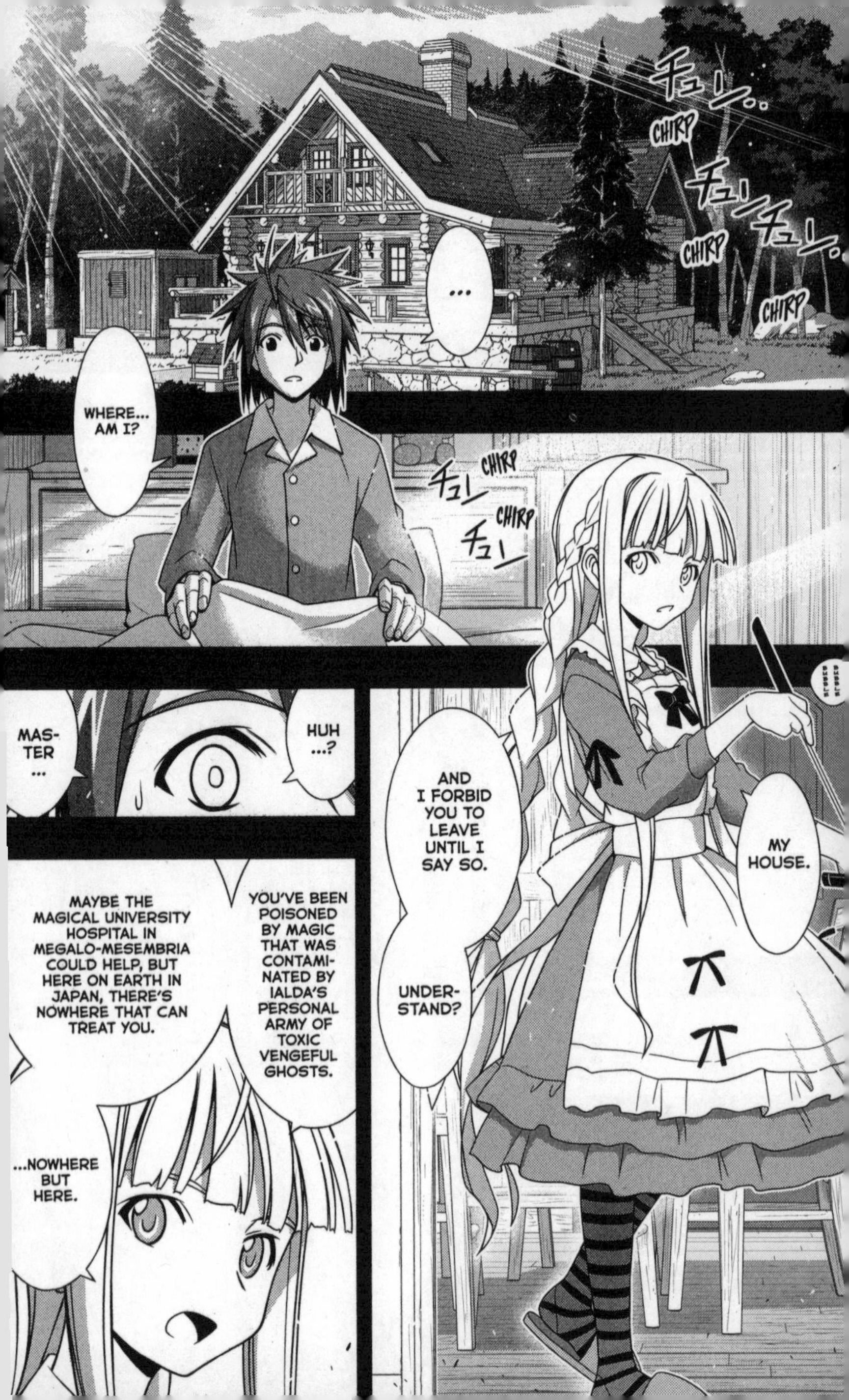
チュン。。
CHIRP
チュンチュン。
CHIRP
CHIRP
...
WHERE... AM I?
チュン
CHIRP
チュン
CHIRP
BUBBLE BUBBLE
MY HOUSE.
AND I FORBID YOU TO LEAVE UNTIL I SAY SO.
UNDERSTAND?
HUH ...?
MAS-TER ...
YOU'VE BEEN POISONED BY MAGIC THAT WAS CONTAMI-NATED BY IALDA'S PERSONAL ARMY OF TOXIC VENGEFUL GHOSTS.
MAYBE THE MAGICAL UNIVERSITY HOSPITAL IN MEGALO-MESEMBRIA COULD HELP, BUT HERE ON EARTH IN JAPAN, THERE'S NOWHERE THAT CAN TREAT YOU.
...NOWHERE BUT HERE.

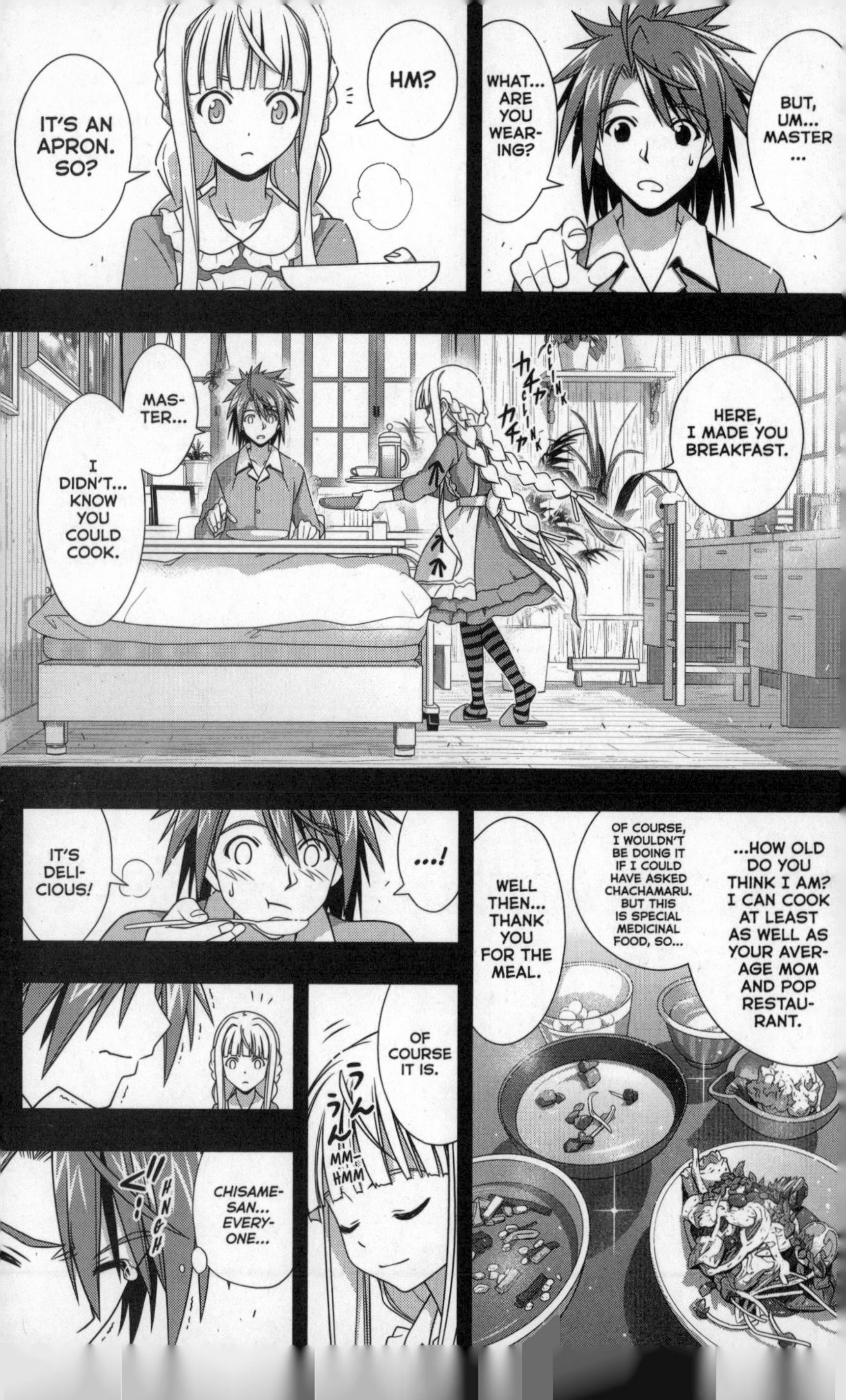
BUT, UM... MASTER ...
WHAT... ARE YOU WEAR-ING?
HM?
IT'S AN APRON. SO?
HERE, I MADE YOU BREAKFAST.
カチャ カチャ CLINK CLINK
MAS-TER...
I DIDN'T... KNOW YOU COULD COOK.
...HOW OLD DO YOU THINK I AM? I CAN COOK AT LEAST AS WELL AS YOUR AVER-AGE MOM AND POP RESTAU-RANT.
OF COURSE, I WOULDN'T BE DOING IT IF I COULD HAVE ASKED CHACHAMARU. BUT THIS IS SPECIAL MEDICINAL FOOD, SO...
WELL THEN... THANK YOU FOR THE MEAL.
...!
IT'S DELI-CIOUS!
OF COURSE IT IS.
うんうん MM-HMM
HNGH
CHISAME-SAN... EVERY-ONE...

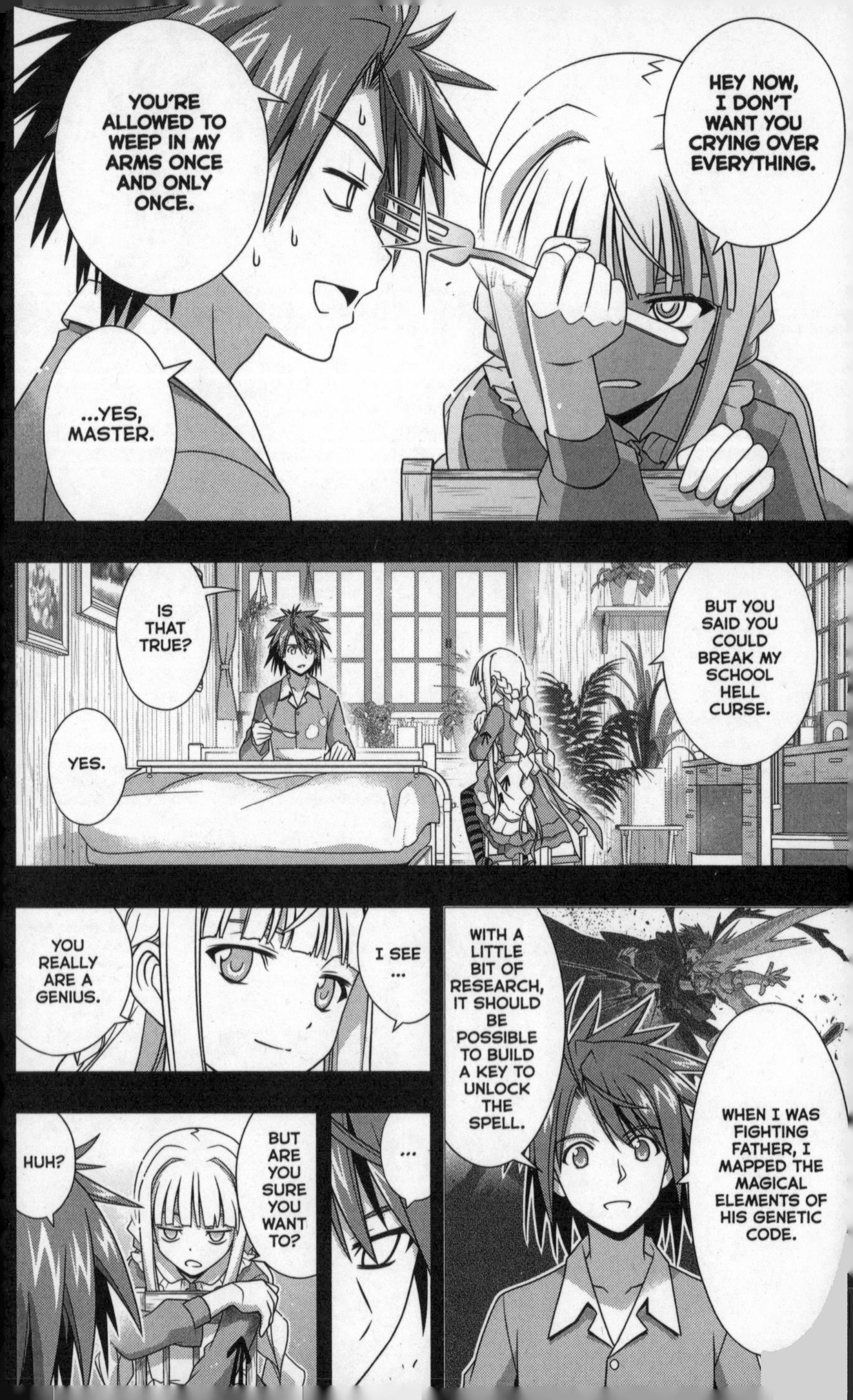
HEY NOW, I DON'T WANT YOU CRYING OVER EVERYTHING.
YOU'RE ALLOWED TO WEEP IN MY ARMS ONCE AND ONLY ONCE.
...YES, MASTER.
BUT YOU SAID YOU COULD BREAK MY SCHOOL HELL CURSE.
IS THAT TRUE?
YES.
WHEN I WAS FIGHTING FATHER, I MAPPED THE MAGICAL ELEMENTS OF HIS GENETIC CODE.
WITH A LITTLE BIT OF RESEARCH, IT SHOULD BE POSSIBLE TO BUILD A KEY TO UNLOCK THE SPELL.
I SEE ...
YOU REALLY ARE A GENIUS.
...
BUT ARE YOU SURE YOU WANT TO?
HUH?

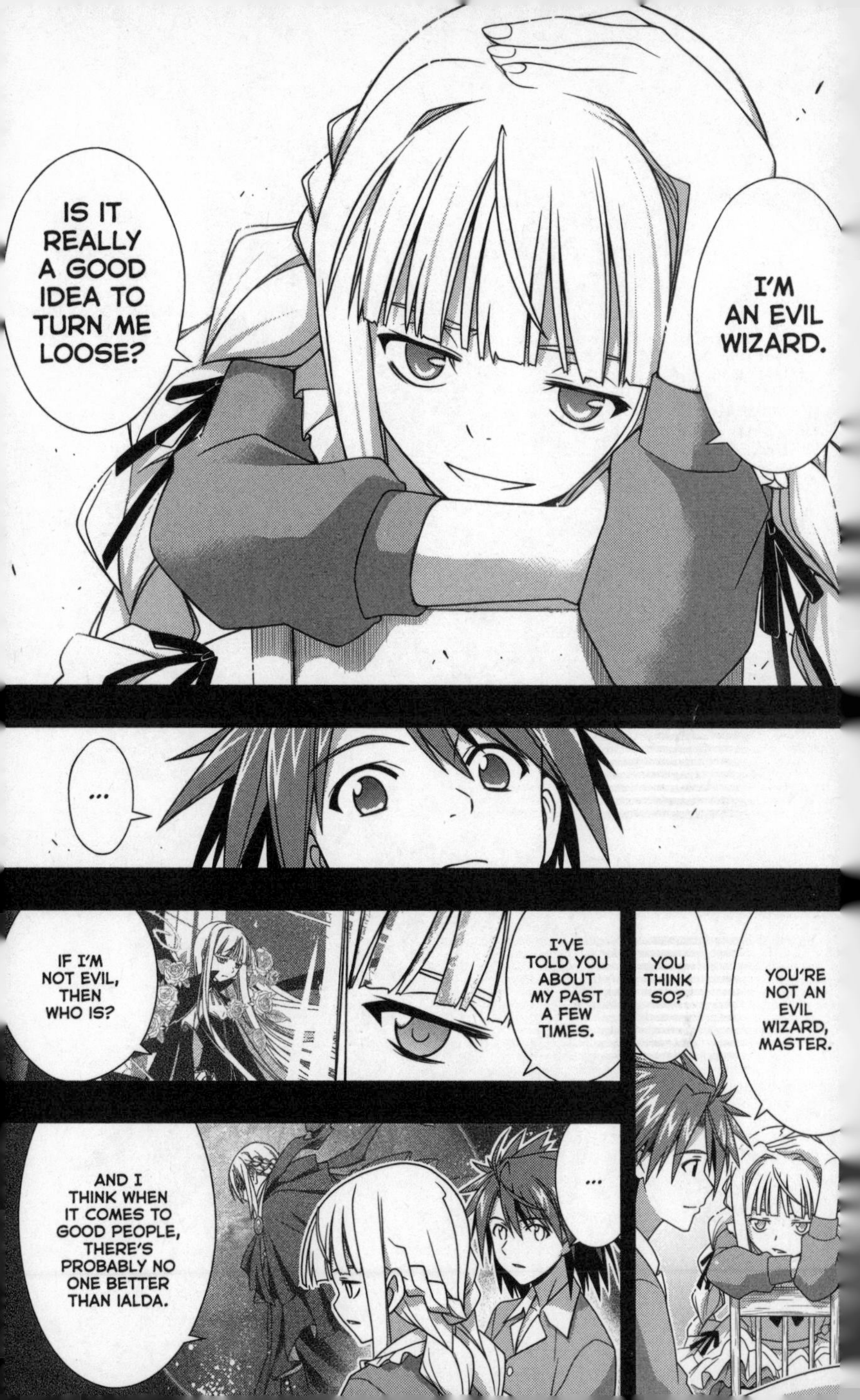
I'M AN EVIL WIZARD.
IS IT REALLY A GOOD IDEA TO TURN ME LOOSE?
...
YOU'RE NOT AN EVIL WIZARD, MASTER.
YOU THINK SO?
I'VE TOLD YOU ABOUT MY PAST A FEW TIMES.
IF I'M NOT EVIL, THEN WHO IS?
...
AND I THINK WHEN IT COMES TO GOOD PEOPLE, THERE'S PROBABLY NO ONE BETTER THAN IALDA.

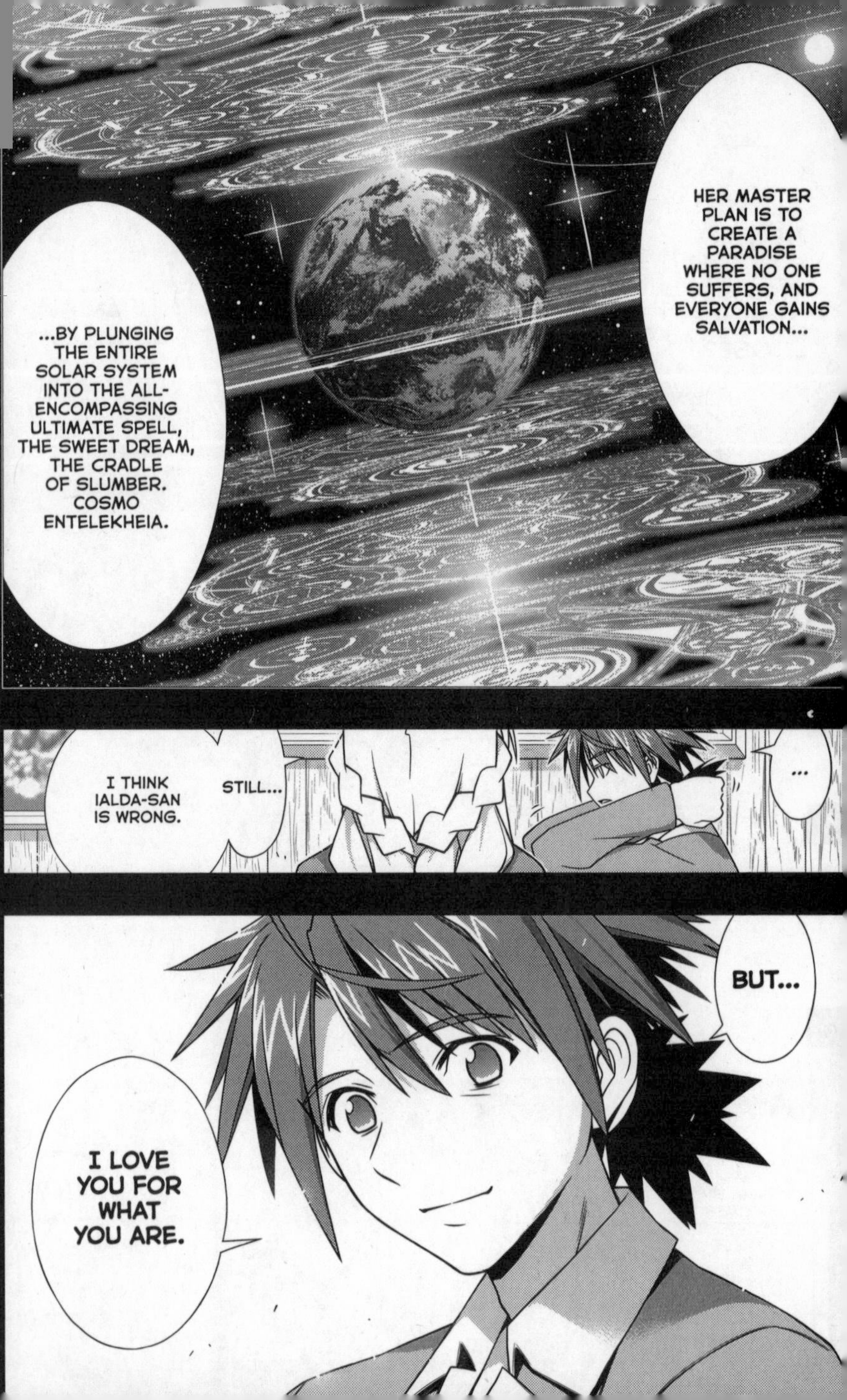
HER MASTER PLAN IS TO CREATE A PARADISE WHERE NO ONE SUFFERS, AND EVERYONE GAINS SALVATION...
...BY PLUNGING THE ENTIRE SOLAR SYSTEM INTO THE ALL-ENCOMPASSING ULTIMATE SPELL, THE SWEET DREAM, THE CRADLE OF SLUMBER. COSMO ENTELEKHEIA.
...
STILL...
I THINK IALDA-SAN IS WRONG.
BUT...
I LOVE YOU FOR WHAT YOU ARE.

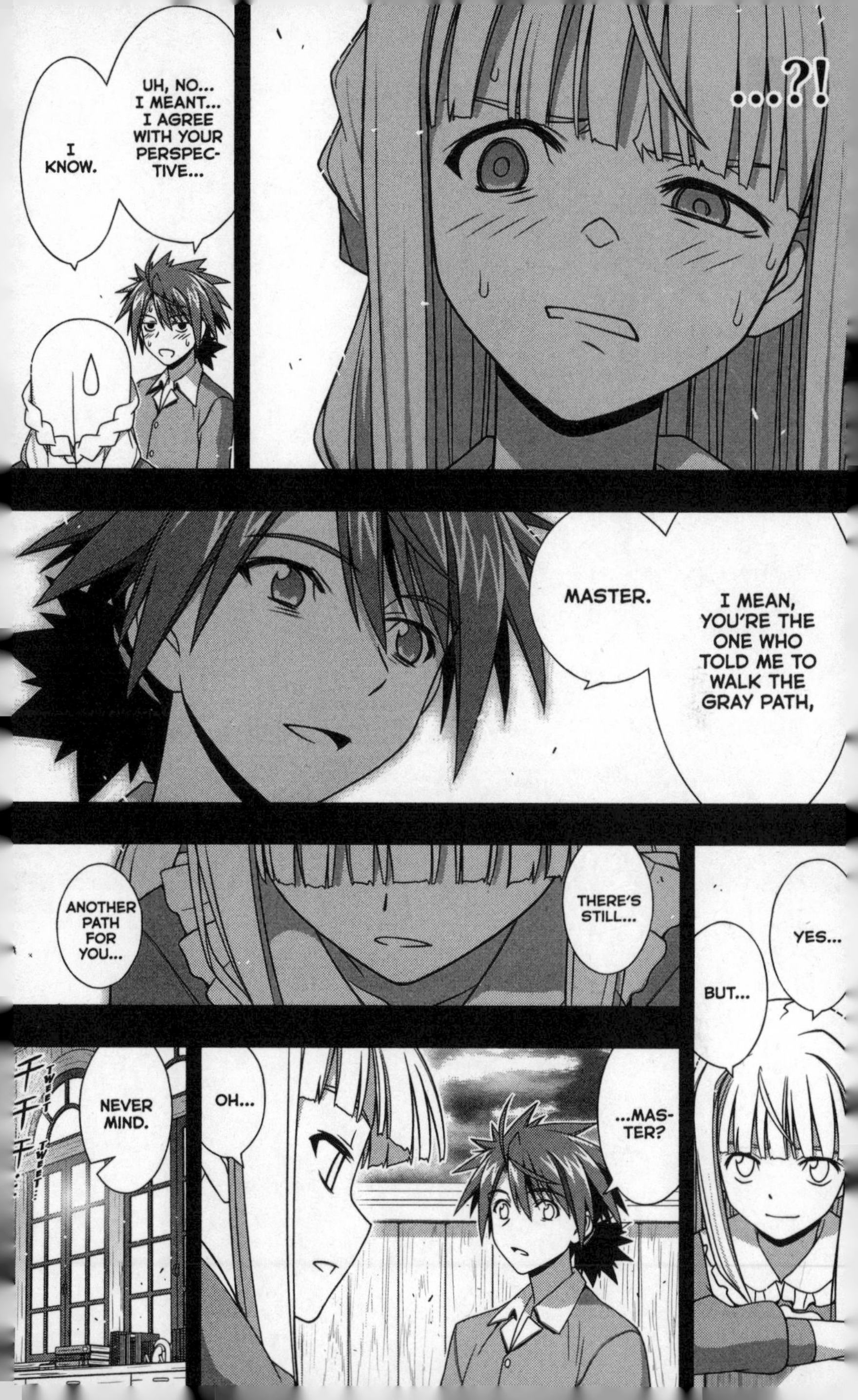
...?!
UH, NO... I MEANT... I AGREE WITH YOUR PERSPECTIVE...
I KNOW.
I MEAN, YOU'RE THE ONE WHO TOLD ME TO WALK THE GRAY PATH,
MASTER.
YES...
BUT...
THERE'S STILL...
ANOTHER PATH FOR YOU...
...MASTER?
OH...
NEVER MIND.
チチチ
TWEET TWEET...

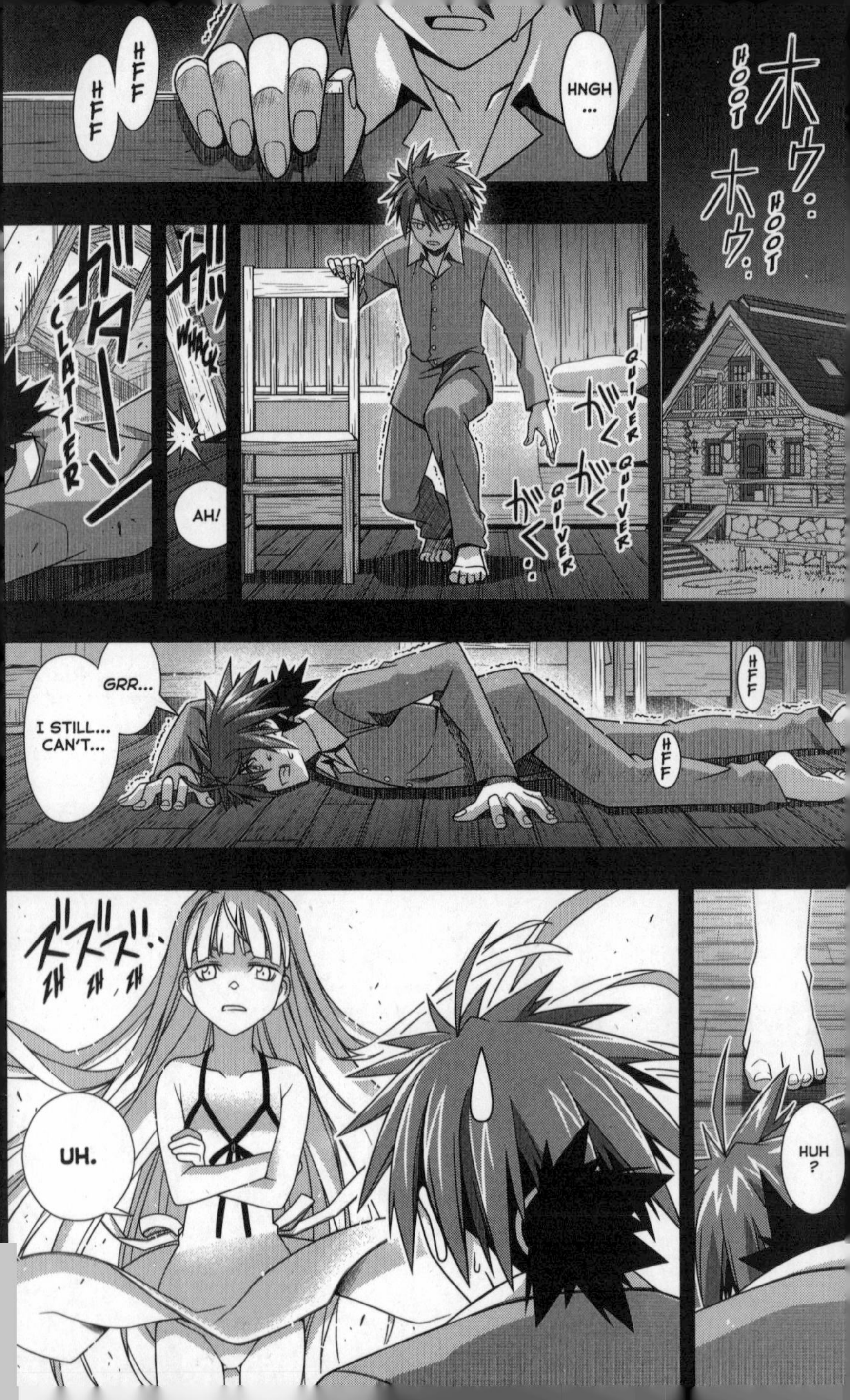

HOOT
HOOT
HNGH...
HFF
HFF
QUIVER
QUIVER
QUIVER
WHACK
AH!
CLATTER
HFF
HFF
GRR...
I STILL... CAN'T...
HUH?
ZH ZH ZH
UH.

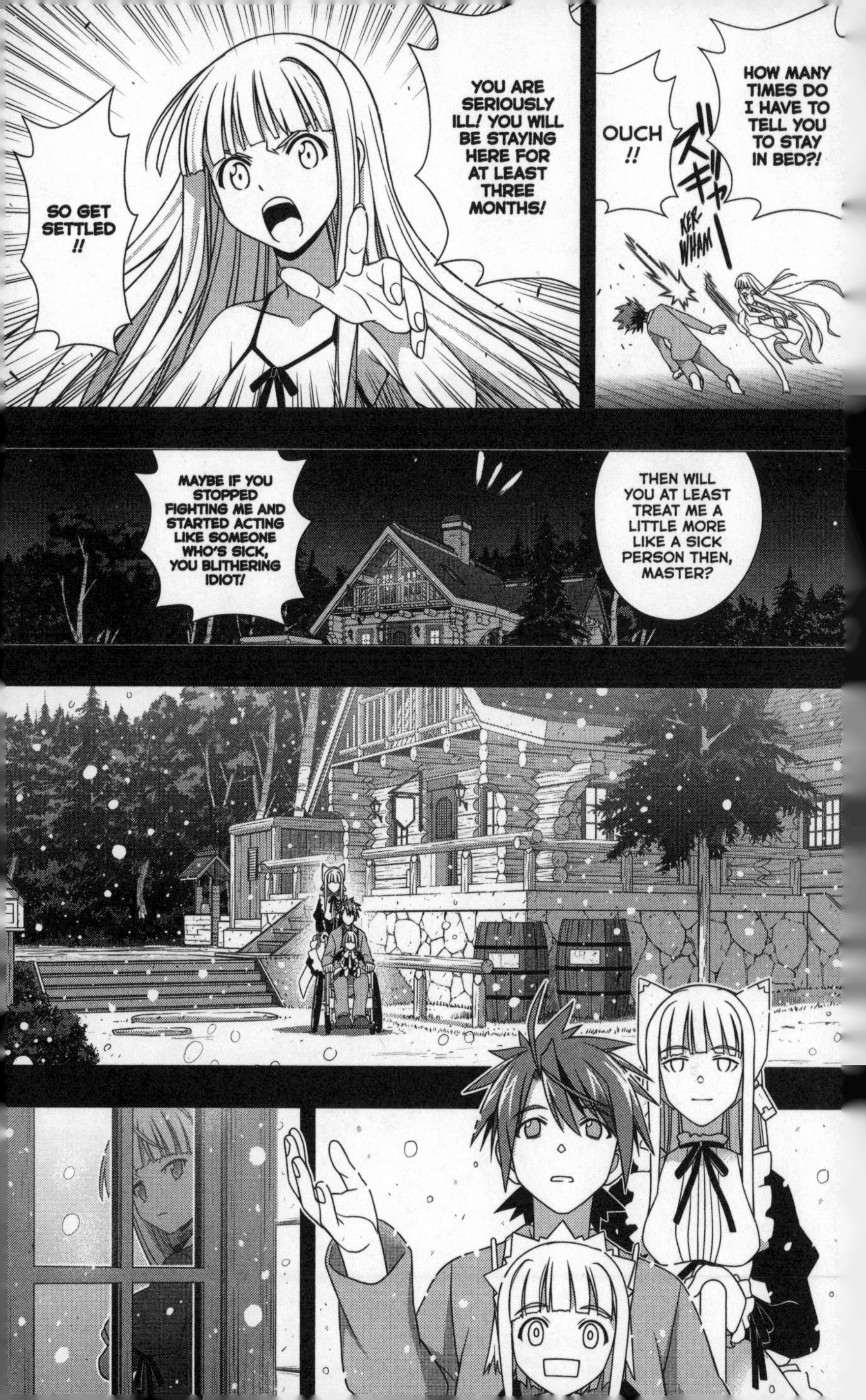
HOW MANY TIMES DO I HAVE TO TELL YOU TO STAY IN BED?!
OUCH !!
ズギャー
KER-WHAM
YOU ARE SERIOUSLY ILL! YOU WILL BE STAYING HERE FOR AT LEAST THREE MONTHS!
SO GET SETTLED !!
THEN WILL YOU AT LEAST TREAT ME A LITTLE MORE LIKE A SICK PERSON THEN, MASTER?
MAYBE IF YOU STOPPED FIGHTING ME AND STARTED ACTING LIKE SOMEONE WHO'S SICK, YOU BLITHERING IDIOT!

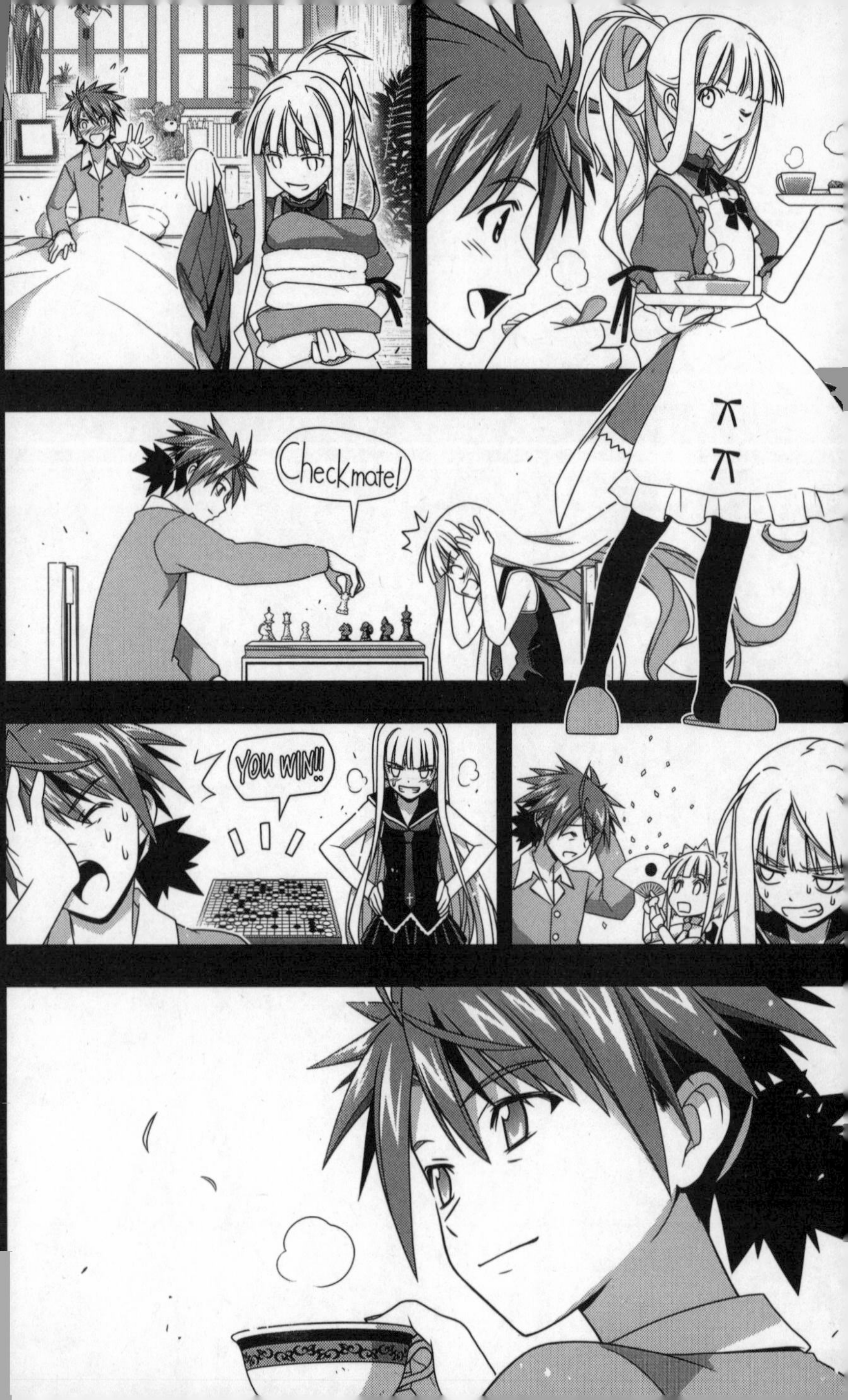
Checkmate!
YOU WIN!!

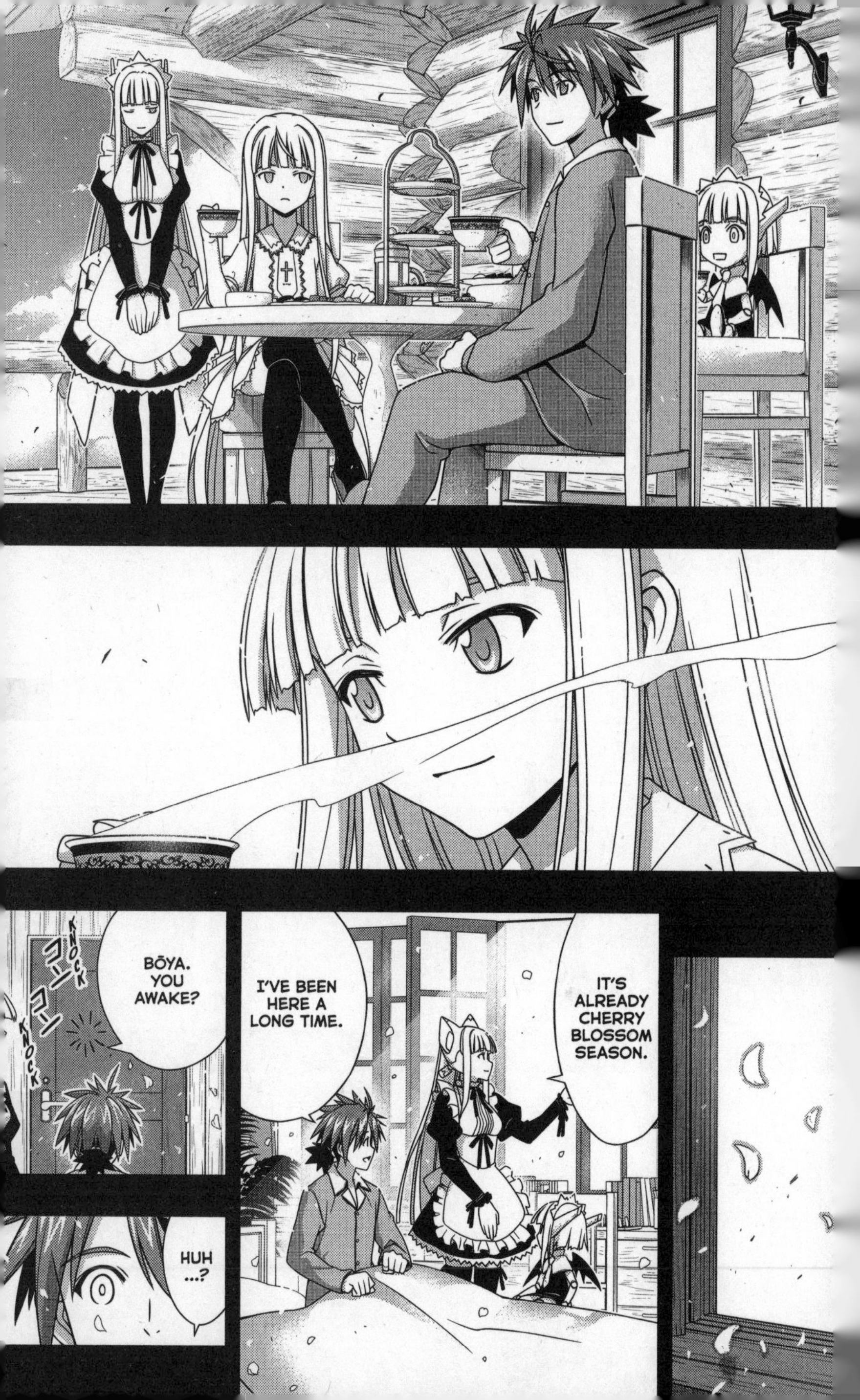
IT'S ALREADY CHERRY BLOSSOM SEASON.
I'VE BEEN HERE A LONG TIME.
KNOCK
KNOCK
BŌYA. YOU AWAKE?
HUH ...?

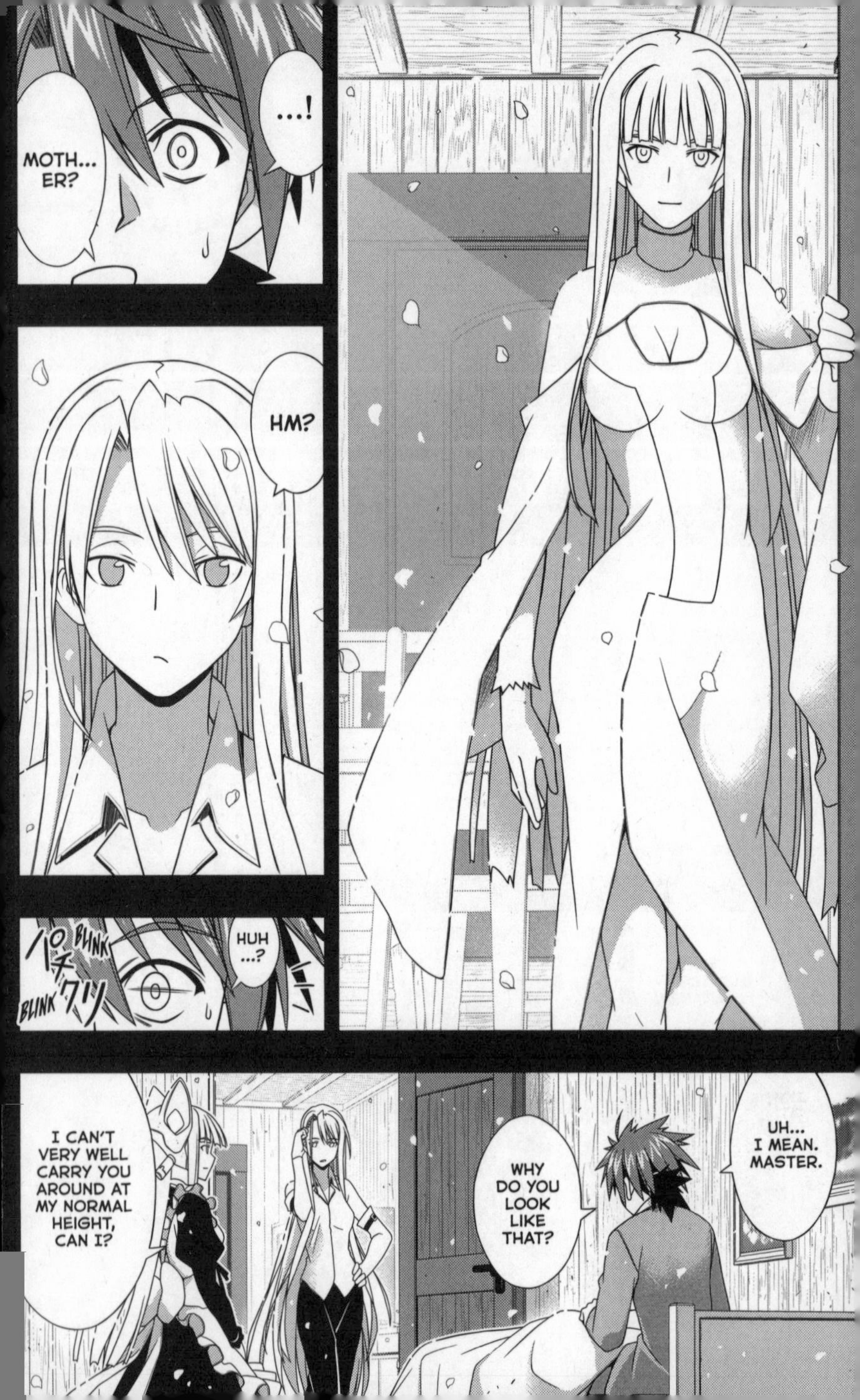
...!
MOTH... ER?
HM?
HUH ...?
パチ BLINK
BLINK クリ
UH... I MEAN. MASTER.
WHY DO YOU LOOK LIKE THAT?
I CAN'T VERY WELL CARRY YOU AROUND AT MY NORMAL HEIGHT, CAN I?

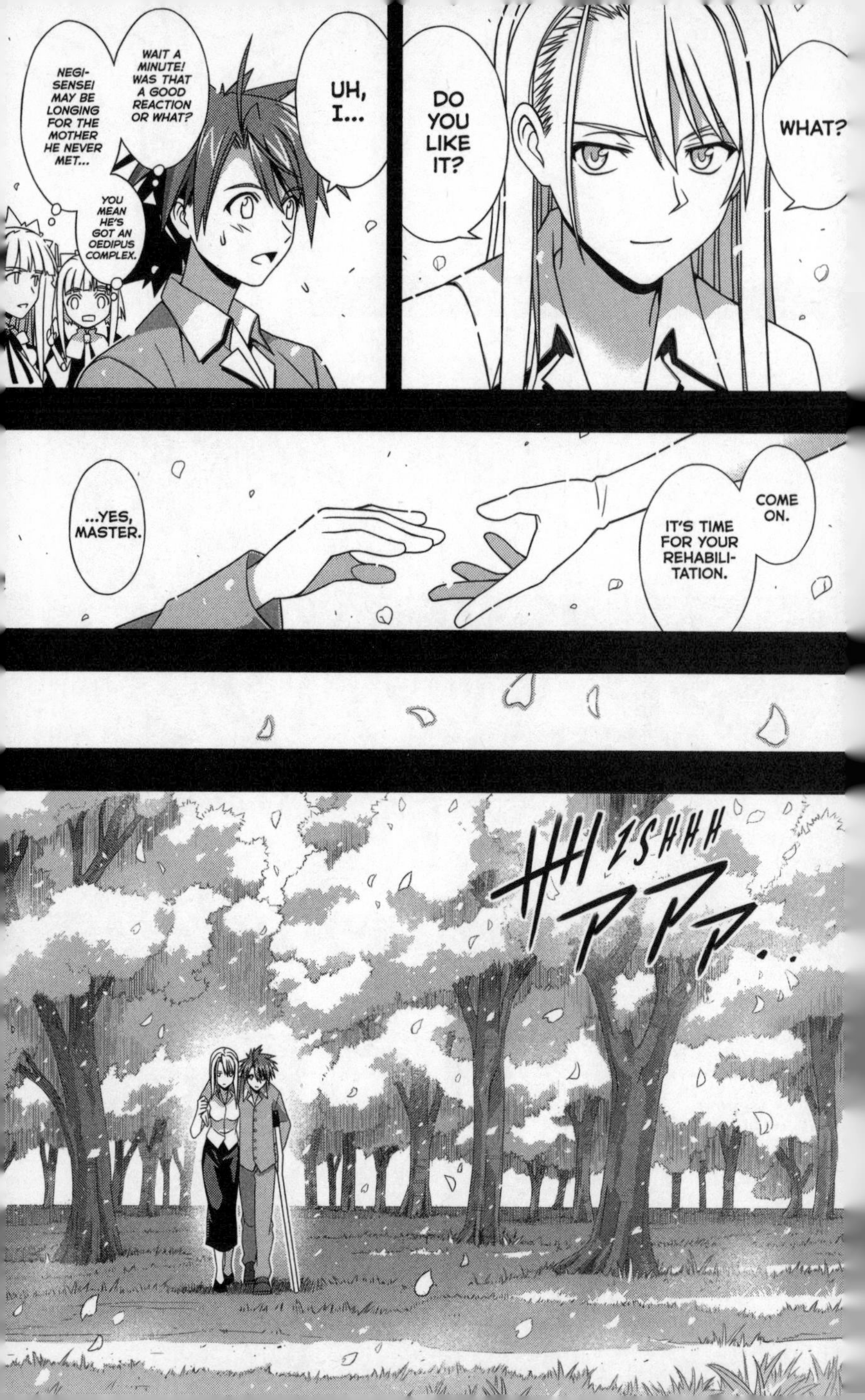
WHAT?
DO YOU LIKE IT?
UH, I...
WAIT A MINUTE! WAS THAT A GOOD REACTION OR WHAT?
NEGI-SENSEI MAY BE LONGING FOR THE MOTHER HE NEVER MET...
YOU MEAN HE'S GOT AN OEDIPUS COMPLEX.
COME ON.
IT'S TIME FOR YOUR REHABILI-TATION.
...YES, MASTER.

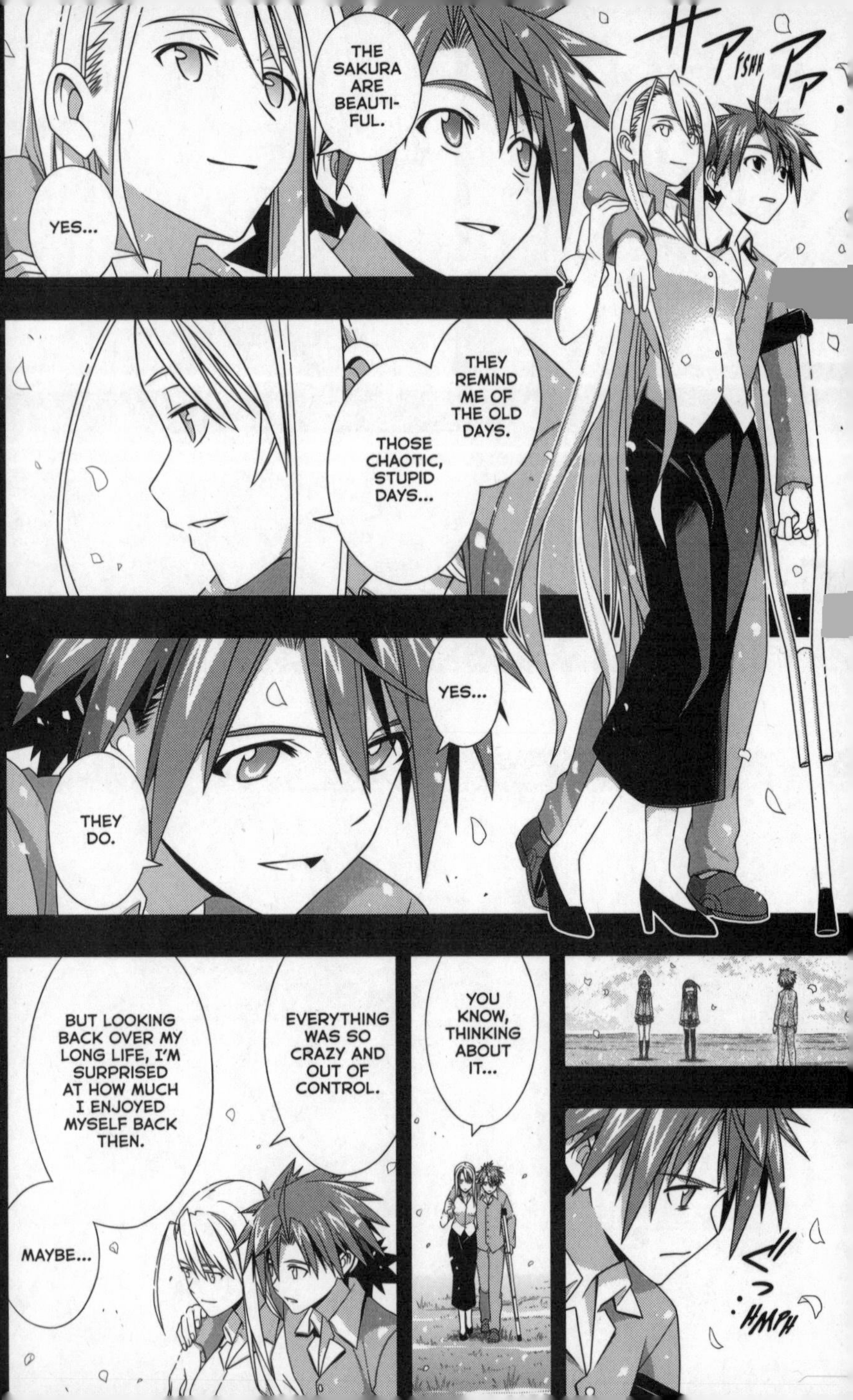
PSHH
THE SAKURA ARE BEAUTI-FUL.
YES...
THEY REMIND ME OF THE OLD DAYS.
THOSE CHAOTIC, STUPID DAYS...
YES...
THEY DO.
HMPH
YOU KNOW, THINKING ABOUT IT...
EVERYTHING WAS SO CRAZY AND OUT OF CONTROL.
BUT LOOKING BACK OVER MY LONG LIFE, I'M SURPRISED AT HOW MUCH I ENJOYED MYSELF BACK THEN.
MAYBE...

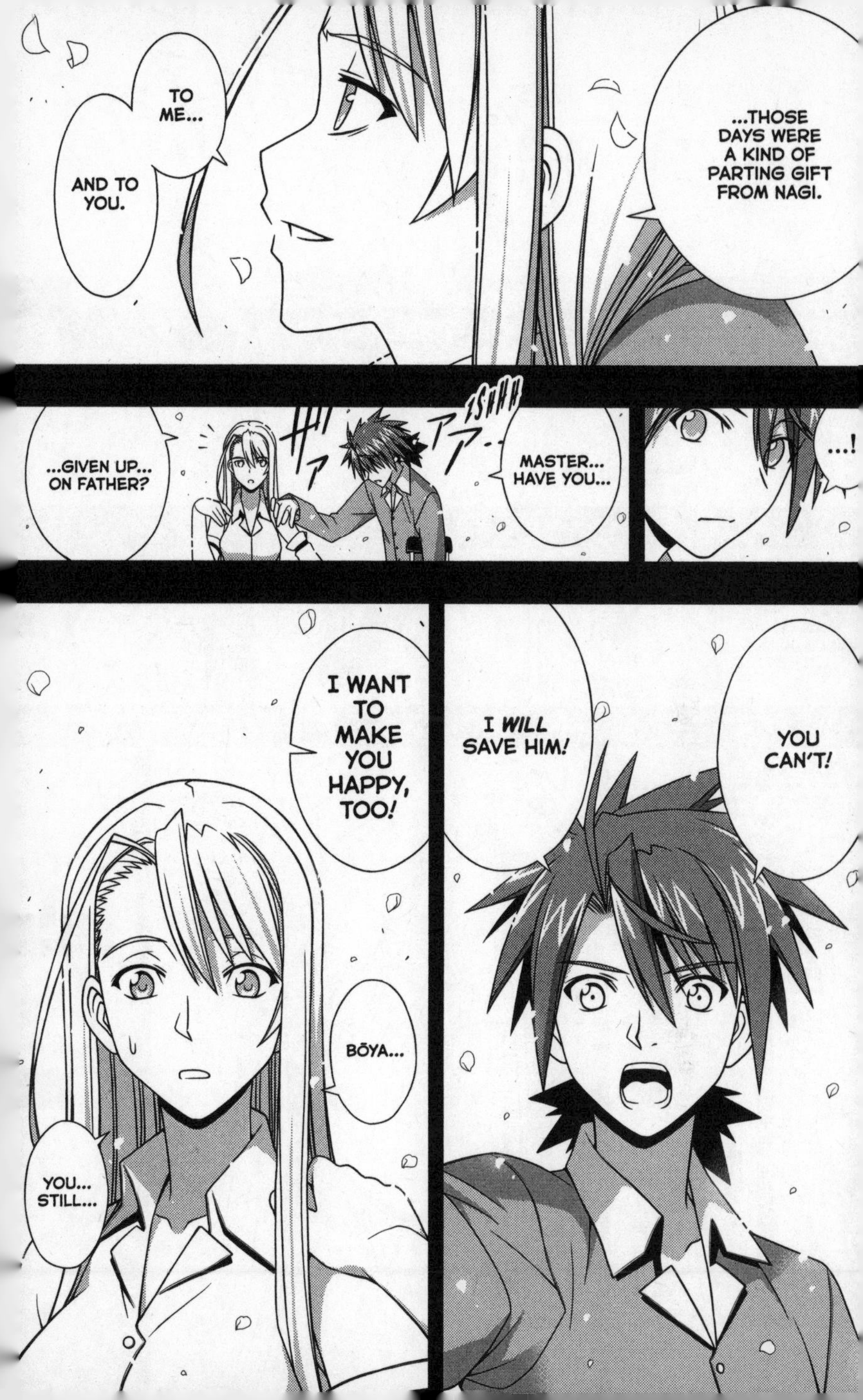
...THOSE DAYS WERE A KIND OF PARTING GIFT FROM NAGI.
TO ME...
AND TO YOU.
...!
MASTER... HAVE YOU...
FSHHH
...GIVEN UP... ON FATHER?
YOU CAN'T!
I *WILL* SAVE HIM!
I WANT TO MAKE YOU HAPPY, TOO!
BŌYA...
YOU... STILL...

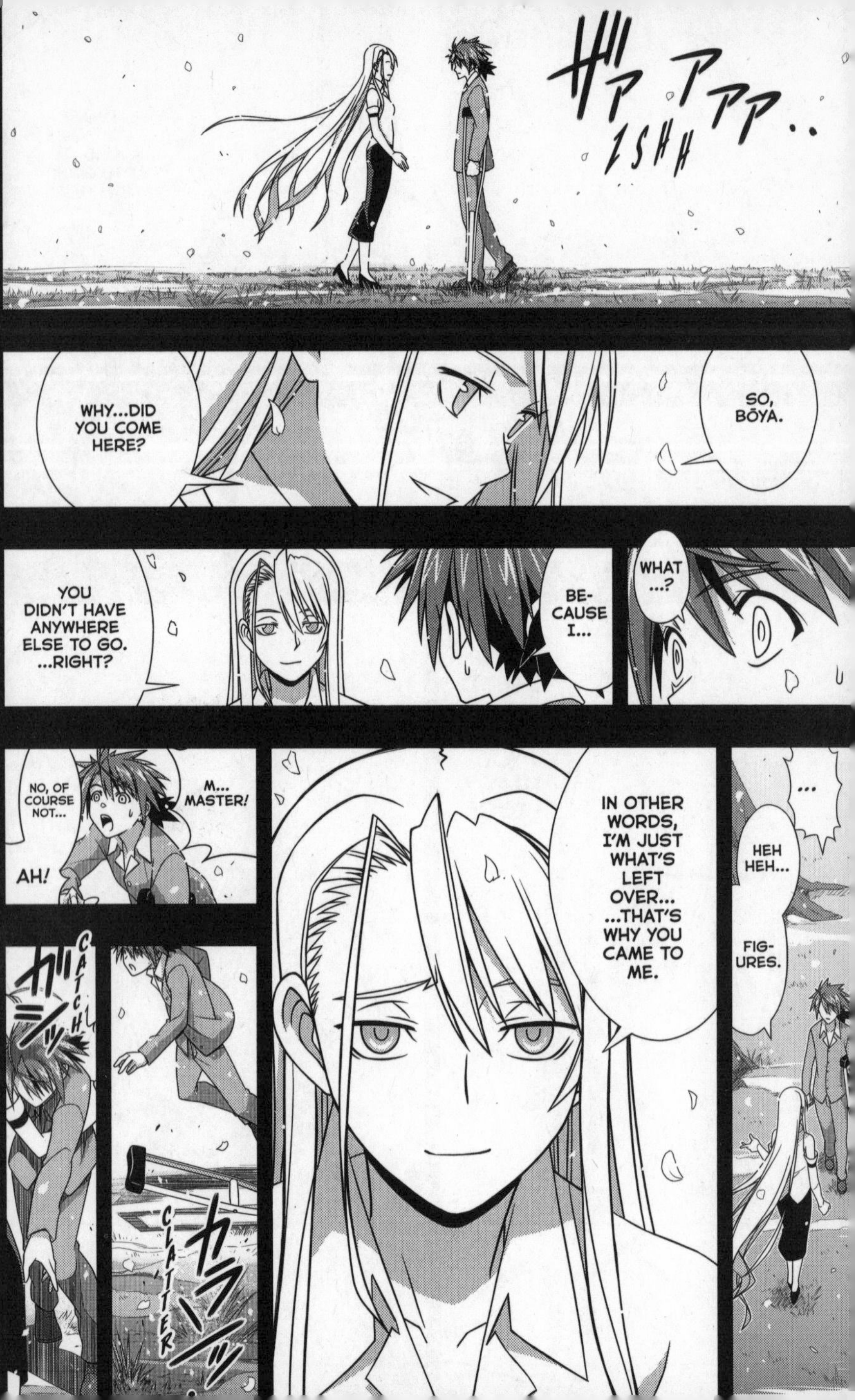
ザァ アァァ..
ISHH
SO, BŌYA.
WHY...DID YOU COME HERE?
WHAT ...?
BE-CAUSE I...
YOU DIDN'T HAVE ANYWHERE ELSE TO GO. ...RIGHT?
...
HEH HEH...
FIG-URES.
IN OTHER WORDS, I'M JUST WHAT'S LEFT OVER... ...THAT'S WHY YOU CAME TO ME.
M... MASTER!
NO, OF COURSE NOT...
AH!
カラーンッ
CLATTER
ガシッ
CATCH

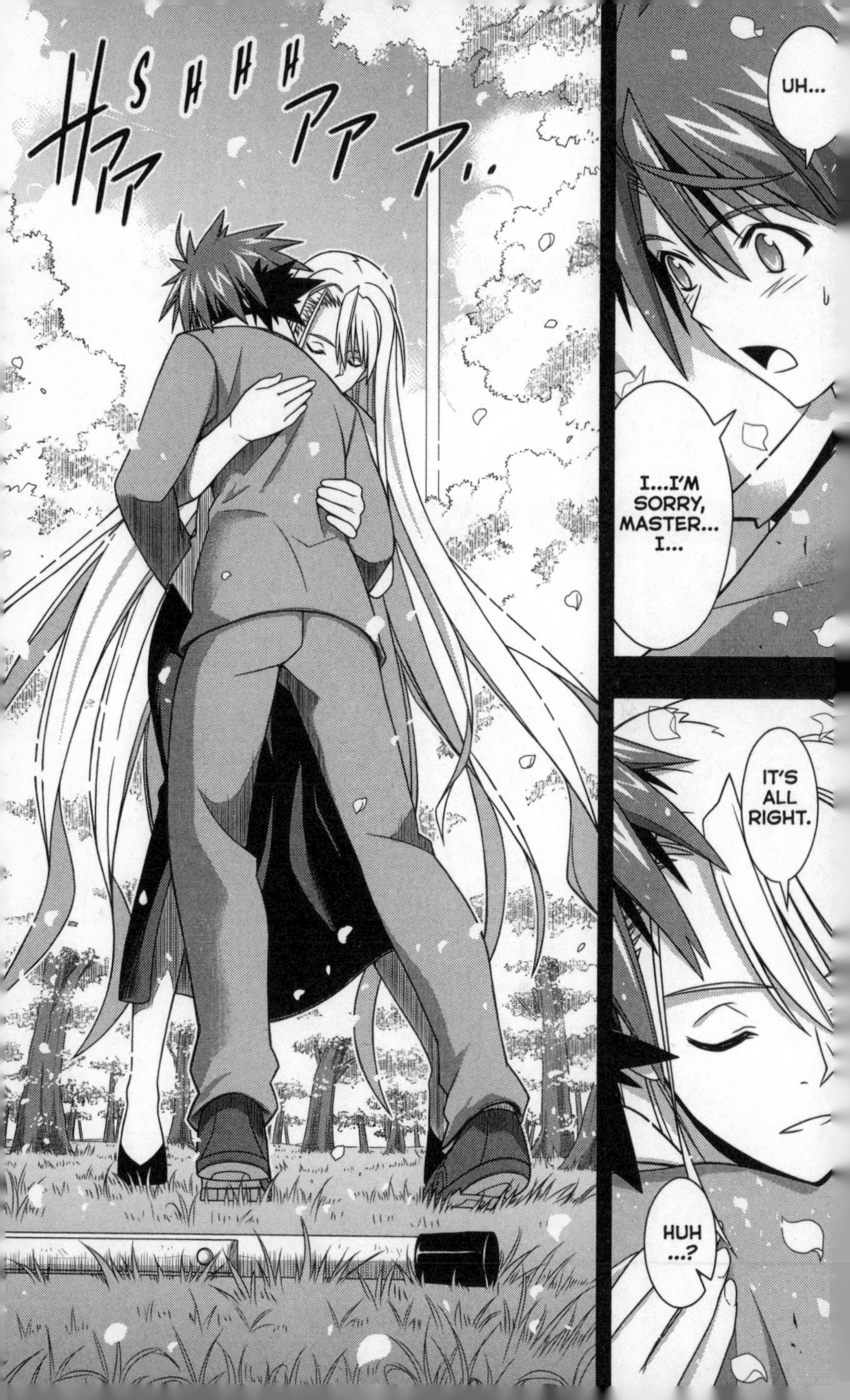
UH...
I...I'M SORRY, MASTER... I...
IT'S ALL RIGHT.
HUH ...?
HSHHH
サァァァ..

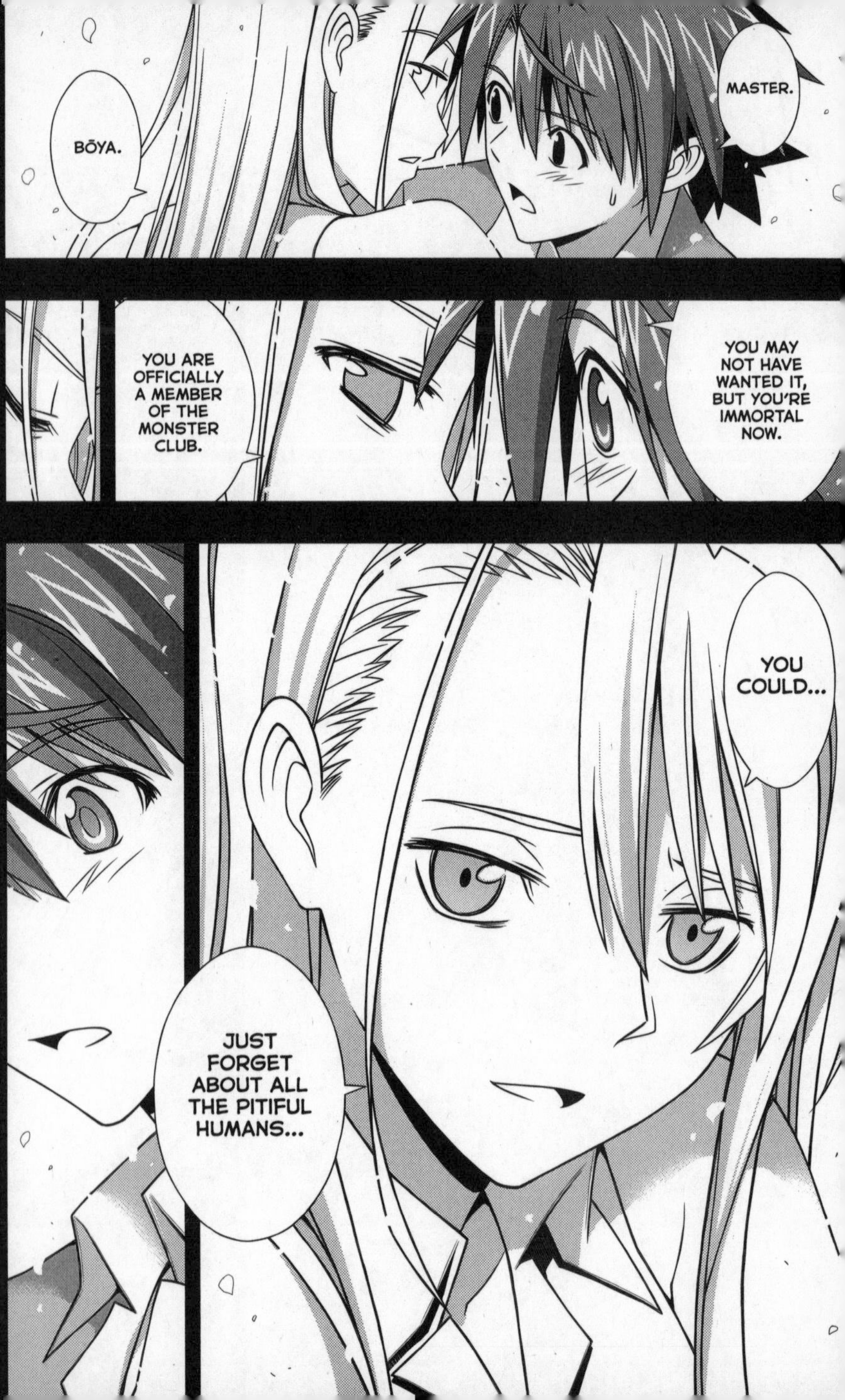
MASTER.
BŌYA.
YOU MAY NOT HAVE WANTED IT, BUT YOU'RE IMMORTAL NOW.
YOU ARE OFFICIALLY A MEMBER OF THE MONSTER CLUB.
YOU COULD...
JUST FORGET ABOUT ALL THE PITIFUL HUMANS...

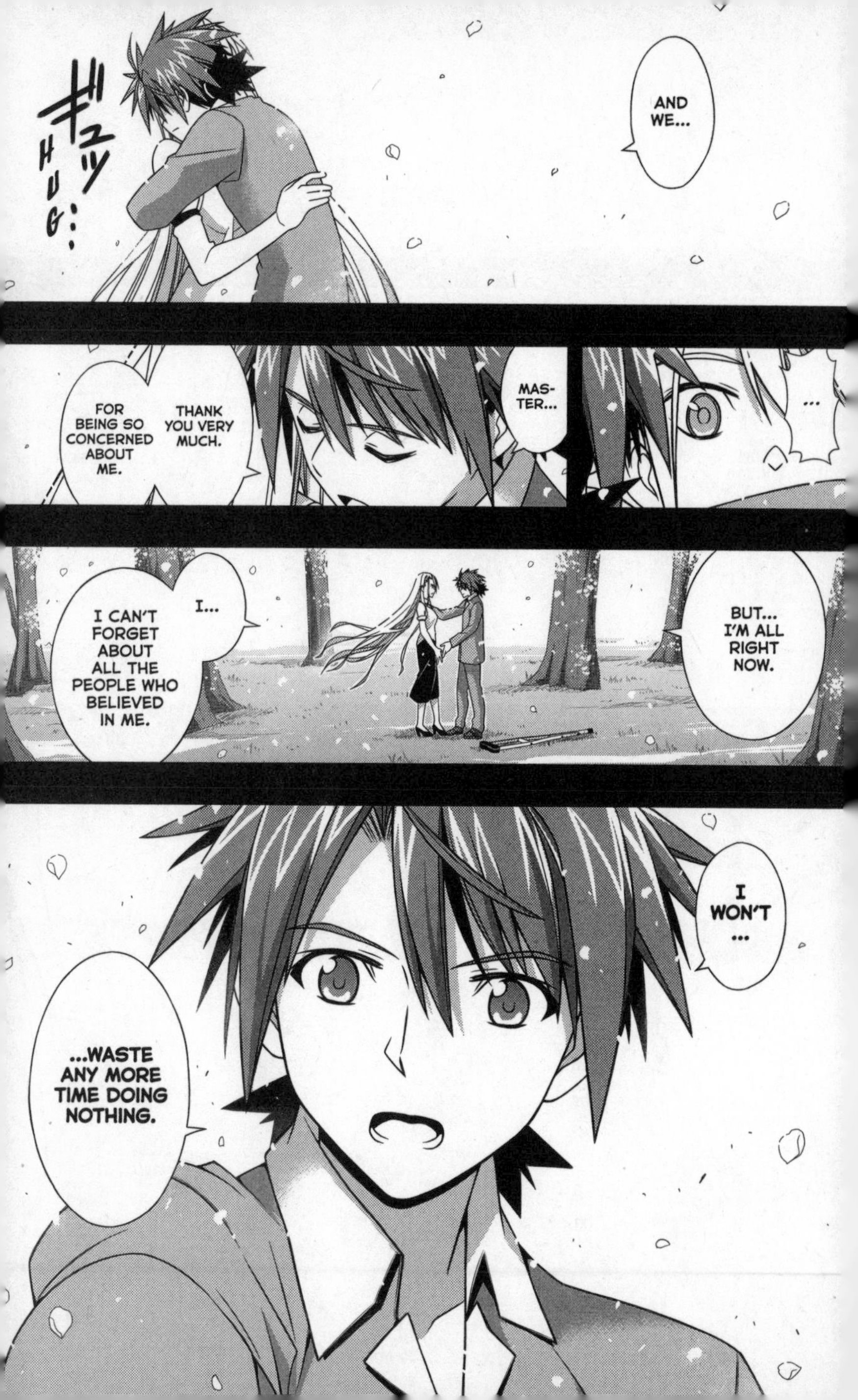
AND WE...
ギュッ
HUG...
...
MAS-TER...
THANK YOU VERY MUCH.
FOR BEING SO CONCERNED ABOUT ME.
BUT... I'M ALL RIGHT NOW.
I...
I CAN'T FORGET ABOUT ALL THE PEOPLE WHO BELIEVED IN ME.
I WON'T ...
...WASTE ANY MORE TIME DOING NOTHING.

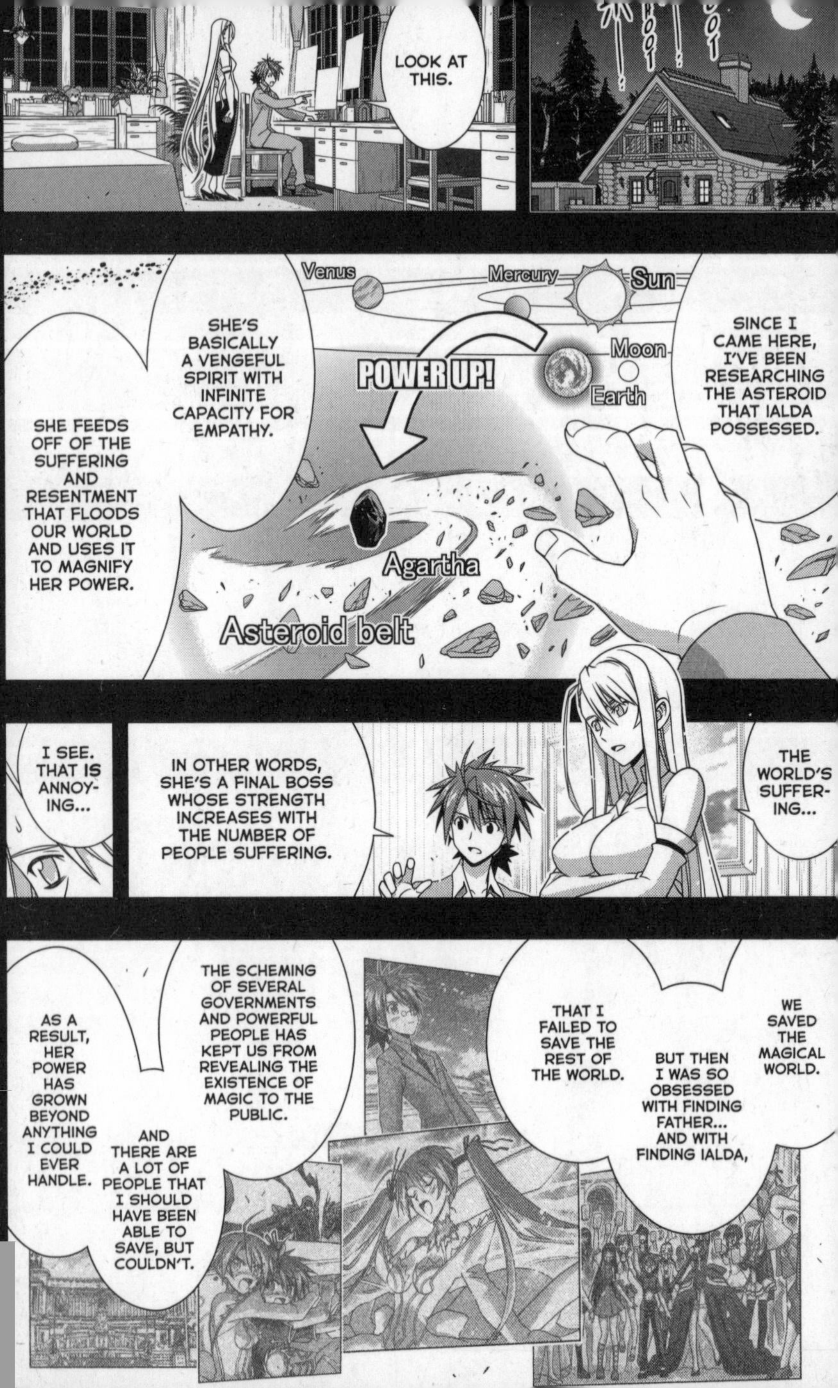
LOOK AT THIS.
SINCE I CAME HERE, I'VE BEEN RESEARCHING THE ASTEROID THAT IALDA POSSESSED.
Venus
Mercury
Sun
Moon
Earth
POWER UP!
Agartha
Asteroid belt
SHE'S BASICALLY A VENGEFUL SPIRIT WITH INFINITE CAPACITY FOR EMPATHY.
SHE FEEDS OFF OF THE SUFFERING AND RESENTMENT THAT FLOODS OUR WORLD AND USES IT TO MAGNIFY HER POWER.
THE WORLD'S SUFFERING...
IN OTHER WORDS, SHE'S A FINAL BOSS WHOSE STRENGTH INCREASES WITH THE NUMBER OF PEOPLE SUFFERING.
I SEE. THAT IS ANNOYING...
WE SAVED THE MAGICAL WORLD.
BUT THEN I WAS SO OBSESSED WITH FINDING FATHER... AND WITH FINDING IALDA,
THAT I FAILED TO SAVE THE REST OF THE WORLD.
THE SCHEMING OF SEVERAL GOVERNMENTS AND POWERFUL PEOPLE HAS KEPT US FROM REVEALING THE EXISTENCE OF MAGIC TO THE PUBLIC.
AS A RESULT, HER POWER HAS GROWN BEYOND ANYTHING I COULD EVER HANDLE.
AND THERE ARE A LOT OF PEOPLE THAT I SHOULD HAVE BEEN ABLE TO SAVE, BUT COULDN'T.

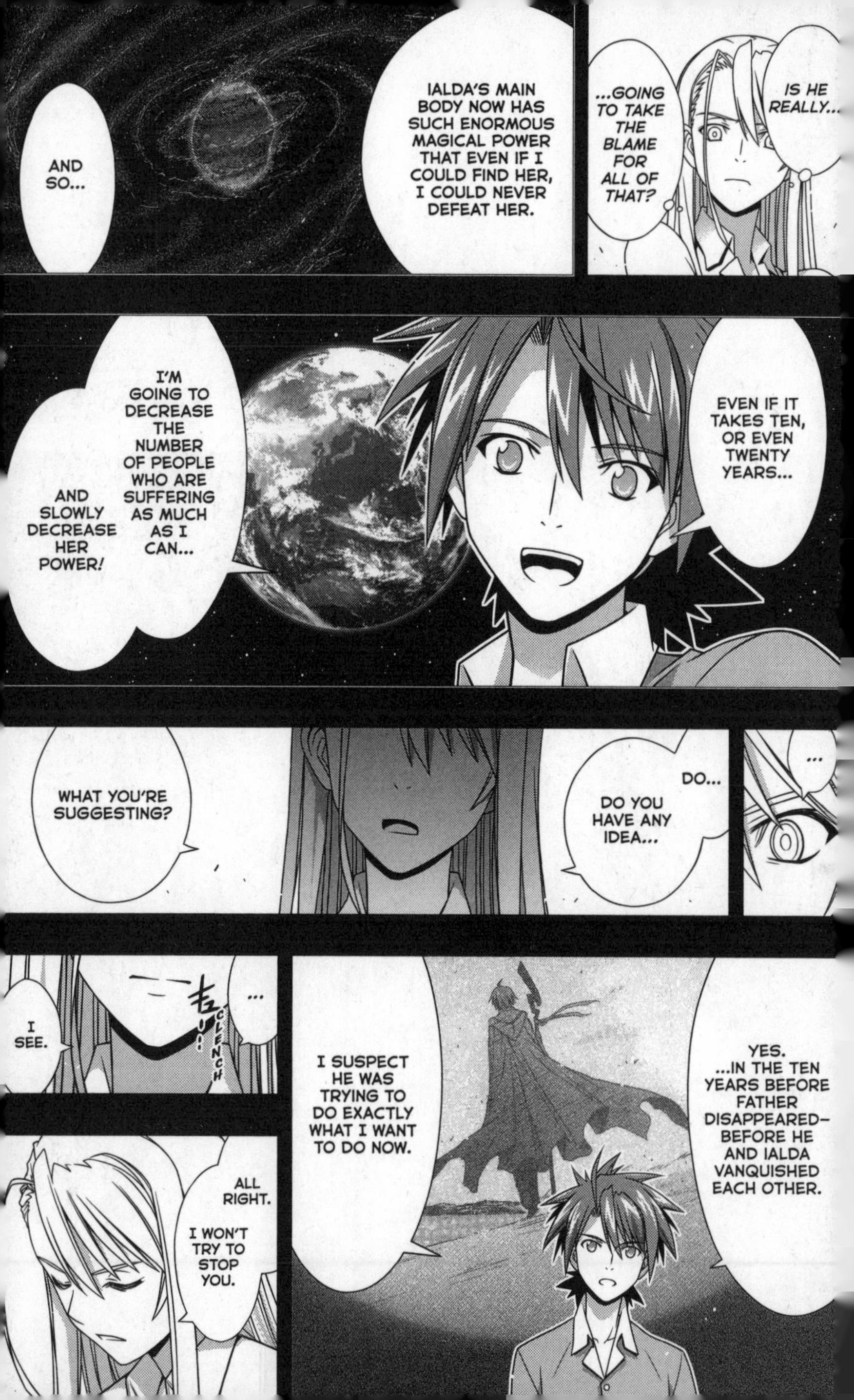
IS HE REALLY...
...GOING TO TAKE THE BLAME FOR ALL OF THAT?
IALDA'S MAIN BODY NOW HAS SUCH ENORMOUS MAGICAL POWER THAT EVEN IF I COULD FIND HER, I COULD NEVER DEFEAT HER.
AND SO...
EVEN IF IT TAKES TEN, OR EVEN TWENTY YEARS...
I'M GOING TO DECREASE THE NUMBER OF PEOPLE WHO ARE SUFFERING AS MUCH AS I CAN...
AND SLOWLY DECREASE HER POWER!
...
DO...
DO YOU HAVE ANY IDEA...
WHAT YOU'RE SUGGESTING?
YES. ...IN THE TEN YEARS BEFORE FATHER DISAPPEARED—BEFORE HE AND IALDA VANQUISHED EACH OTHER.
I SUSPECT HE WAS TRYING TO DO EXACTLY WHAT I WANT TO DO NOW.
...
CLENCH
I SEE.
ALL RIGHT.
I WON'T TRY TO STOP YOU.

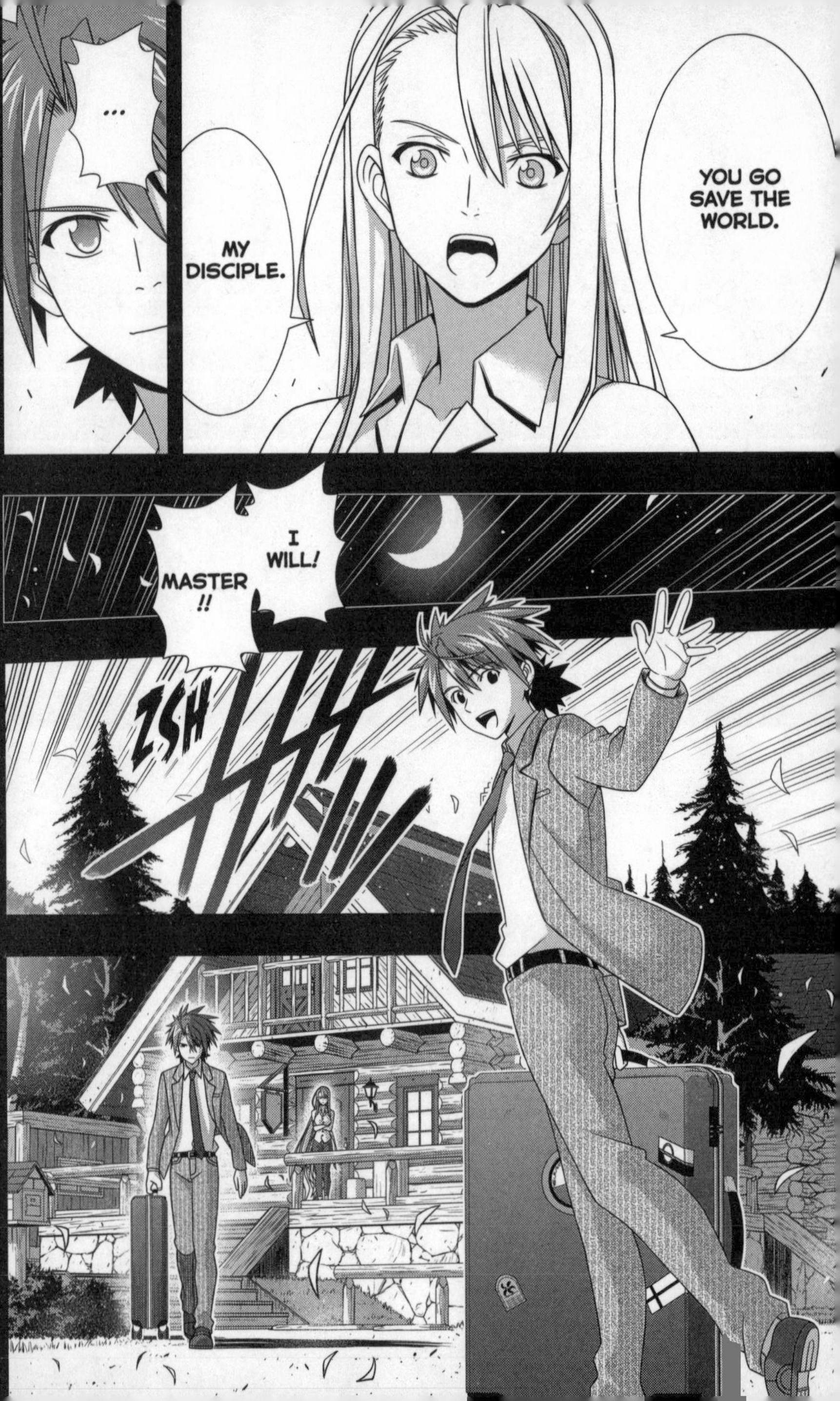
YOU GO SAVE THE WORLD.
MY DISCIPLE.
...
I WILL!
MASTER !!
ZSH

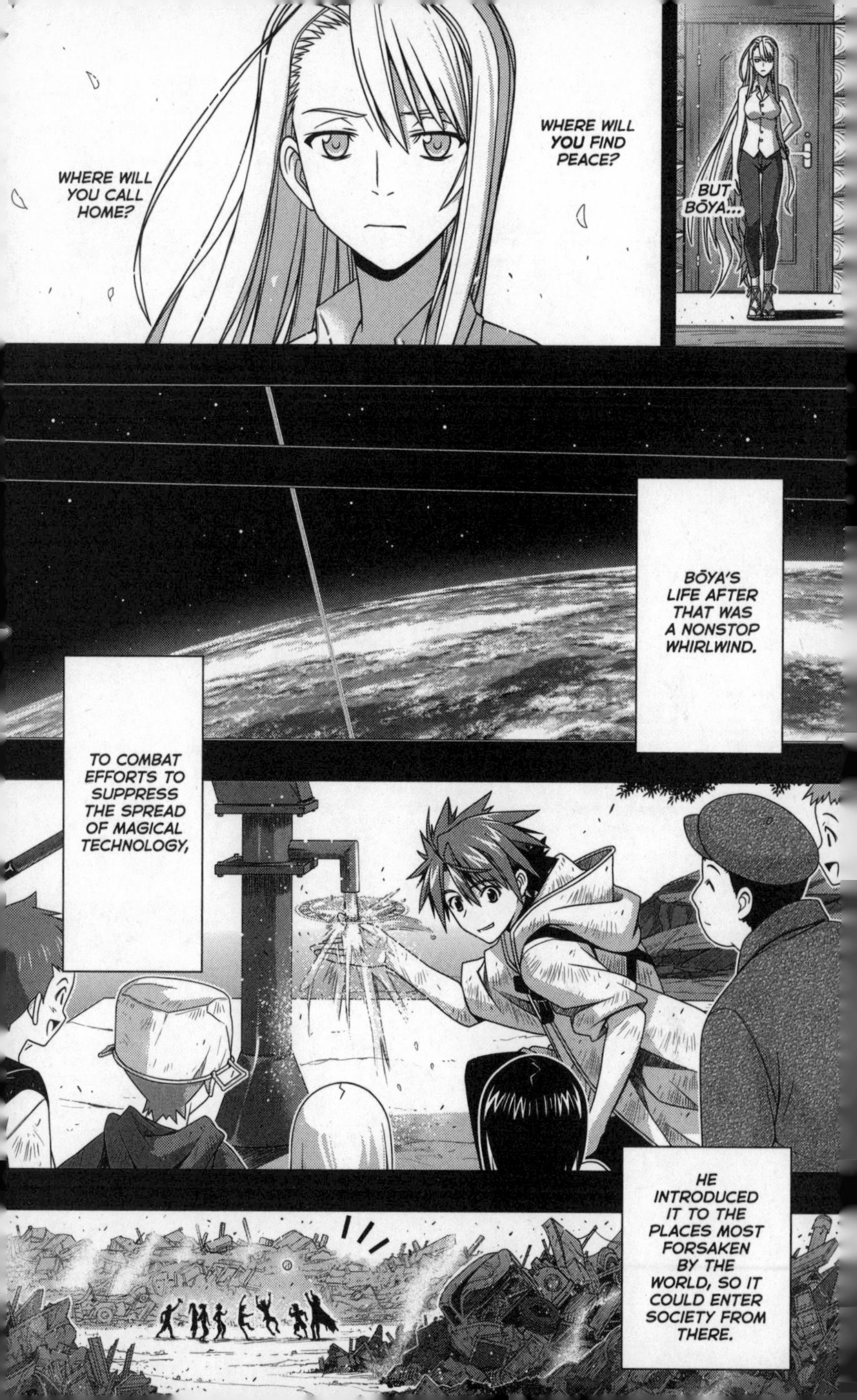
BUT BŌYA...
WHERE WILL YOU FIND PEACE?
WHERE WILL YOU CALL HOME?
BŌYA'S LIFE AFTER THAT WAS A NONSTOP WHIRLWIND.
TO COMBAT EFFORTS TO SUPPRESS THE SPREAD OF MAGICAL TECHNOLOGY,
HE INTRODUCED IT TO THE PLACES MOST FORSAKEN BY THE WORLD, SO IT COULD ENTER SOCIETY FROM THERE.

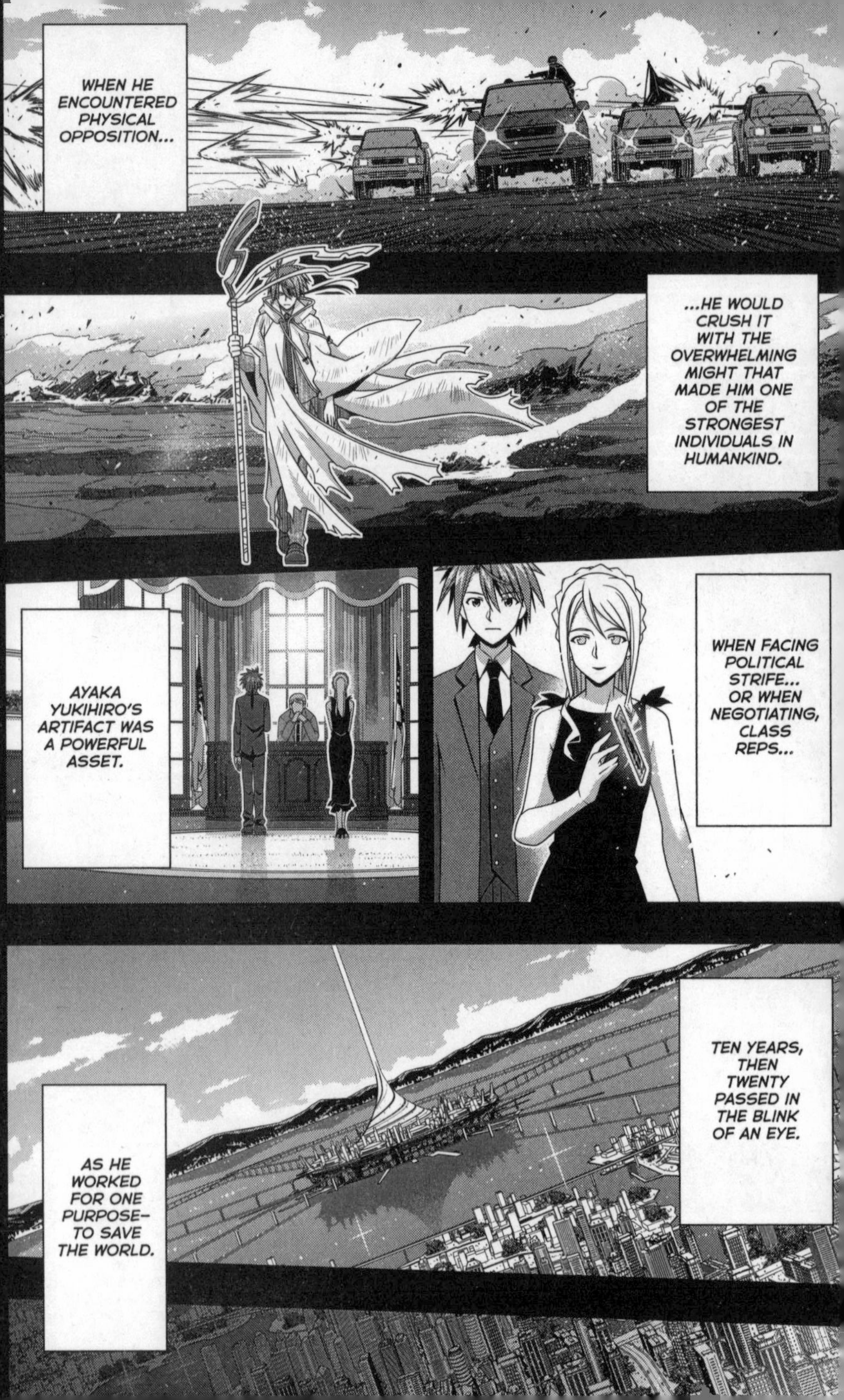
WHEN HE ENCOUNTERED PHYSICAL OPPOSITION...
...HE WOULD CRUSH IT WITH THE OVERWHELMING MIGHT THAT MADE HIM ONE OF THE STRONGEST INDIVIDUALS IN HUMANKIND.
WHEN FACING POLITICAL STRIFE... OR WHEN NEGOTIATING, CLASS REPS...
AYAKA YUKIHIRO'S ARTIFACT WAS A POWERFUL ASSET.
TEN YEARS, THEN TWENTY PASSED IN THE BLINK OF AN EYE.
AS HE WORKED FOR ONE PURPOSE— TO SAVE THE WORLD.

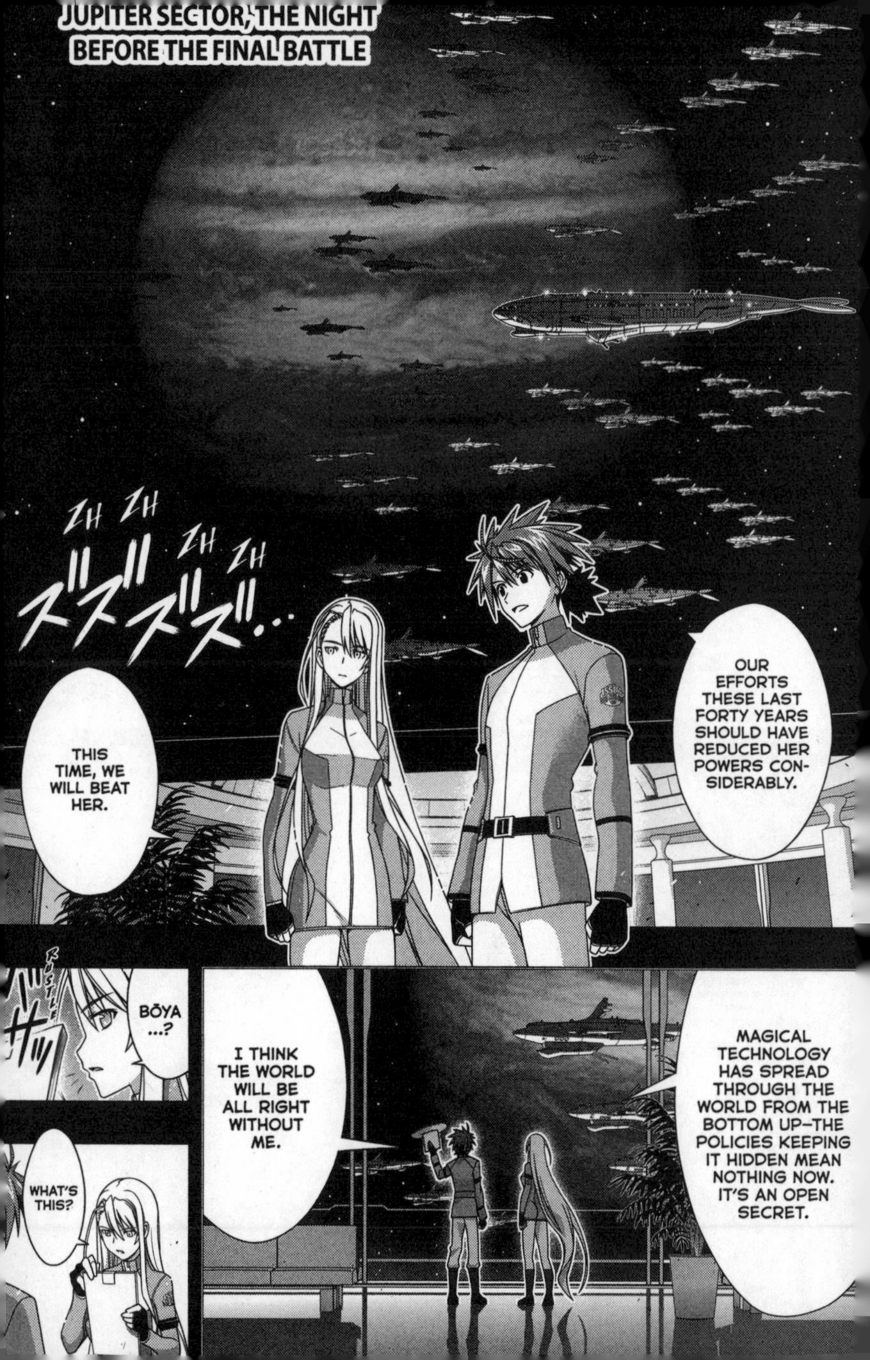
JUPITER SECTOR, THE NIGHT BEFORE THE FINAL BATTLE
ZH ZH ZH ZH
ズズズズ…
OUR EFFORTS THESE LAST FORTY YEARS SHOULD HAVE REDUCED HER POWERS CONSIDERABLY.
THIS TIME, WE WILL BEAT HER.
MAGICAL TECHNOLOGY HAS SPREAD THROUGH THE WORLD FROM THE BOTTOM UP–THE POLICIES KEEPING IT HIDDEN MEAN NOTHING NOW. IT'S AN OPEN SECRET.
I THINK THE WORLD WILL BE ALL RIGHT WITHOUT ME.
RUSTLE
BŌYA ...?
WHAT'S THIS?

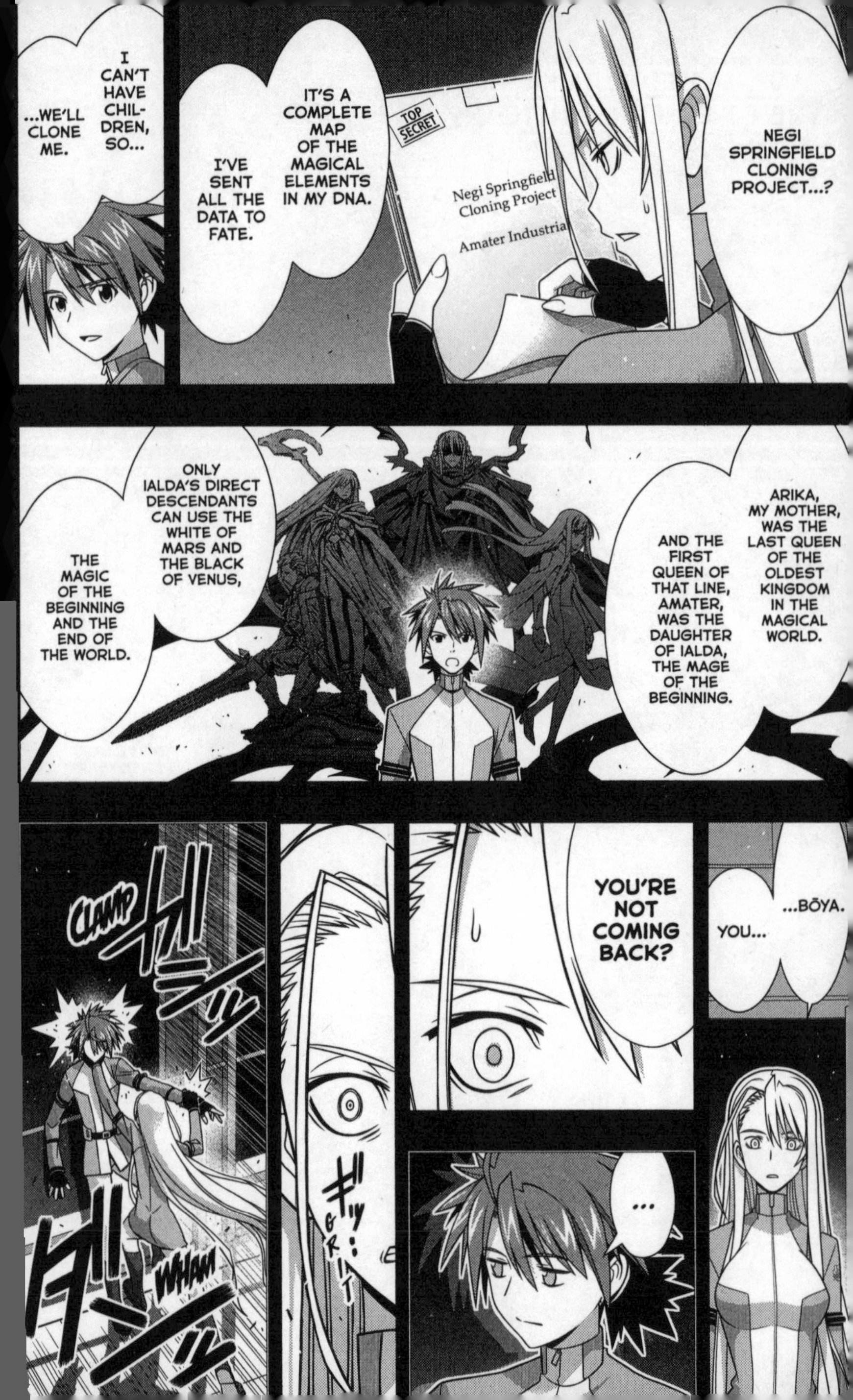
NEGI SPRINGFIELD CLONING PROJECT...?
TOP SECRET
Negi Springfield Cloning Project
Amater Industria
IT'S A COMPLETE MAP OF THE MAGICAL ELEMENTS IN MY DNA.
I'VE SENT ALL THE DATA TO FATE.
I CAN'T HAVE CHIL-DREN, SO...
...WE'LL CLONE ME.
ARIKA, MY MOTHER, WAS THE LAST QUEEN OF THE OLDEST KINGDOM IN THE MAGICAL WORLD.
AND THE FIRST QUEEN OF THAT LINE, AMATER, WAS THE DAUGHTER OF IALDA, THE MAGE OF THE BEGINNING.
ONLY IALDA'S DIRECT DESCENDANTS CAN USE THE WHITE OF MARS AND THE BLACK OF VENUS,
THE MAGIC OF THE BEGINNING AND THE END OF THE WORLD.
...BŌYA.
YOU...
YOU'RE NOT COMING BACK?
...
GRIT
CLAMP
WHAM

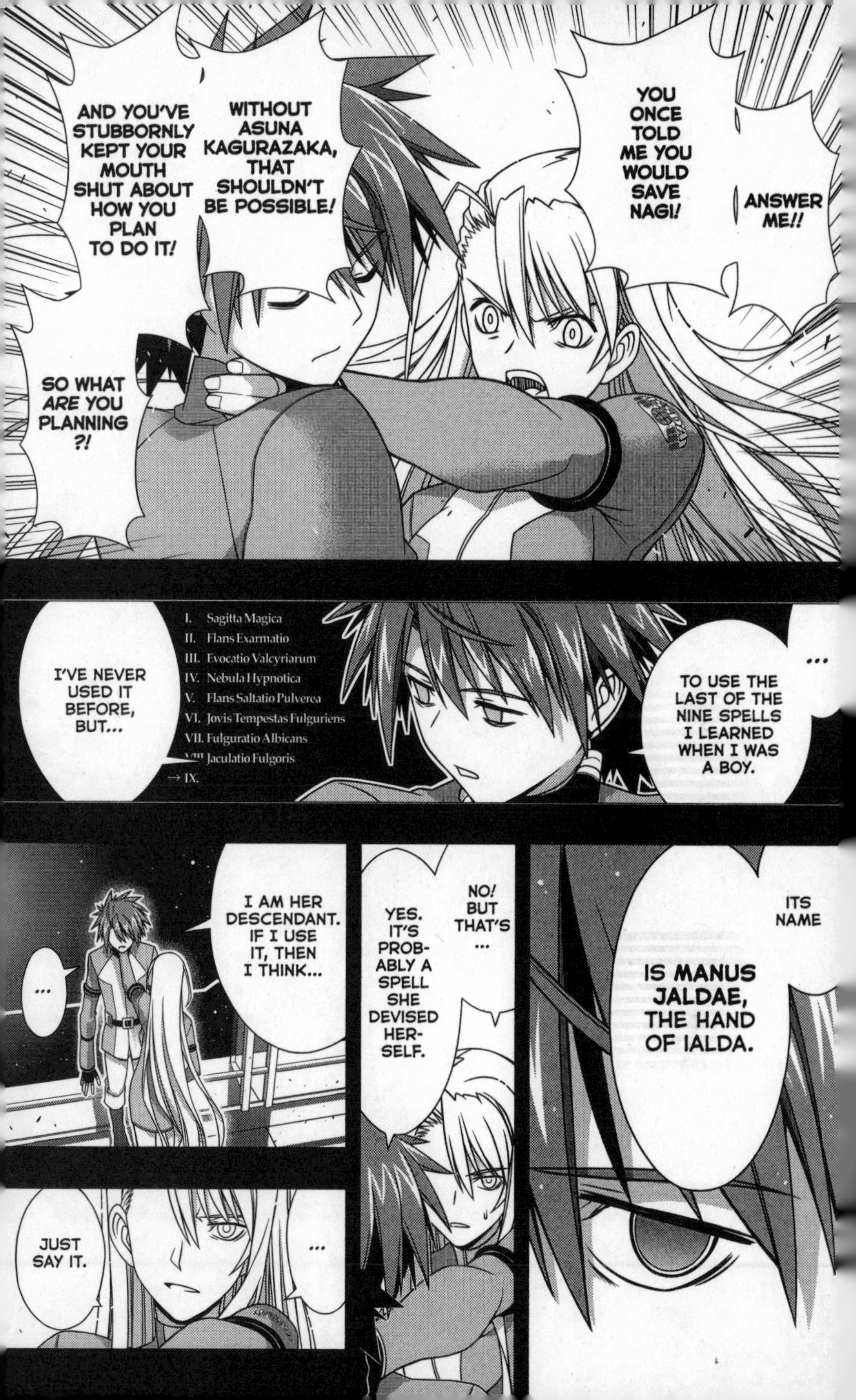
YOU ONCE TOLD ME YOU WOULD SAVE NAGI!
ANSWER ME!!
WITHOUT ASUNA KAGURAZAKA, THAT SHOULDN'T BE POSSIBLE!
AND YOU'VE STUBBORNLY KEPT YOUR MOUTH SHUT ABOUT HOW YOU PLAN TO DO IT!
SO WHAT *ARE* YOU PLANNING?!
...
TO USE THE LAST OF THE NINE SPELLS I LEARNED WHEN I WAS A BOY.
I. Sagitta Magica
II. Flans Exarmatio
III. Evocatio Valcyriarum
IV. Nebula Hypnotica
V. Flans Saltatio Pulverea
VI. Jovis Tempestas Fulguriens
VII. Fulguratio Albicans
VIII Jaculatio Fulgoris
→ IX.
I'VE NEVER USED IT BEFORE, BUT...
ITS NAME
IS MANUS JALDAE, THE HAND OF IALDA.
NO! BUT THAT'S...
YES. IT'S PROBABLY A SPELL SHE DEVISED HERSELF.
I AM HER DESCENDANT. IF I USE IT, THEN I THINK...
...
...
JUST SAY IT.

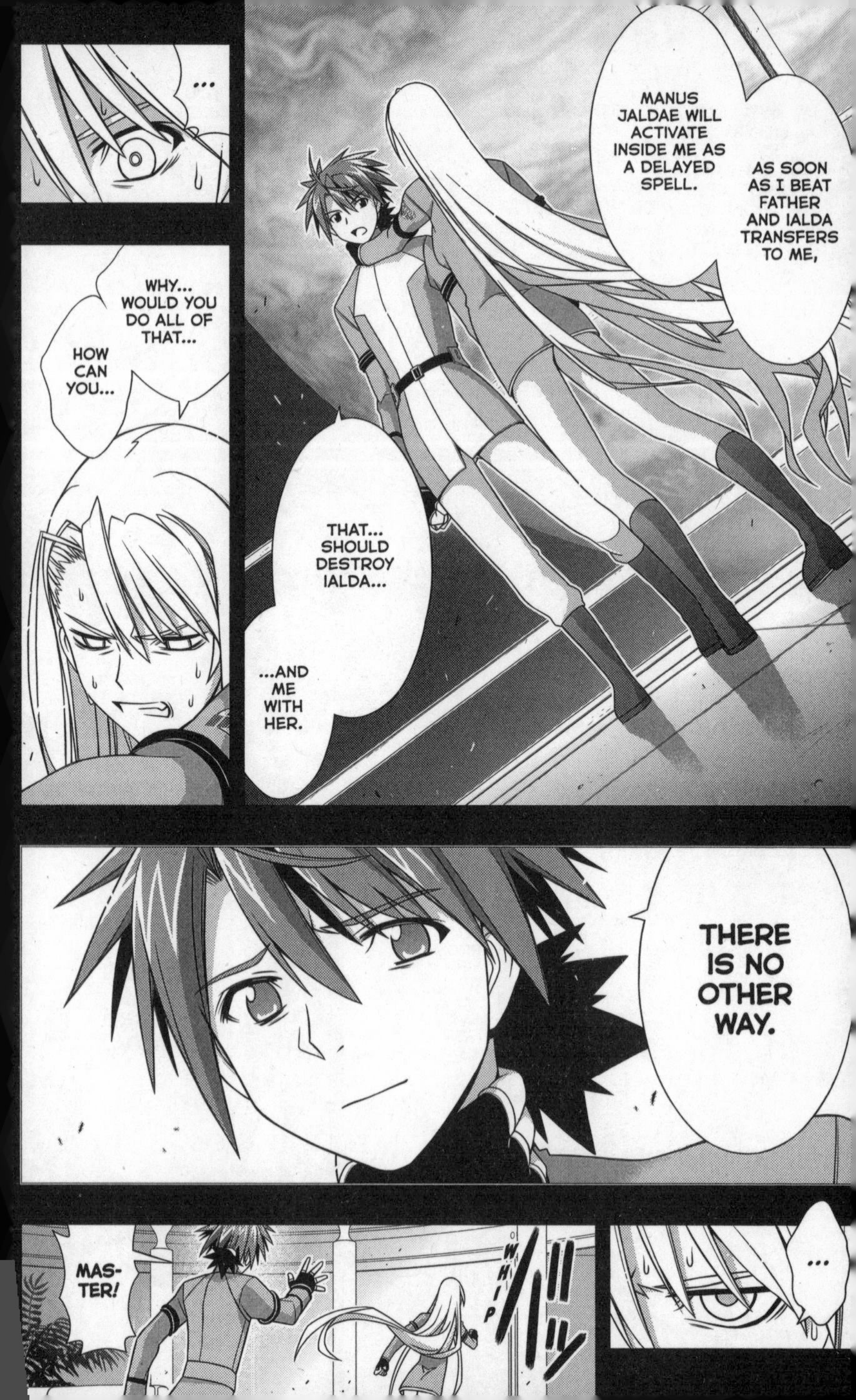
AS SOON AS I BEAT FATHER AND IALDA TRANSFERS TO ME,
MANUS JALDAE WILL ACTIVATE INSIDE ME AS A DELAYED SPELL.
THAT... SHOULD DESTROY IALDA...
...AND ME WITH HER.
...
WHY... WOULD YOU DO ALL OF THAT...
HOW CAN YOU...
THERE IS NO OTHER WAY.
...
WHIP
MAS-TER!

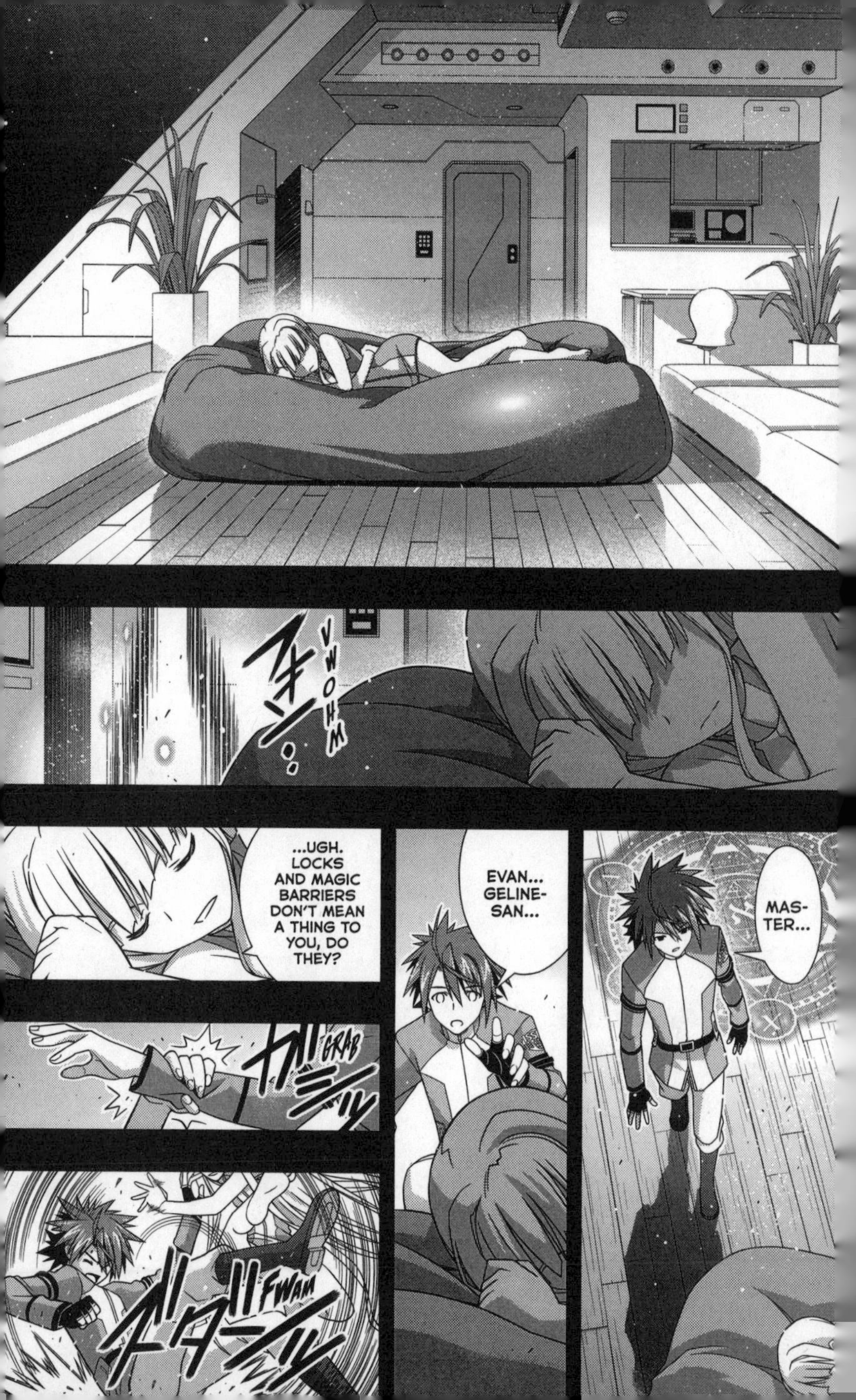
VWOHM
MAS-TER...
EVAN... GELINE-SAN...
...UGH. LOCKS AND MAGIC BARRIERS DON'T MEAN A THING TO YOU, DO THEY?
GRAB
FWAM

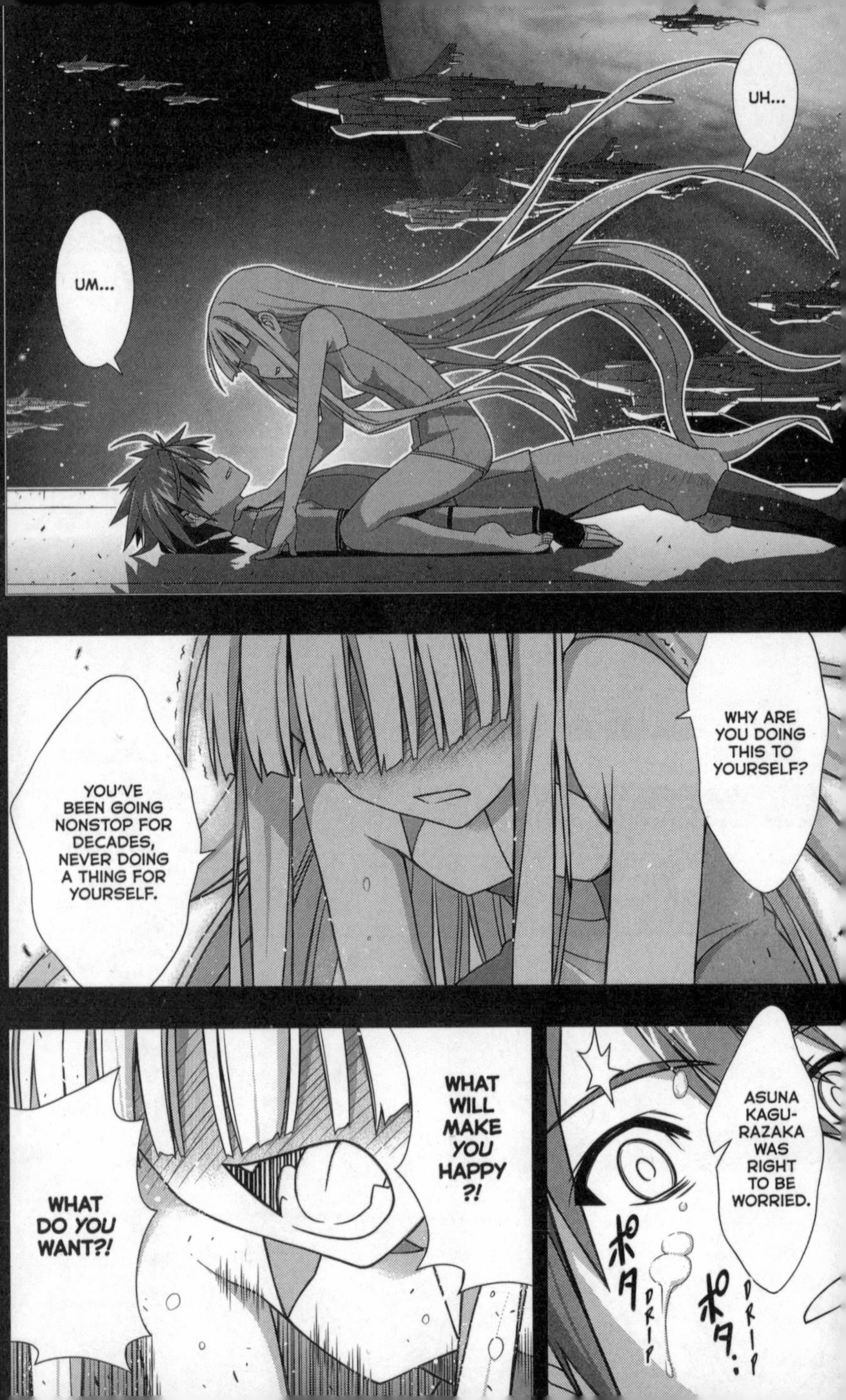
UH...
UM...
WHY ARE YOU DOING THIS TO YOURSELF?
YOU'VE BEEN GOING NONSTOP FOR DECADES, NEVER DOING A THING FOR YOURSELF.
ASUNA KAGURA-ZAKA WAS RIGHT TO BE WORRIED.
ポタ DRIP
ポタ DRIP
WHAT WILL MAKE *YOU* HAPPY?!
WHAT DO *YOU* WANT?!

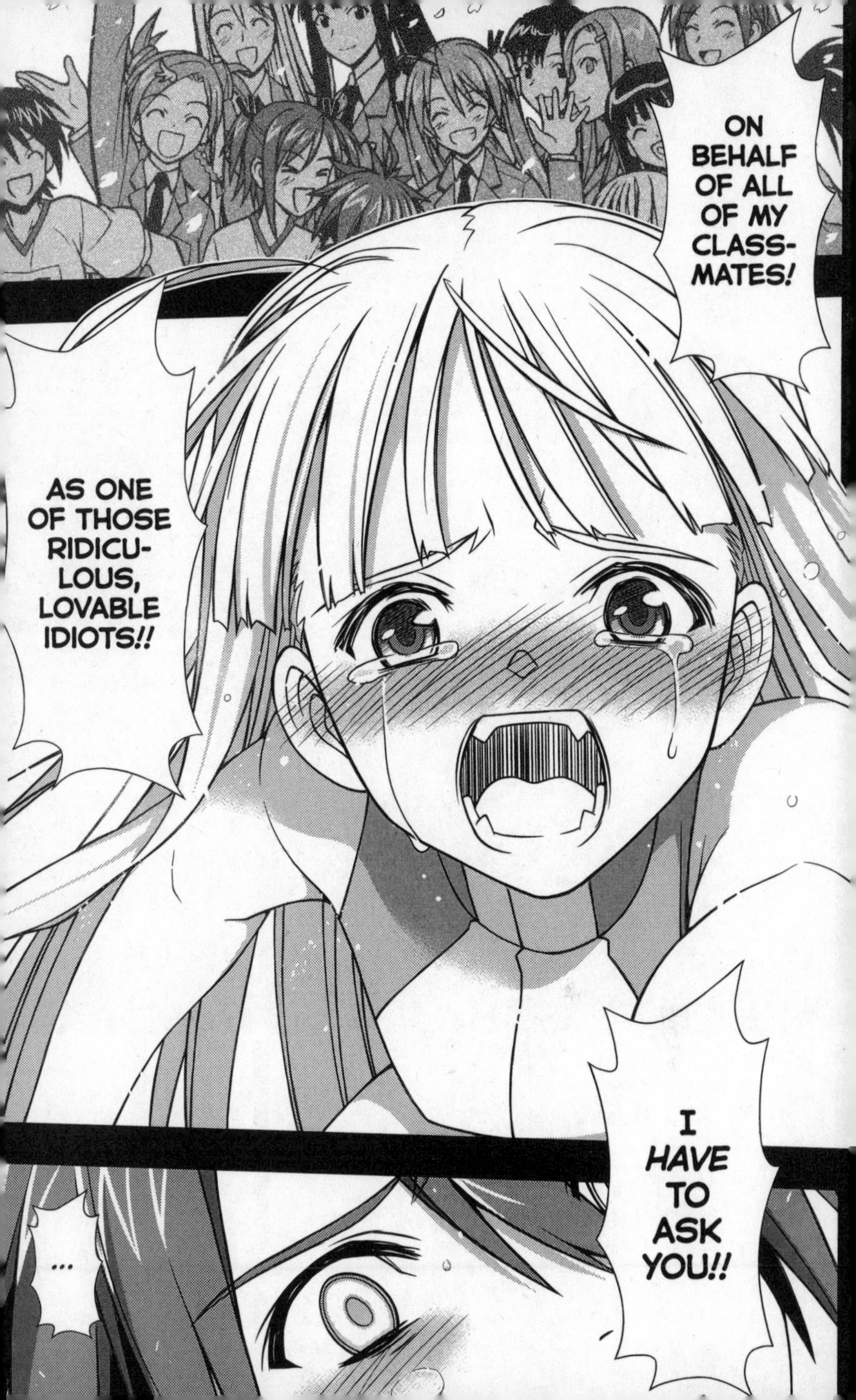
ON BEHALF OF ALL OF MY CLASSMATES!
AS ONE OF THOSE RIDICULOUS, LOVABLE IDIOTS!!
I HAVE TO ASK YOU!!
...

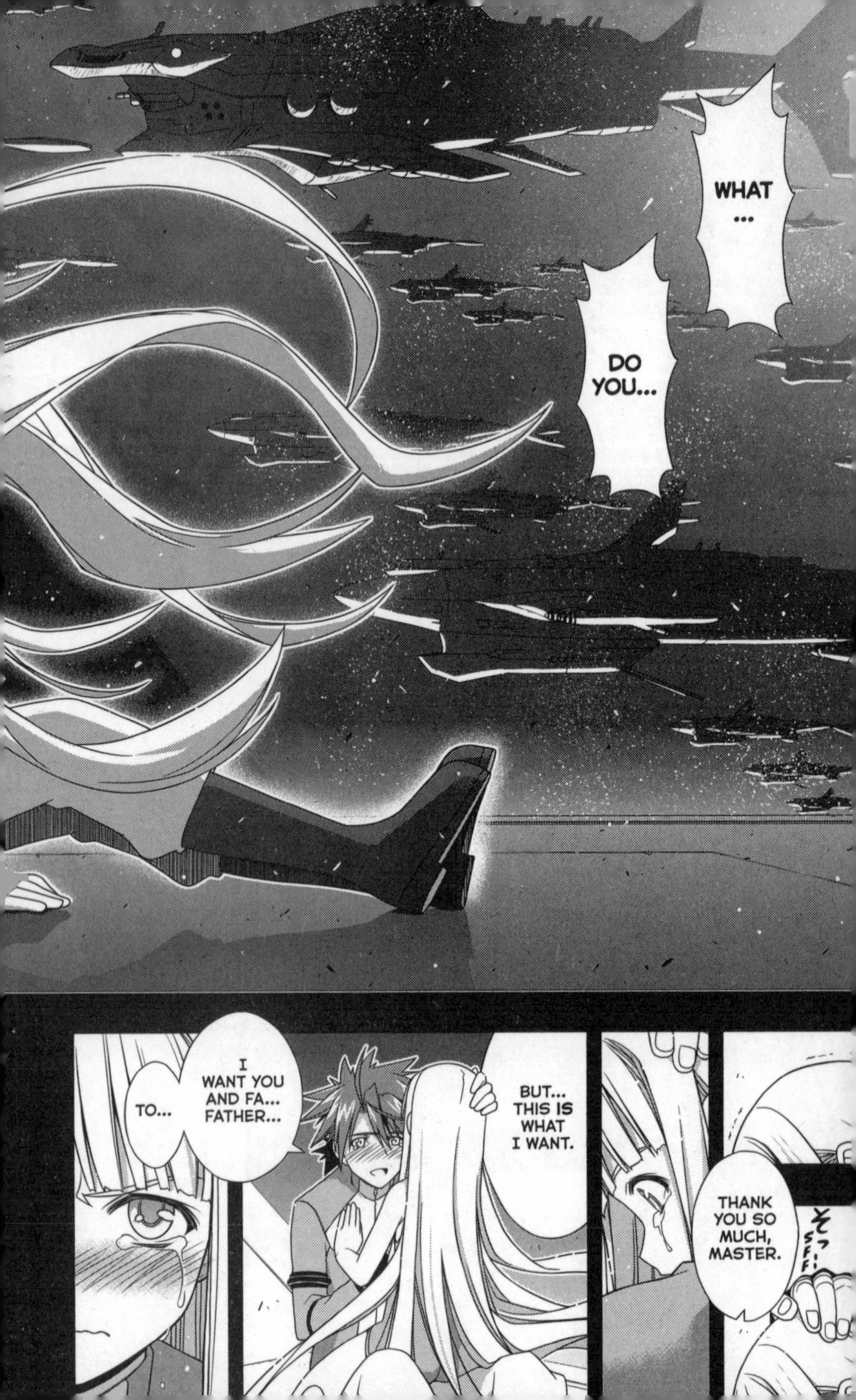
WHAT...
DO YOU...
THANK YOU SO MUCH, MASTER.
SFF
BUT... THIS IS WHAT I WANT.
I WANT YOU AND FA... FATHER...
TO...

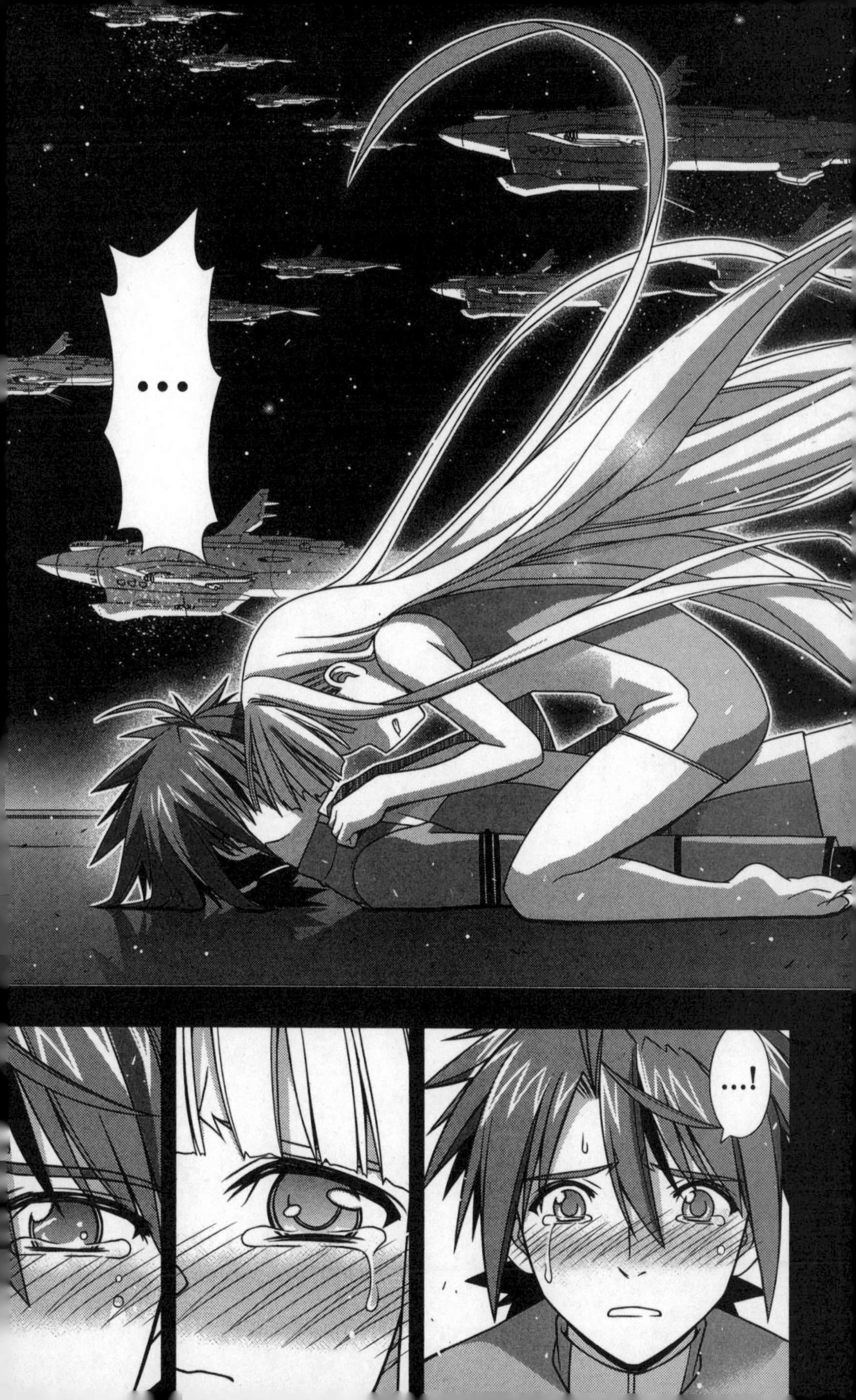
...
...!

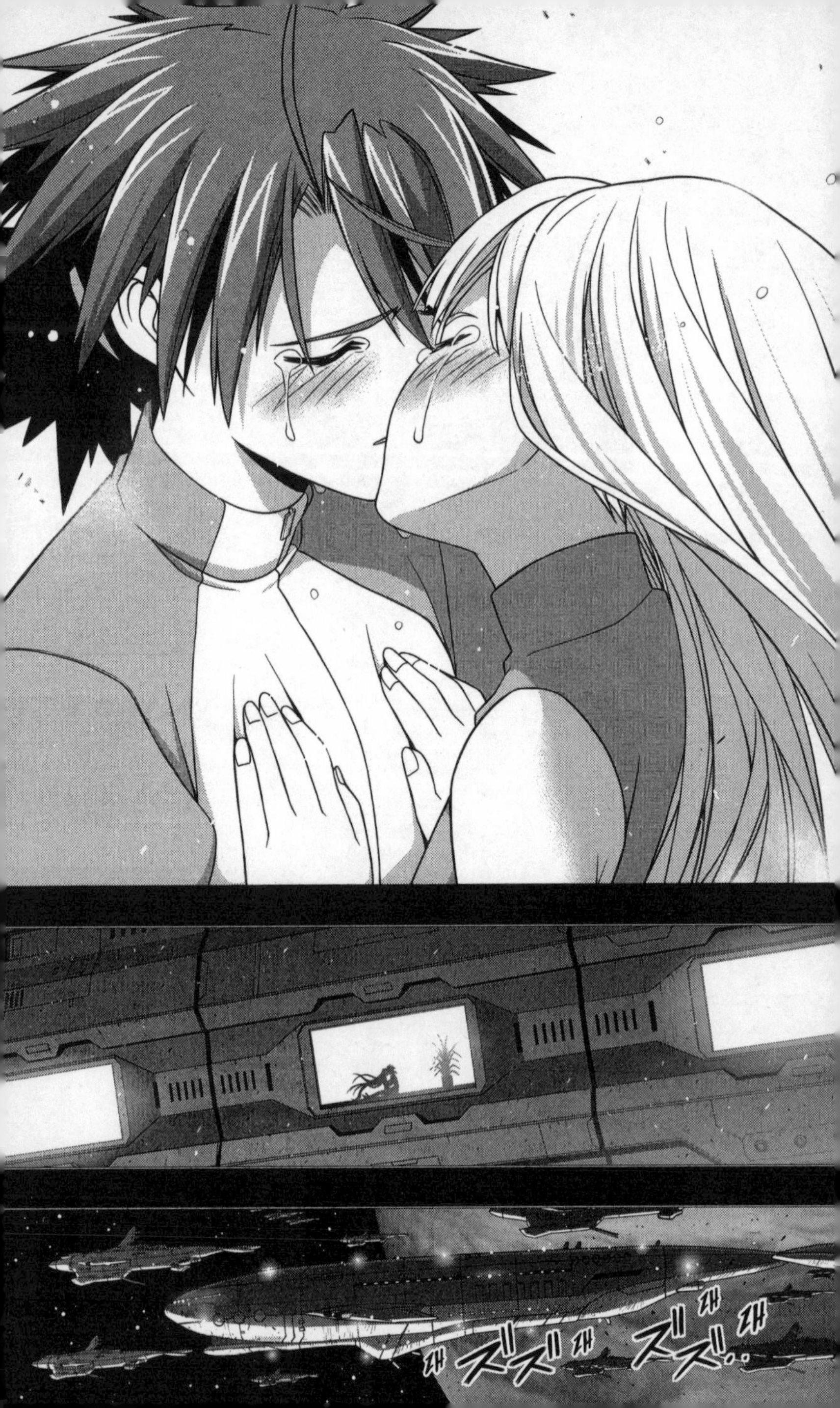
ズズ..
ZH ZH
ズズ
ZH ZH

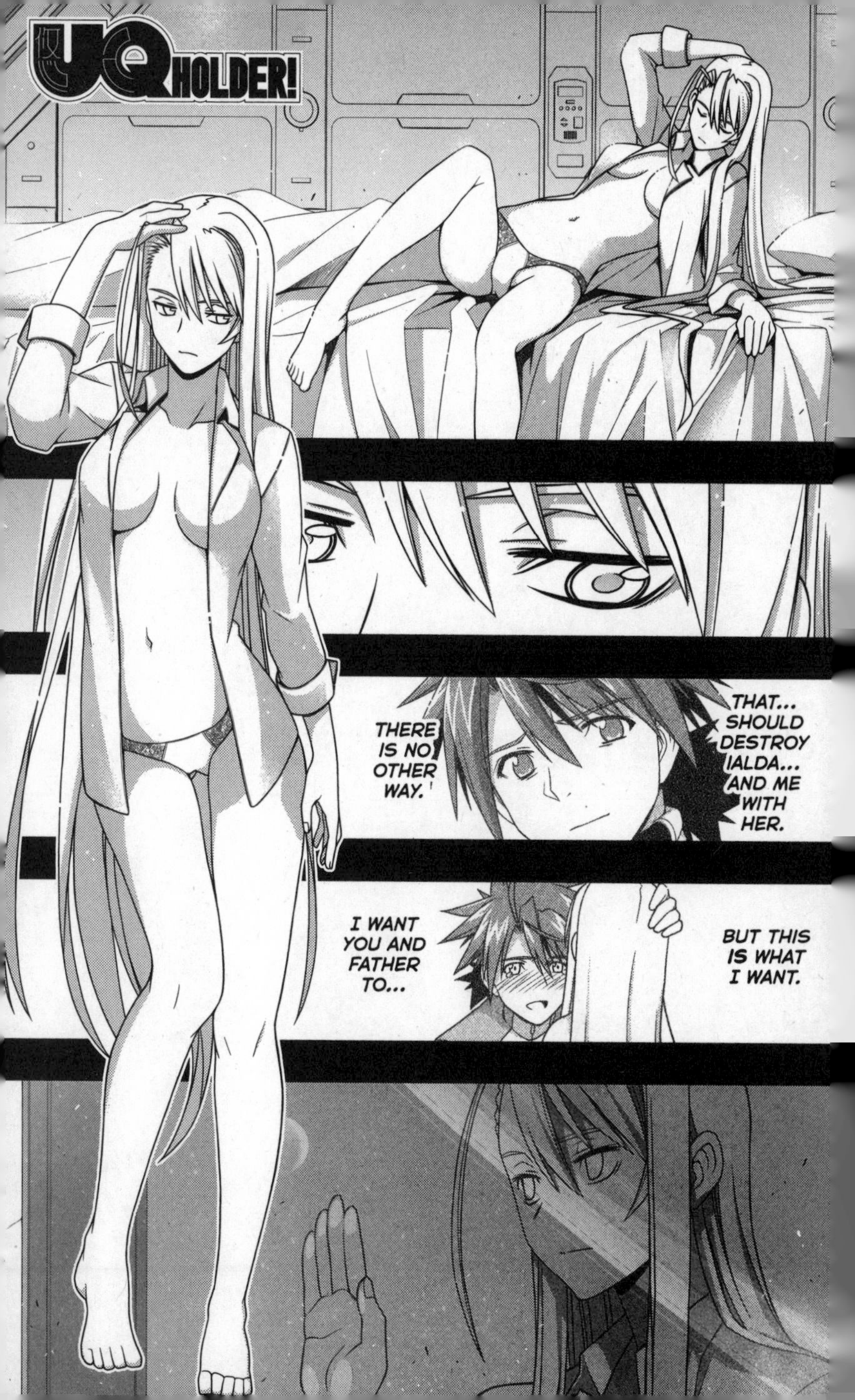
UQ HOLDER!
THAT... SHOULD DESTROY IALDA... AND ME WITH HER.
THERE IS NO OTHER WAY.
BUT THIS IS WHAT I WANT.
I WANT YOU AND FATHER TO...

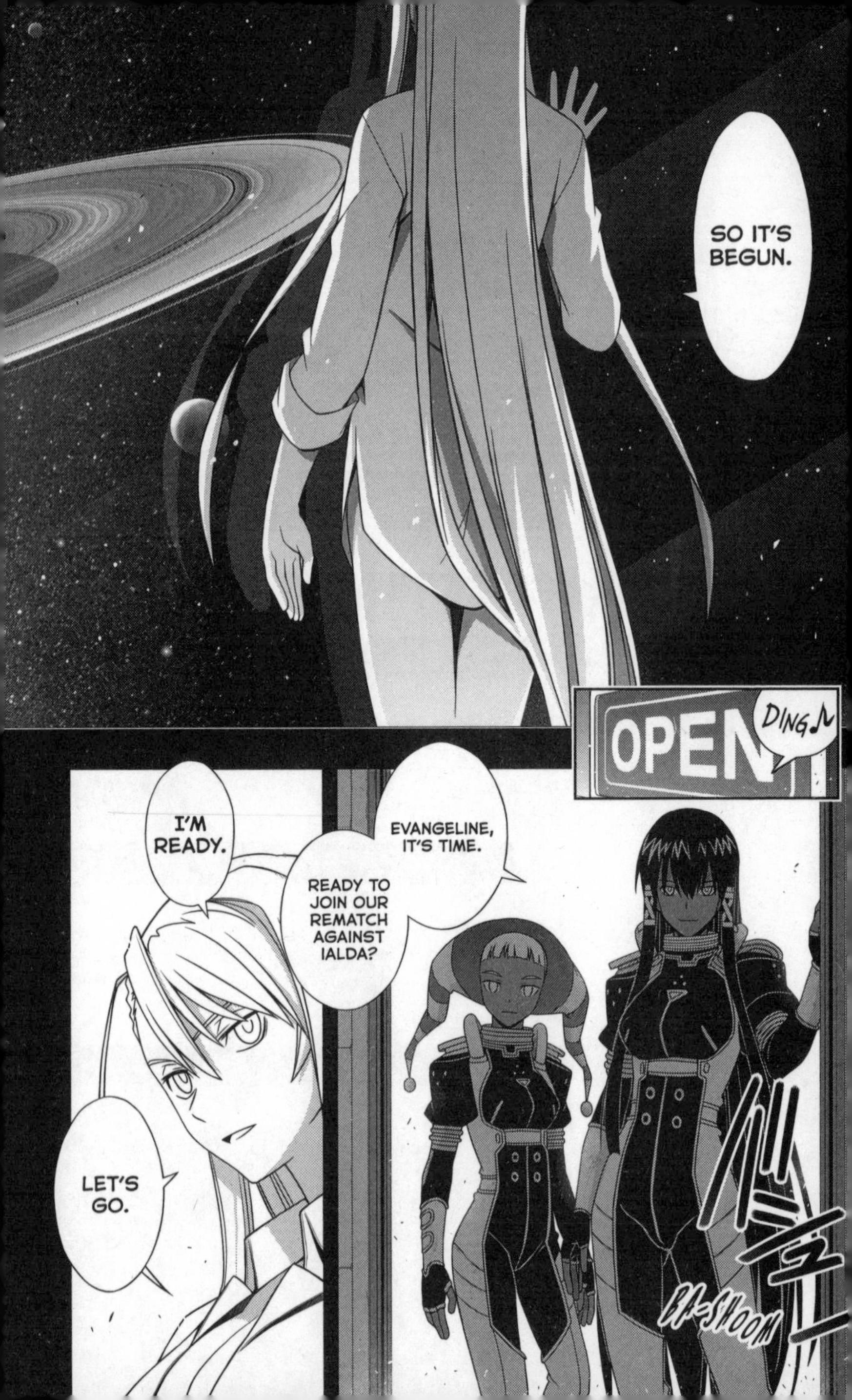
SO IT'S BEGUN.
DING♪
OPEN
EVANGELINE, IT'S TIME.
READY TO JOIN OUR REMATCH AGAINST IALDA?
I'M READY.
LET'S GO.
BA-SHOOM

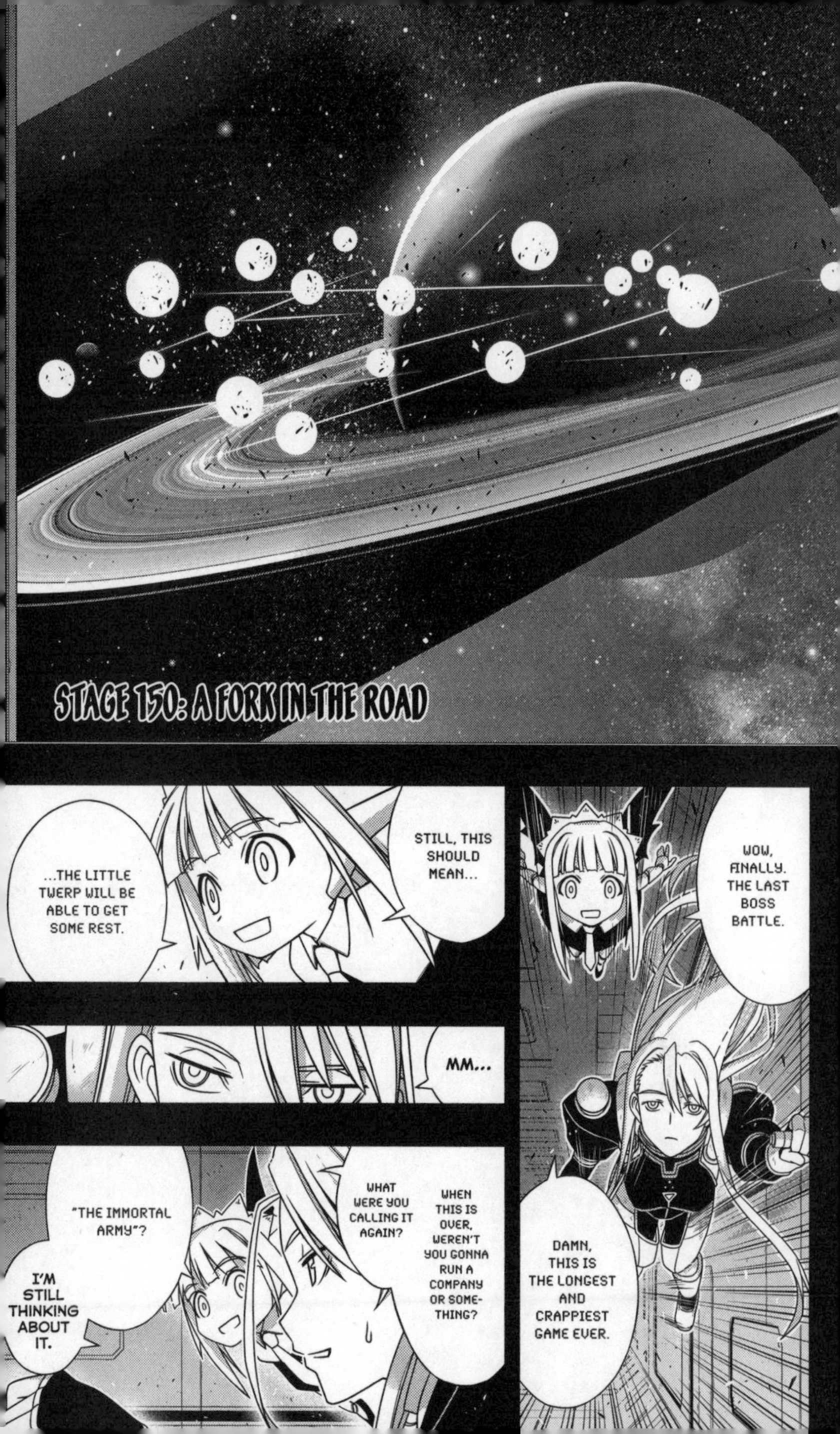
STAGE 150: A FORK IN THE ROAD
WOW, FINALLY. THE LAST BOSS BATTLE.
DAMN, THIS IS THE LONGEST AND CRAPPIEST GAME EVER.
STILL, THIS SHOULD MEAN...
...THE LITTLE TWERP WILL BE ABLE TO GET SOME REST.
MM...
WHEN THIS IS OVER, WEREN'T YOU GONNA RUN A COMPANY OR SOME-THING?
WHAT WERE YOU CALLING IT AGAIN?
"THE IMMORTAL ARMY"?
I'M STILL THINKING ABOUT IT.

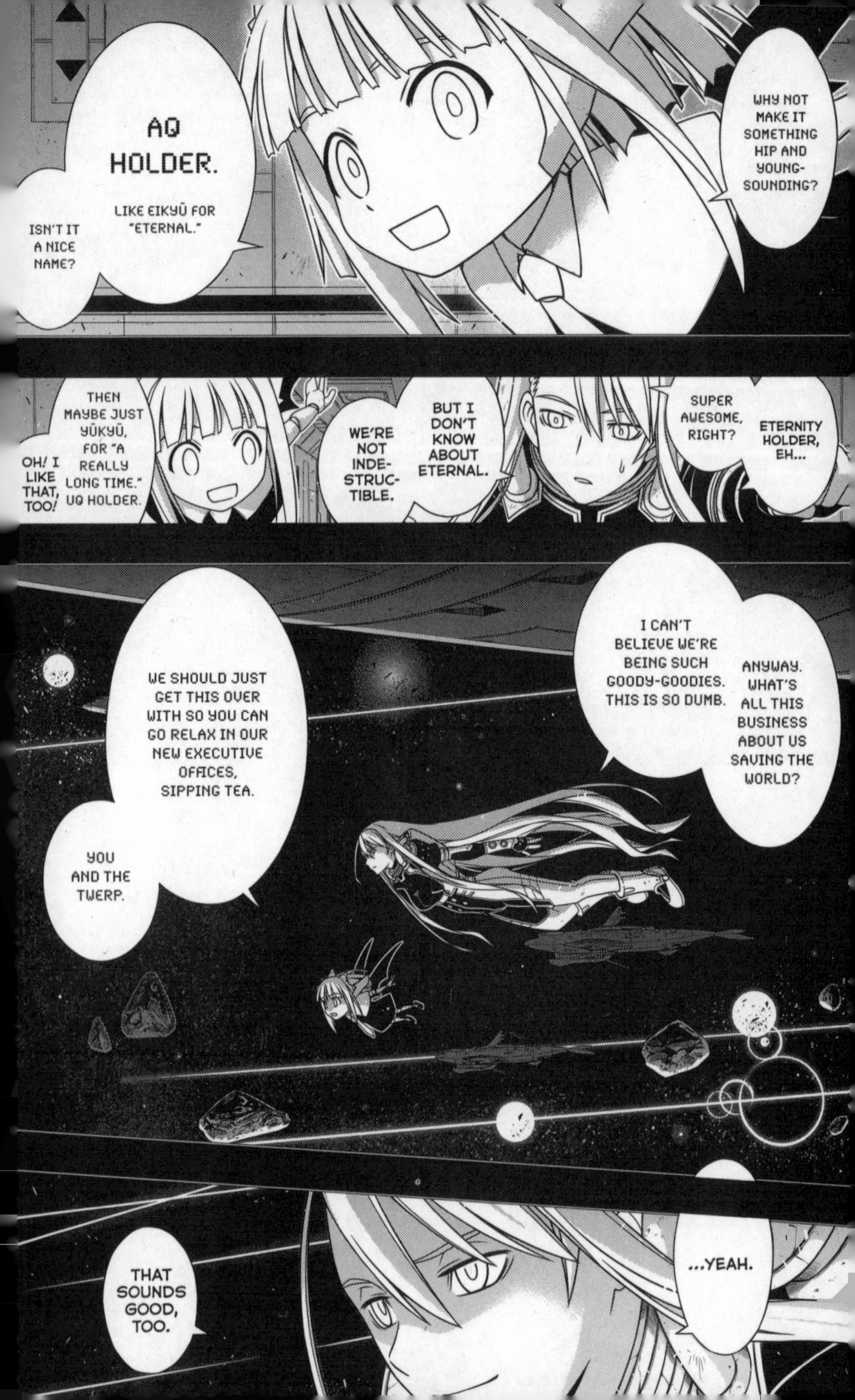
WHY NOT MAKE IT SOMETHING HIP AND YOUNG-SOUNDING?
AQ HOLDER.
LIKE EIKYŪ FOR "ETERNAL."
ISN'T IT A NICE NAME?
ETERNITY HOLDER, EH...
SUPER AWESOME, RIGHT?
BUT I DON'T KNOW ABOUT ETERNAL.
WE'RE NOT INDE-STRUC-TIBLE.
THEN MAYBE JUST YŪKYŪ, FOR "A REALLY LONG TIME." UQ HOLDER.
OH! I LIKE THAT, TOO!
I CAN'T BELIEVE WE'RE BEING SUCH GOODY-GOODIES. THIS IS SO DUMB.
ANYWAY. WHAT'S ALL THIS BUSINESS ABOUT US SAVING THE WORLD?
WE SHOULD JUST GET THIS OVER WITH SO YOU CAN GO RELAX IN OUR NEW EXECUTIVE OFFICES, SIPPING TEA.
YOU AND THE TWERP.
...YEAH.
THAT SOUNDS GOOD, TOO.

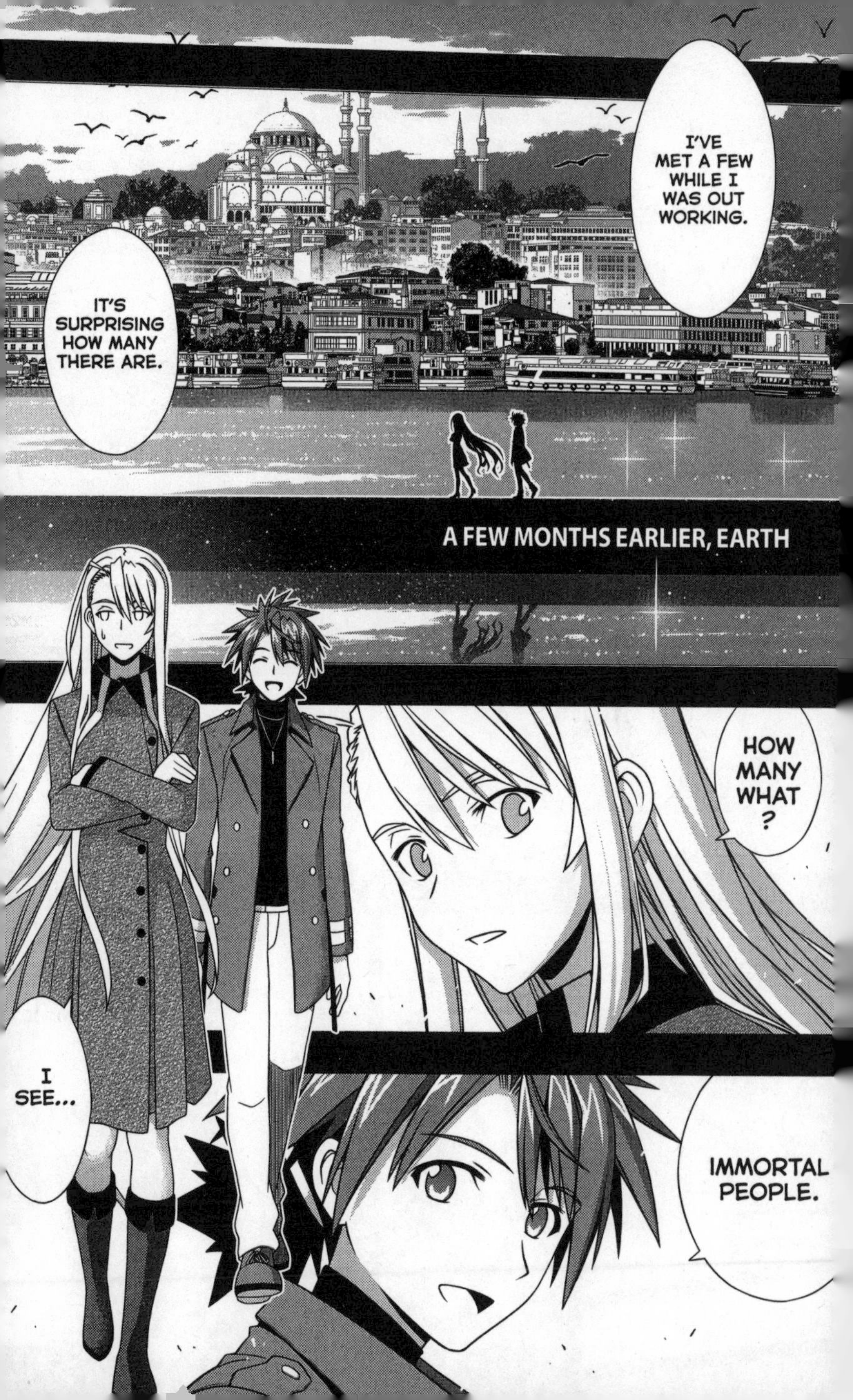
I'VE MET A FEW WHILE I WAS OUT WORKING.
IT'S SURPRISING HOW MANY THERE ARE.
A FEW MONTHS EARLIER, EARTH
HOW MANY WHAT?
IMMORTAL PEOPLE.
I SEE...

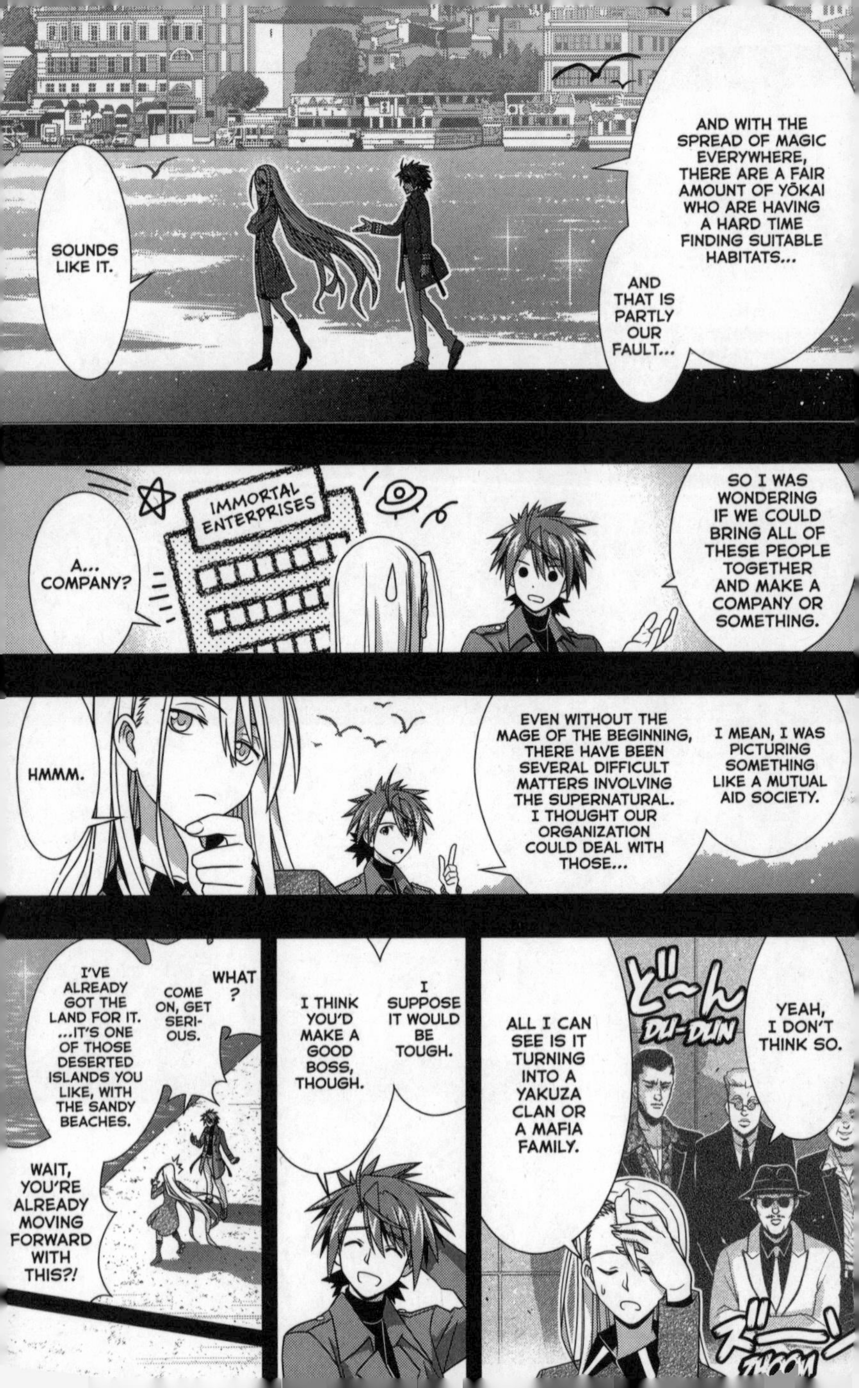
AND WITH THE SPREAD OF MAGIC EVERYWHERE, THERE ARE A FAIR AMOUNT OF YŌKAI WHO ARE HAVING A HARD TIME FINDING SUITABLE HABITATS...
AND THAT IS PARTLY OUR FAULT...
SOUNDS LIKE IT.
SO I WAS WONDERING IF WE COULD BRING ALL OF THESE PEOPLE TOGETHER AND MAKE A COMPANY OR SOMETHING.
IMMORTAL ENTERPRISES
A... COMPANY?
I MEAN, I WAS PICTURING SOMETHING LIKE A MUTUAL AID SOCIETY.
EVEN WITHOUT THE MAGE OF THE BEGINNING, THERE HAVE BEEN SEVERAL DIFFICULT MATTERS INVOLVING THE SUPERNATURAL. I THOUGHT OUR ORGANIZATION COULD DEAL WITH THOSE...
HMMM.
YEAH, I DON'T THINK SO.
どーん
DU-DUN
ALL I CAN SEE IS IT TURNING INTO A YAKUZA CLAN OR A MAFIA FAMILY.
ズーン
I SUPPOSE IT WOULD BE TOUGH.
I THINK YOU'D MAKE A GOOD BOSS, THOUGH.
WHAT?
COME ON, GET SERI-OUS.
I'VE ALREADY GOT THE LAND FOR IT. ...IT'S ONE OF THOSE DESERTED ISLANDS YOU LIKE, WITH THE SANDY BEACHES.
WAIT, YOU'RE ALREADY MOVING FORWARD WITH THIS?!

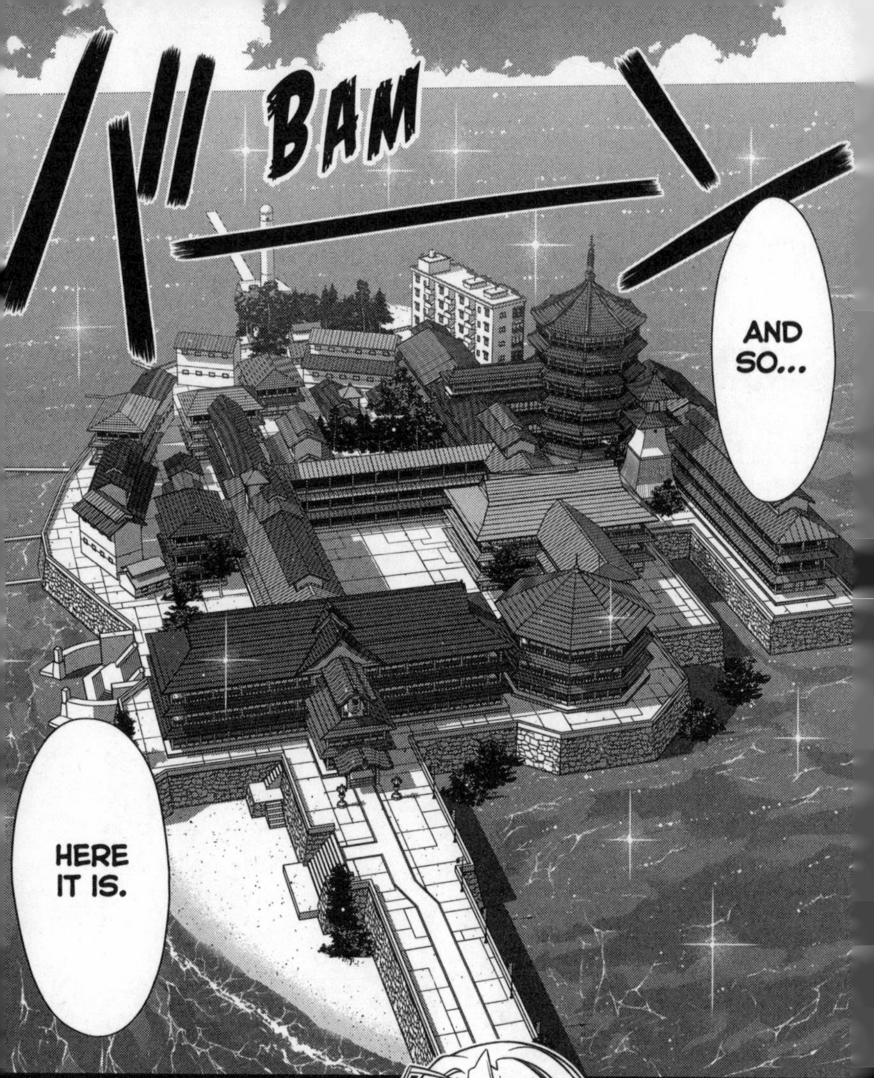
BAM
AND SO...
HERE IT IS.

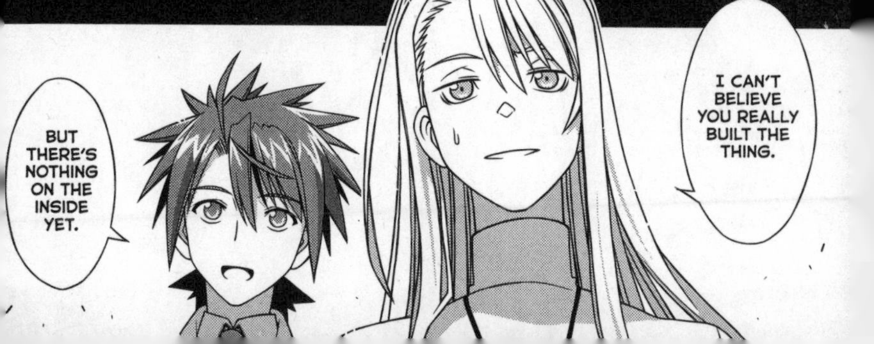
I CAN'T BELIEVE YOU REALLY BUILT THE THING.
BUT THERE'S NOTHING ON THE INSIDE YET.

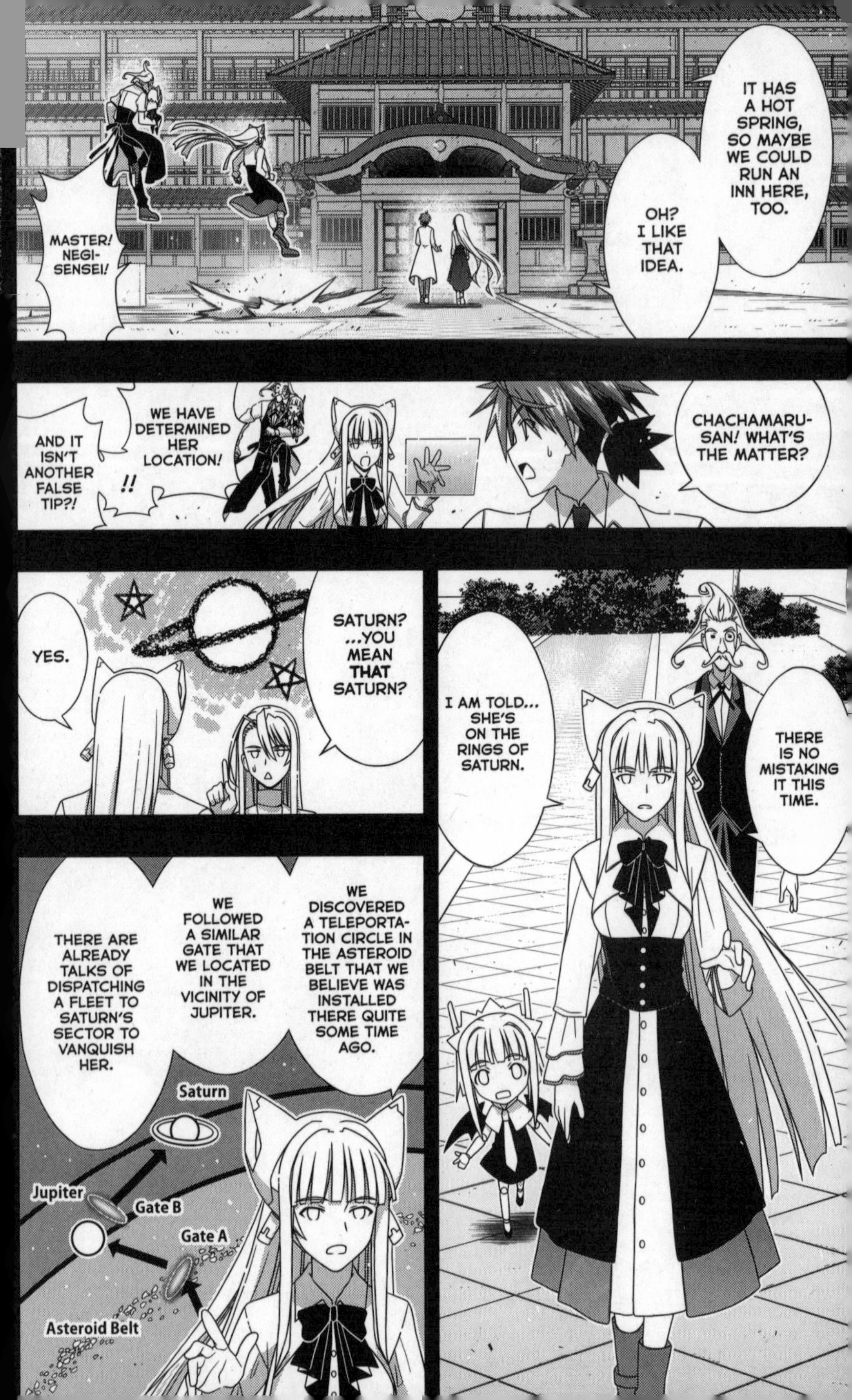
IT HAS A HOT SPRING, SO MAYBE WE COULD RUN AN INN HERE, TOO.
OH? I LIKE THAT IDEA.
MASTER! NEGI-SENSEI!
CHACHAMARU-SAN! WHAT'S THE MATTER?
WE HAVE DETERMINED HER LOCATION!
!!
AND IT ISN'T ANOTHER FALSE TIP?!
THERE IS NO MISTAKING IT THIS TIME.
I AM TOLD... SHE'S ON THE RINGS OF SATURN.
SATURN? ...YOU MEAN THAT SATURN?
YES.
WE DISCOVERED A TELEPORTATION CIRCLE IN THE ASTEROID BELT THAT WE BELIEVE WAS INSTALLED THERE QUITE SOME TIME AGO.
WE FOLLOWED A SIMILAR GATE THAT WE LOCATED IN THE VICINITY OF JUPITER.
THERE ARE ALREADY TALKS OF DISPATCHING A FLEET TO SATURN'S SECTOR TO VANQUISH HER.
Saturn
Jupiter
Gate B
Gate A
Asteroid Belt

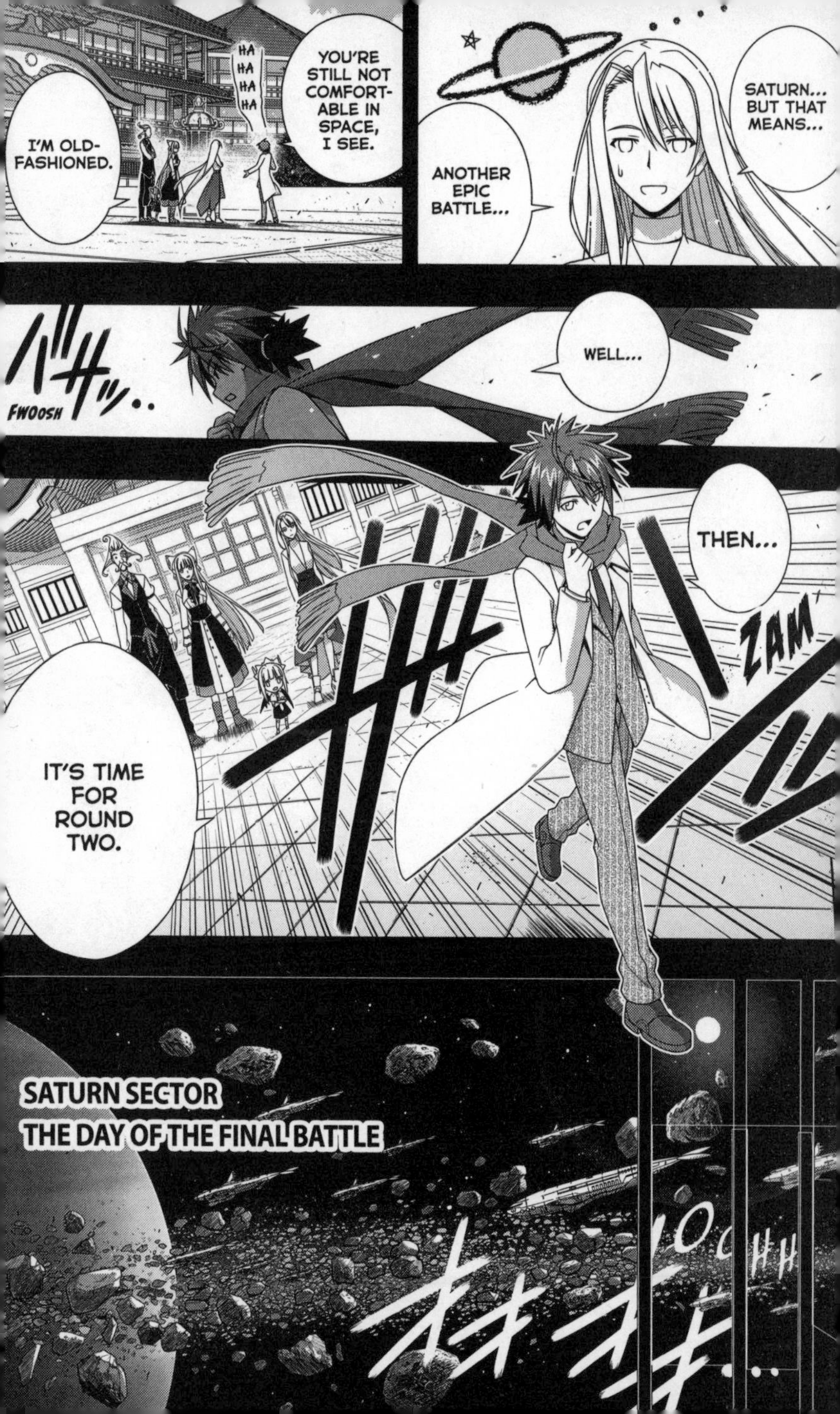
SATURN... BUT THAT MEANS...
ANOTHER EPIC BATTLE...
YOU'RE STILL NOT COMFORTABLE IN SPACE, I SEE.
HA HA HA HA
I'M OLD-FASHIONED.
WELL...
FWOOSH
THEN...
ZAM
IT'S TIME FOR ROUND TWO.
SATURN SECTOR
THE DAY OF THE FINAL BATTLE

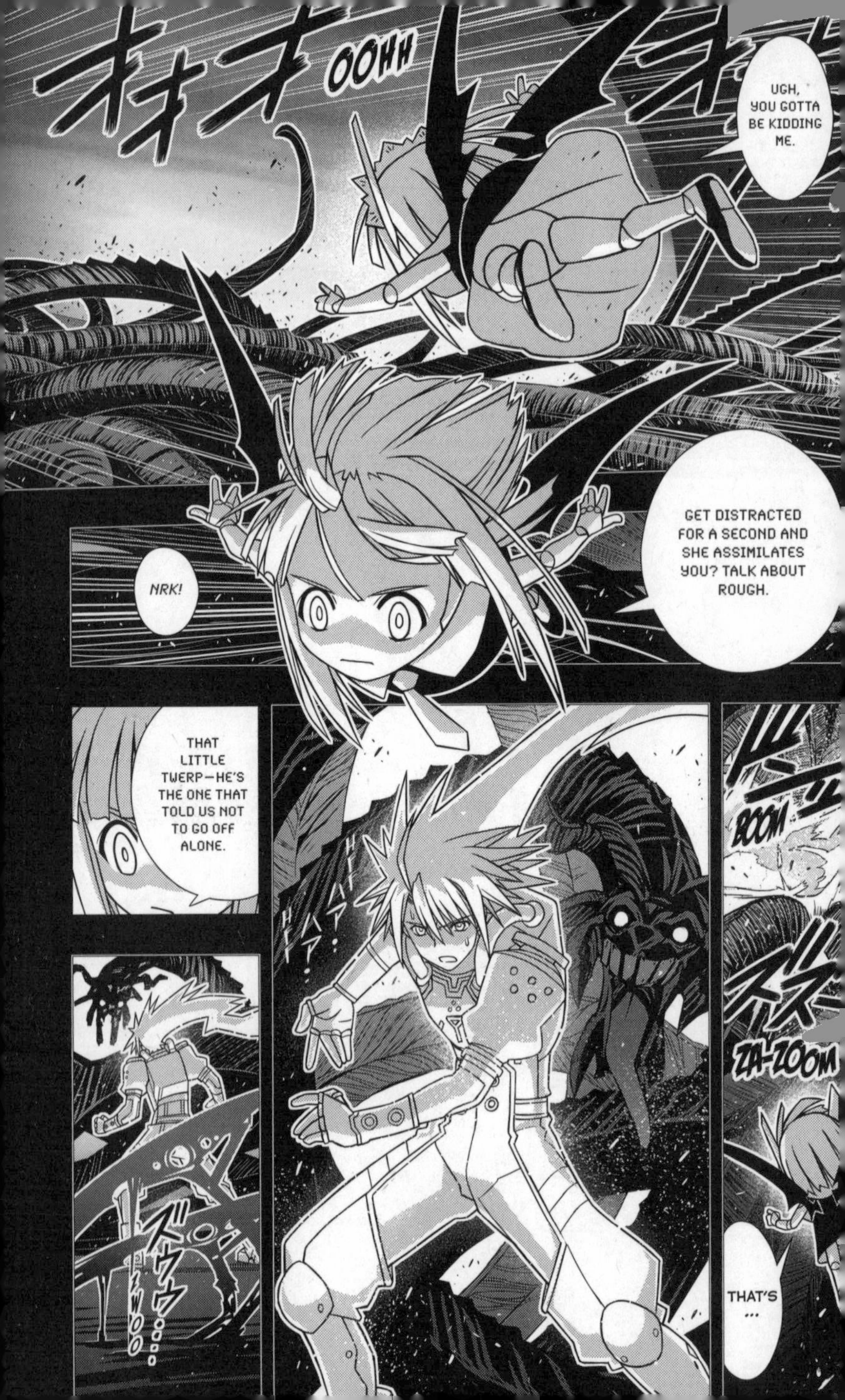

OOHH
UGH, YOU GOTTA BE KIDDING ME.
GET DISTRACTED FOR A SECOND AND SHE ASSIMILATES YOU? TALK ABOUT ROUGH.
NRK!
BOOM
ZA-ZOOM
THAT'S...
THAT LITTLE TWERP—HE'S THE ONE THAT TOLD US NOT TO GO OFF ALONE.

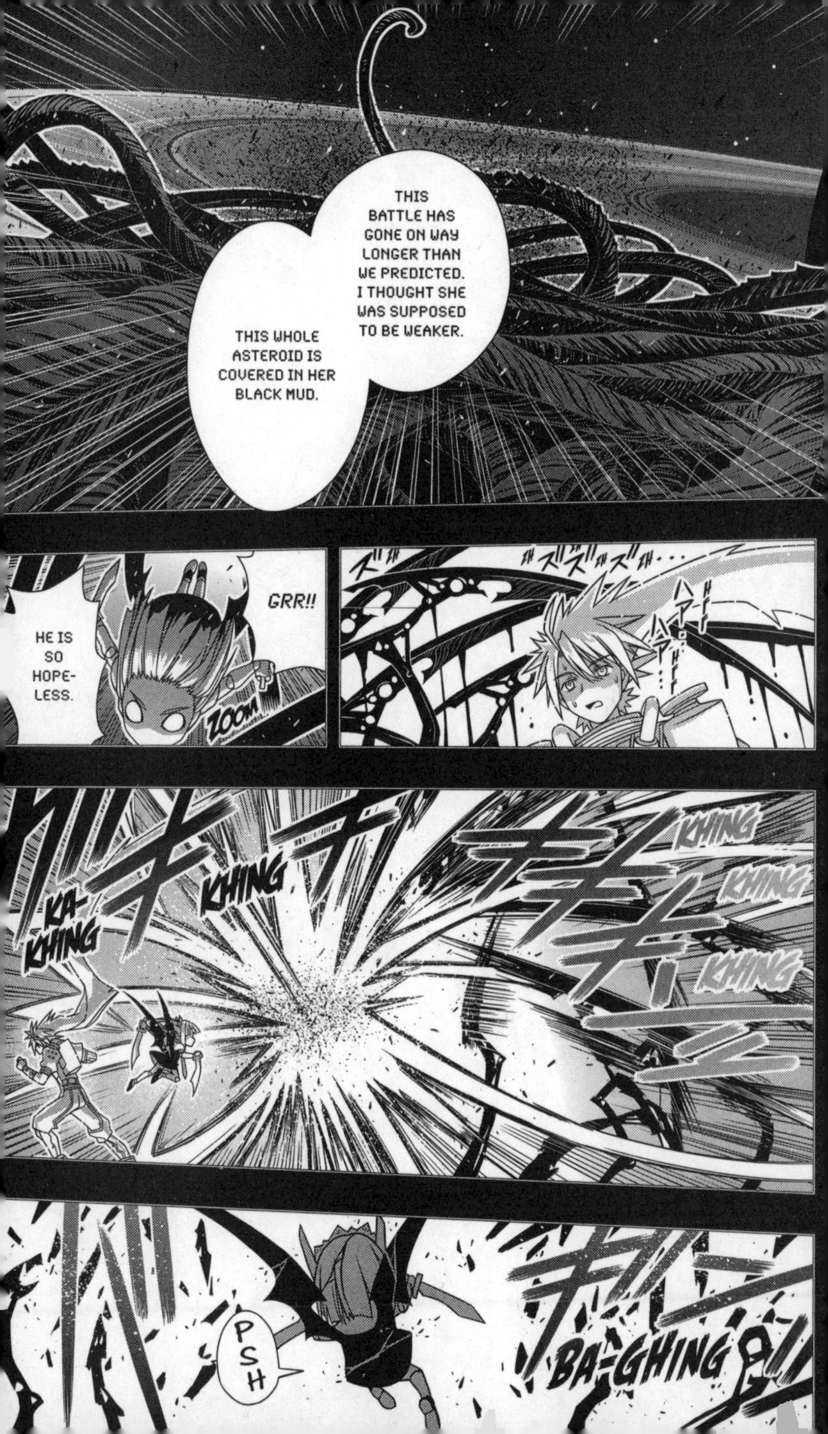
THIS BATTLE HAS GONE ON WAY LONGER THAN WE PREDICTED. I THOUGHT SHE WAS SUPPOSED TO BE WEAKER.
THIS WHOLE ASTEROID IS COVERED IN HER BLACK MUD.
GRR!!
HE IS SO HOPE-LESS.
ZOOM
KHING
KHING
KHING
KHING
KA-KHING
BA-GHING
PSH

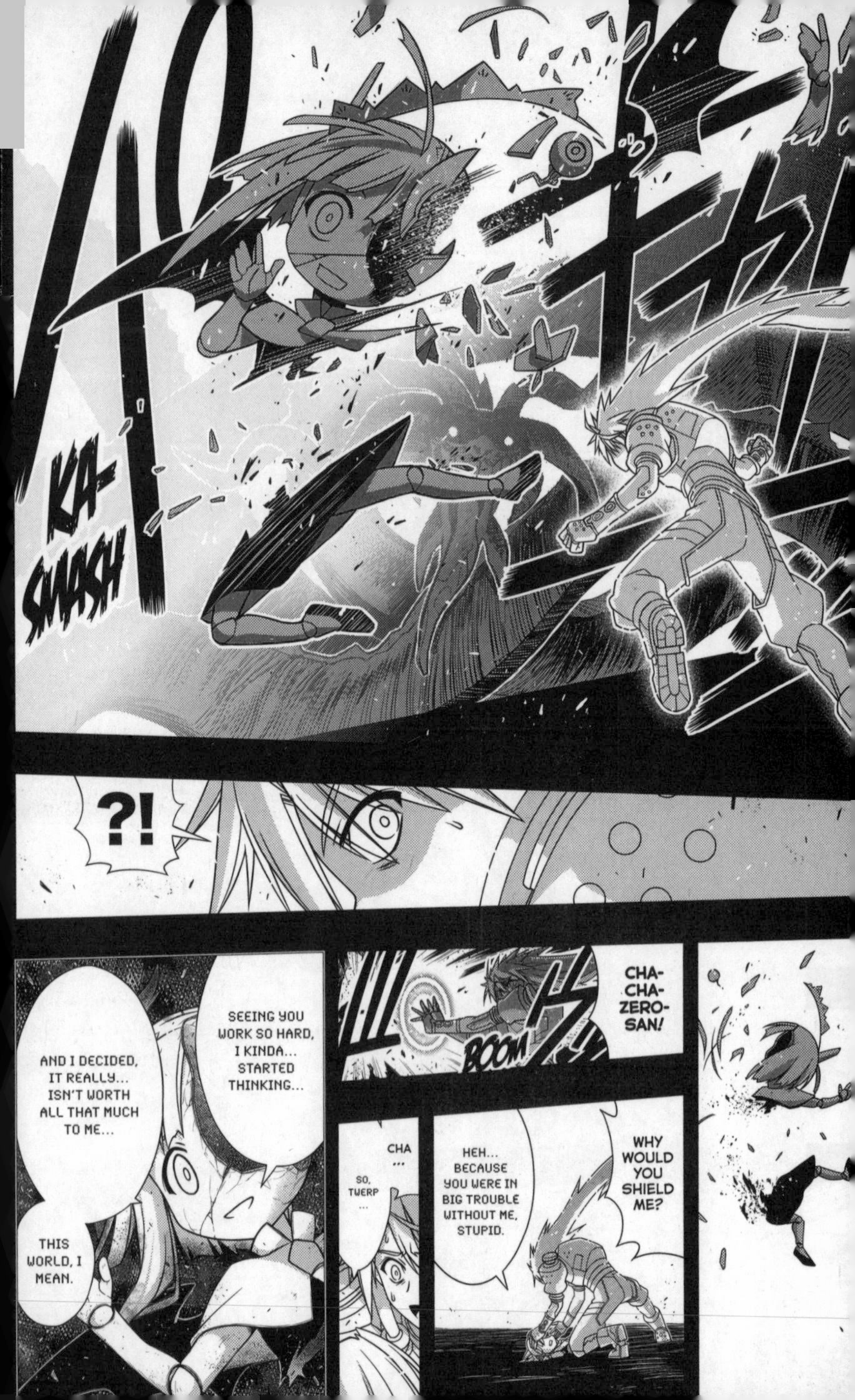
KA-SMASH
?!
BOOM
CHA-CHA-ZERO-SAN!
WHY WOULD YOU SHIELD ME?
HEH... BECAUSE YOU WERE IN BIG TROUBLE WITHOUT ME, STUPID.
CHA...
SO, TWERP...
SEEING YOU WORK SO HARD, I KINDA... STARTED THINKING...
AND I DECIDED, IT REALLY... ISN'T WORTH ALL THAT MUCH TO ME...
THIS WORLD, I MEAN.

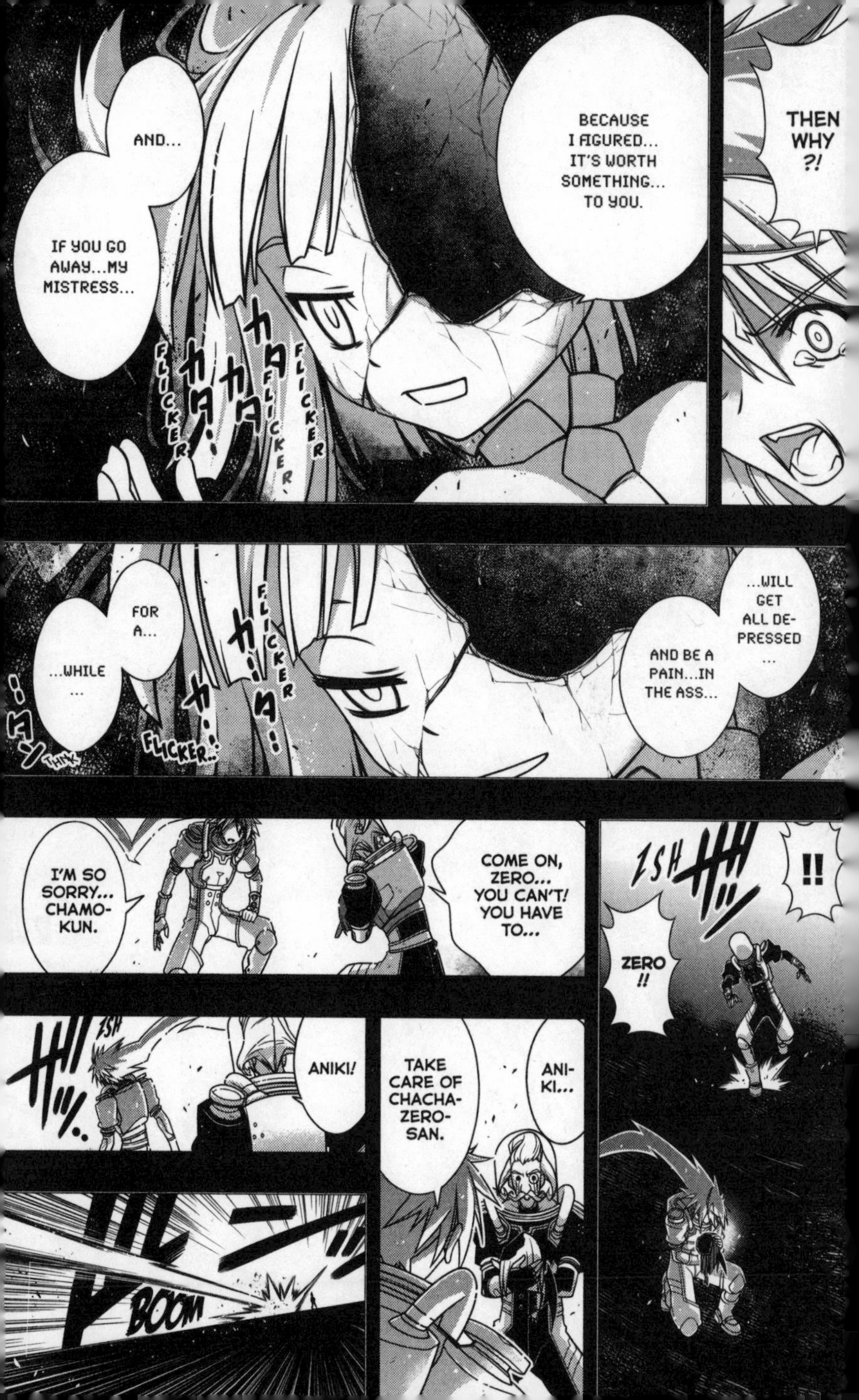
THEN WHY ?!
BECAUSE I FIGURED... IT'S WORTH SOMETHING... TO YOU.
AND...
IF YOU GO AWAY...MY MISTRESS...
FLICKER
FLICKER
FLICKER
...WILL GET ALL DE-PRESSED ...
AND BE A PAIN...IN THE ASS...
FOR A...
...WHILE ...
FLICKER
FLICKER..
THNK
!!
ZSH
ZERO !!
COME ON, ZERO... YOU CAN'T! YOU HAVE TO...
I'M SO SORRY... CHAMO-KUN.
ANI-KI...
TAKE CARE OF CHACHA-ZERO-SAN.
ANIKI!
ZSH
BOOM

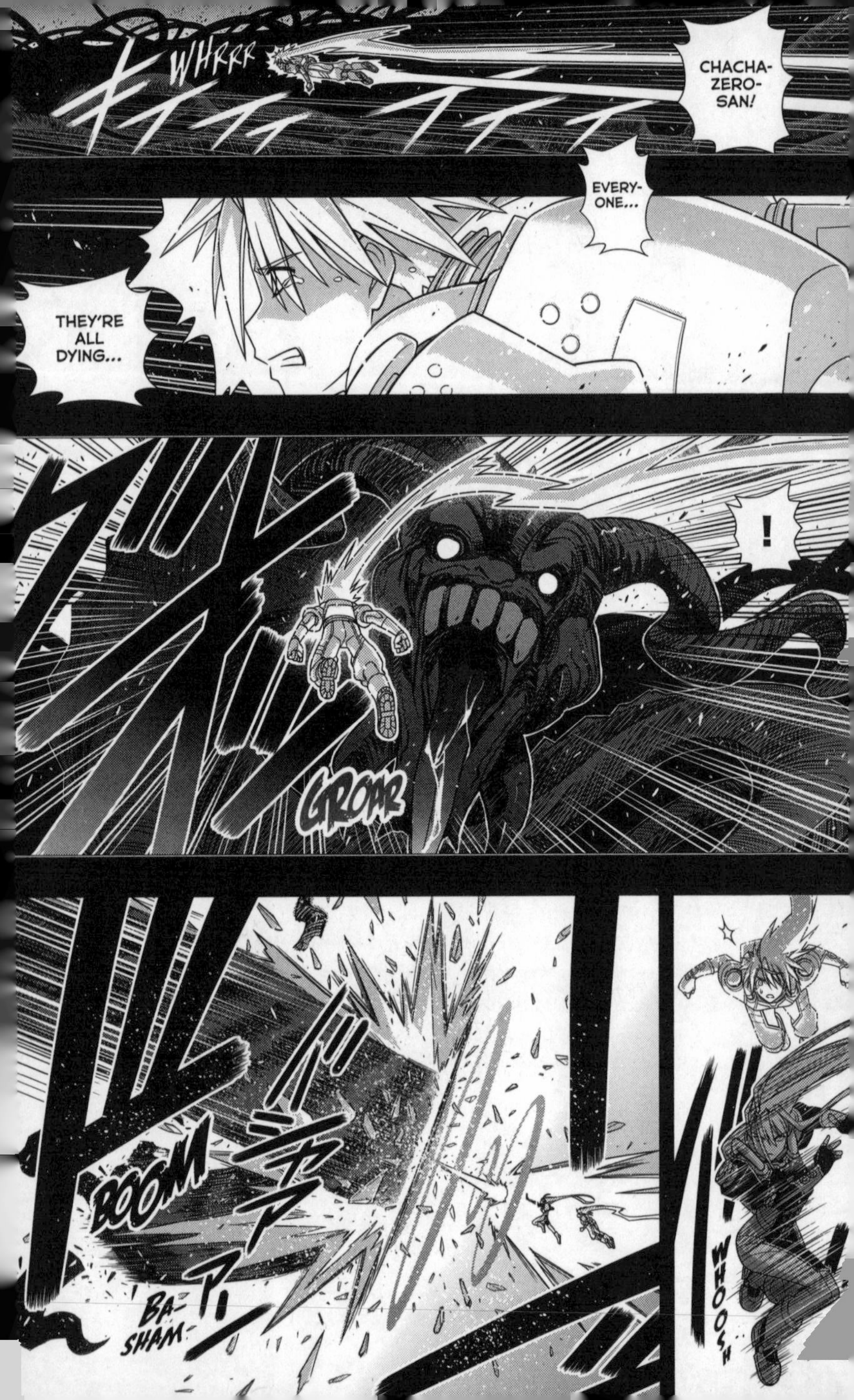
CHACHA-ZERO-SAN!
WHRRR
EVERY-ONE...
THEY'RE ALL DYING...
!
GROAR
WHOOSH
BOOM
BA-SHAM

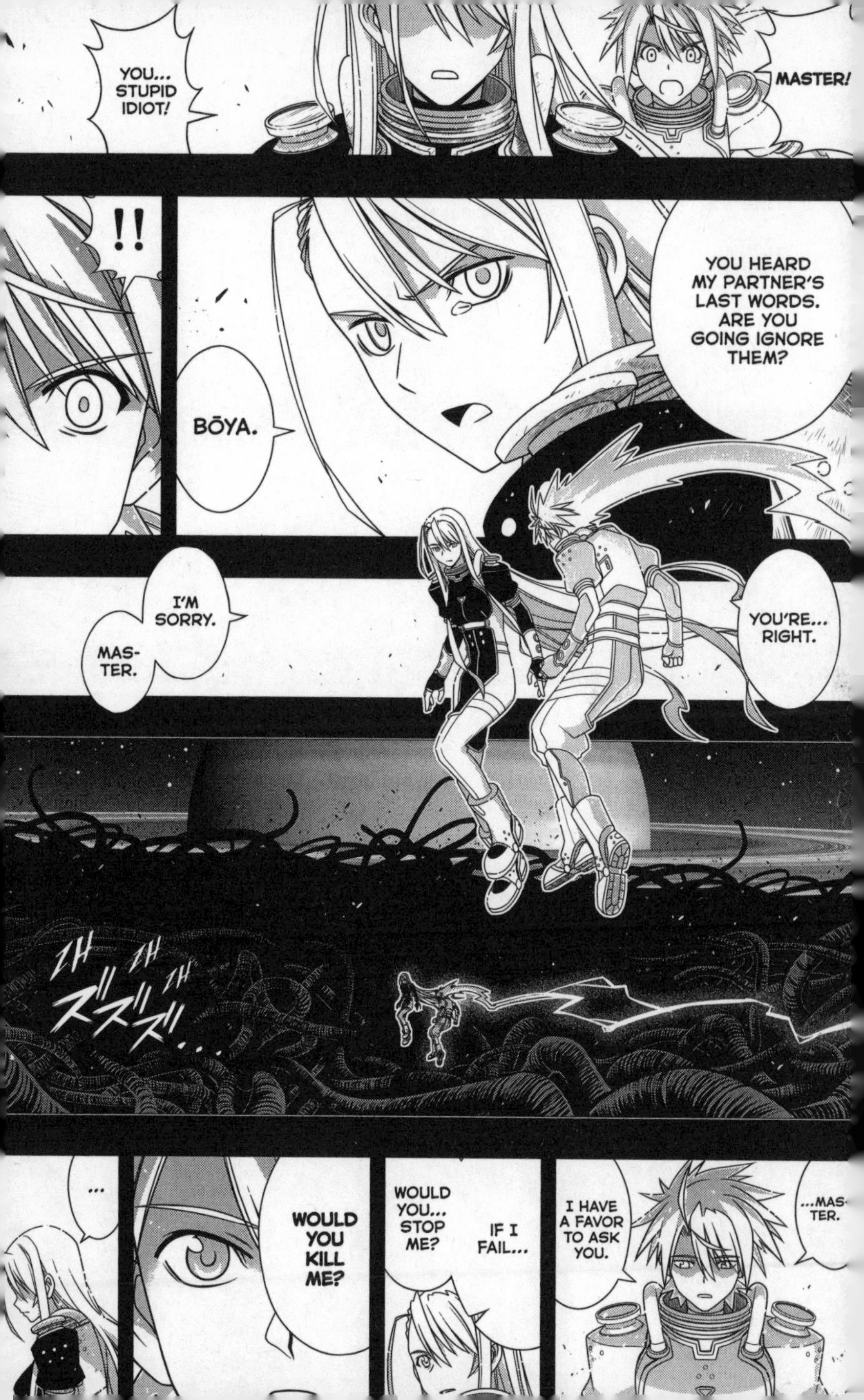
MASTER!
YOU... STUPID IDIOT!
YOU HEARD MY PARTNER'S LAST WORDS. ARE YOU GOING IGNORE THEM?
BŌYA.
!!
YOU'RE... RIGHT.
I'M SORRY.
MAS-TER.
ズズズ...
...MAS-TER.
I HAVE A FAVOR TO ASK YOU.
IF I FAIL...
WOULD YOU... STOP ME?
WOULD YOU KILL ME?
...

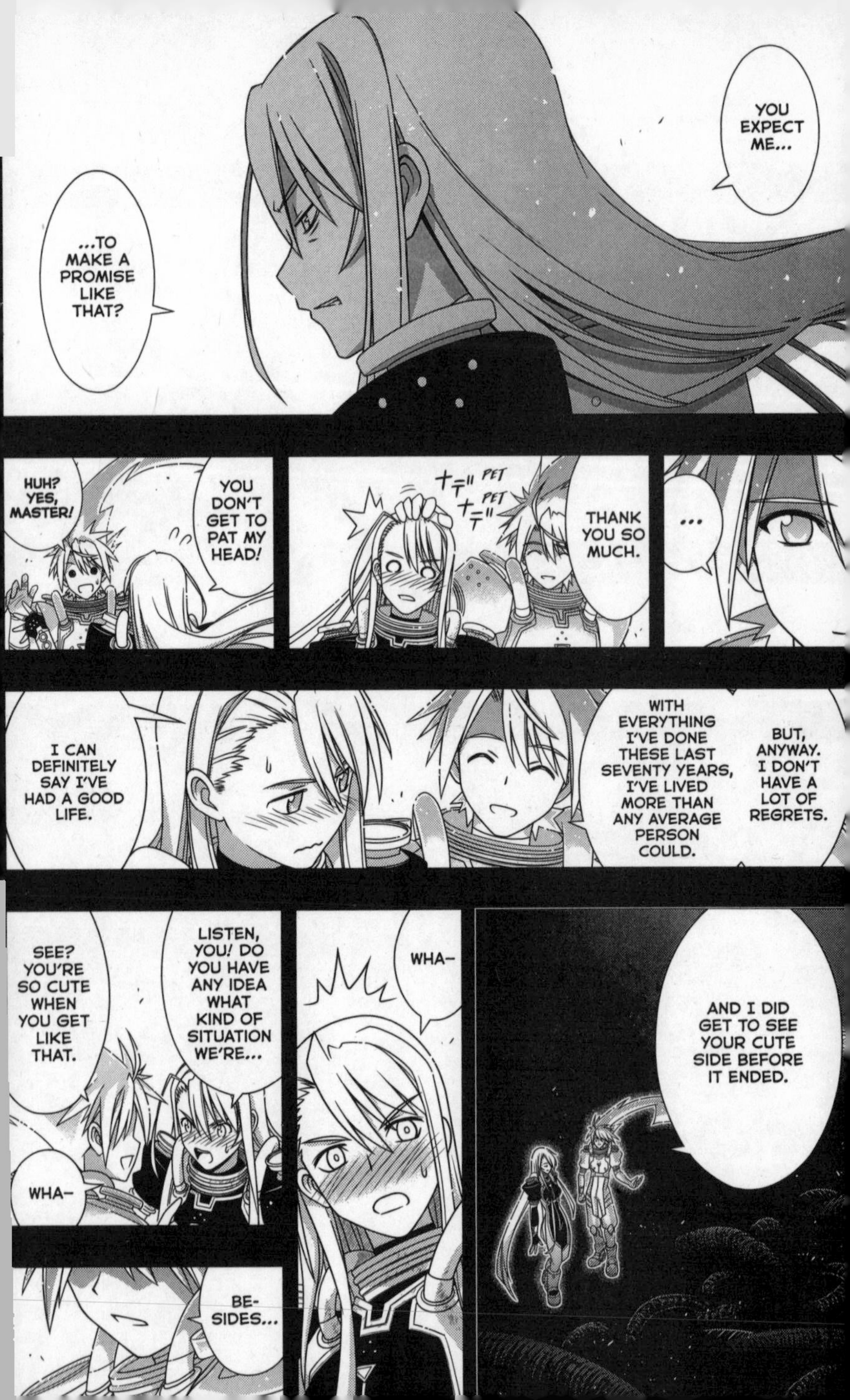
YOU EXPECT ME...
...TO MAKE A PROMISE LIKE THAT?
...
PET PET
THANK YOU SO MUCH.
YOU DON'T GET TO PAT MY HEAD!
HUH? YES, MASTER!
BUT, ANYWAY. I DON'T HAVE A LOT OF REGRETS.
WITH EVERYTHING I'VE DONE THESE LAST SEVENTY YEARS, I'VE LIVED MORE THAN ANY AVERAGE PERSON COULD.
I CAN DEFINITELY SAY I'VE HAD A GOOD LIFE.
AND I DID GET TO SEE YOUR CUTE SIDE BEFORE IT ENDED.
WHA-
LISTEN, YOU! DO YOU HAVE ANY IDEA WHAT KIND OF SITUATION WE'RE...
SEE? YOU'RE SO CUTE WHEN YOU GET LIKE THAT.
WHA-
BE-SIDES...

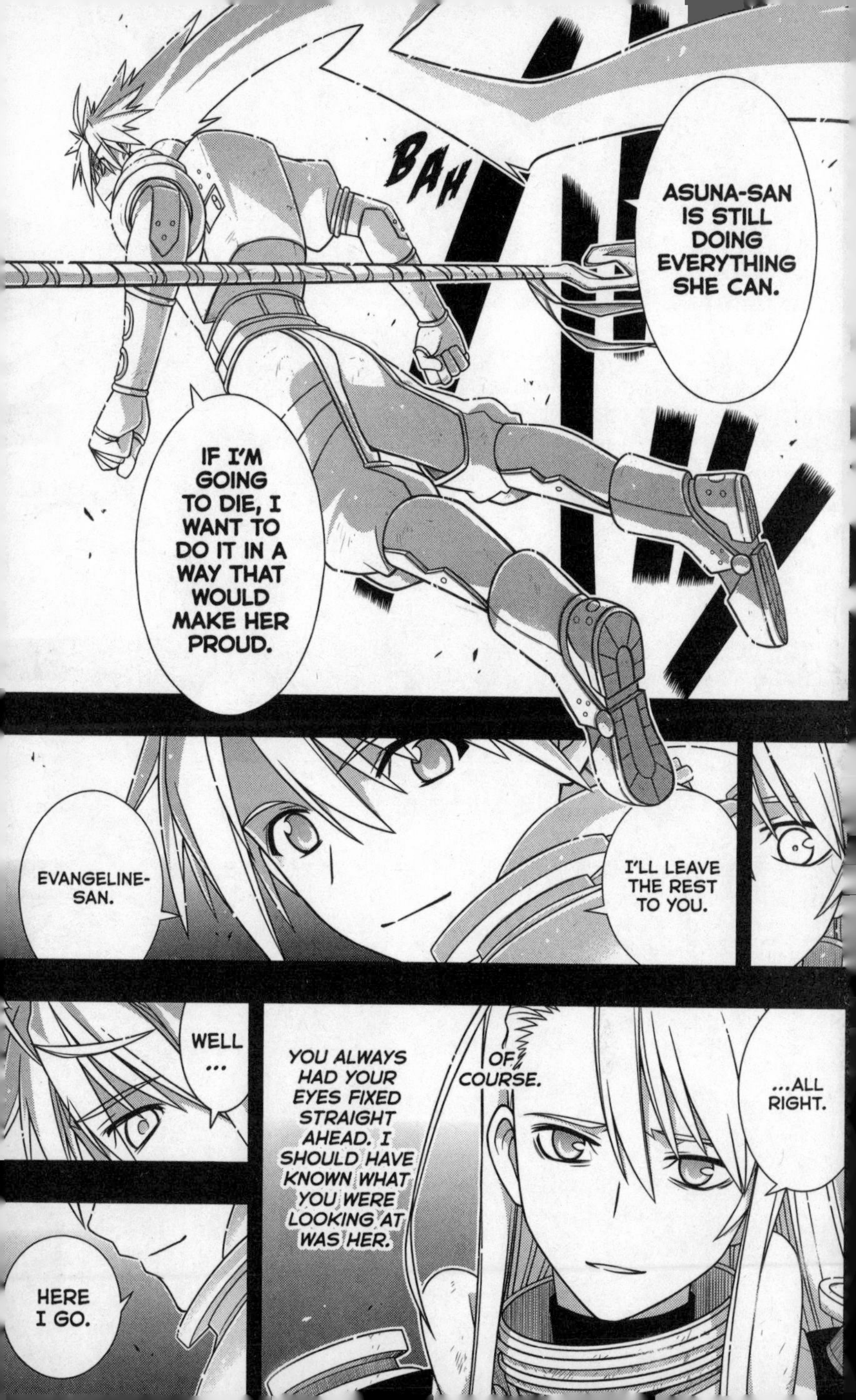
BAH
ASUNA-SAN IS STILL DOING EVERYTHING SHE CAN.
IF I'M GOING TO DIE, I WANT TO DO IT IN A WAY THAT WOULD MAKE HER PROUD.
I'LL LEAVE THE REST TO YOU.
EVANGELINE-SAN.
...ALL RIGHT.
OF COURSE.
YOU ALWAYS HAD YOUR EYES FIXED STRAIGHT AHEAD. I SHOULD HAVE KNOWN WHAT YOU WERE LOOKING AT WAS HER.
WELL ...
HERE I GO.

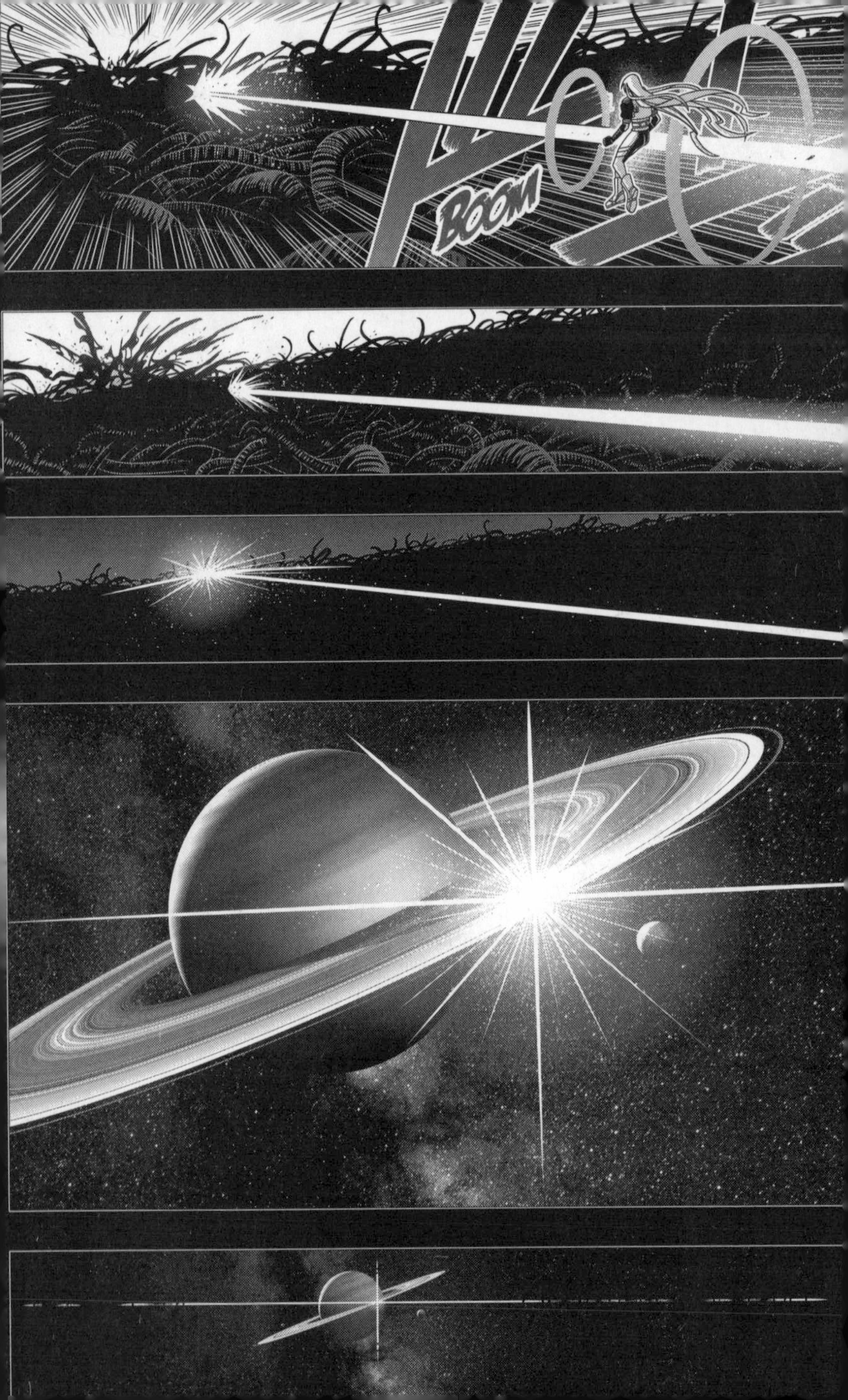
BOOM

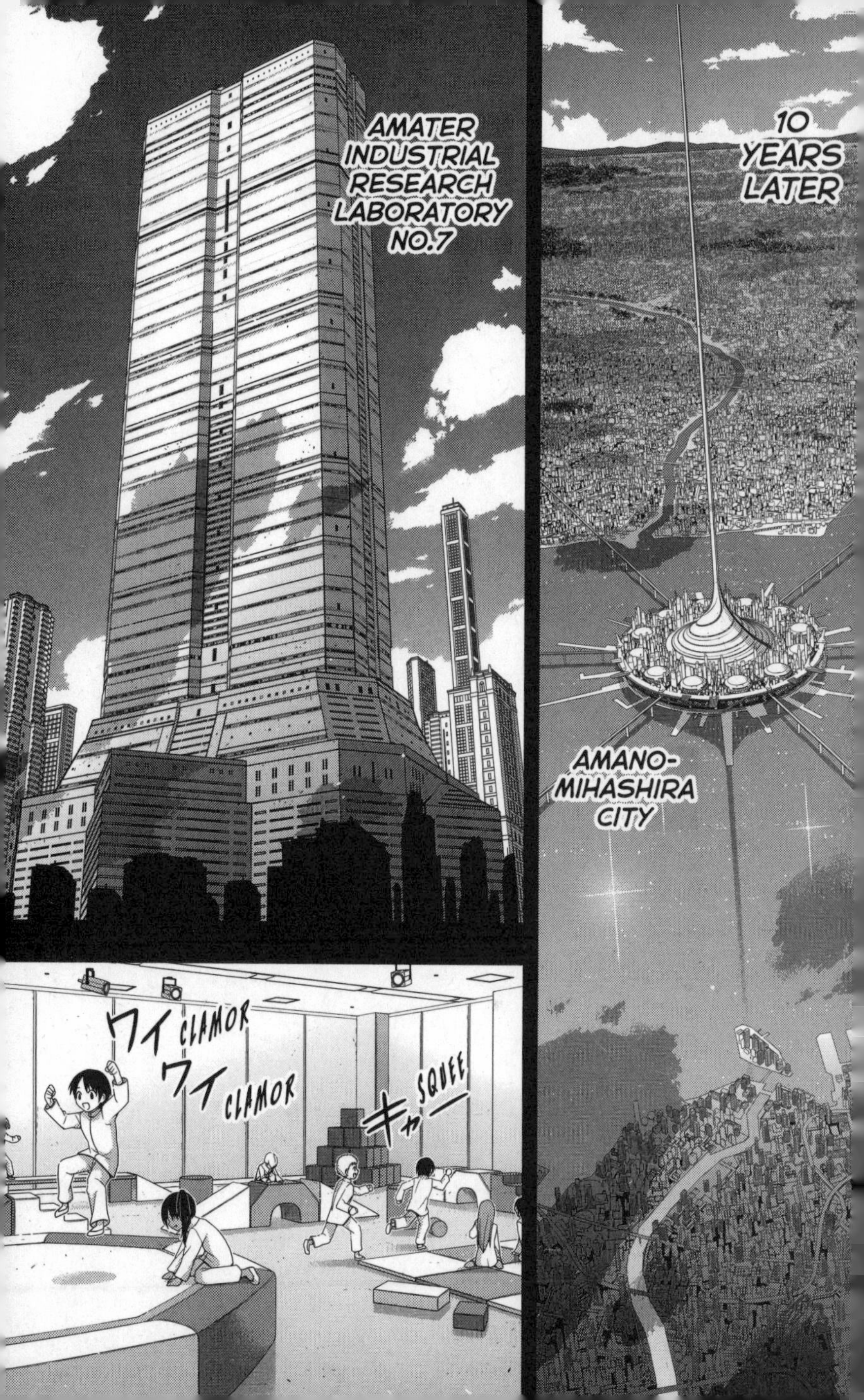
10 YEARS LATER
AMANO-MIHASHIRA CITY
AMATER INDUSTRIAL RESEARCH LABORATORY NO.7
キャー
SQUEE
ワイ
CLAMOR
ワイ
CLAMOR

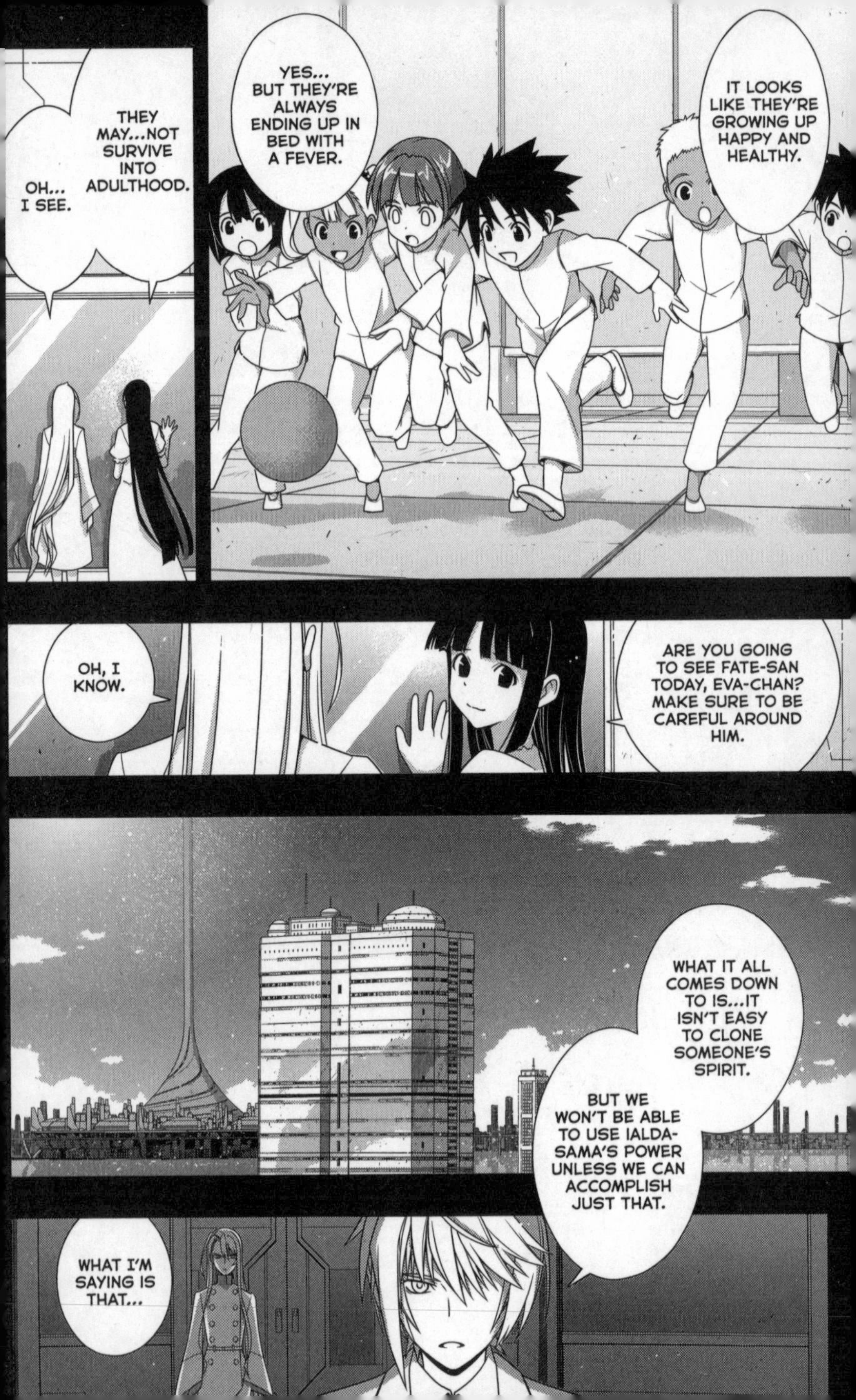

IT LOOKS LIKE THEY'RE GROWING UP HAPPY AND HEALTHY.
YES... BUT THEY'RE ALWAYS ENDING UP IN BED WITH A FEVER.
THEY MAY...NOT SURVIVE INTO ADULTHOOD.
OH... I SEE.
ARE YOU GOING TO SEE FATE-SAN TODAY, EVA-CHAN? MAKE SURE TO BE CAREFUL AROUND HIM.
OH, I KNOW.
WHAT IT ALL COMES DOWN TO IS...IT ISN'T EASY TO CLONE SOMEONE'S SPIRIT.
BUT WE WON'T BE ABLE TO USE IALDA-SAMA'S POWER UNLESS WE CAN ACCOMPLISH JUST THAT.
WHAT I'M SAYING IS THAT...

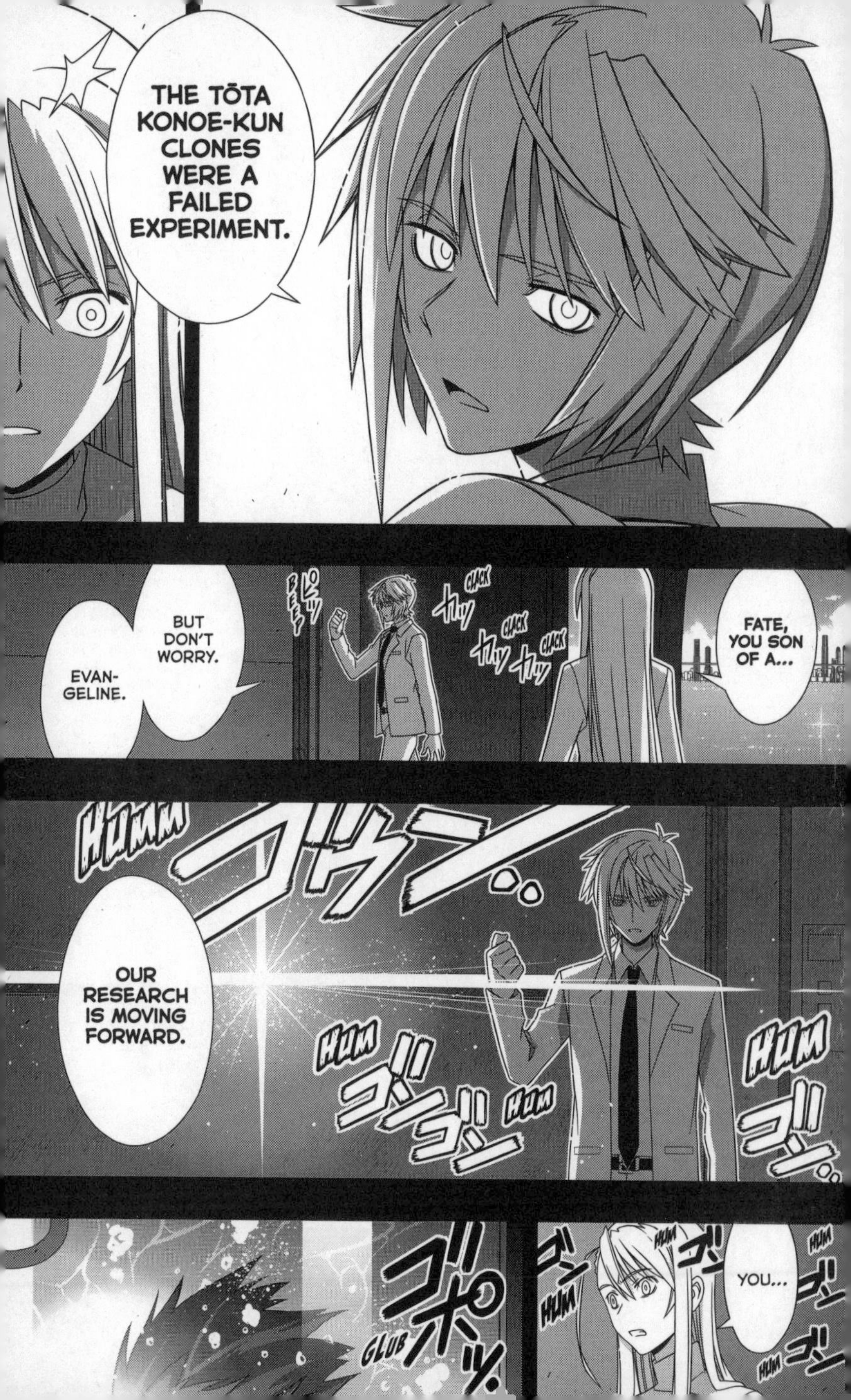
THE TŌTA KONOE-KUN CLONES WERE A FAILED EXPERIMENT.
FATE, YOU SON OF A...
CLACK
CLACK
CLACK
CLACK
BEEP
BUT DON'T WORRY.
EVAN-GELINE.
HUMM
OUR RESEARCH IS MOVING FORWARD.
HUM
HUM
HUM
HUM
YOU...
HUM
HUM
HUM
HUM
GLUB

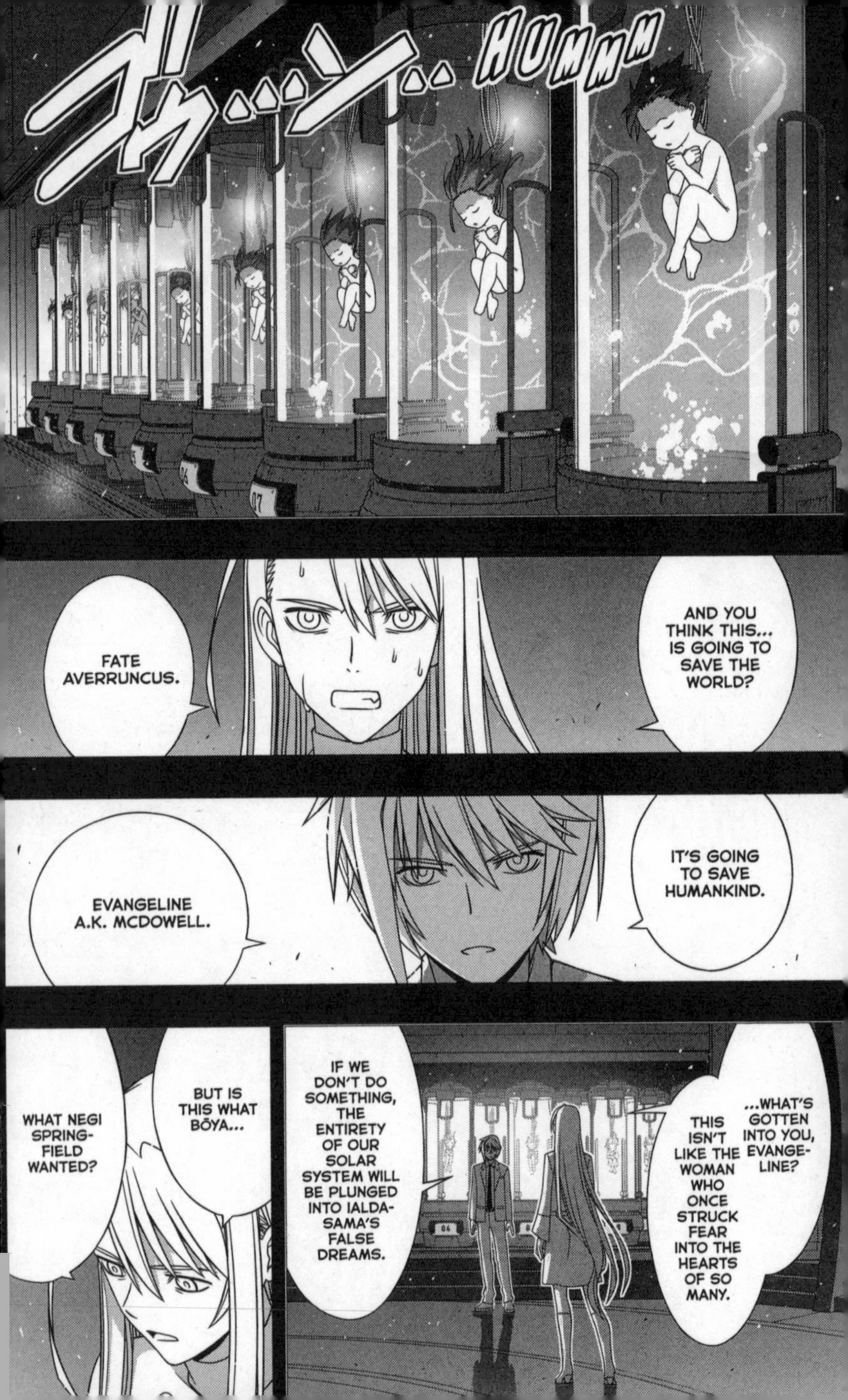
ゴゥ…ン..
HUMMM
AND YOU THINK THIS... IS GOING TO SAVE THE WORLD?
FATE AVERRUNCUS.
IT'S GOING TO SAVE HUMANKIND.
EVANGELINE A.K. MCDOWELL.
...WHAT'S GOTTEN INTO YOU, EVANGELINE?
THIS ISN'T LIKE THE WOMAN WHO ONCE STRUCK FEAR INTO THE HEARTS OF SO MANY.
IF WE DON'T DO SOMETHING, THE ENTIRETY OF OUR SOLAR SYSTEM WILL BE PLUNGED INTO IALDA-SAMA'S FALSE DREAMS.
BUT IS THIS WHAT BŌYA...
WHAT NEGI SPRINGFIELD WANTED?

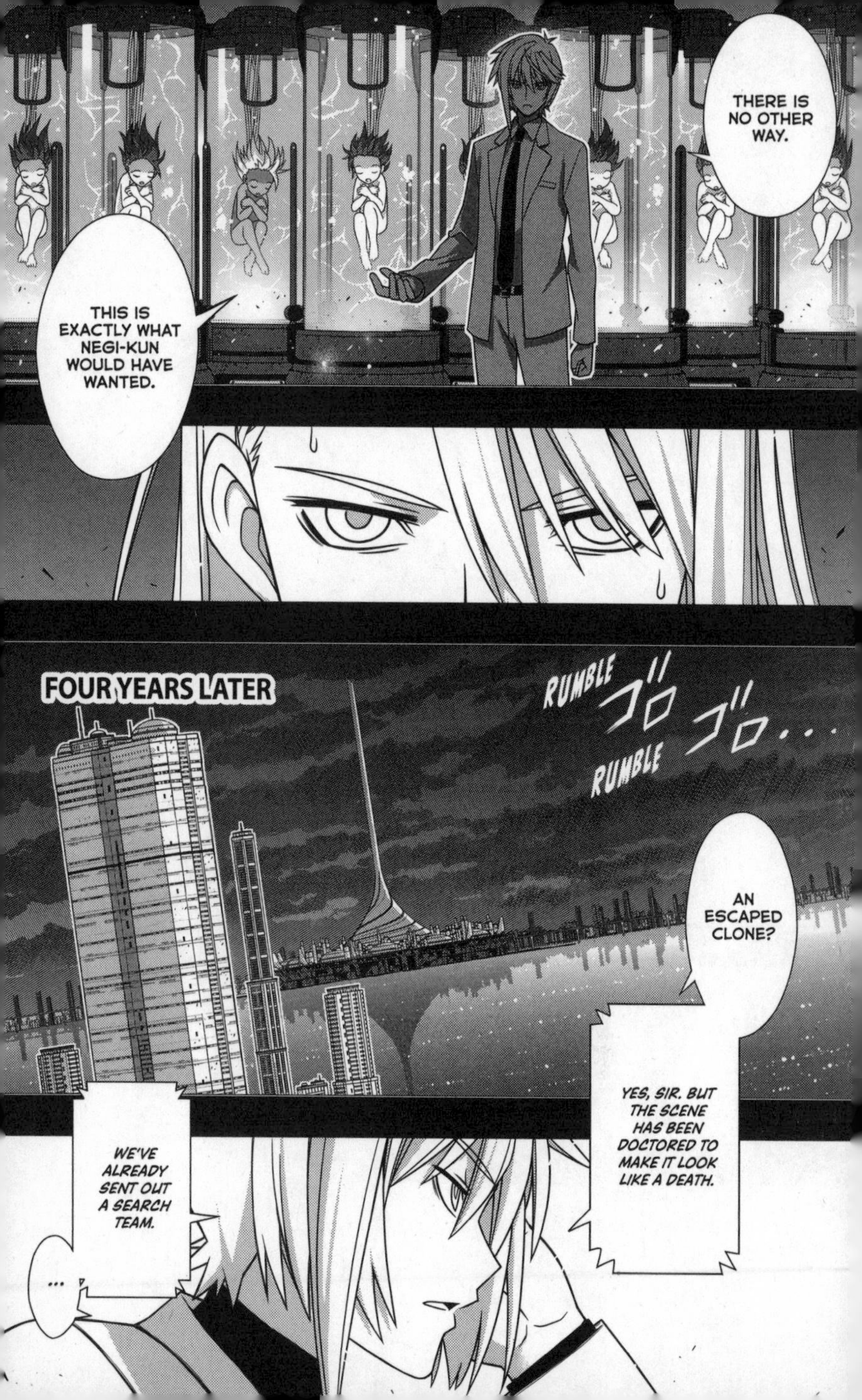
THERE IS NO OTHER WAY.
THIS IS EXACTLY WHAT NEGI-KUN WOULD HAVE WANTED.
RUMBLE ゴロ
RUMBLE ゴロ...
FOUR YEARS LATER
AN ESCAPED CLONE?
YES, SIR. BUT THE SCENE HAS BEEN DOCTORED TO MAKE IT LOOK LIKE A DEATH.
WE'VE ALREADY SENT OUT A SEARCH TEAM.
...

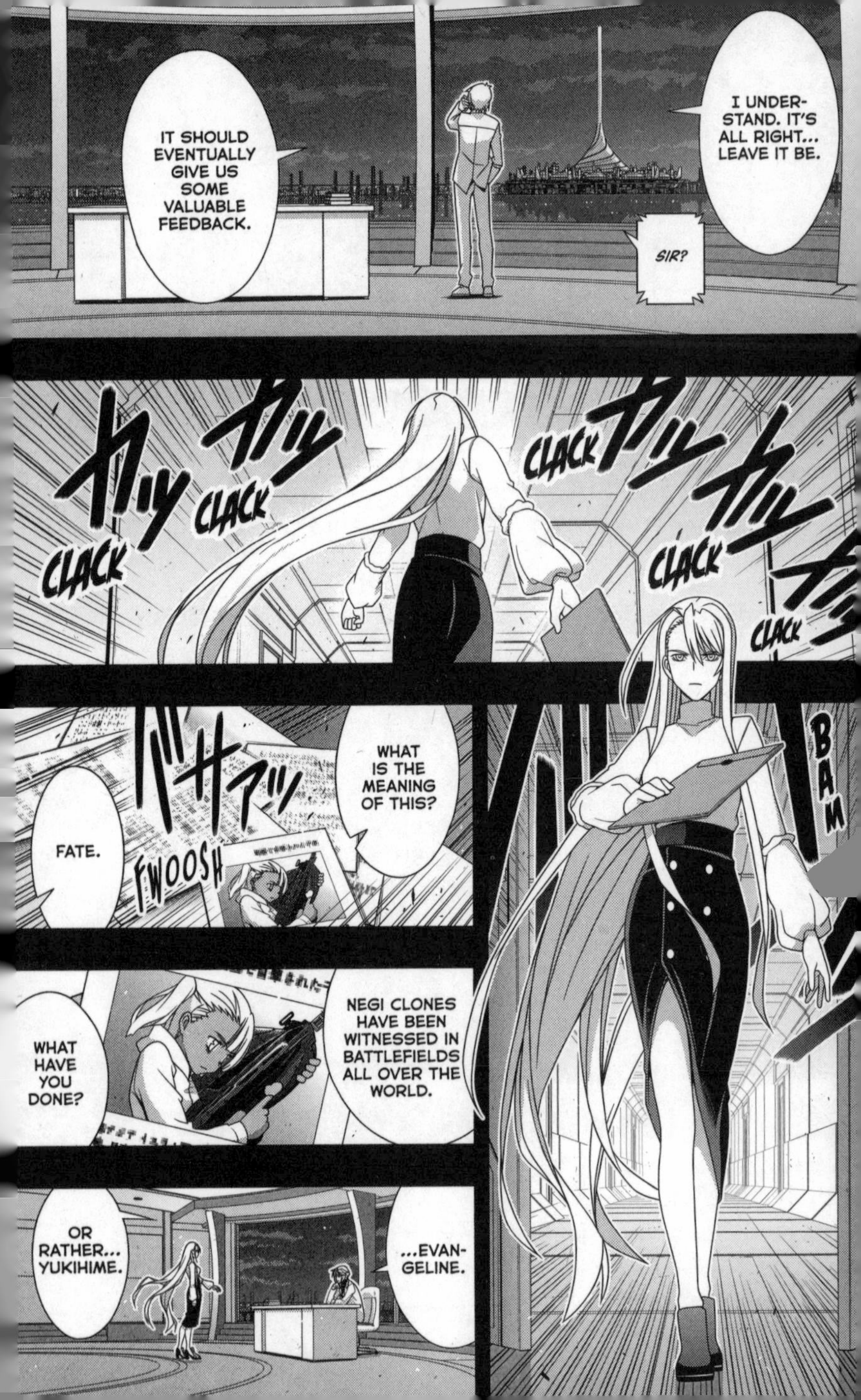
I UNDER-STAND. IT'S ALL RIGHT... LEAVE IT BE.
SIR?
IT SHOULD EVENTUALLY GIVE US SOME VALUABLE FEEDBACK.
CLACK
CLACK
CLACK
CLACK
CLACK
BAM
WHAT IS THE MEANING OF THIS?
FWOOSH
FATE.
NEGI CLONES HAVE BEEN WITNESSED IN BATTLEFIELDS ALL OVER THE WORLD.
WHAT HAVE YOU DONE?
...EVAN-GELINE.
OR RATHER... YUKIHIME.

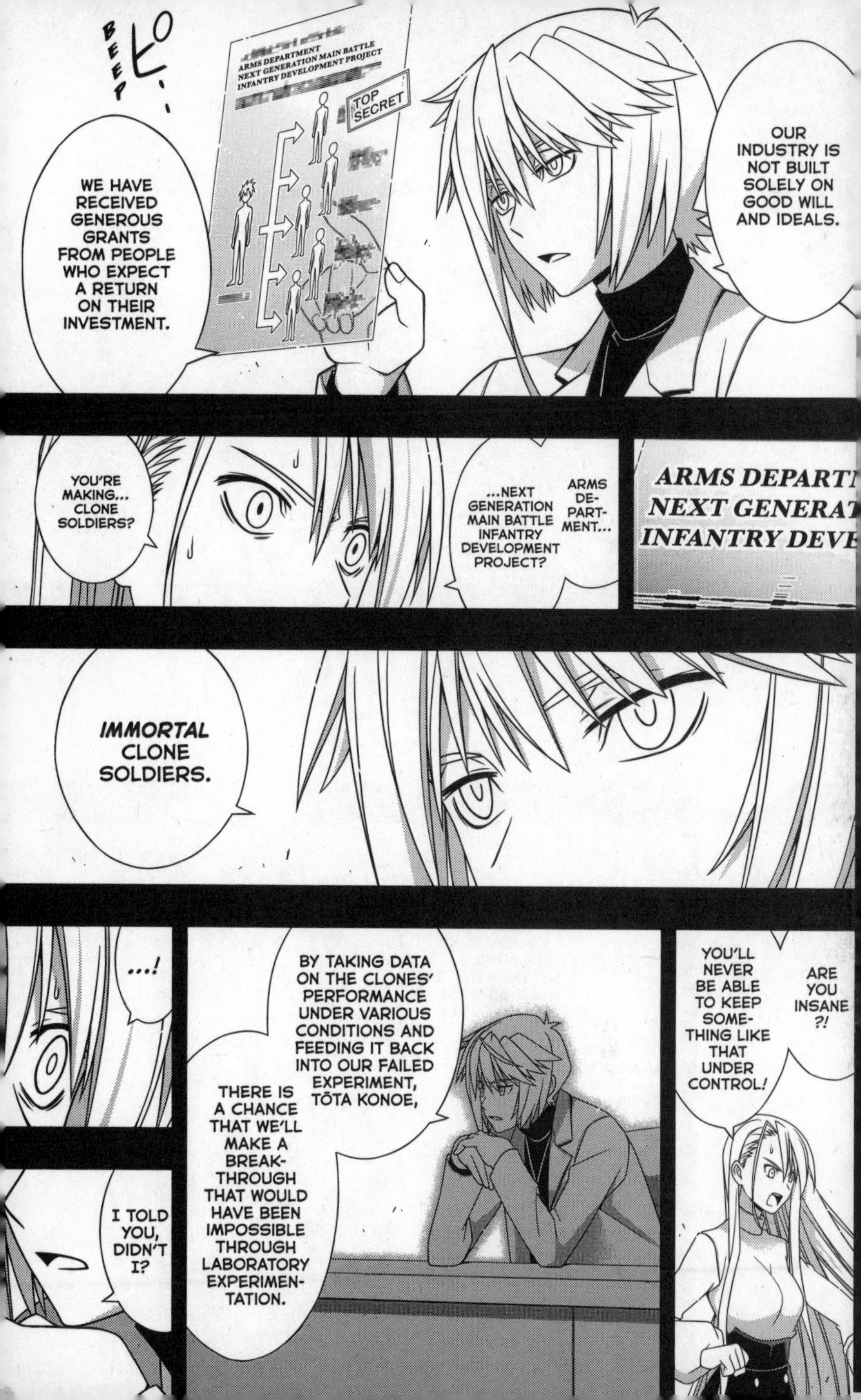

OUR INDUSTRY IS NOT BUILT SOLELY ON GOOD WILL AND IDEALS.
ARMS DEPARTMENT NEXT GENERATION MAIN BATTLE INFANTRY DEVELOPMENT PROJECT
TOP SECRET
BEEP
WE HAVE RECEIVED GENEROUS GRANTS FROM PEOPLE WHO EXPECT A RETURN ON THEIR INVESTMENT.
ARMS DEPART
NEXT GENERAT
INFANTRY DEVE
ARMS DE-PART-MENT...
...NEXT GENERATION MAIN BATTLE INFANTRY DEVELOPMENT PROJECT?
YOU'RE MAKING... CLONE SOLDIERS?
*IMMORTAL* CLONE SOLDIERS.
ARE YOU INSANE?!
YOU'LL NEVER BE ABLE TO KEEP SOME-THING LIKE THAT UNDER CONTROL!
BY TAKING DATA ON THE CLONES' PERFORMANCE UNDER VARIOUS CONDITIONS AND FEEDING IT BACK INTO OUR FAILED EXPERIMENT, TŌTA KONOE,
THERE IS A CHANCE THAT WE'LL MAKE A BREAK-THROUGH THAT WOULD HAVE BEEN IMPOSSIBLE THROUGH LABORATORY EXPERIMEN-TATION.
...!
I TOLD YOU, DIDN'T I?

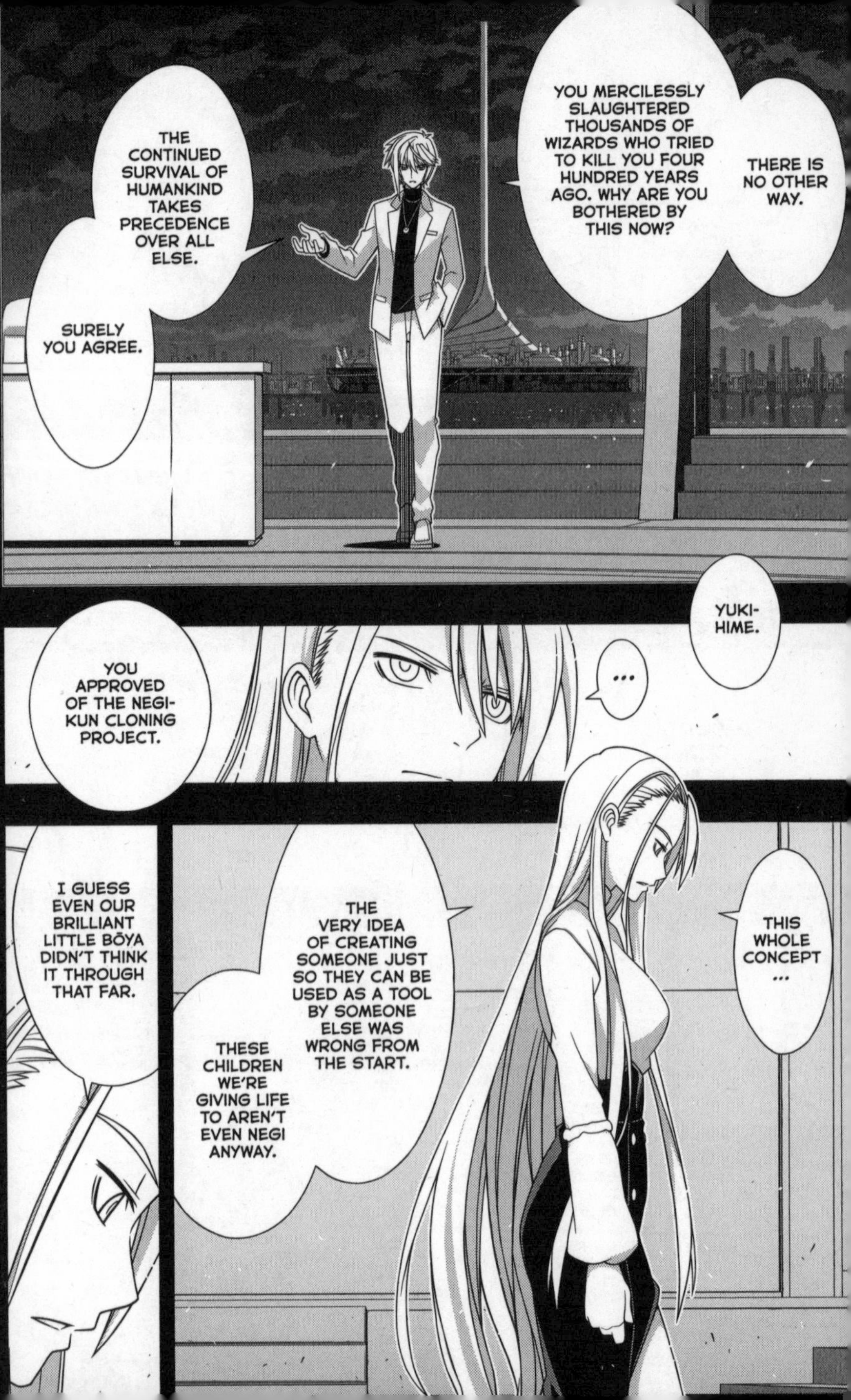
THERE IS NO OTHER WAY.
YOU MERCILESSLY SLAUGHTERED THOUSANDS OF WIZARDS WHO TRIED TO KILL YOU FOUR HUNDRED YEARS AGO. WHY ARE YOU BOTHERED BY THIS NOW?
THE CONTINUED SURVIVAL OF HUMANKIND TAKES PRECEDENCE OVER ALL ELSE.
SURELY YOU AGREE.
YUKI-HIME.
...
YOU APPROVED OF THE NEGI-KUN CLONING PROJECT.
THIS WHOLE CONCEPT ...
THE VERY IDEA OF CREATING SOMEONE JUST SO THEY CAN BE USED AS A TOOL BY SOMEONE ELSE WAS WRONG FROM THE START.
THESE CHILDREN WE'RE GIVING LIFE TO AREN'T EVEN NEGI ANYWAY.
I GUESS EVEN OUR BRILLIANT LITTLE BŌYA DIDN'T THINK IT THROUGH THAT FAR.

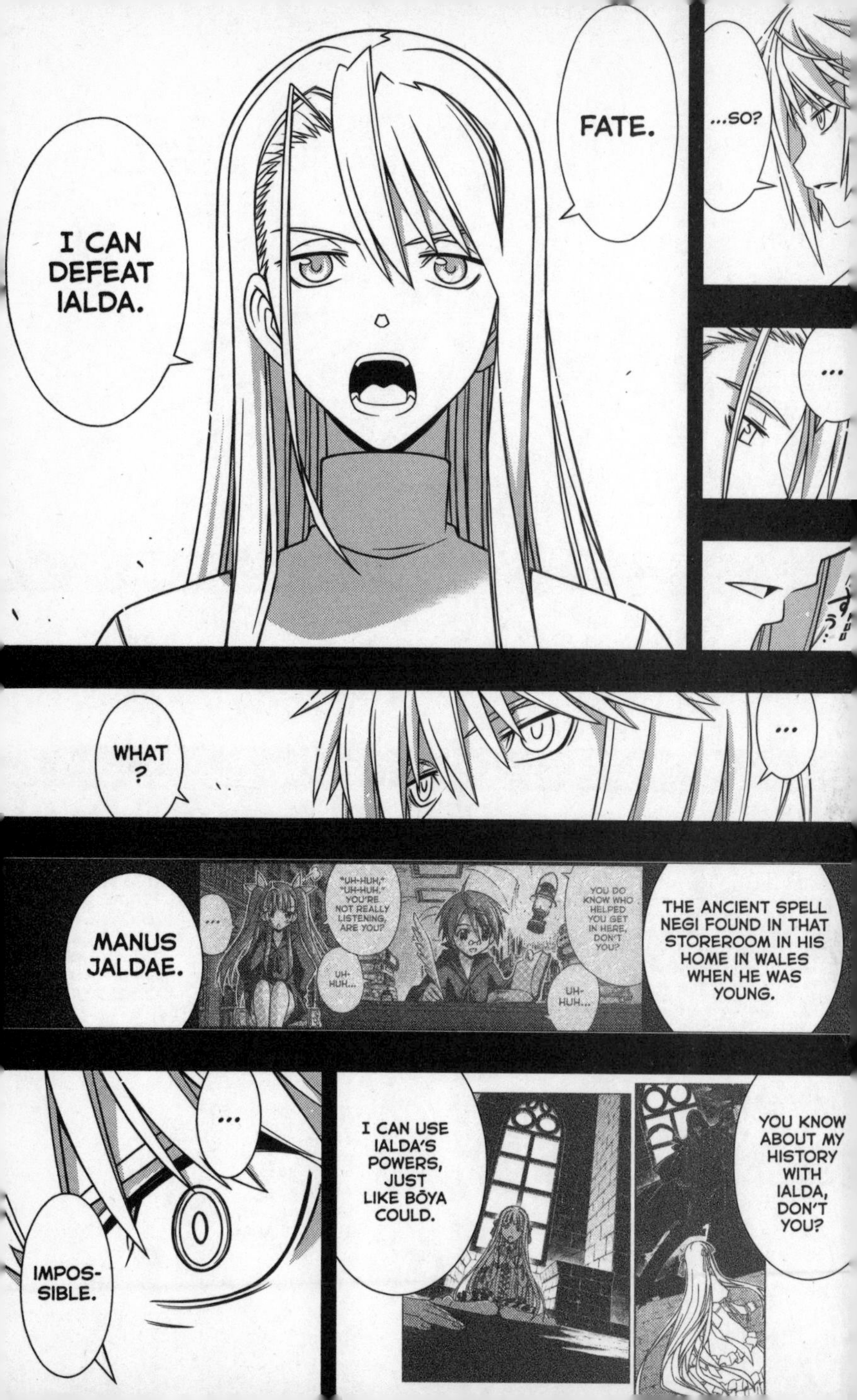
...SO?
...
FATE.
I CAN DEFEAT IALDA.
...
WHAT?
THE ANCIENT SPELL NEGI FOUND IN THAT STOREROOM IN HIS HOME IN WALES WHEN HE WAS YOUNG.
YOU DO KNOW WHO HELPED YOU GET IN HERE, DON'T YOU?
UH-HUH...
"UH-HUH," "UH-HUH." YOU'RE NOT REALLY LISTENING, ARE YOU?
UH-HUH...
...
MANUS JALDAE.
YOU KNOW ABOUT MY HISTORY WITH IALDA, DON'T YOU?
I CAN USE IALDA'S POWERS, JUST LIKE BŌYA COULD.
...
IMPOSSIBLE.

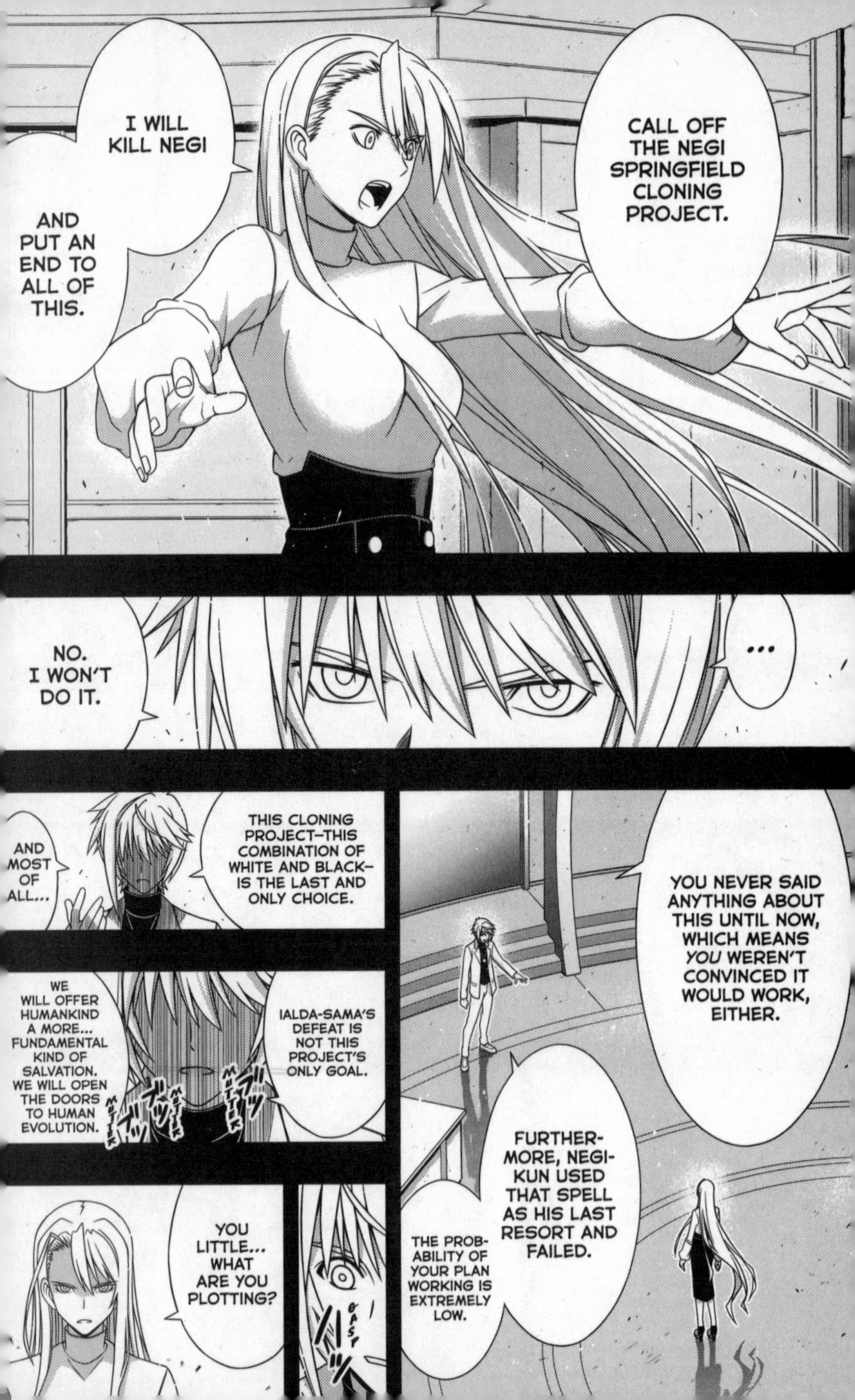
CALL OFF THE NEGI SPRINGFIELD CLONING PROJECT.
I WILL KILL NEGI
AND PUT AN END TO ALL OF THIS.
...
NO. I WON'T DO IT.
YOU NEVER SAID ANYTHING ABOUT THIS UNTIL NOW, WHICH MEANS *YOU* WEREN'T CONVINCED IT WOULD WORK, EITHER.
FURTHER-MORE, NEGI-KUN USED THAT SPELL AS HIS LAST RESORT AND FAILED.
THE PROB-ABILITY OF YOUR PLAN WORKING IS EXTREMELY LOW.
THIS CLONING PROJECT—THIS COMBINATION OF WHITE AND BLACK—IS THE LAST AND ONLY CHOICE.
AND MOST OF ALL...
IALDA-SAMA'S DEFEAT IS NOT THIS PROJECT'S ONLY GOAL.
WE WILL OFFER HUMANKIND A MORE... FUNDAMENTAL KIND OF SALVATION. WE WILL OPEN THE DOORS TO HUMAN EVOLUTION.
GASP
YOU LITTLE... WHAT ARE YOU PLOTTING?

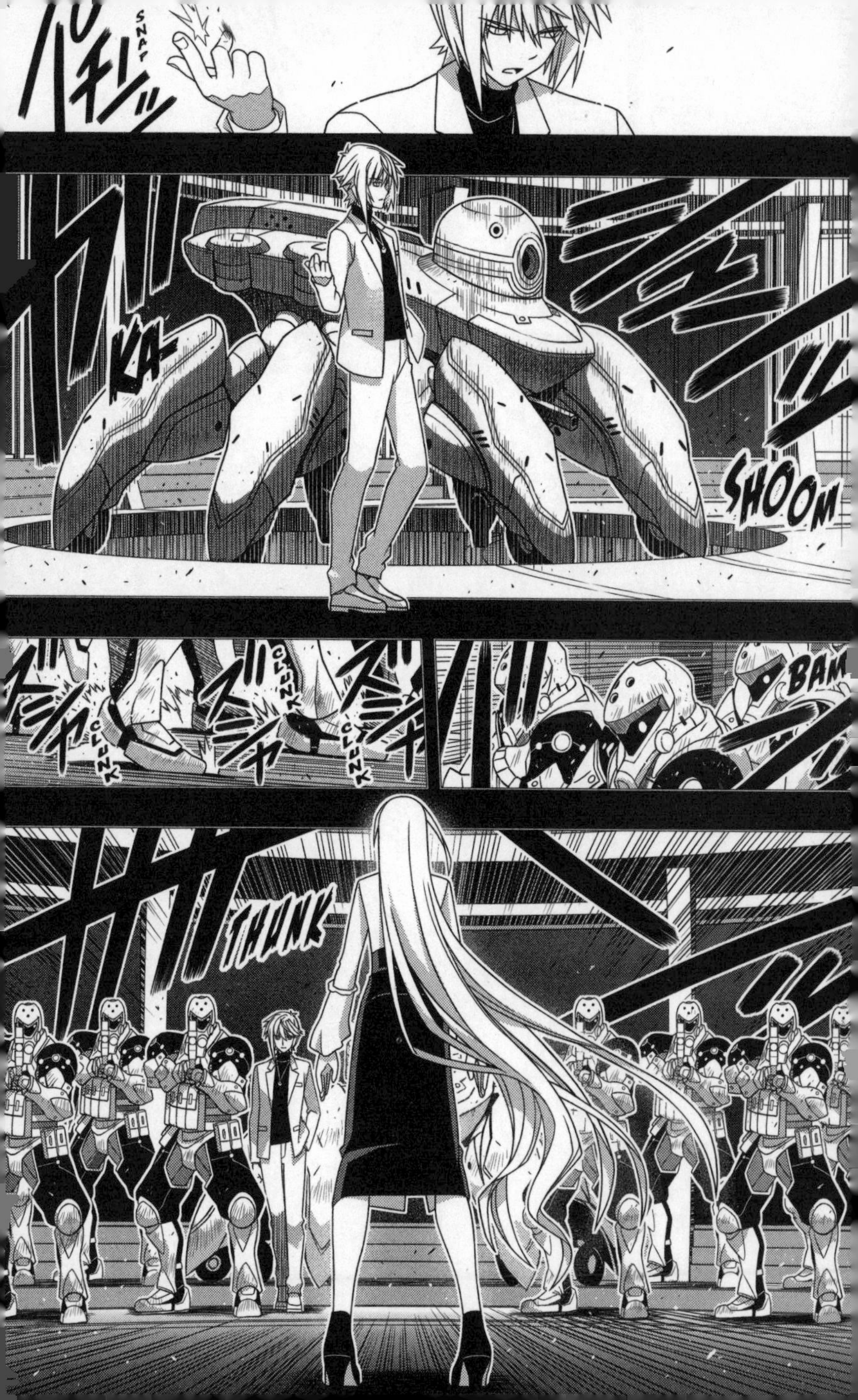
SNAP
SHOOM
KA
BAM
CLUNK
CLUNK
CLUNK
THUNK

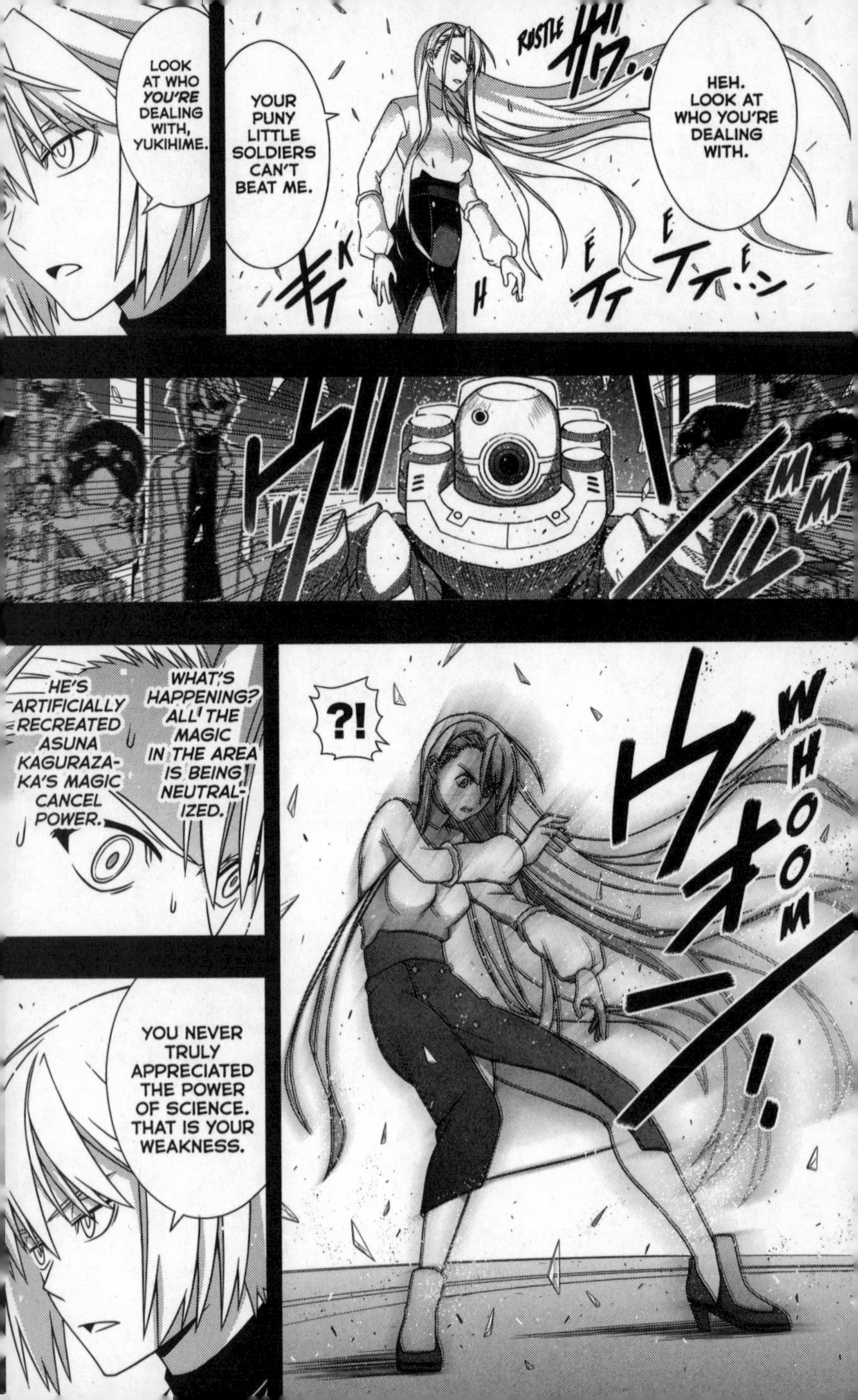

HEH. LOOK AT WHO YOU'RE DEALING WITH.
RUSTLE
YOUR PUNY LITTLE SOLDIERS CAN'T BEAT ME.
LOOK AT WHO *YOU'RE* DEALING WITH, YUKIHIME.
WHOOOM
?!
WHAT'S HAPPENING? ALL THE MAGIC IN THE AREA IS BEING NEUTRAL-IZED.
HE'S ARTIFICIALLY RECREATED ASUNA KAGURAZA-KA'S MAGIC CANCEL POWER.
YOU NEVER TRULY APPRECIATED THE POWER OF SCIENCE. THAT IS YOUR WEAKNESS.

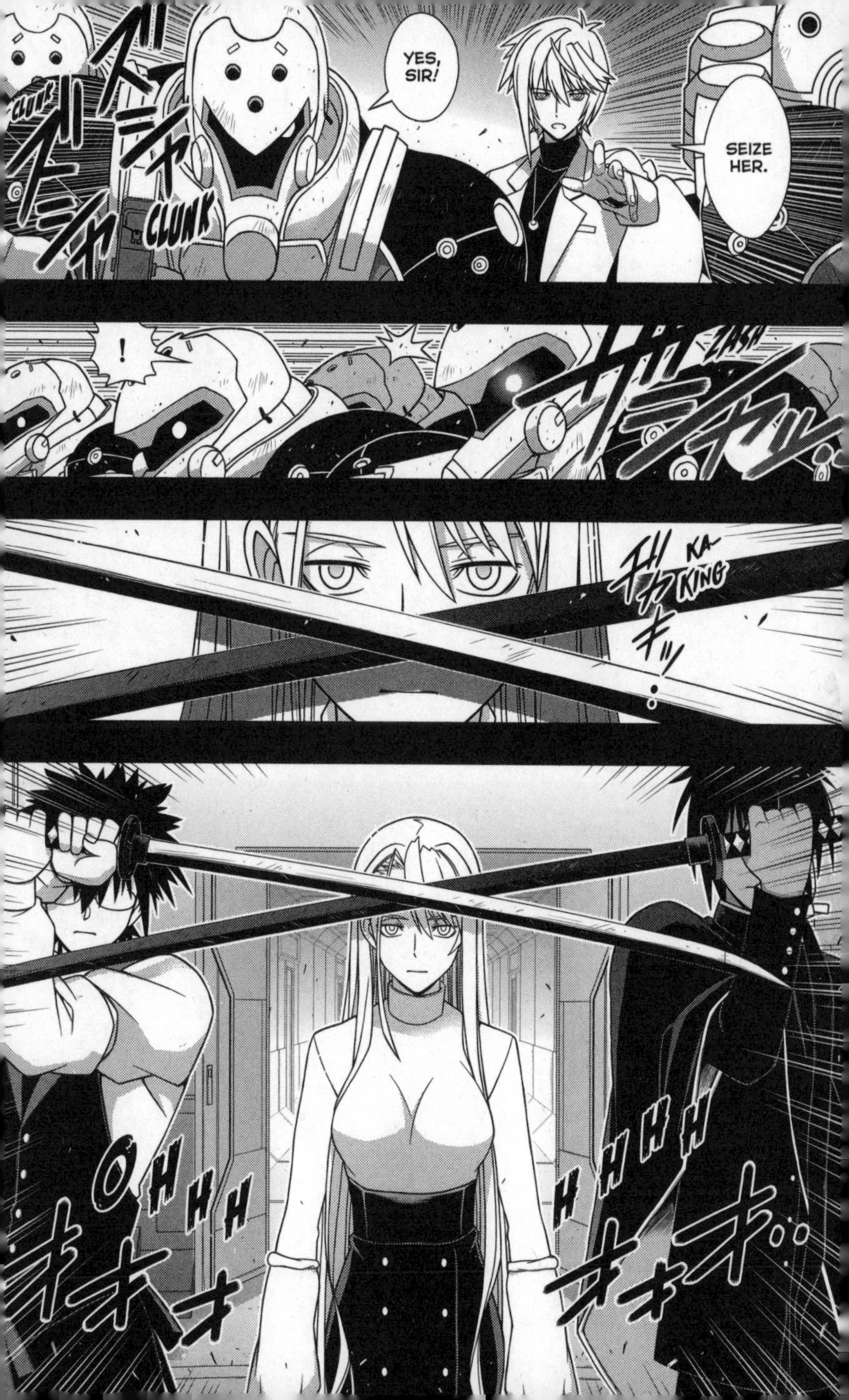
SEIZE HER.
YES, SIR!
CLUNK
CLUNK
ZASH
!
KA-KING
HHHH
OHHH

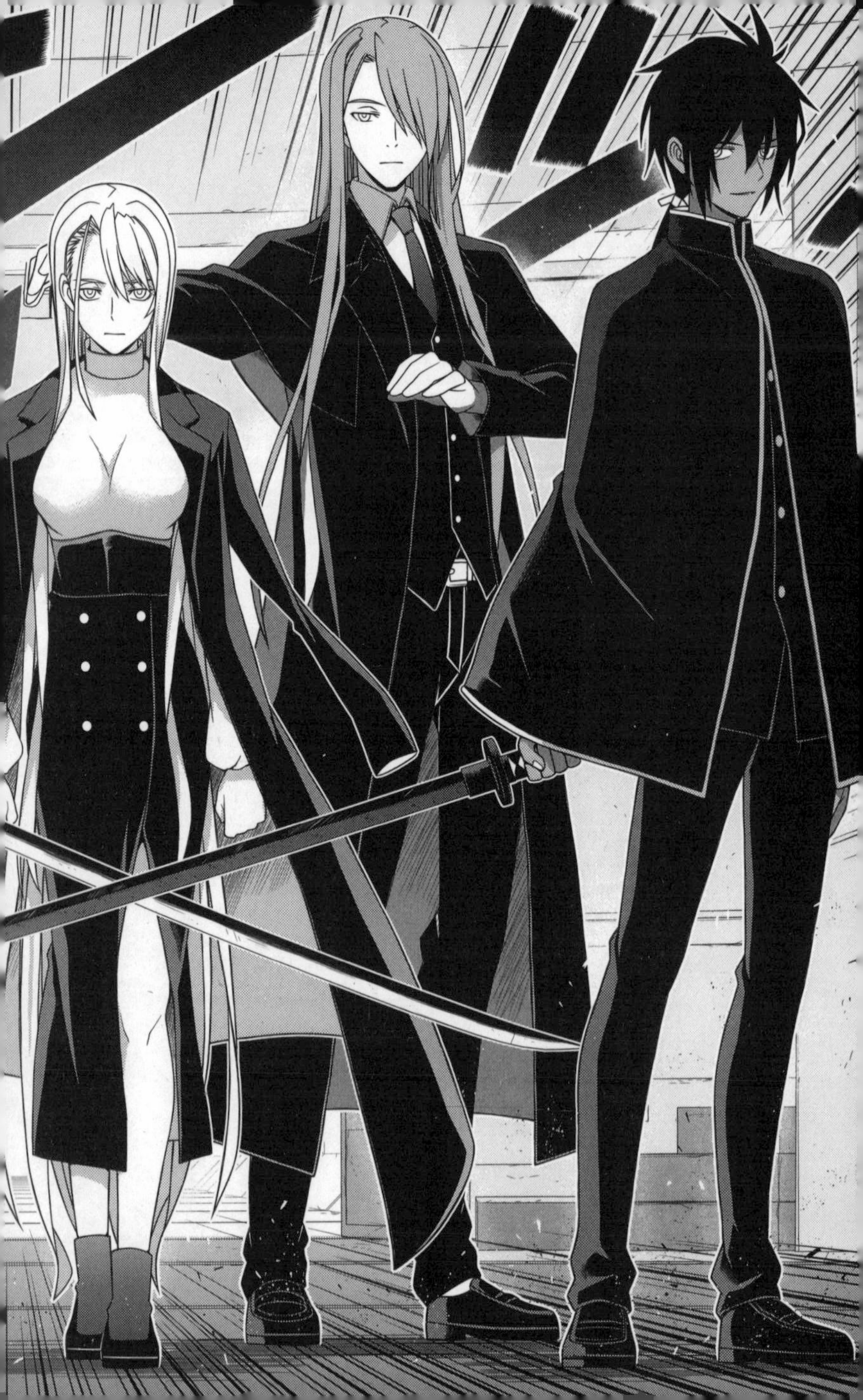

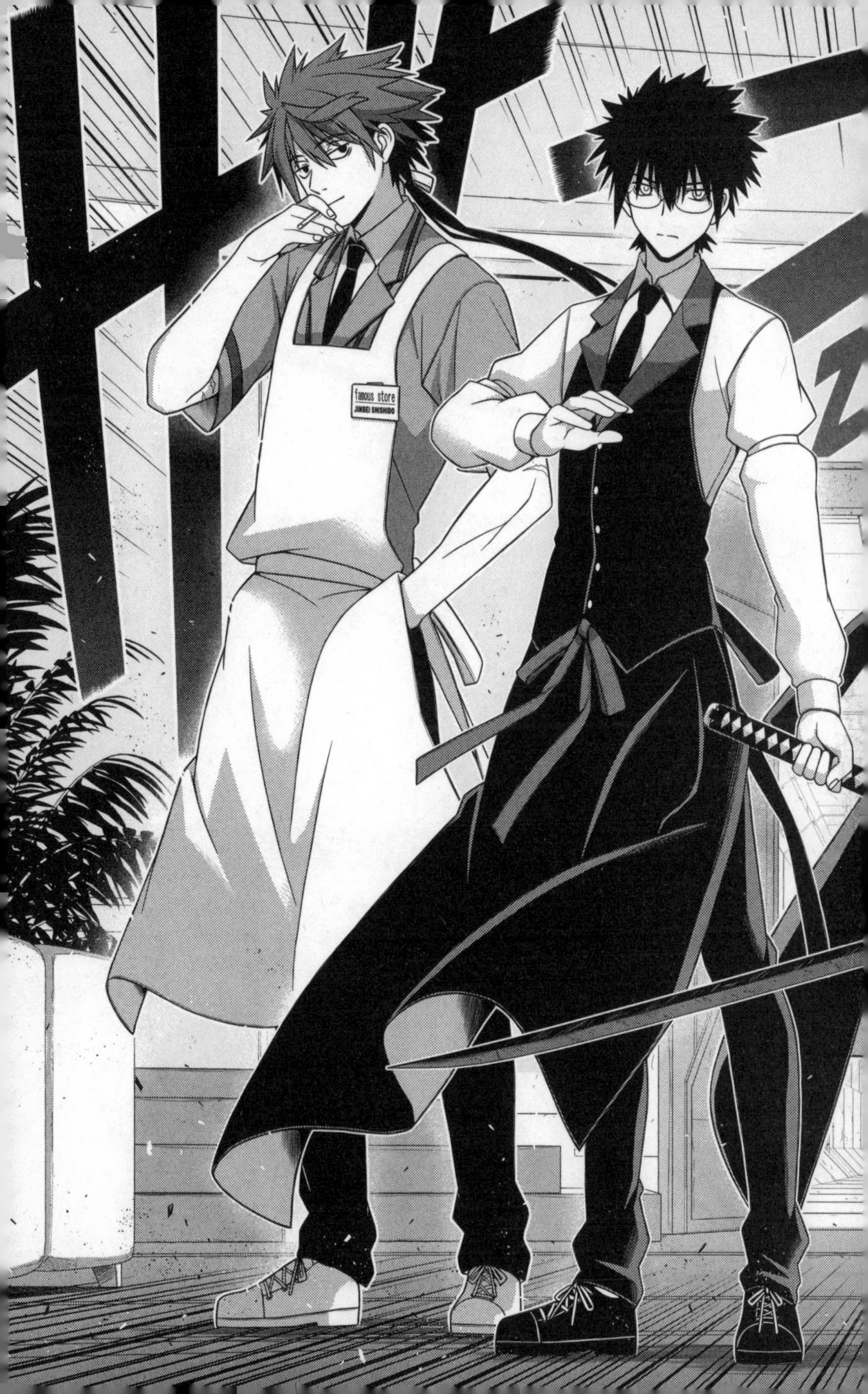
famous store
JINBEI SHISHIDO

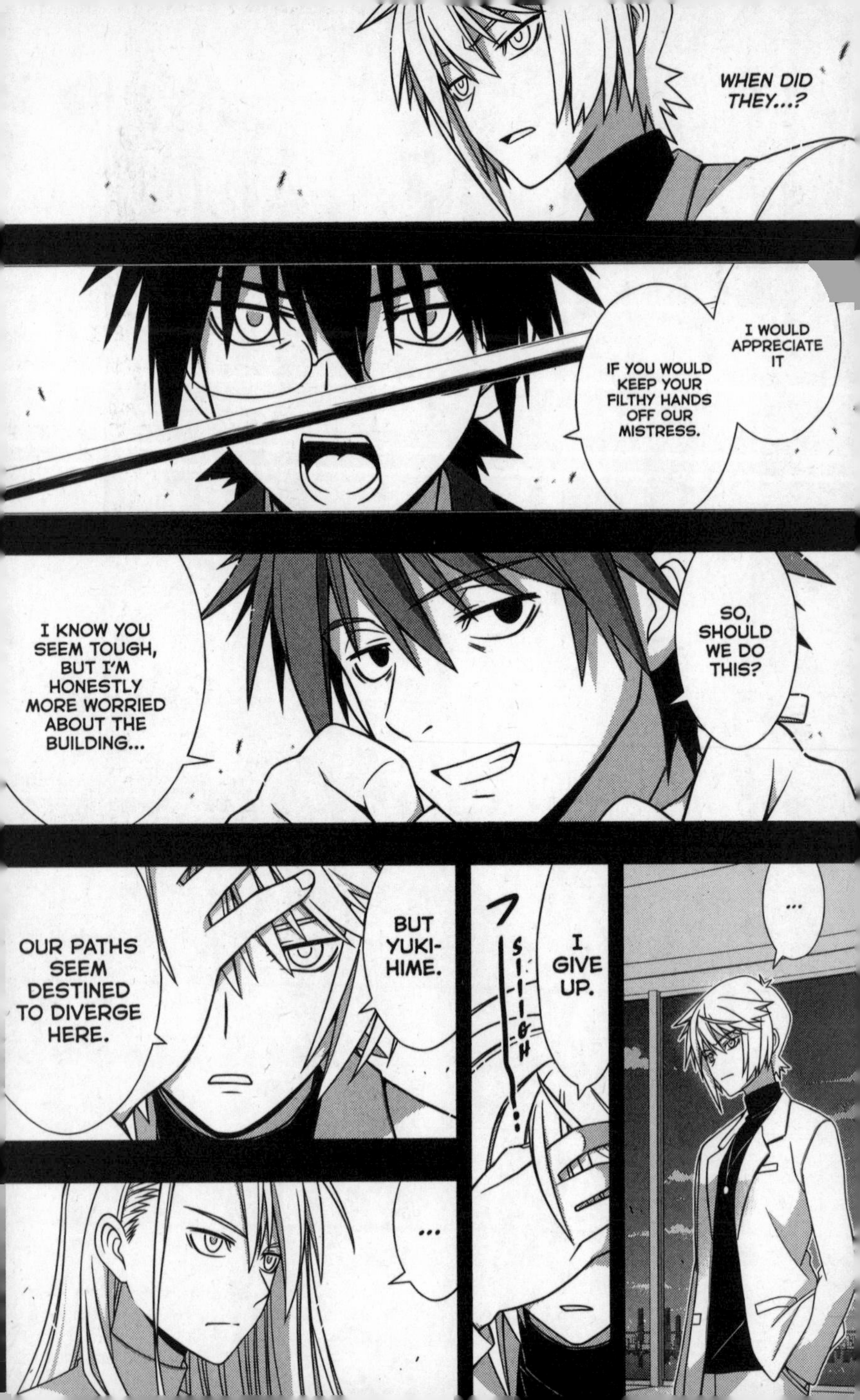
WHEN DID THEY...?
I WOULD APPRECIATE IT
IF YOU WOULD KEEP YOUR FILTHY HANDS OFF OUR MISTRESS.
SO, SHOULD WE DO THIS?
I KNOW YOU SEEM TOUGH, BUT I'M HONESTLY MORE WORRIED ABOUT THE BUILDING...
...
I GIVE UP.
SIIIGH...!
BUT YUKI-HIME.
OUR PATHS SEEM DESTINED TO DIVERGE HERE.
...

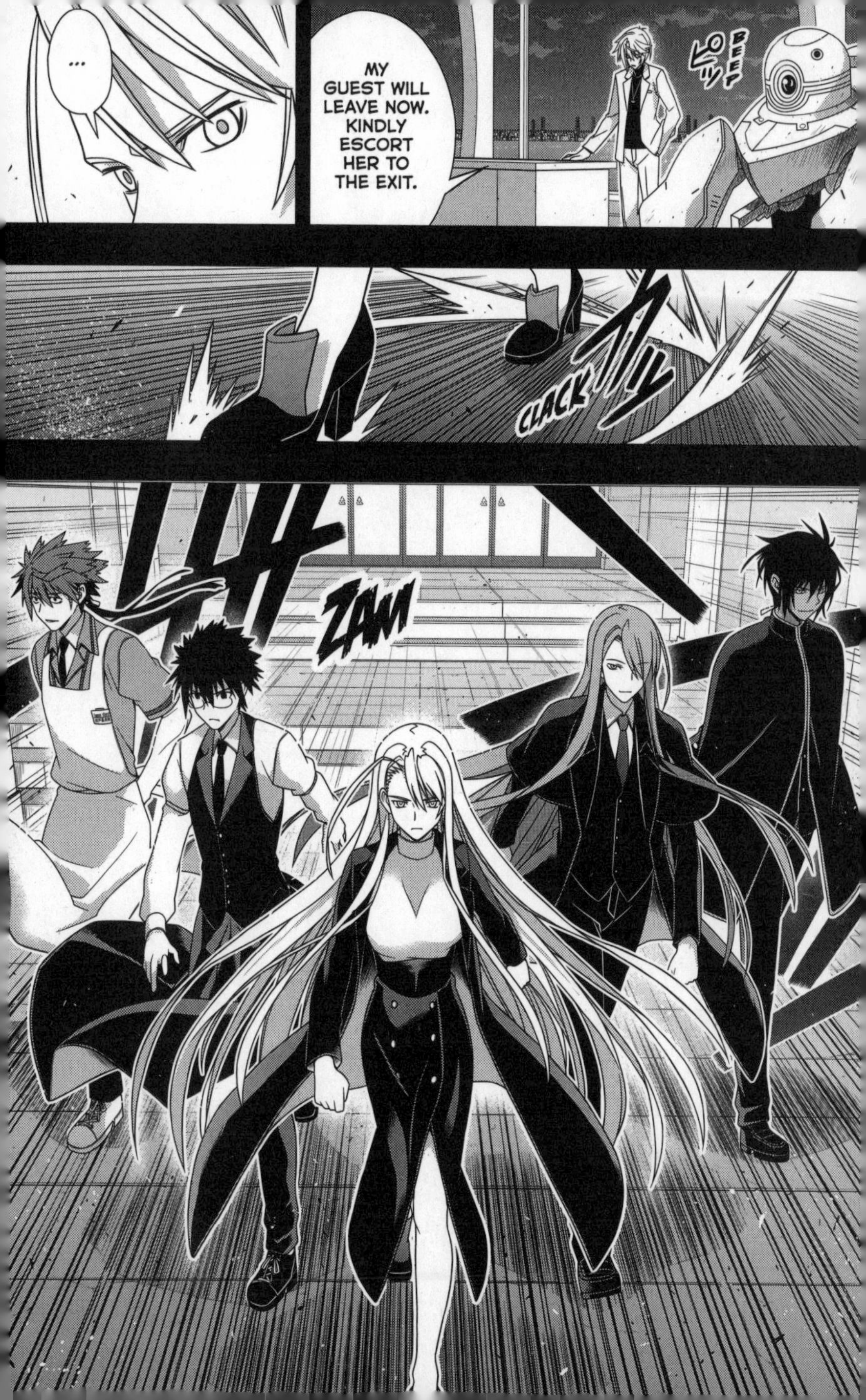
BEEP
ピッ
MY GUEST WILL LEAVE NOW. KINDLY ESCORT HER TO THE EXIT.
...
CLACK
ZAM

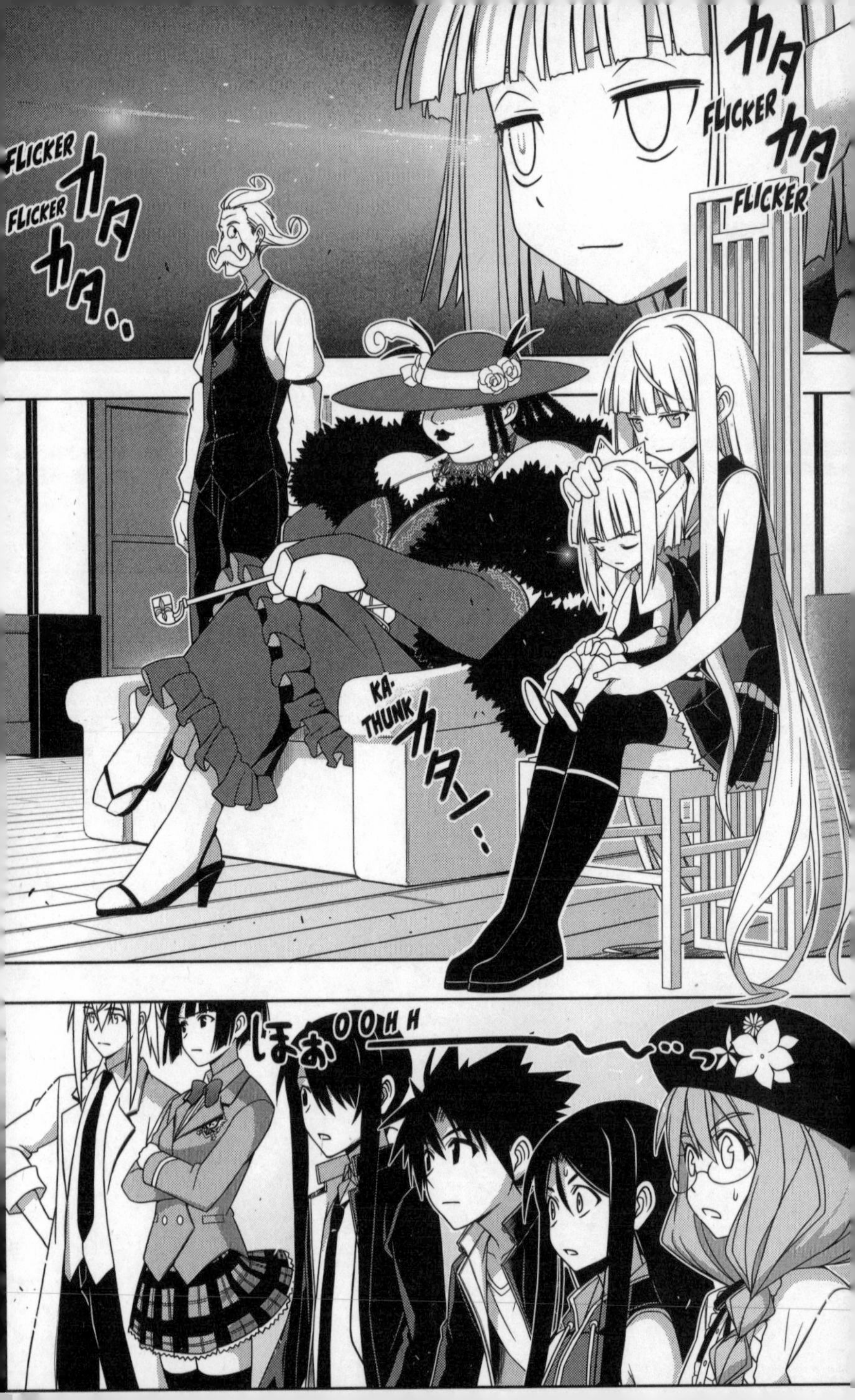
カタ
FLICKER
カタ
FLICKER
FLICKER
FLICKER
カタ
カタ..
KA-THUNK
カタン..
ほぉ OOHH ~~っ

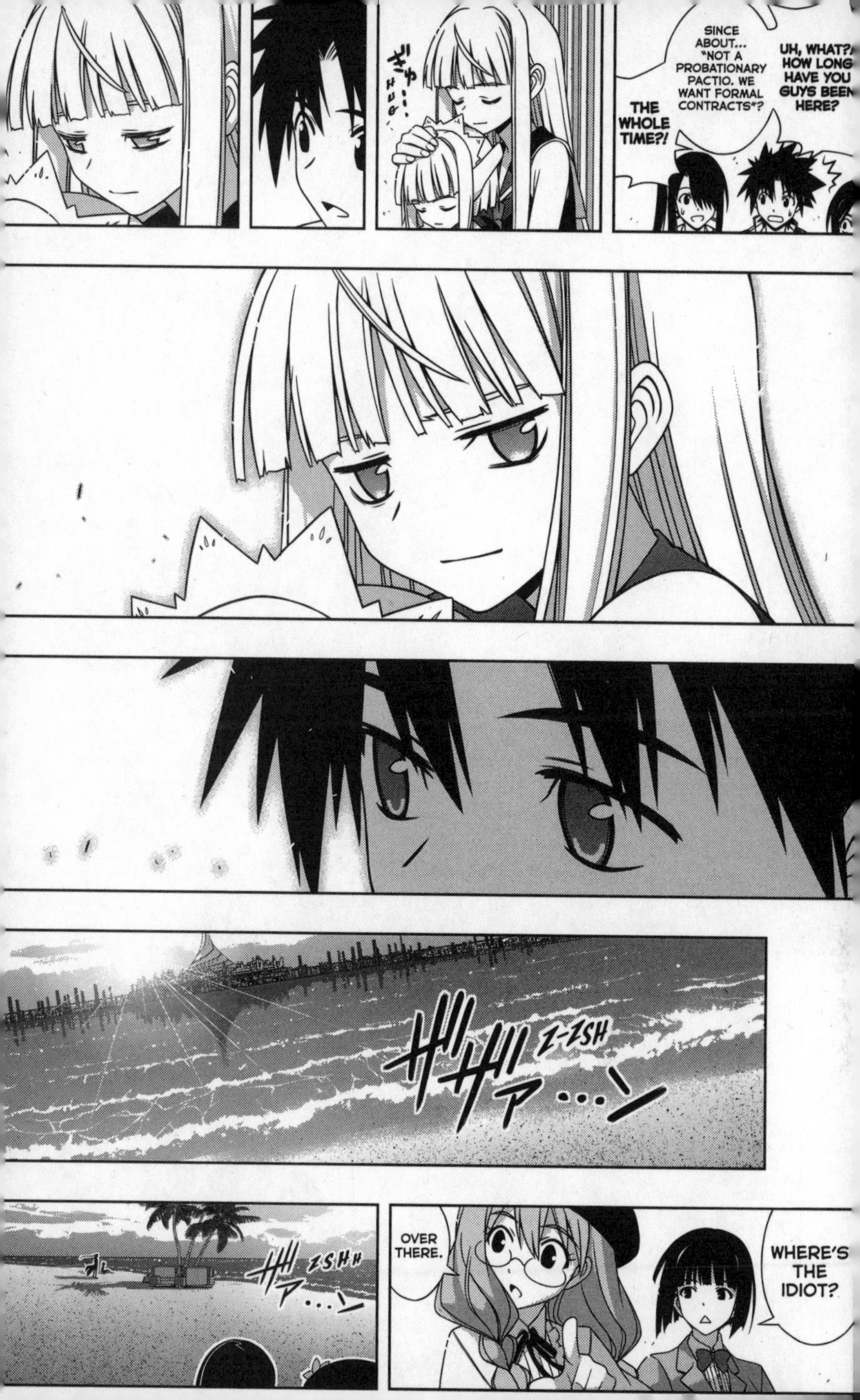
UH, WHAT?! HOW LONG HAVE YOU GUYS BEEN HERE?
SINCE ABOUT... "NOT A PROBATIONARY PACTIO. WE WANT FORMAL CONTRACTS"?
THE WHOLE TIME?!
ぎゅ…
HUG
ザザァ…ン
Z-ZSH
WHERE'S THE IDIOT?
OVER THERE.
ザァ…ン
ZSHH

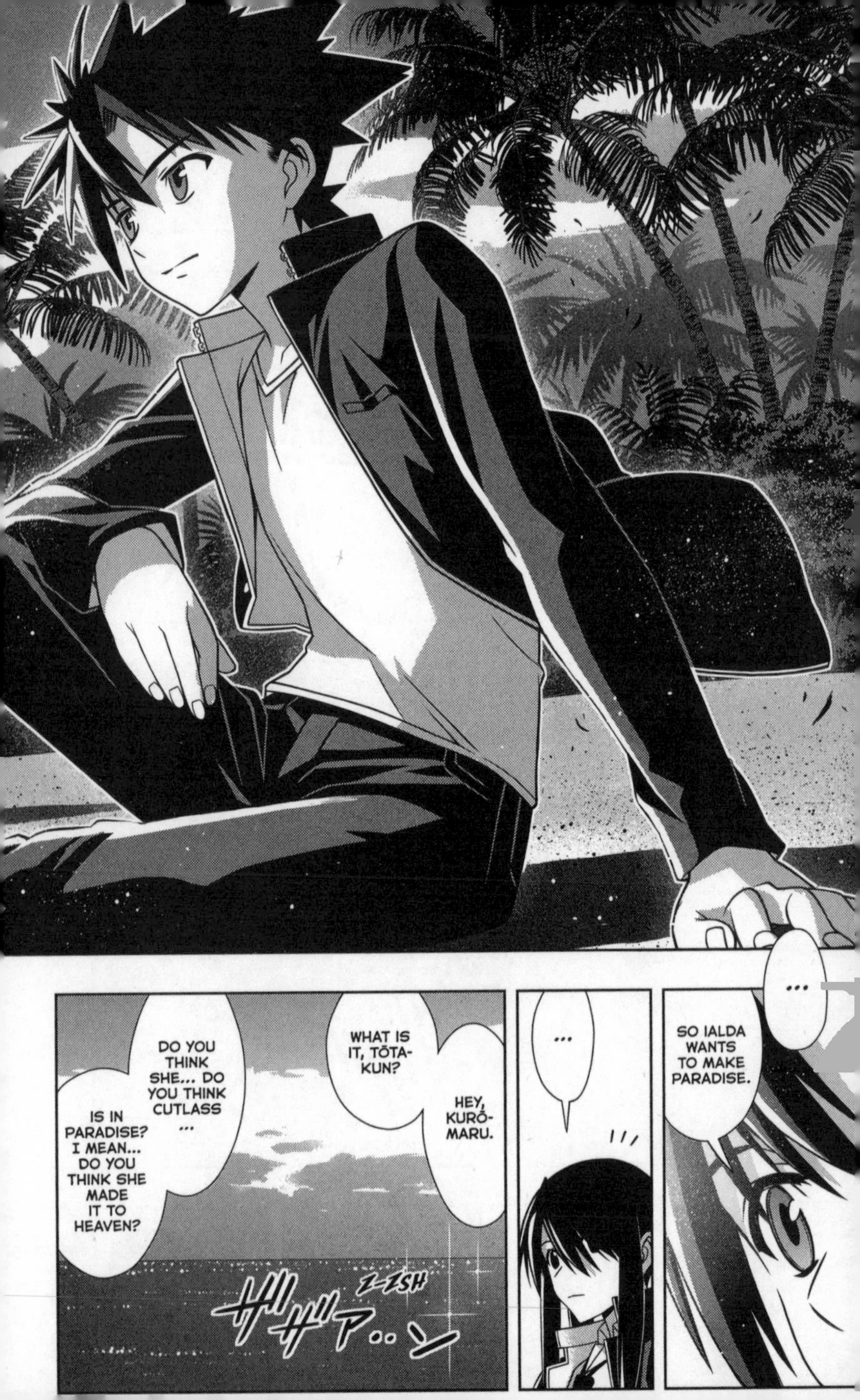
...
SO IALDA WANTS TO MAKE PARADISE.
...
HEY, KURŌ-MARU.
WHAT IS IT, TŌTA-KUN?
DO YOU THINK SHE... DO YOU THINK CUTLASS ...
IS IN PARADISE? I MEAN... DO YOU THINK SHE MADE IT TO HEAVEN?
Z-ZSH

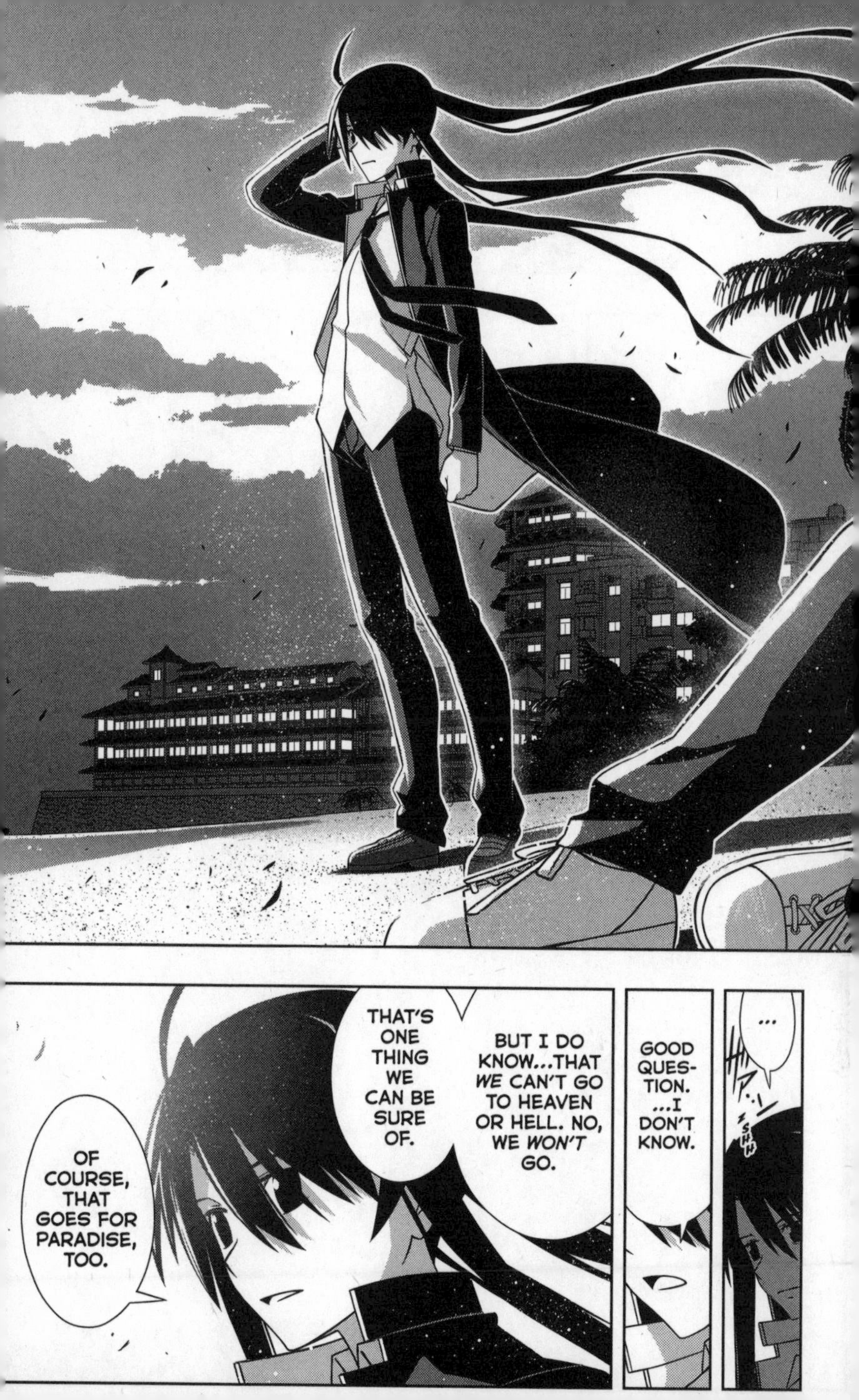
...
ZSHH
GOOD QUESTION. ...I DON'T KNOW.
BUT I DO KNOW...THAT WE CAN'T GO TO HEAVEN OR HELL. NO, WE WON'T GO.
THAT'S ONE THING WE CAN BE SURE OF.
OF COURSE, THAT GOES FOR PARADISE, TOO.

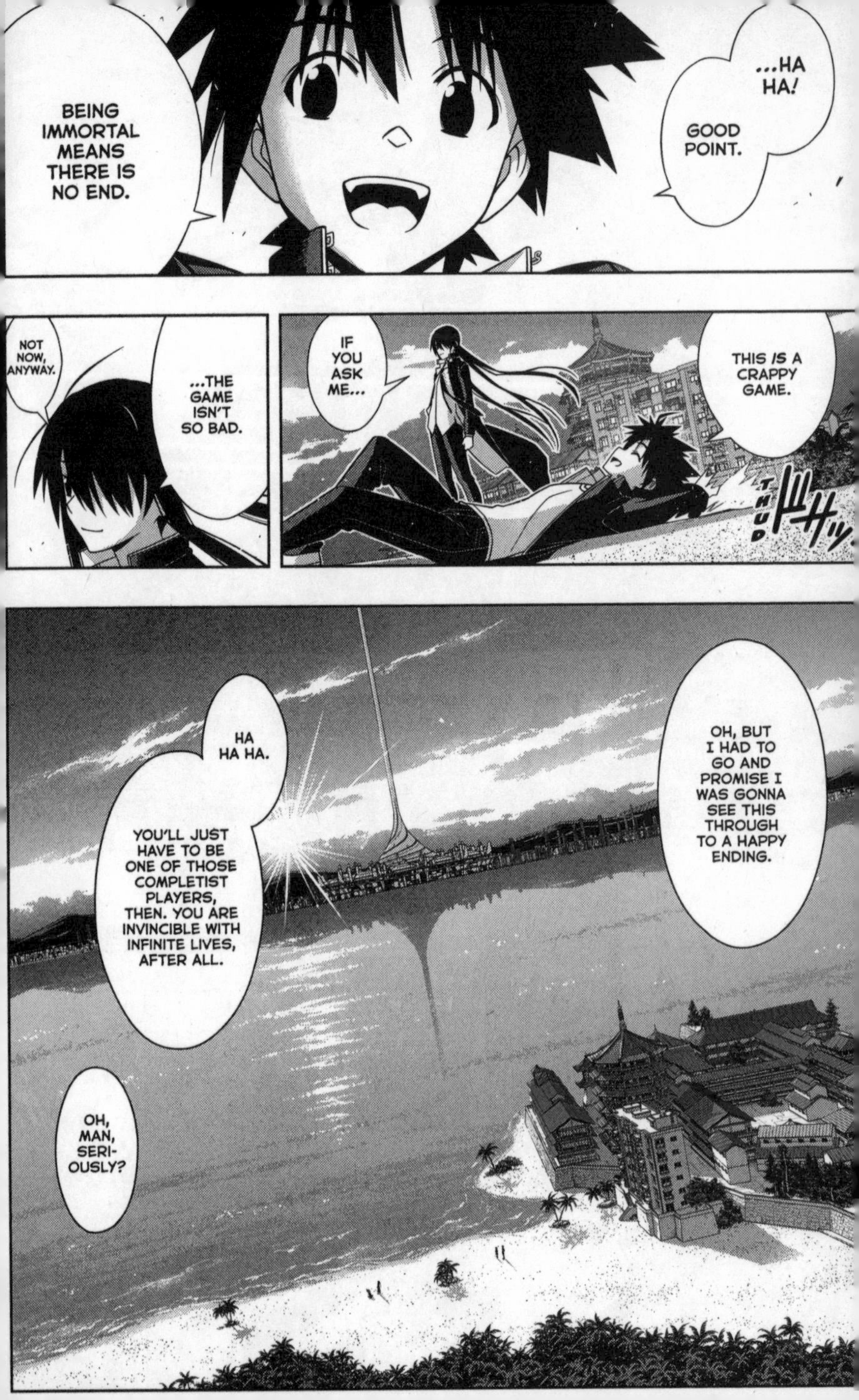
...HA HA!
GOOD POINT.
BEING IMMORTAL MEANS THERE IS NO END.
THIS *IS* A CRAPPY GAME.
IF YOU ASK ME...
THUD
...THE GAME ISN'T SO BAD.
NOT NOW, ANYWAY.
OH, BUT I HAD TO GO AND PROMISE I WAS GONNA SEE THIS THROUGH TO A HAPPY ENDING.
HA HA HA.
YOU'LL JUST HAVE TO BE ONE OF THOSE COMPLETIST PLAYERS, THEN. YOU ARE INVINCIBLE WITH INFINITE LIVES, AFTER ALL.
OH, MAN, SERI-OUSLY?

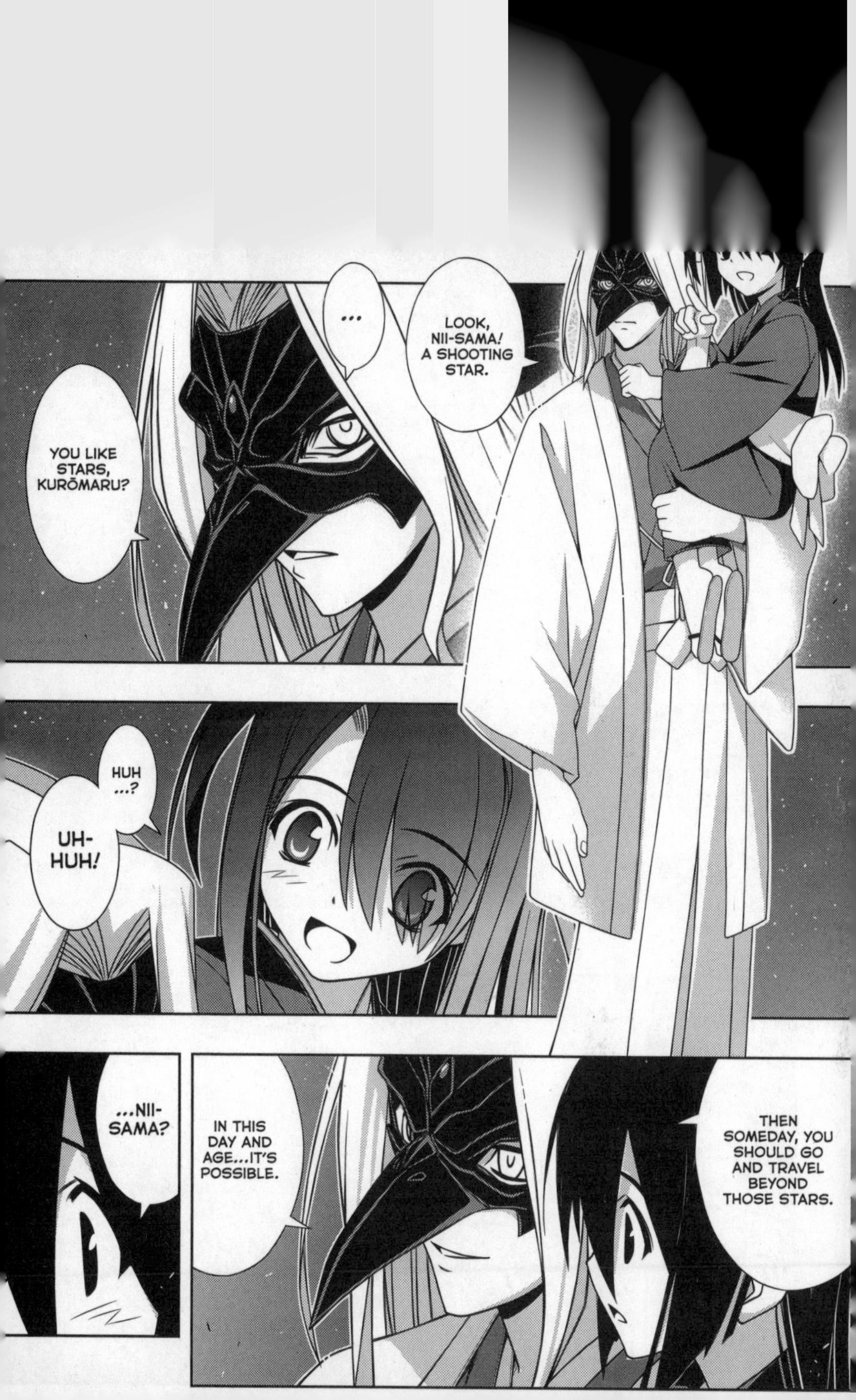
LOOK, NII-SAMA! A SHOOTING STAR.
...
YOU LIKE STARS, KURŌMARU?
HUH ...?
UH-HUH!
THEN SOMEDAY, YOU SHOULD GO AND TRAVEL BEYOND THOSE STARS.
IN THIS DAY AND AGE...IT'S POSSIBLE.
...NII-SAMA?

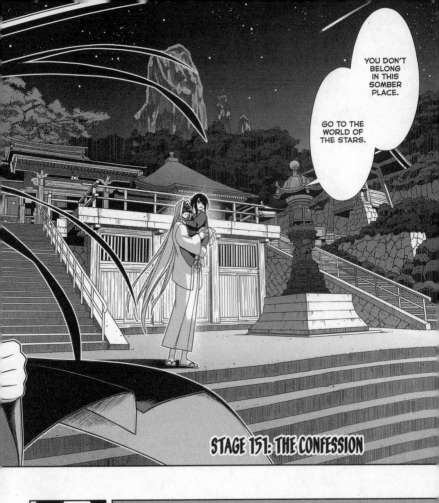

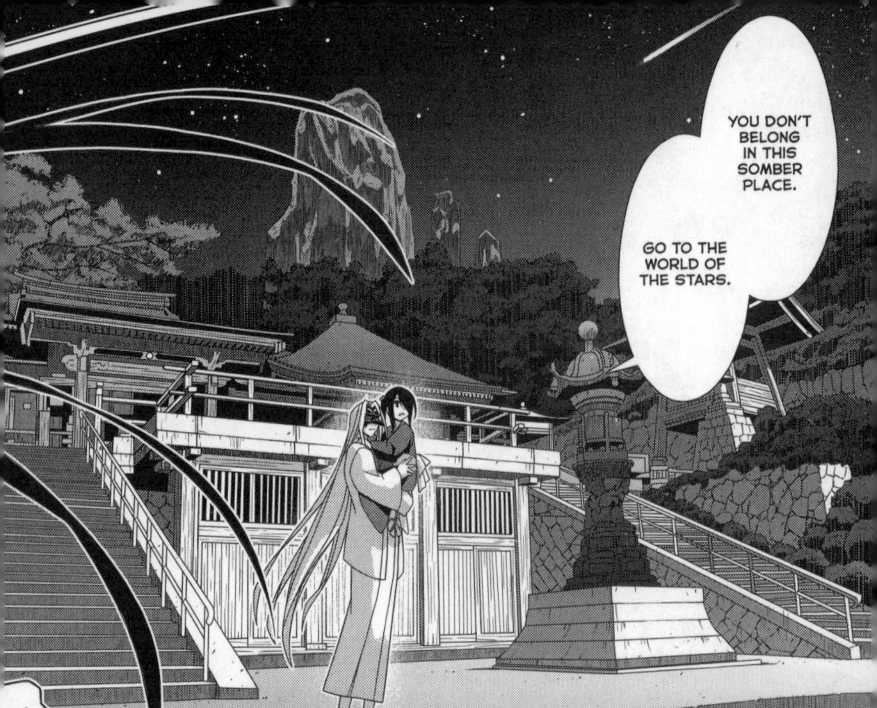
YOU DON'T BELONG IN THIS SOMBER PLACE.
GO TO THE WORLD OF THE STARS.
STAGE 151: THE CONFESSION

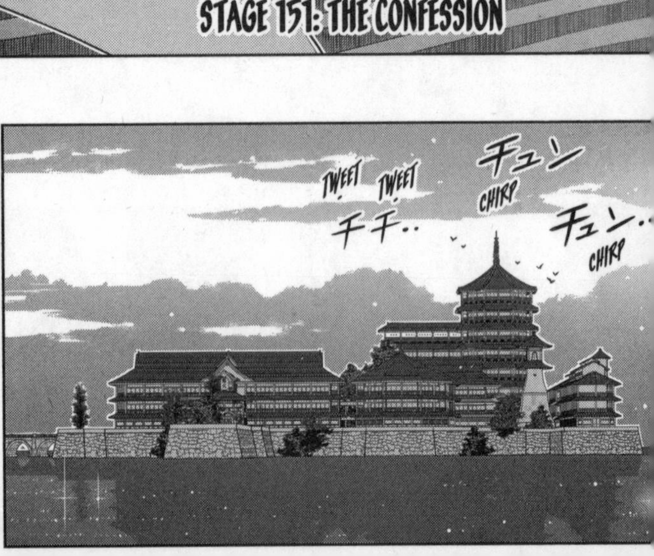
チュン
CHIRP
チュン..
CHIRP
チチ..
TWEET TWEET

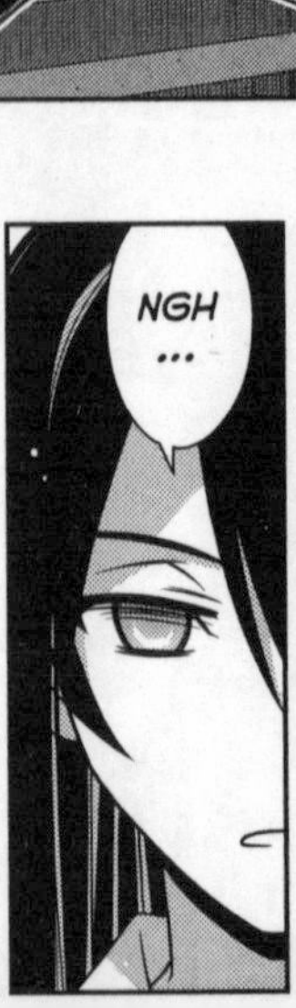
NGH ...

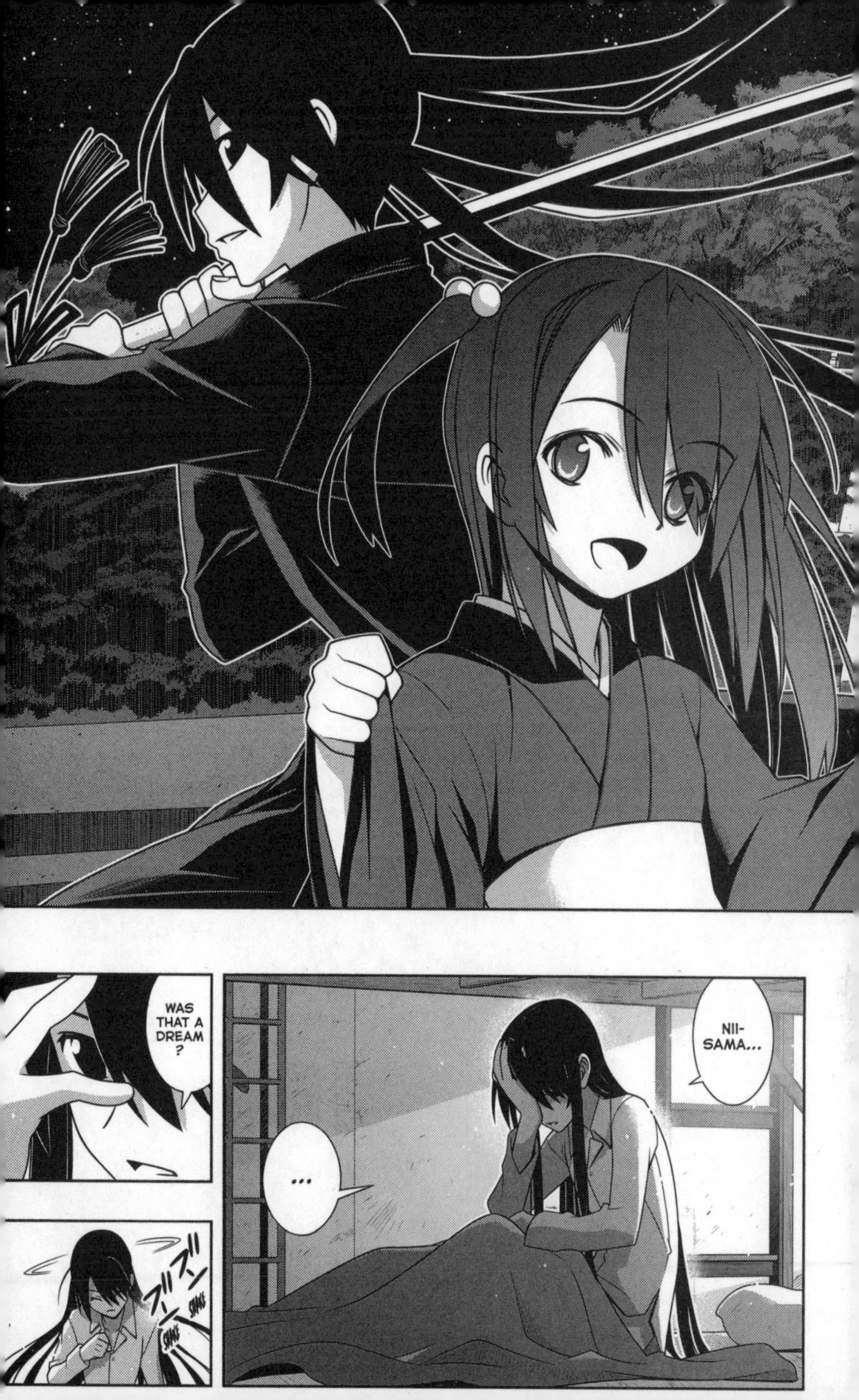
NII-SAMA...
...
WAS THAT A DREAM?
ブン
ブン
SHAKE
SHAKE

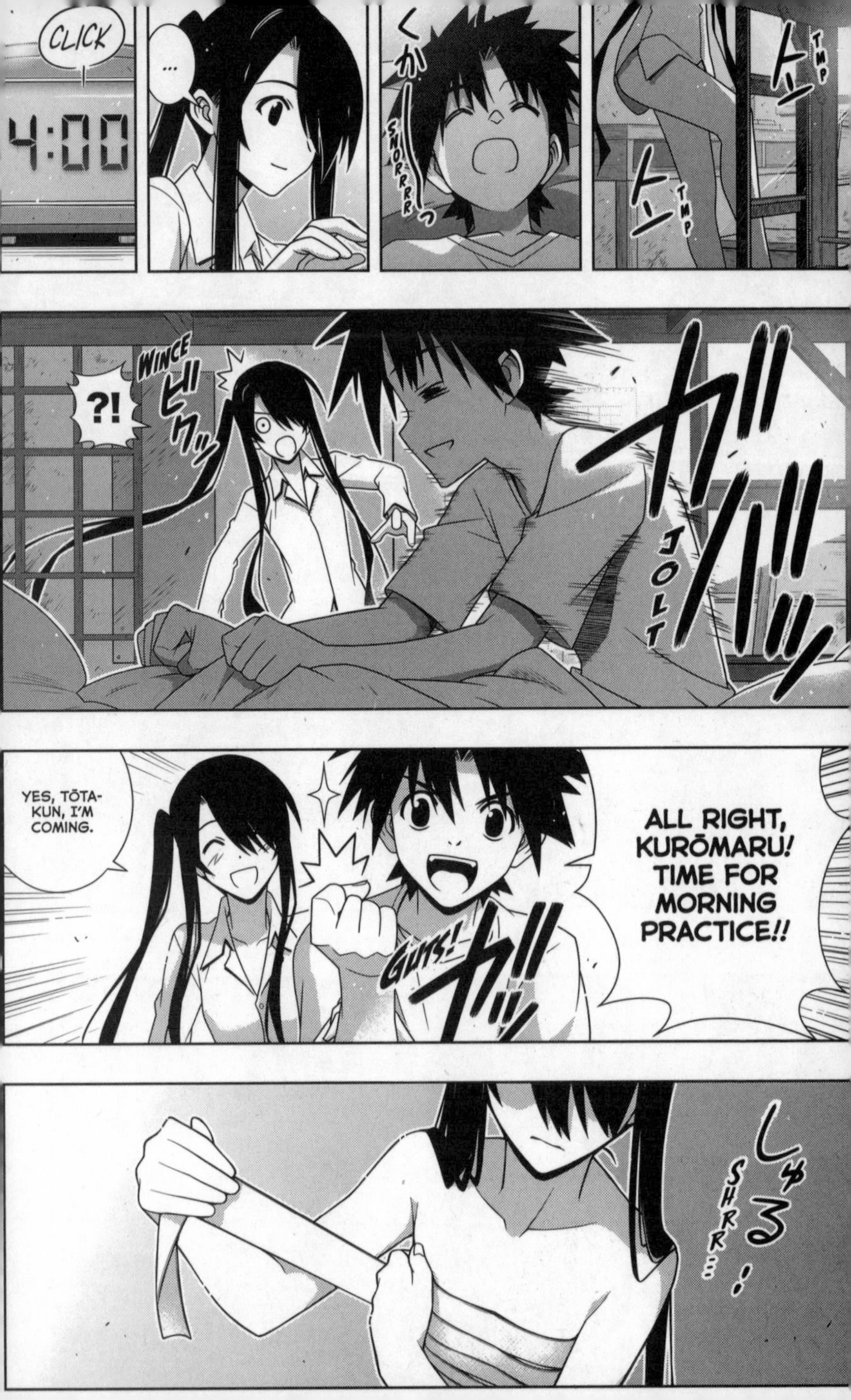
TMP
TMP
SNORRRR
...
CLICK
4:00
JOLT
?!
WINCE
ALL RIGHT, KURŌMARU! TIME FOR MORNING PRACTICE!!
GUTS!
YES, TŌTA-KUN, I'M COMING.
SHRR...

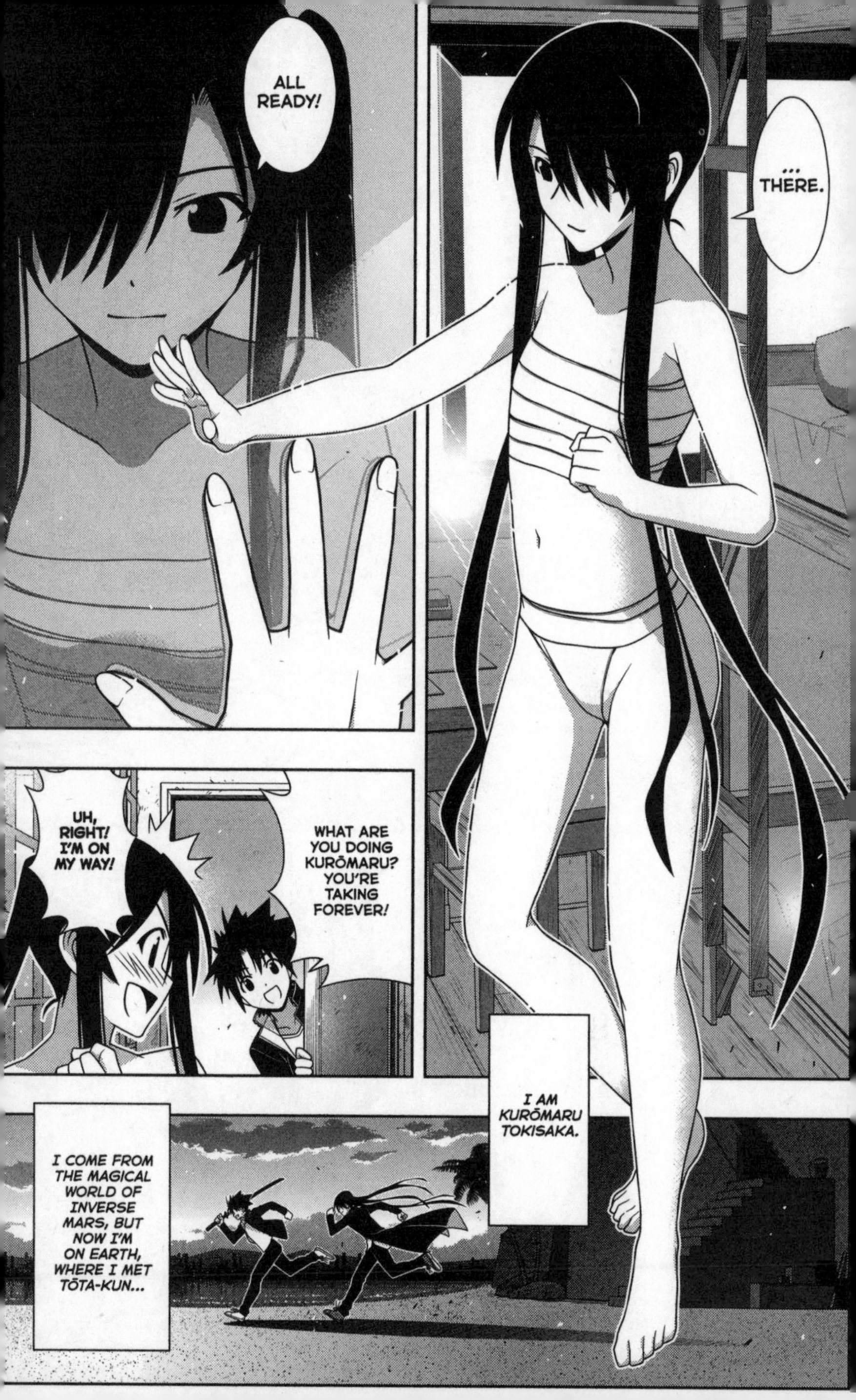
...THERE.
ALL READY!
WHAT ARE YOU DOING KURŌMARU? YOU'RE TAKING FOREVER!
UH, RIGHT! I'M ON MY WAY!
I AM KURŌMARU TOKISAKA.
I COME FROM THE MAGICAL WORLD OF INVERSE MARS, BUT NOW I'M ON EARTH, WHERE I MET TŌTA-KUN...

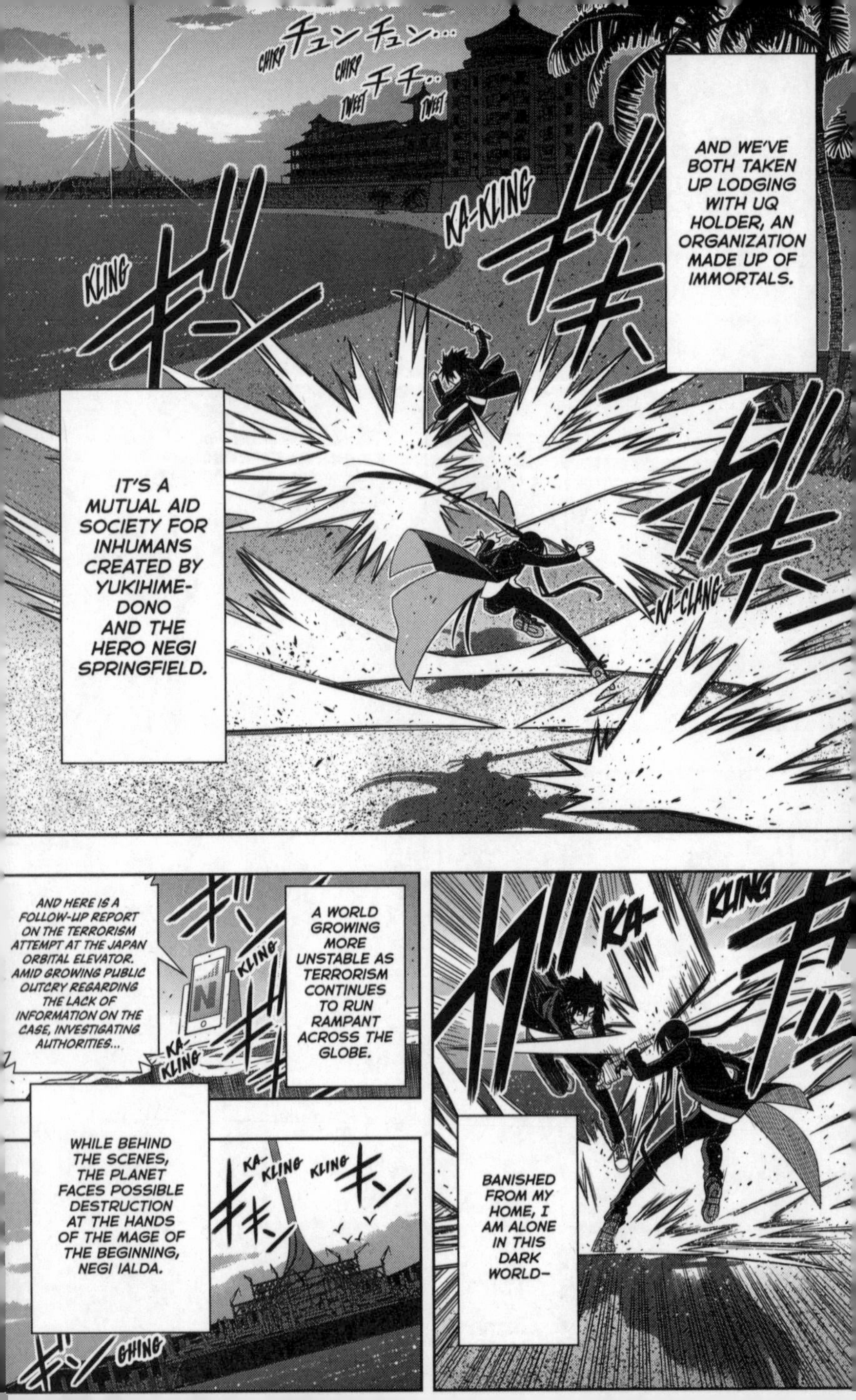

CHIRP チュンチュン…
CHIRP チチ…
TWEET
TWEET
AND WE'VE BOTH TAKEN UP LODGING WITH UQ HOLDER, AN ORGANIZATION MADE UP OF IMMORTALS.
KA-KLING
KLING
IT'S A MUTUAL AID SOCIETY FOR INHUMANS CREATED BY YUKIHIME-DONO AND THE HERO NEGI SPRINGFIELD.
KA-CLANG
KA-
KLING
BANISHED FROM MY HOME, I AM ALONE IN THIS DARK WORLD–
A WORLD GROWING MORE UNSTABLE AS TERRORISM CONTINUES TO RUN RAMPANT ACROSS THE GLOBE.
AND HERE IS A FOLLOW-UP REPORT ON THE TERRORISM ATTEMPT AT THE JAPAN ORBITAL ELEVATOR. AMID GROWING PUBLIC OUTCRY REGARDING THE LACK OF INFORMATION ON THE CASE, INVESTIGATING AUTHORITIES...
KLING
KA-KLING
WHILE BEHIND THE SCENES, THE PLANET FACES POSSIBLE DESTRUCTION AT THE HANDS OF THE MAGE OF THE BEGINNING, NEGI IALDA.
KLING
KA-KLING
CHING

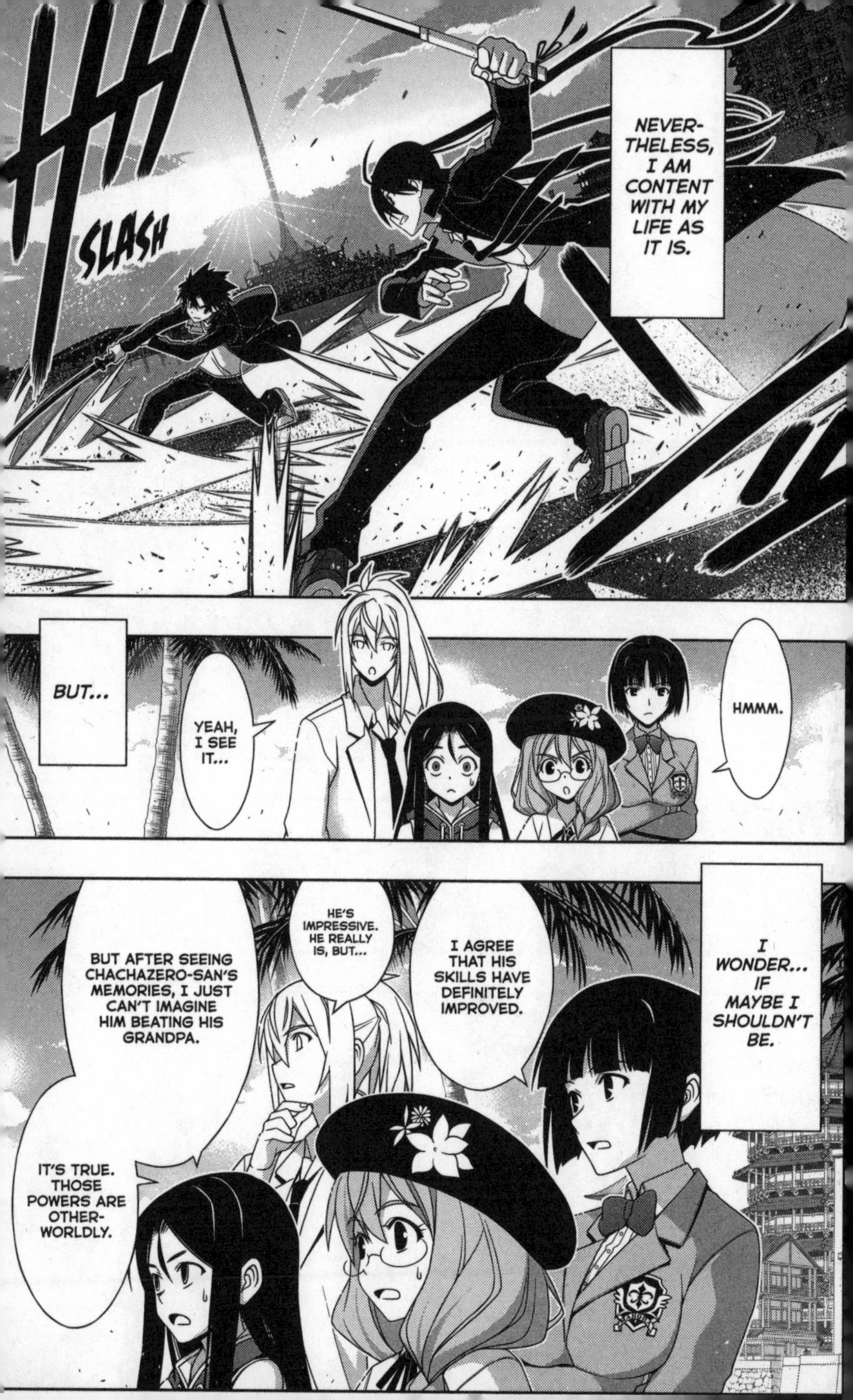
NEVER-THELESS, I AM CONTENT WITH MY LIFE AS IT IS.
SLASH
HMMM.
YEAH, I SEE IT...
BUT...
I WONDER... IF MAYBE I SHOULDN'T BE.
I AGREE THAT HIS SKILLS HAVE DEFINITELY IMPROVED.
HE'S IMPRESSIVE. HE REALLY IS, BUT...
BUT AFTER SEEING CHACHAZERO-SAN'S MEMORIES, I JUST CAN'T IMAGINE HIM BEATING HIS GRANDPA.
IT'S TRUE. THOSE POWERS ARE OTHER-WORLDLY.

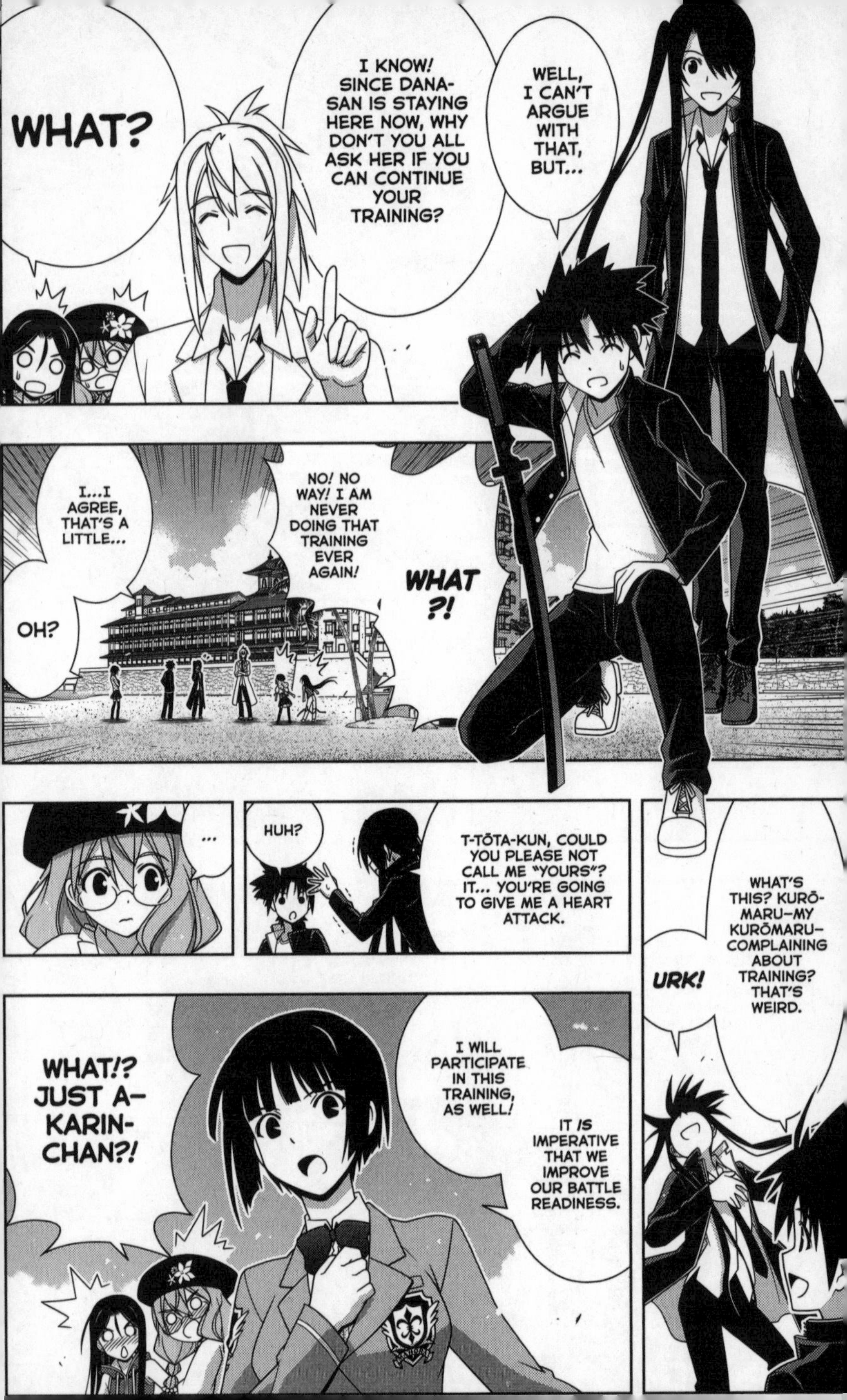
WELL, I CAN'T ARGUE WITH THAT, BUT...
I KNOW! SINCE DANA-SAN IS STAYING HERE NOW, WHY DON'T YOU ALL ASK HER IF YOU CAN CONTINUE YOUR TRAINING?
WHAT?
NO! NO WAY! I AM NEVER DOING THAT TRAINING EVER AGAIN!
WHAT ?!
I...I AGREE, THAT'S A LITTLE...
OH?
WHAT'S THIS? KURŌ-MARU—MY KURŌMARU—COMPLAINING ABOUT TRAINING? THAT'S WEIRD.
URK!
T-TŌTA-KUN, COULD YOU PLEASE NOT CALL ME "YOURS"? IT... YOU'RE GOING TO GIVE ME A HEART ATTACK.
HUH?
...
I WILL PARTICIPATE IN THIS TRAINING, AS WELL!
IT IS IMPERATIVE THAT WE IMPROVE OUR BATTLE READINESS.
WHAT!? JUST A-KARIN-CHAN?!

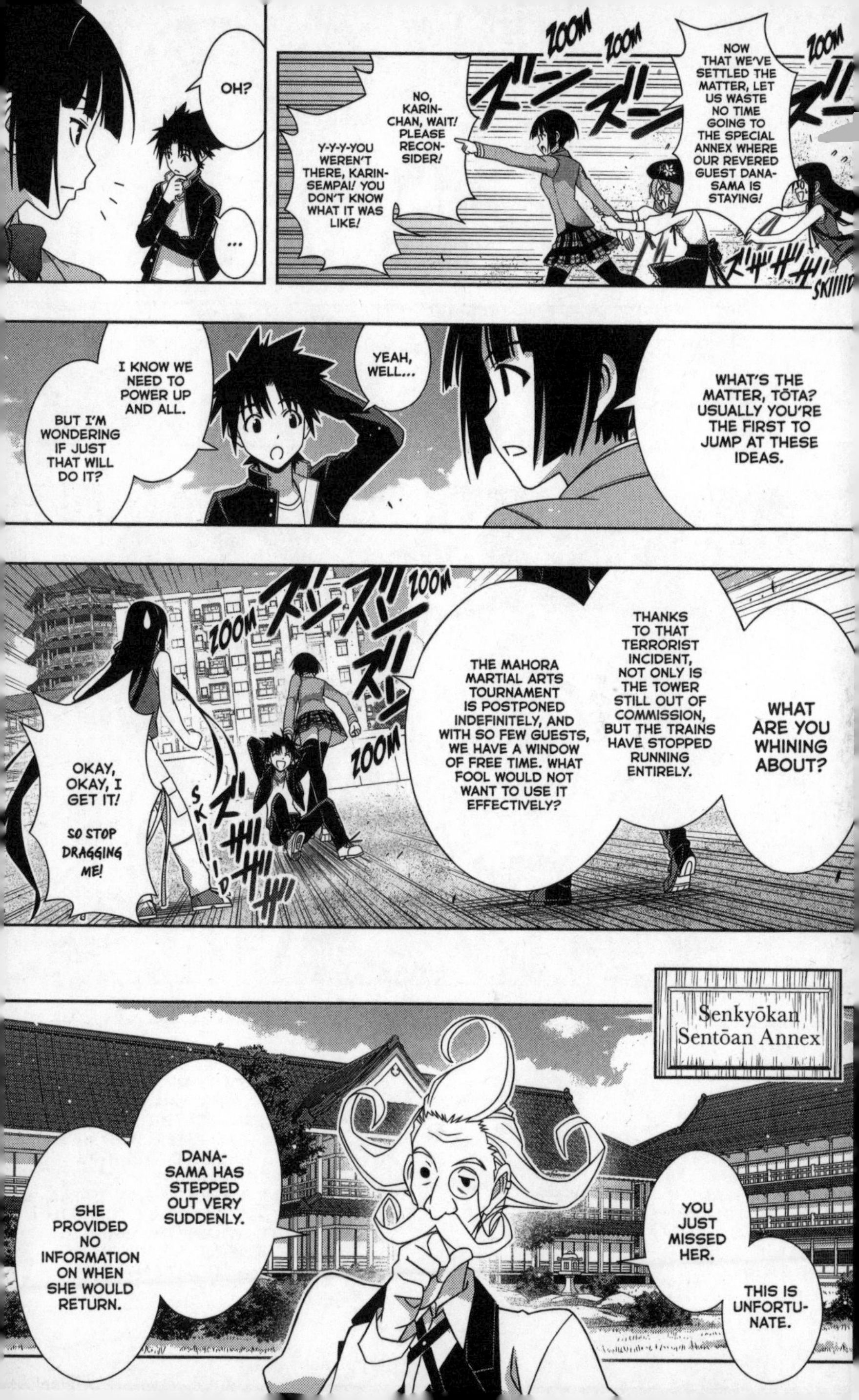
ZOOM
ZOOM
ZOOM
NOW THAT WE'VE SETTLED THE MATTER, LET US WASTE NO TIME GOING TO THE SPECIAL ANNEX WHERE OUR REVERED GUEST DANA-SAMA IS STAYING!
NO, KARIN-CHAN, WAIT! PLEASE RECONSIDER!
Y-Y-Y-YOU WEREN'T THERE, KARIN-SEMPAI! YOU DON'T KNOW WHAT IT WAS LIKE!
SKIIIID
OH?
...
WHAT'S THE MATTER, TŌTA? USUALLY YOU'RE THE FIRST TO JUMP AT THESE IDEAS.
YEAH, WELL...
I KNOW WE NEED TO POWER UP AND ALL.
BUT I'M WONDERING IF JUST THAT WILL DO IT?
WHAT ARE YOU WHINING ABOUT?
THANKS TO THAT TERRORIST INCIDENT, NOT ONLY IS THE TOWER STILL OUT OF COMMISSION, BUT THE TRAINS HAVE STOPPED RUNNING ENTIRELY.
THE MAHORA MARTIAL ARTS TOURNAMENT IS POSTPONED INDEFINITELY, AND WITH SO FEW GUESTS, WE HAVE A WINDOW OF FREE TIME. WHAT FOOL WOULD NOT WANT TO USE IT EFFECTIVELY?
ZOOM
ZOOM
ZOOM
OKAY, OKAY, I GET IT!
SO STOP DRAGGING ME!
SKIIID
Senkyōkan Sentōan Annex
YOU JUST MISSED HER.
THIS IS UNFORTUNATE.
DANA-SAMA HAS STEPPED OUT VERY SUDDENLY.
SHE PROVIDED NO INFORMATION ON WHEN SHE WOULD RETURN.

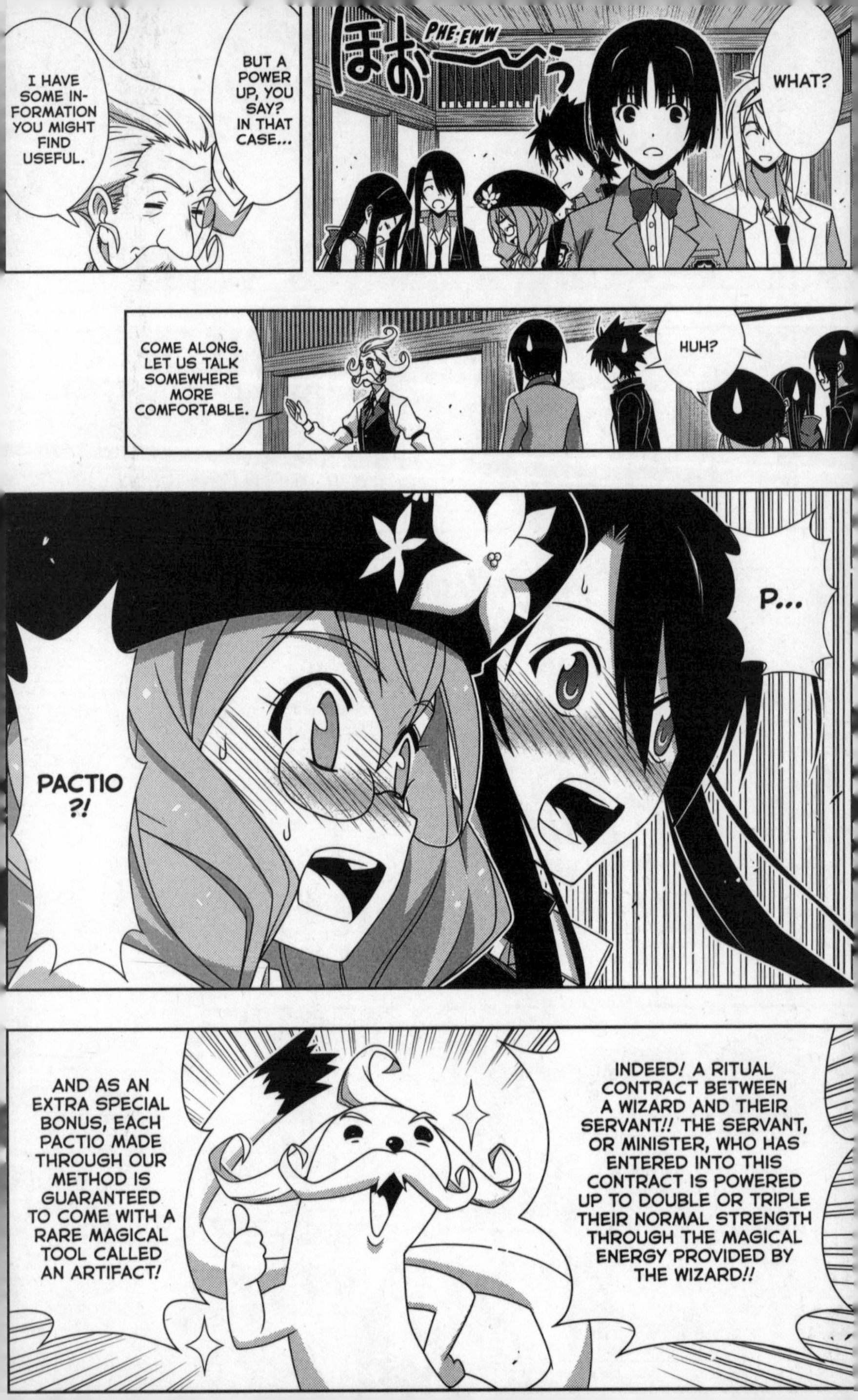
WHAT?
ほぉ～～ぅ
PHE-EWW
BUT A POWER UP, YOU SAY? IN THAT CASE...
I HAVE SOME IN-FORMATION YOU MIGHT FIND USEFUL.
HUH?
COME ALONG. LET US TALK SOMEWHERE MORE COMFORTABLE.
P...
PACTIO ?!
INDEED! A RITUAL CONTRACT BETWEEN A WIZARD AND THEIR SERVANT!! THE SERVANT, OR MINISTER, WHO HAS ENTERED INTO THIS CONTRACT IS POWERED UP TO DOUBLE OR TRIPLE THEIR NORMAL STRENGTH THROUGH THE MAGICAL ENERGY PROVIDED BY THE WIZARD!!
AND AS AN EXTRA SPECIAL BONUS, EACH PACTIO MADE THROUGH OUR METHOD IS GUARANTEED TO COME WITH A RARE MAGICAL TOOL CALLED AN ARTIFACT!

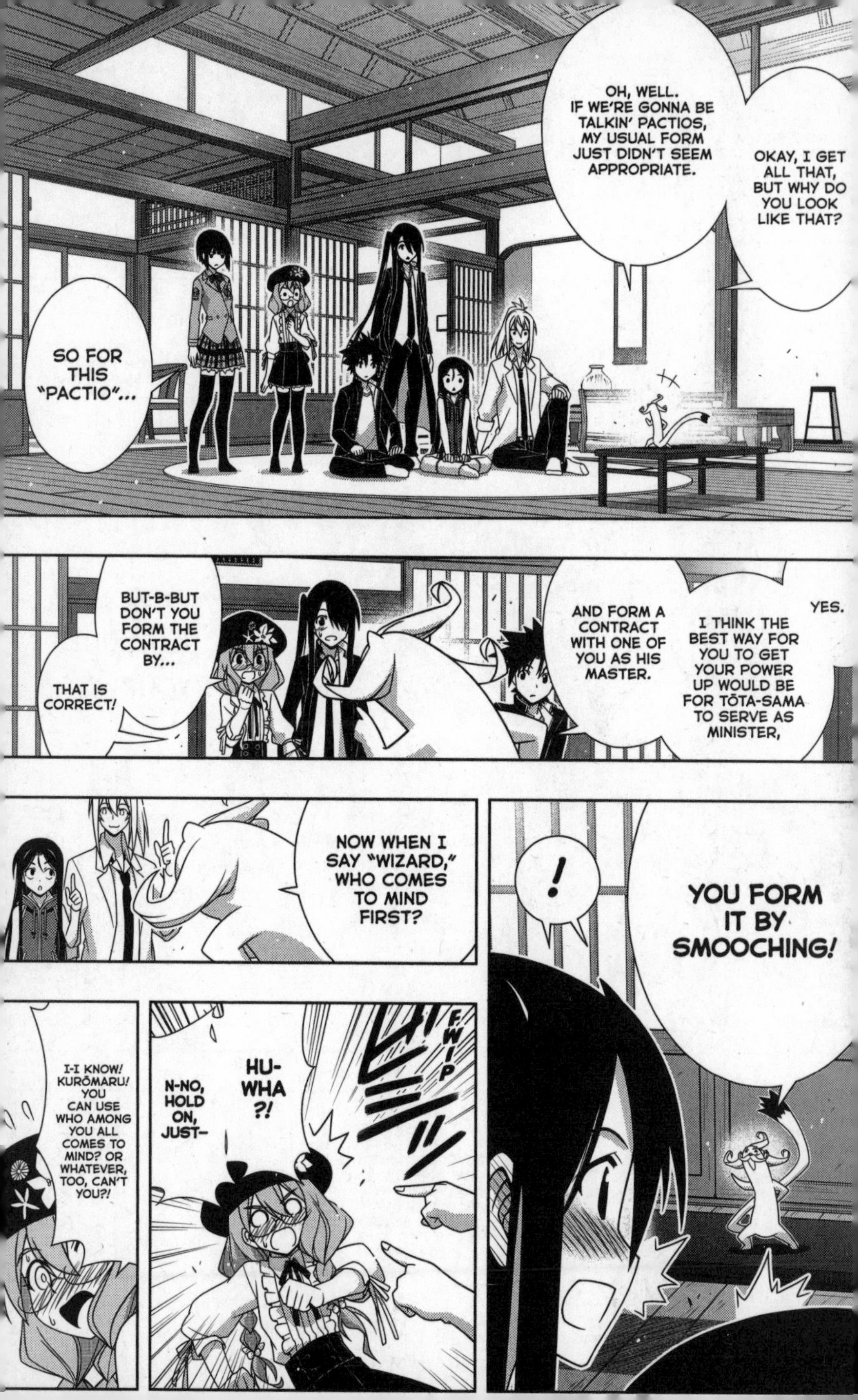
OKAY, I GET ALL THAT, BUT WHY DO YOU LOOK LIKE THAT?
OH, WELL. IF WE'RE GONNA BE TALKIN' PACTIOS, MY USUAL FORM JUST DIDN'T SEEM APPROPRIATE.
SO FOR THIS "PACTIO"...
YES.
I THINK THE BEST WAY FOR YOU TO GET YOUR POWER UP WOULD BE FOR TŌTA-SAMA TO SERVE AS MINISTER,
AND FORM A CONTRACT WITH ONE OF YOU AS HIS MASTER.
BUT-B-BUT DON'T YOU FORM THE CONTRACT BY...
THAT IS CORRECT!
YOU FORM IT BY SMOOCHING!
!
NOW WHEN I SAY "WIZARD," WHO COMES TO MIND FIRST?
HU-WHA?!
FWIP
N-NO, HOLD ON, JUST-
I-I KNOW! KURŌMARU! YOU CAN USE WHO AMONG YOU ALL COMES TO MIND? OR WHATEVER, TOO, CAN'T YOU?!

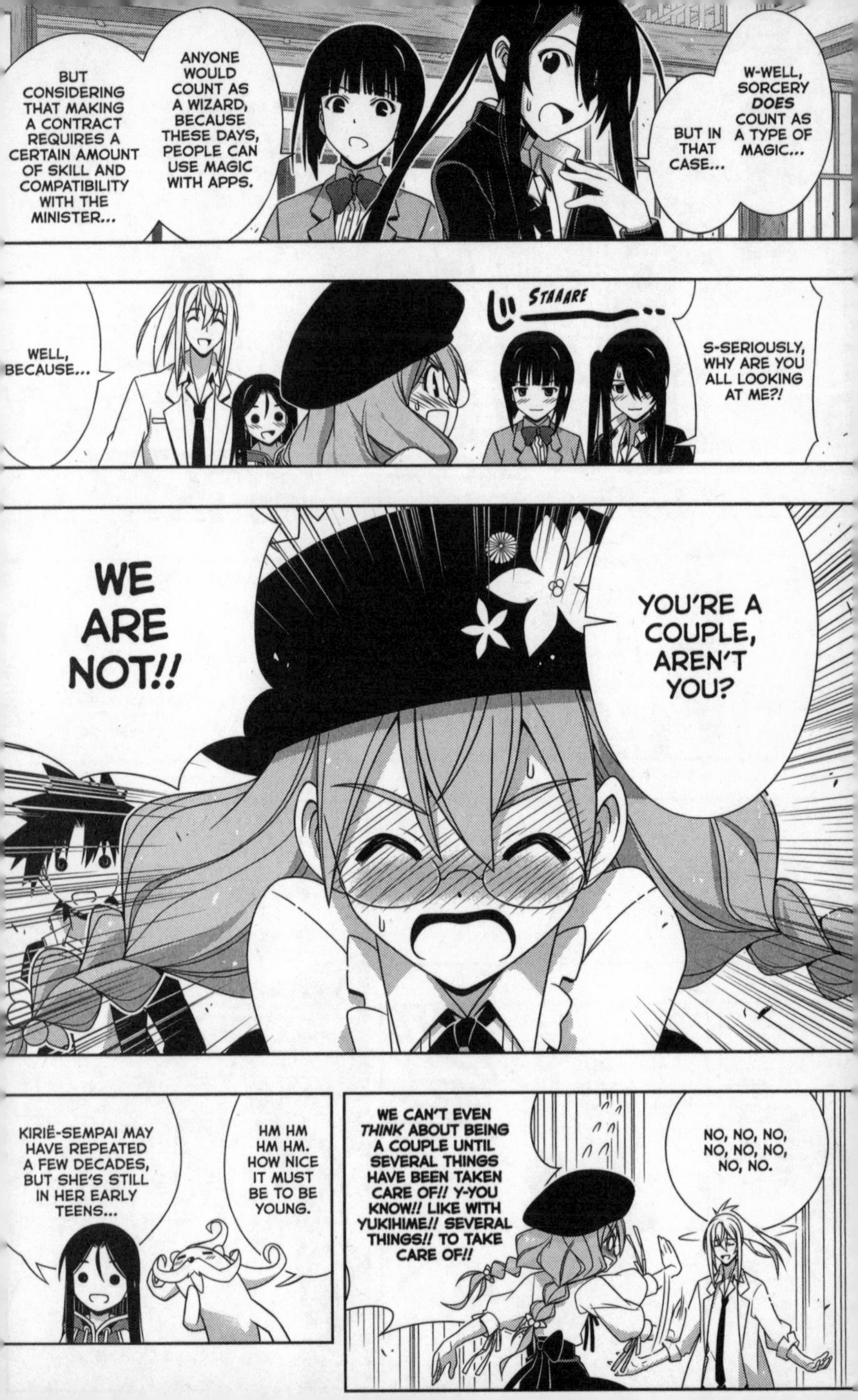
W-WELL, SORCERY *DOES* COUNT AS A TYPE OF MAGIC...
BUT IN THAT CASE...
ANYONE WOULD COUNT AS A WIZARD, BECAUSE THESE DAYS, PEOPLE CAN USE MAGIC WITH APPS.
BUT CONSIDERING THAT MAKING A CONTRACT REQUIRES A CERTAIN AMOUNT OF SKILL AND COMPATIBILITY WITH THE MINISTER...
S-SERIOUSLY, WHY ARE YOU ALL LOOKING AT ME?!
STAAARE
WELL, BECAUSE...
YOU'RE A COUPLE, AREN'T YOU?
WE ARE NOT!!
NO, NO, NO, NO, NO, NO, NO, NO.
WE CAN'T EVEN *THINK* ABOUT BEING A COUPLE UNTIL SEVERAL THINGS HAVE BEEN TAKEN CARE OF!! Y-YOU KNOW!! LIKE WITH YUKIHIME!! SEVERAL THINGS!! TO TAKE CARE OF!!
HM HM HM HM. HOW NICE IT MUST BE TO BE YOUNG.
KIRIË-SEMPAI MAY HAVE REPEATED A FEW DECADES, BUT SHE'S STILL IN HER EARLY TEENS...

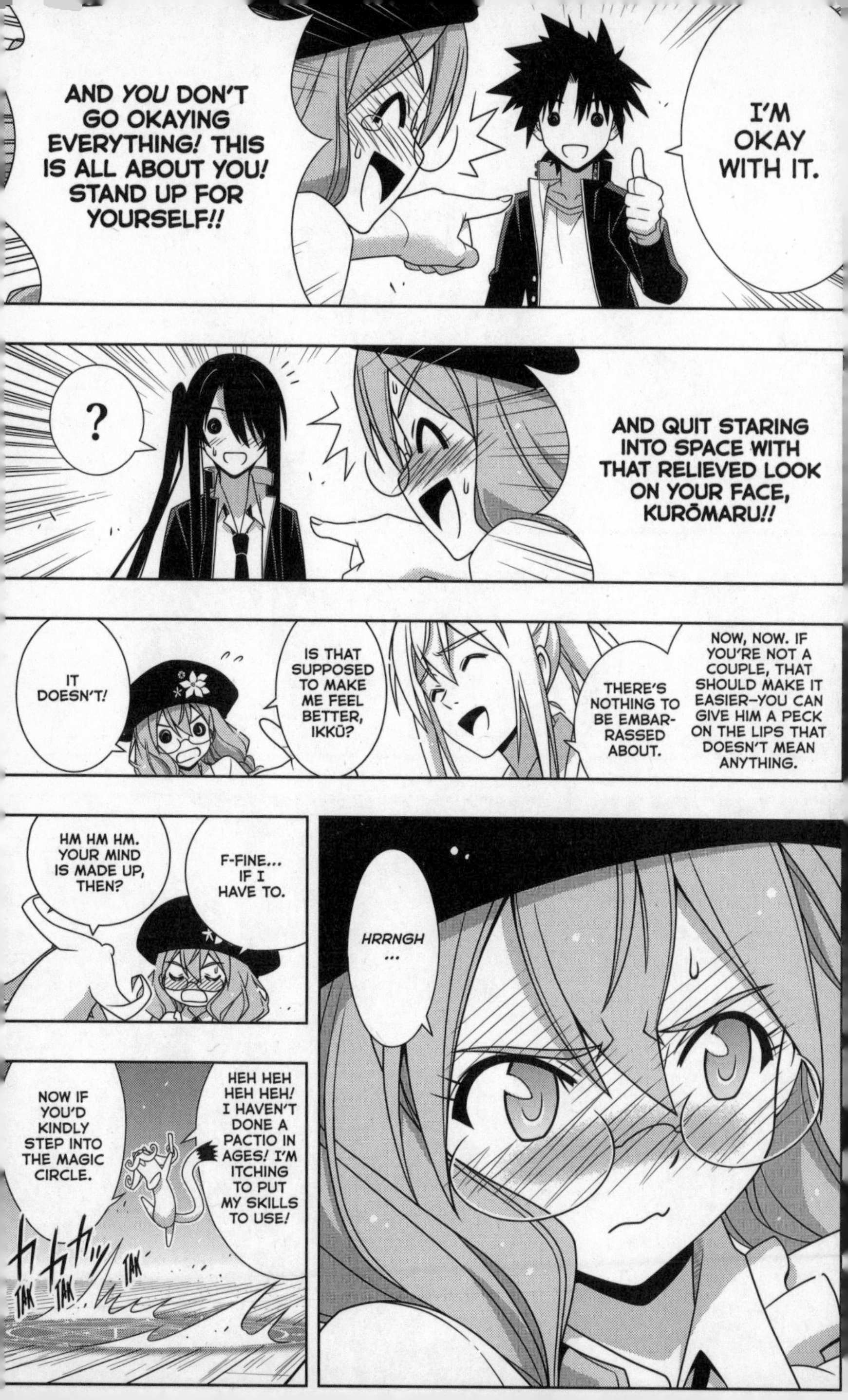
I'M OKAY WITH IT.
AND *YOU* DON'T GO OKAYING EVERYTHING! THIS IS ALL ABOUT YOU! STAND UP FOR YOURSELF!!
AND QUIT STARING INTO SPACE WITH THAT RELIEVED LOOK ON YOUR FACE, KURŌMARU!!
?
NOW, NOW. IF YOU'RE NOT A COUPLE, THAT SHOULD MAKE IT EASIER—YOU CAN GIVE HIM A PECK ON THE LIPS THAT DOESN'T MEAN ANYTHING.
THERE'S NOTHING TO BE EMBARRASSED ABOUT.
IS THAT SUPPOSED TO MAKE ME FEEL BETTER, IKKŪ?
IT DOESN'T!
HRRNGH...
F-FINE... IF I HAVE TO.
HM HM HM. YOUR MIND IS MADE UP, THEN?
HEH HEH HEH HEH! I HAVEN'T DONE A PACTIO IN AGES! I'M ITCHING TO PUT MY SKILLS TO USE!
NOW IF YOU'D KINDLY STEP INTO THE MAGIC CIRCLE.
TAK
TAK
TAK

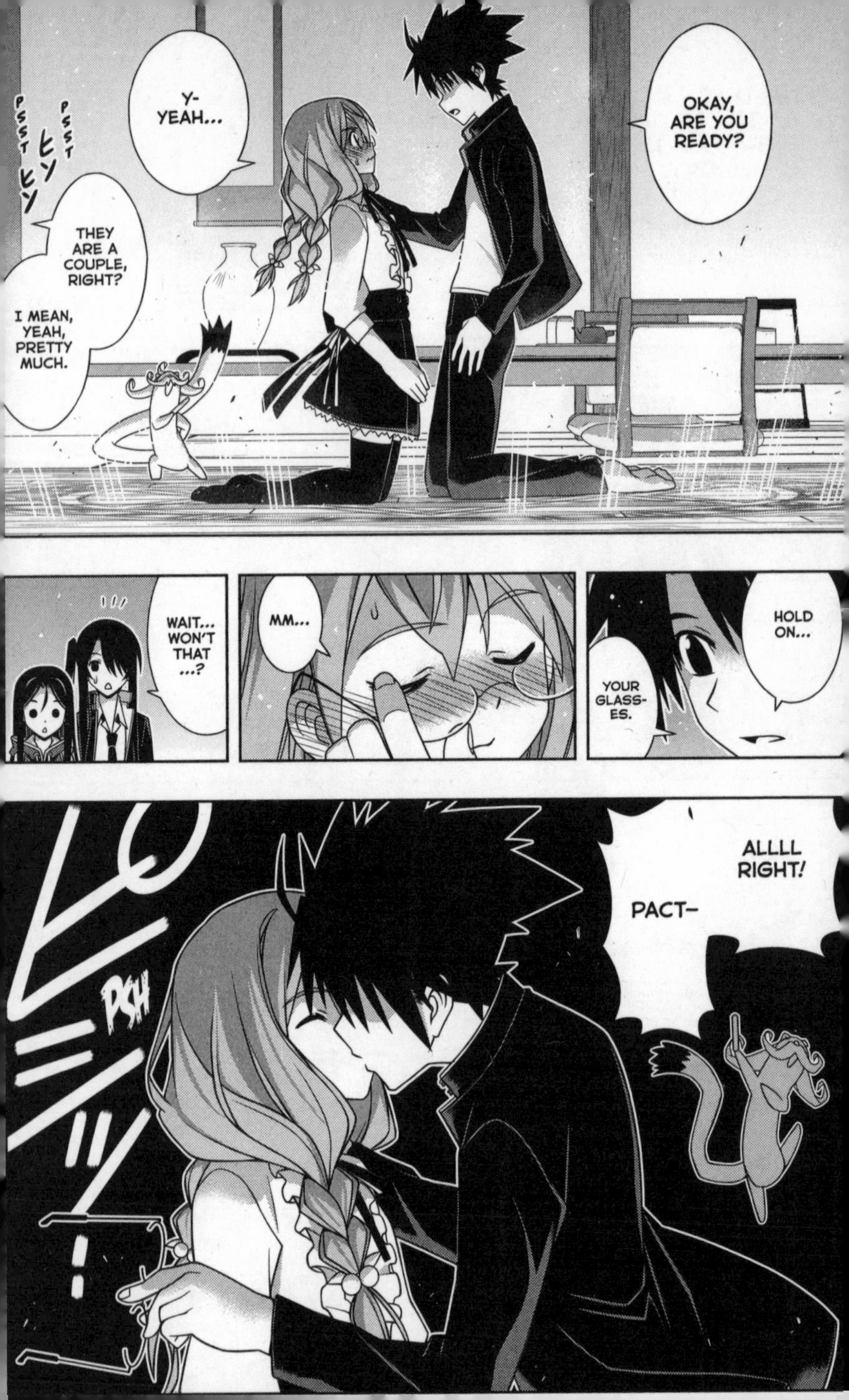
OKAY, ARE YOU READY?
Y-YEAH...
PSST ヒソ
PSST ヒソ
THEY ARE A COUPLE, RIGHT?
I MEAN, YEAH, PRETTY MUCH.
HOLD ON...
YOUR GLASSES.
MM...
WAIT... WON'T THAT ...?
ALLLL RIGHT!
PACT–
DSH

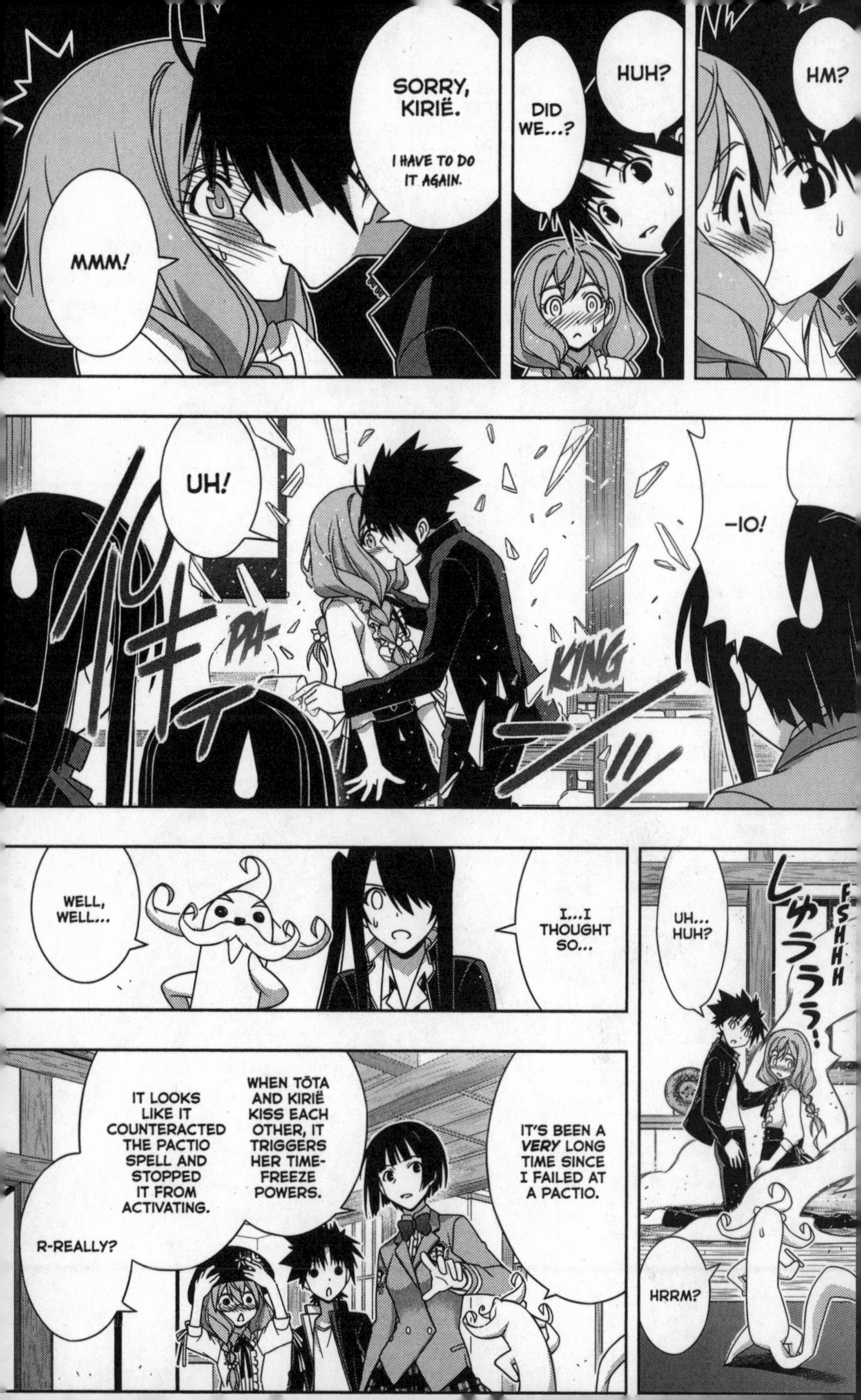
HM?
HUH?
DID WE...?
SORRY, KIRIË.
I HAVE TO DO IT AGAIN.
MMM!
–IO!
KING
PA-
UH!
UH... HUH?
FSHHH
HRRM?
I...I THOUGHT SO...
WELL, WELL...
IT'S BEEN A *VERY* LONG TIME SINCE I FAILED AT A PACTIO.
WHEN TŌTA AND KIRIË KISS EACH OTHER, IT TRIGGERS HER TIME-FREEZE POWERS.
IT LOOKS LIKE IT COUNTERACTED THE PACTIO SPELL AND STOPPED IT FROM ACTIVATING.
R-REALLY?

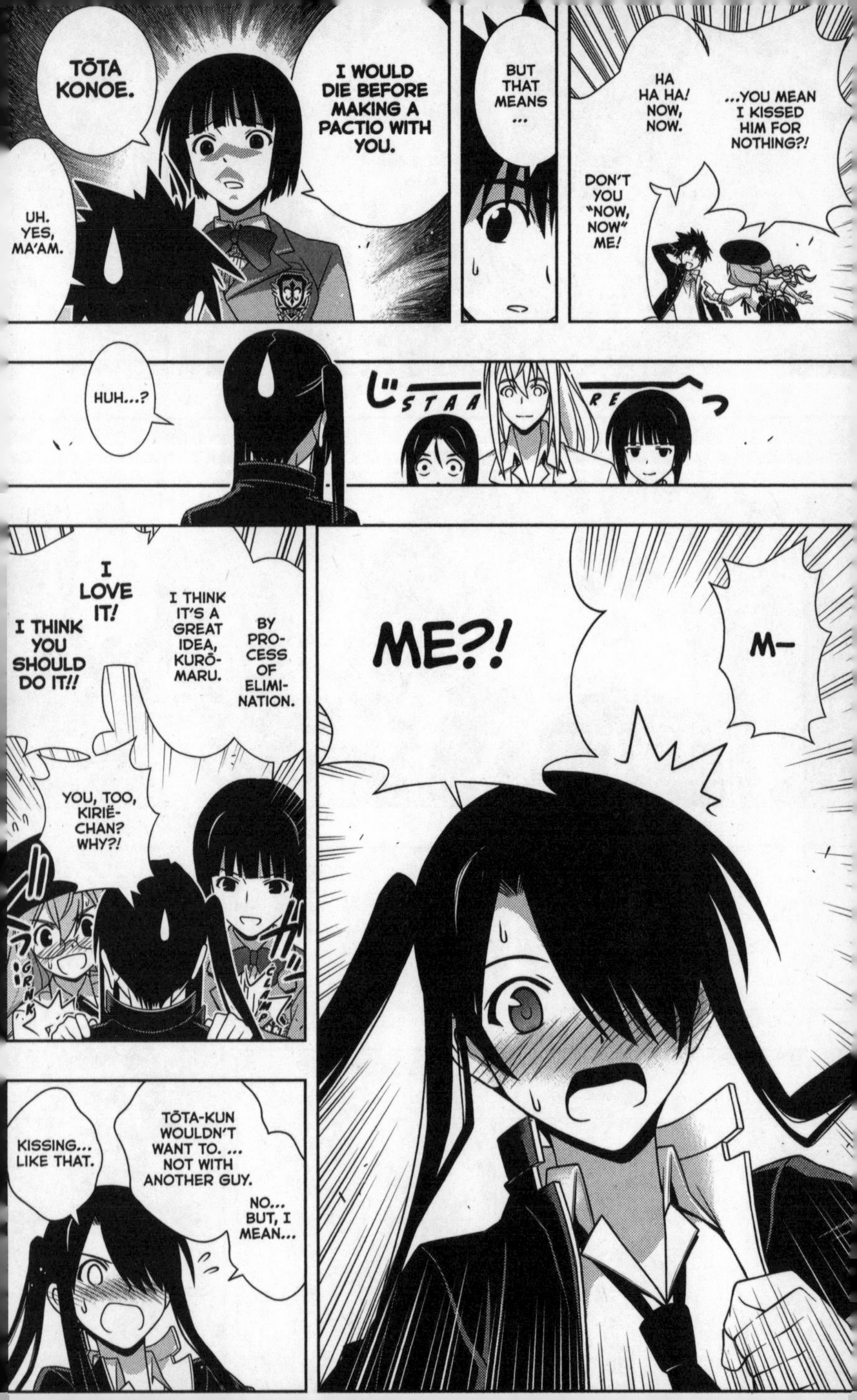
...YOU MEAN I KISSED HIM FOR NOTHING?!
HA HA HA! NOW, NOW.
DON'T YOU "NOW, NOW" ME!
BUT THAT MEANS ...
I WOULD DIE BEFORE MAKING A PACTIO WITH YOU.
TŌTA KONOE.
UH. YES, MA'AM.
じ STAARE つ
HUH...?
M-
ME?!
BY PROCESS OF ELIMINATION.
I THINK IT'S A GREAT IDEA, KURŌMARU.
I LOVE IT!
I THINK YOU SHOULD DO IT!!
YOU, TOO, KIRIË-CHAN? WHY?!
CLAMP
GRNK
TŌTA-KUN WOULDN'T WANT TO. ... NOT WITH ANOTHER GUY.
KISSING... LIKE THAT.
NO... BUT, I MEAN...

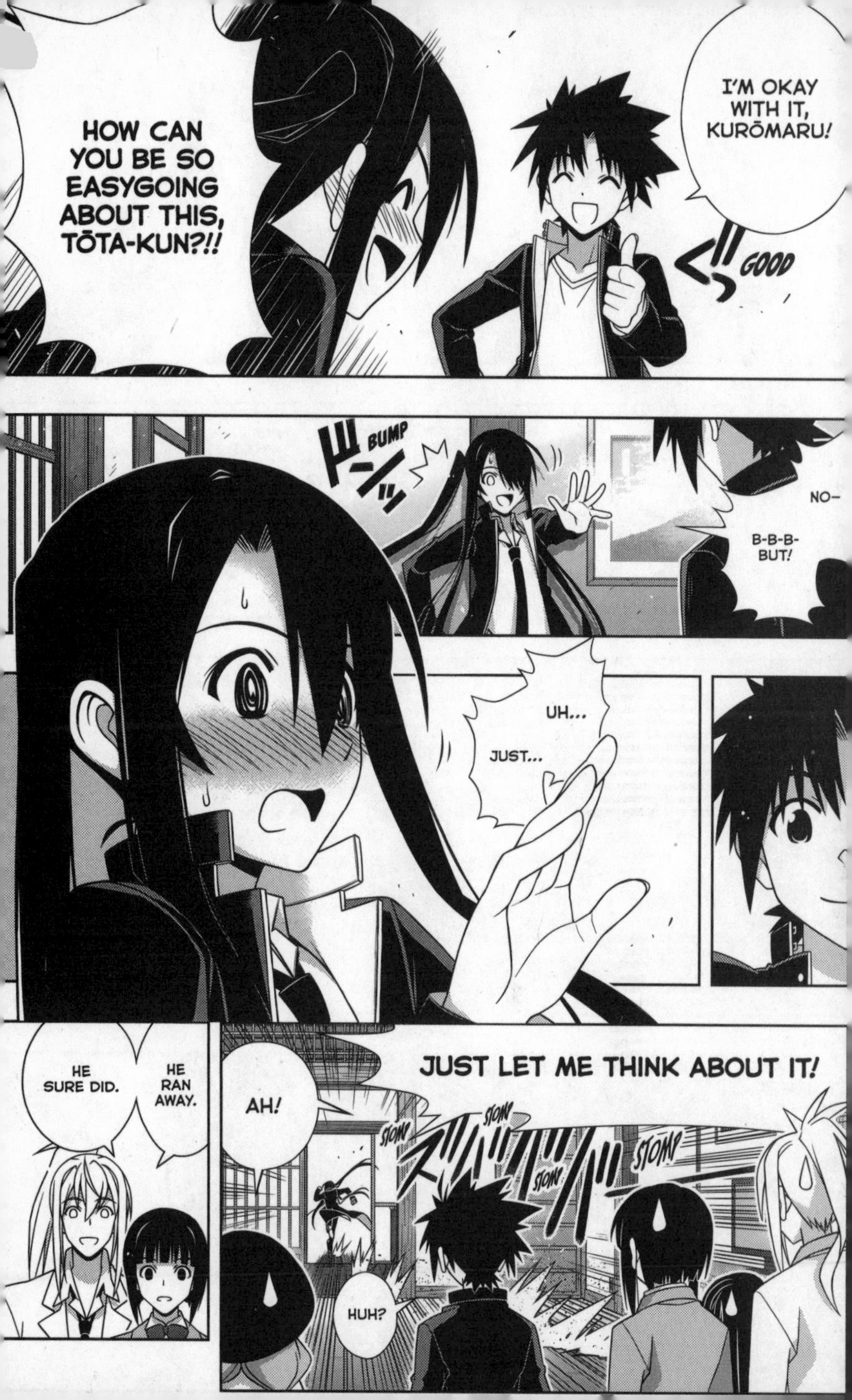
I'M OKAY WITH IT, KURŌMARU!
GOOD
HOW CAN YOU BE SO EASYGOING ABOUT THIS, TŌTA-KUN?!!
NO—
B-B-B-BUT!
BUMP
UH...
JUST...
JUST LET ME THINK ABOUT IT!
STOMP
STOMP
STOMP
STOMP
STOMP
AH!
HUH?
HE RAN AWAY.
HE SURE DID.

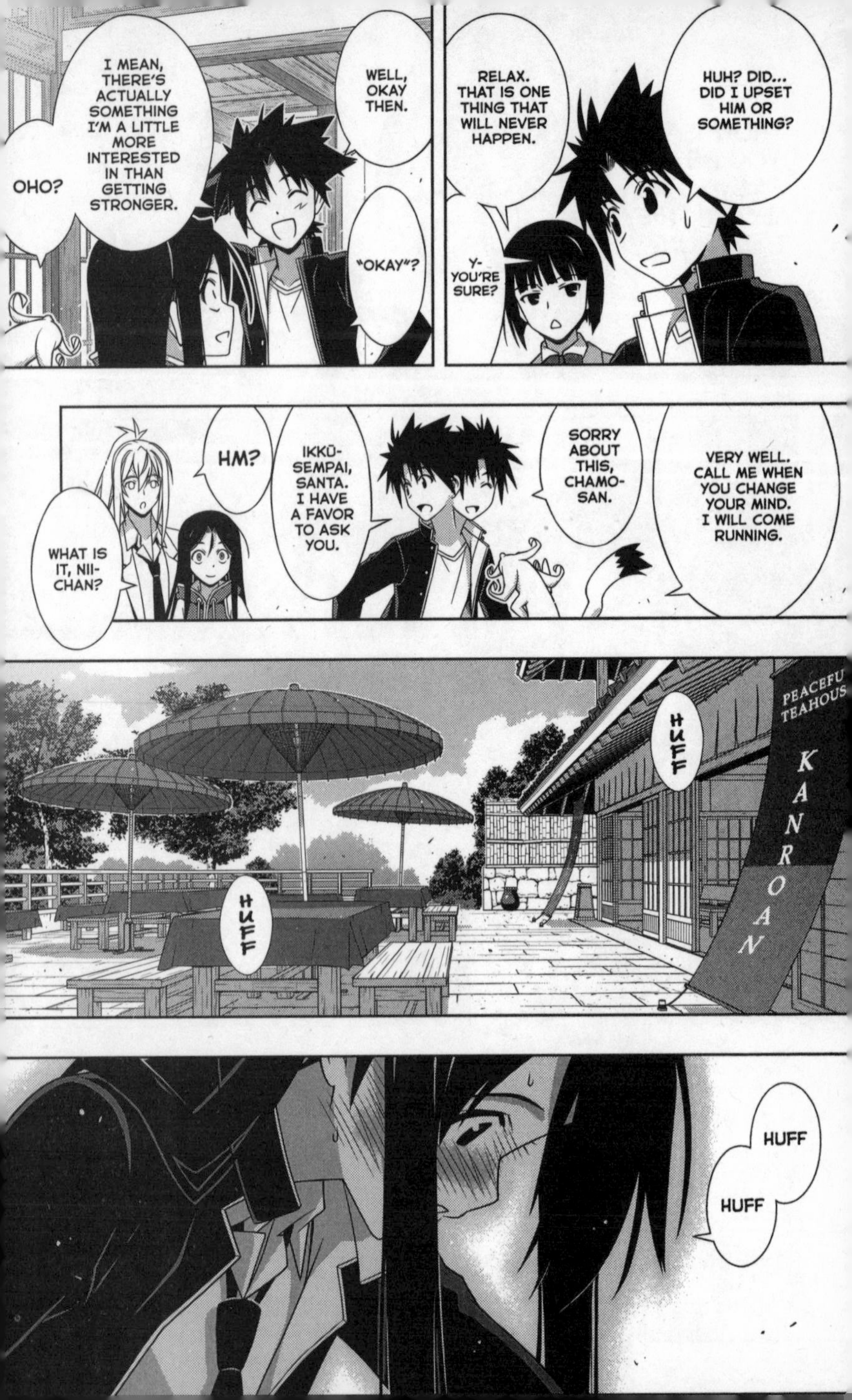
HUH? DID... DID I UPSET HIM OR SOMETHING?
RELAX. THAT IS ONE THING THAT WILL NEVER HAPPEN.
Y-YOU'RE SURE?
WELL, OKAY THEN.
"OKAY"?
I MEAN, THERE'S ACTUALLY SOMETHING I'M A LITTLE MORE INTERESTED IN THAN GETTING STRONGER.
OHO?
VERY WELL. CALL ME WHEN YOU CHANGE YOUR MIND. I WILL COME RUNNING.
SORRY ABOUT THIS, CHAMO-SAN.
IKKŪ-SEMPAI, SANTA. I HAVE A FAVOR TO ASK YOU.
HM?
WHAT IS IT, NII-CHAN?
PEACEFU TEAHOUS
KANROAN
HUFF
HUFF
HUFF
HUFF

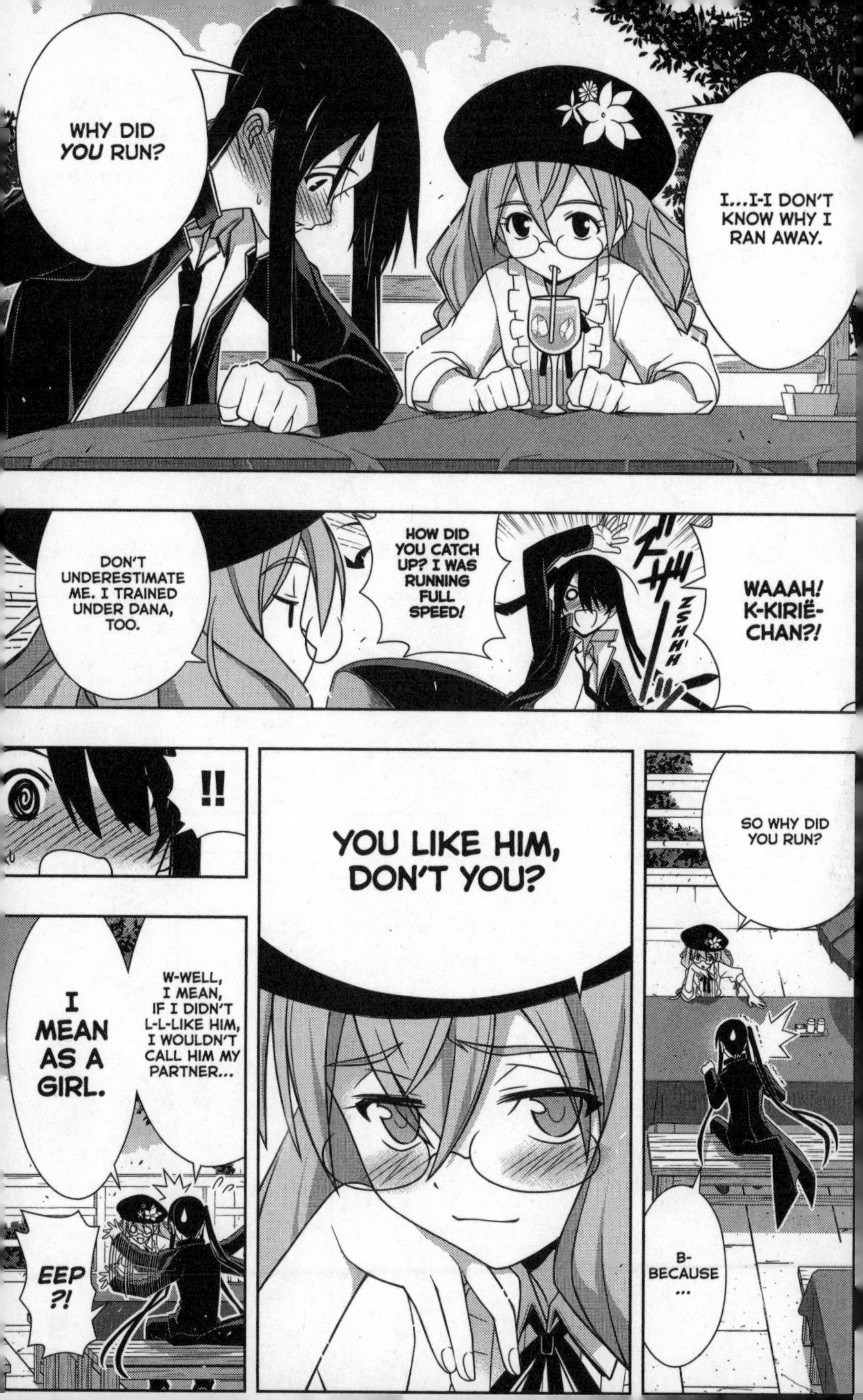

WHY DID *YOU* RUN?
I...I-I DON'T KNOW WHY I RAN AWAY.
WAAAH! K-KIRIË-CHAN?!
ZSHHH
HOW DID YOU CATCH UP? I WAS RUNNING FULL SPEED!
DON'T UNDERESTIMATE ME. I TRAINED UNDER DANA, TOO.
SO WHY DID YOU RUN?
B-BECAUSE ...
YOU LIKE HIM, DON'T YOU?
!!
W-WELL, I MEAN, IF I DIDN'T L-L-LIKE HIM, I WOULDN'T CALL HIM MY PARTNER...
I MEAN AS A GIRL.
EEP ?!

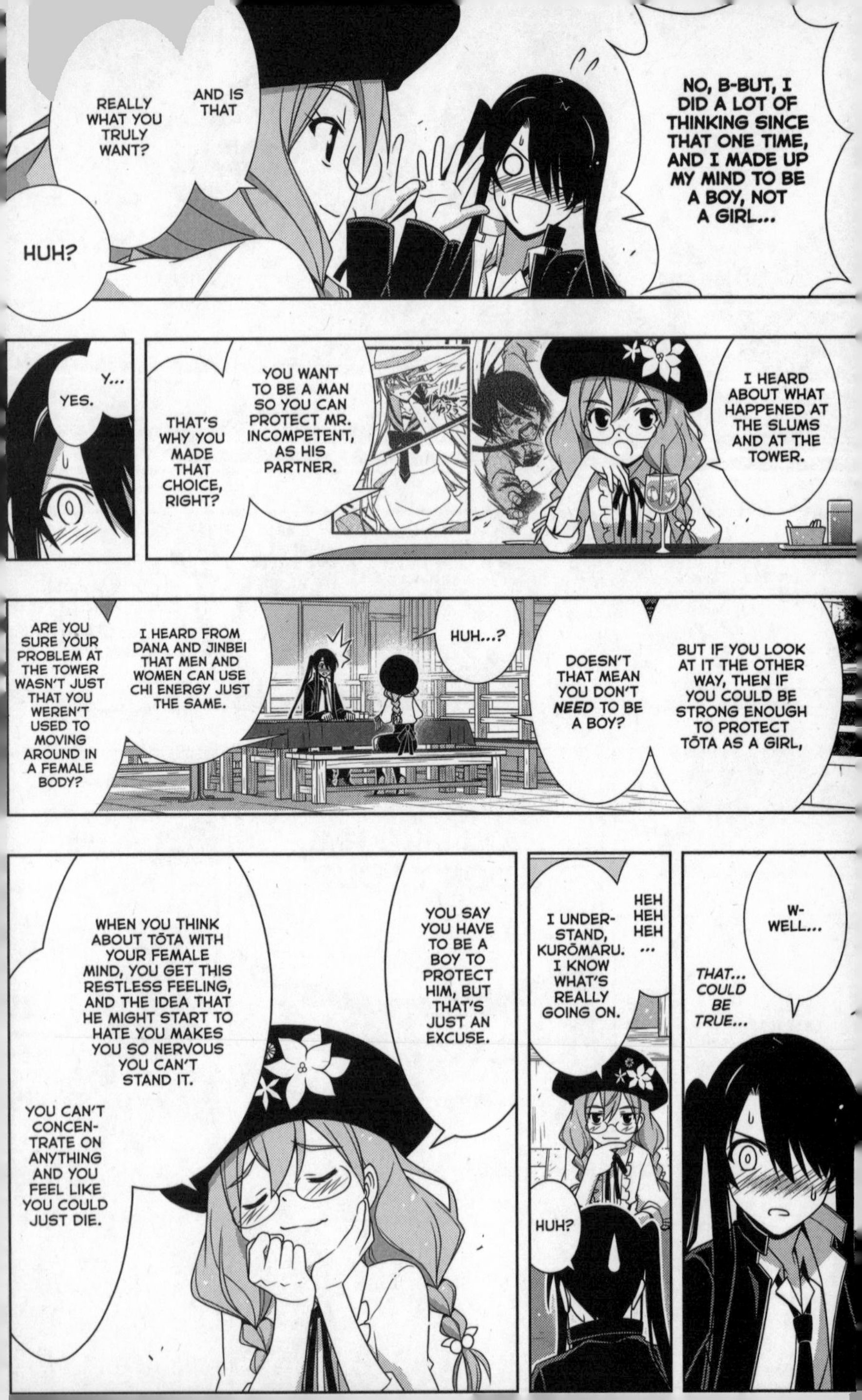
NO, B-BUT, I DID A LOT OF THINKING SINCE THAT ONE TIME, AND I MADE UP MY MIND TO BE A BOY, NOT A GIRL...
AND IS THAT REALLY WHAT YOU TRULY WANT?
HUH?
I HEARD ABOUT WHAT HAPPENED AT THE SLUMS AND AT THE TOWER.
YOU WANT TO BE A MAN SO YOU CAN PROTECT MR. INCOMPETENT, AS HIS PARTNER.
THAT'S WHY YOU MADE THAT CHOICE, RIGHT?
Y... YES.
BUT IF YOU LOOK AT IT THE OTHER WAY, THEN IF YOU COULD BE STRONG ENOUGH TO PROTECT TŌTA AS A GIRL,
DOESN'T THAT MEAN YOU DON'T *NEED* TO BE A BOY?
HUH...?
I HEARD FROM DANA AND JINBEI THAT MEN AND WOMEN CAN USE CHI ENERGY JUST THE SAME.
ARE YOU SURE YOUR PROBLEM AT THE TOWER WASN'T JUST THAT YOU WEREN'T USED TO MOVING AROUND IN A FEMALE BODY?
W-WELL...
*THAT... COULD BE TRUE...*
HEH HEH HEH ...
I UNDERSTAND, KURŌMARU. I KNOW WHAT'S REALLY GOING ON.
HUH?
YOU SAY YOU HAVE TO BE A BOY TO PROTECT HIM, BUT THAT'S JUST AN EXCUSE.
WHEN YOU THINK ABOUT TŌTA WITH YOUR FEMALE MIND, YOU GET THIS RESTLESS FEELING, AND THE IDEA THAT HE MIGHT START TO HATE YOU MAKES YOU SO NERVOUS YOU CAN'T STAND IT.
YOU CAN'T CONCENTRATE ON ANYTHING AND YOU FEEL LIKE YOU COULD JUST DIE.

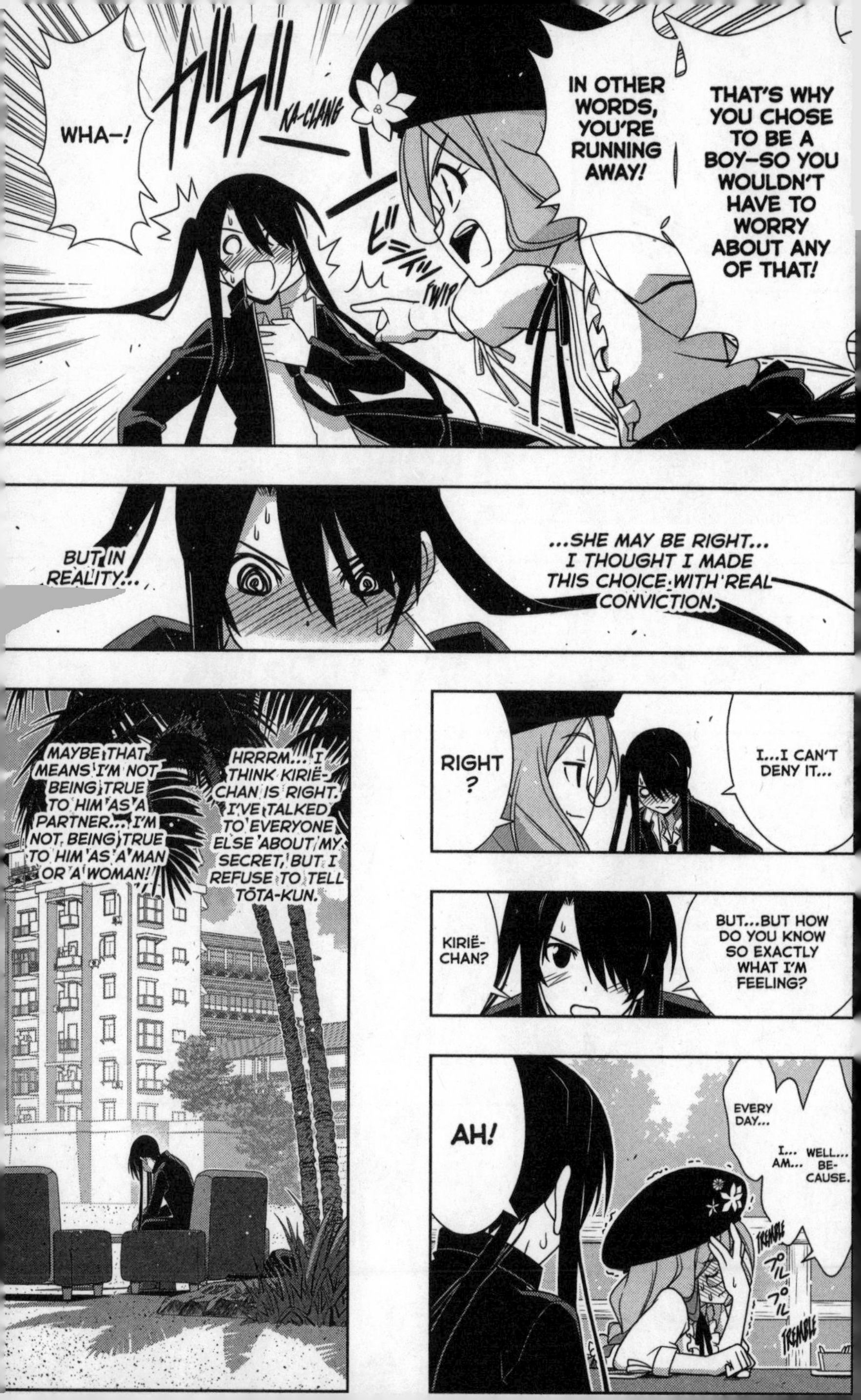
THAT'S WHY YOU CHOSE TO BE A BOY—SO YOU WOULDN'T HAVE TO WORRY ABOUT ANY OF THAT!
IN OTHER WORDS, YOU'RE RUNNING AWAY!
KA-CLANG
WHA–!
FWIP
...SHE MAY BE RIGHT... I THOUGHT I MADE THIS CHOICE WITH REAL CONVICTION.
BUT IN REALITY...
I...I CAN'T DENY IT...
RIGHT?
BUT...BUT HOW DO YOU KNOW SO EXACTLY WHAT I'M FEELING?
KIRIË-CHAN?
EVERY DAY...
WELL... BE-CAUSE.
I... AM...
AH!
TREMBLE
TREMBLE
HRRRM... I THINK KIRIË-CHAN IS RIGHT. I'VE TALKED TO EVERYONE ELSE ABOUT MY SECRET, BUT I REFUSE TO TELL TŌTA-KUN.
MAYBE THAT MEANS I'M NOT BEING TRUE TO HIM AS A PARTNER... I'M NOT BEING TRUE TO HIM AS A MAN OR A WOMAN!

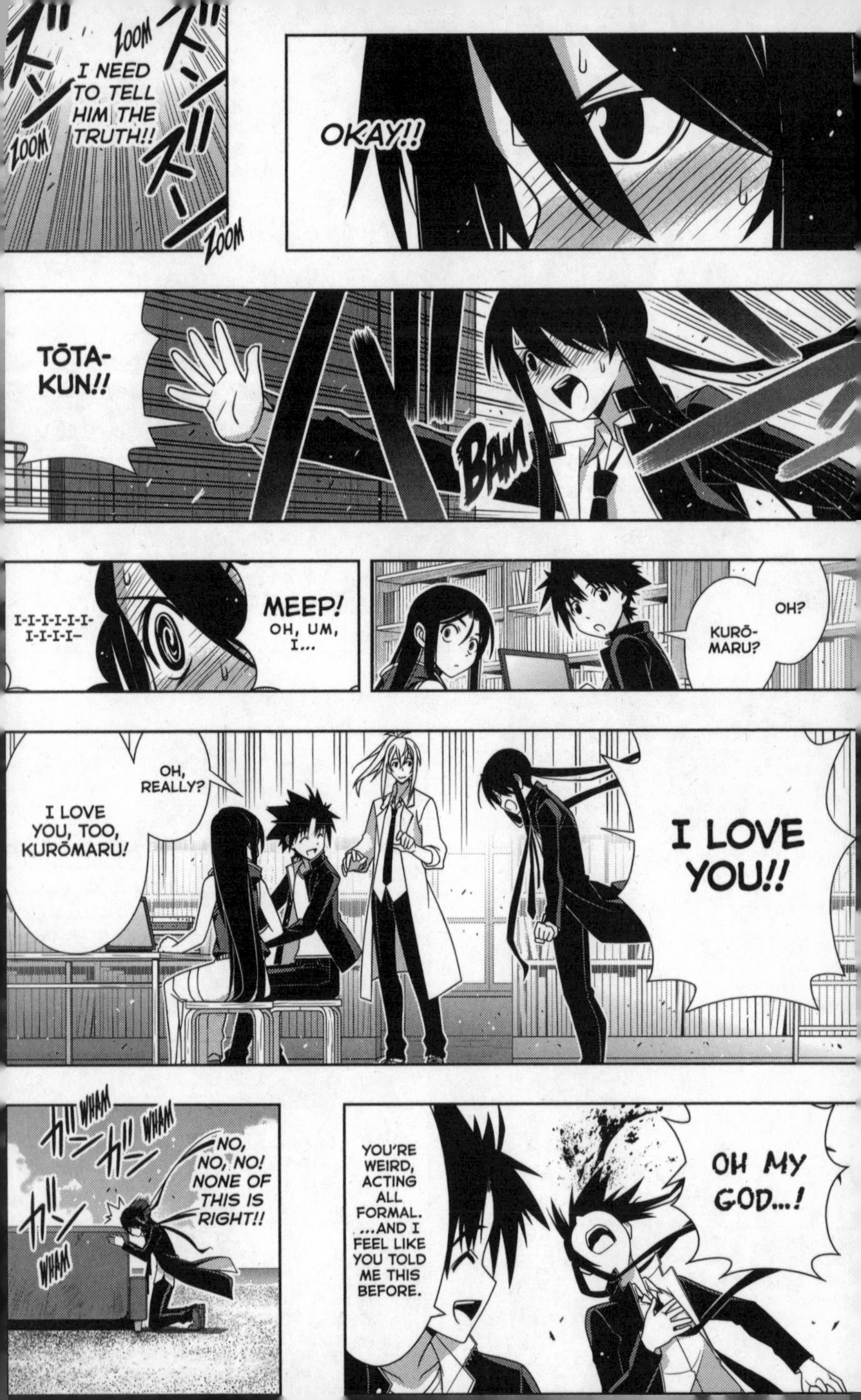
OKAY!!
ZOOM
I NEED TO TELL HIM THE TRUTH!!
ZOOM
ZOOM
BAM
TŌTA-KUN!!
OH?
KURŌ-MARU?
MEEP! OH, UM, I...
I-I-I-I-I-I-I-I-I-I–
I LOVE YOU!!
OH, REALLY?
I LOVE YOU, TOO, KURŌMARU!
OH MY GOD...!
YOU'RE WEIRD, ACTING ALL FORMAL. ...AND I FEEL LIKE YOU TOLD ME THIS BEFORE.
WHAM
WHAM
NO, NO, NO! NONE OF THIS IS RIGHT!!
WHAM

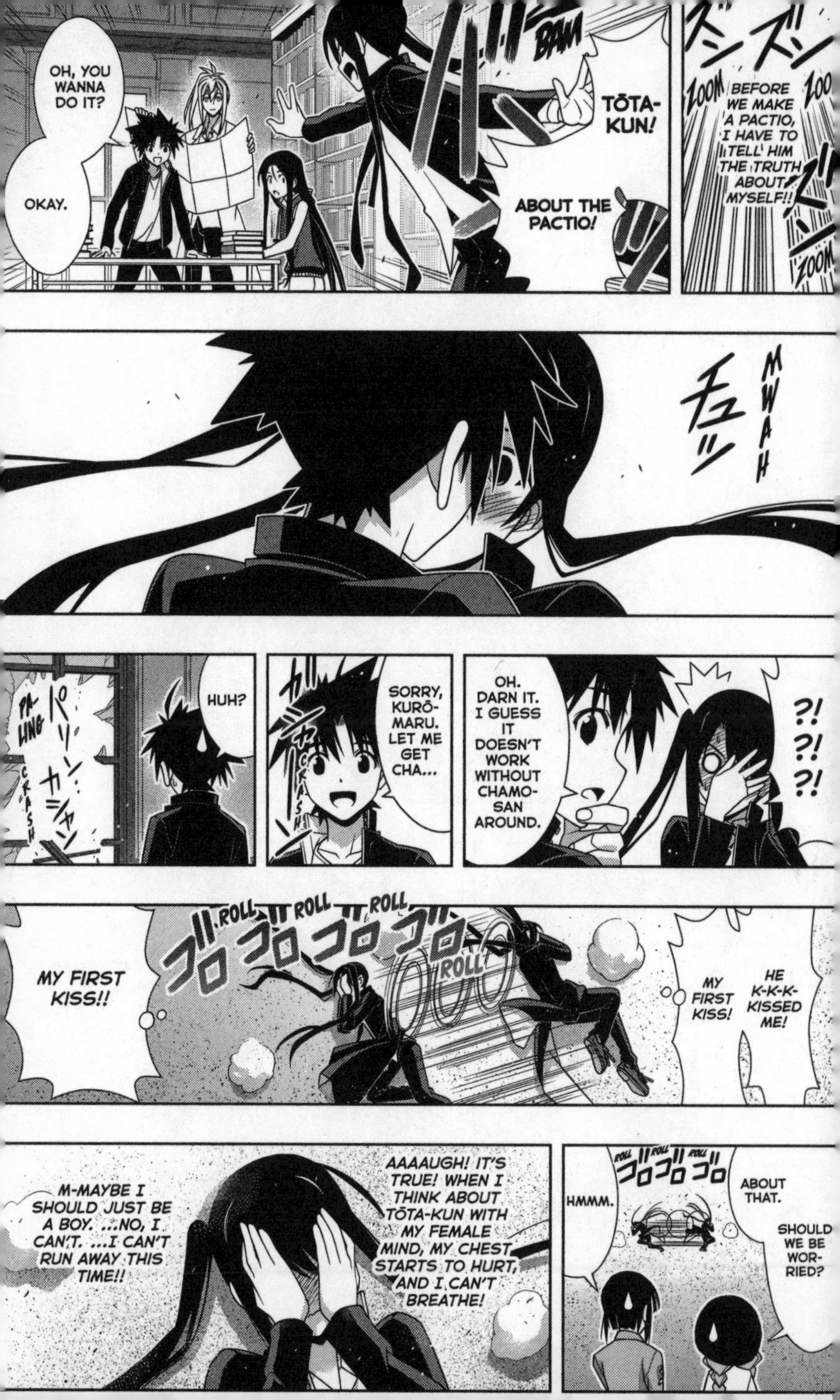
ZOOM
BEFORE WE MAKE A PACTIO, I HAVE TO TELL HIM THE TRUTH ABOUT MYSELF!!
ZOOM
BAM
TŌTA-KUN!
ABOUT THE PACTIO!
OH, YOU WANNA DO IT?
OKAY.
MWAH
?! ?! ?!
OH. DARN IT. I GUESS IT DOESN'T WORK WITHOUT CHAMO-SAN AROUND.
SORRY, KURŌ-MARU. LET ME GET CHA...
CRASH
HUH?
PA-LING
CRASH
HE K-K-K-KISSED ME!
MY FIRST KISS!
ROLL
ROLL
ROLL
ROLL
MY FIRST KISS!!
ABOUT THAT.
SHOULD WE BE WOR-RIED?
ROLL ROLL ROLL
HMMM.
AAAAUGH! IT'S TRUE! WHEN I THINK ABOUT TŌTA-KUN WITH MY FEMALE MIND, MY CHEST STARTS TO HURT, AND I CAN'T BREATHE!
M-MAYBE I SHOULD JUST BE A BOY. ...NO, I CAN'T. ...I CAN'T RUN AWAY THIS TIME!!

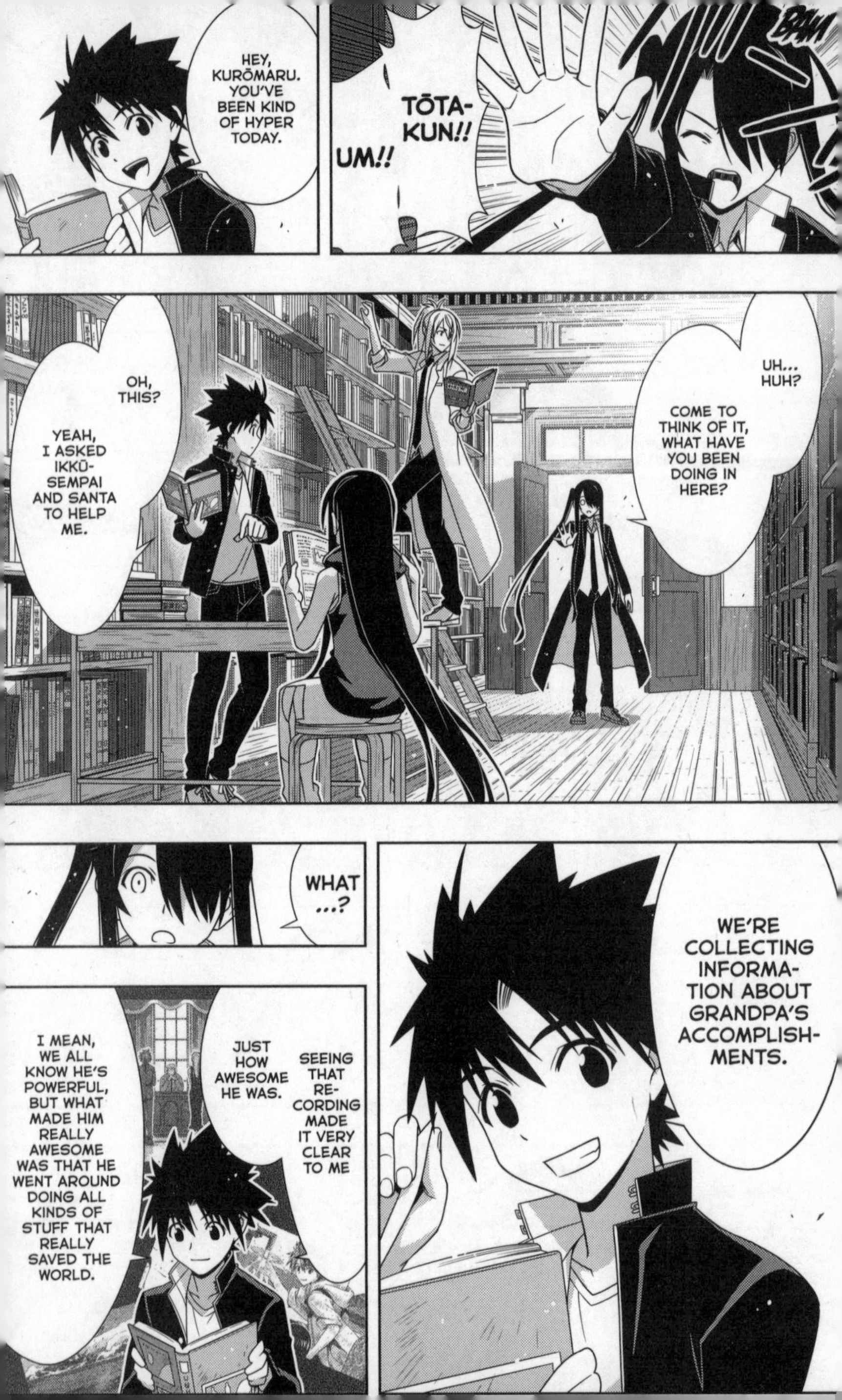
BAM
TŌTA-KUN!!
UM!!
HEY, KURŌMARU. YOU'VE BEEN KIND OF HYPER TODAY.
UH... HUH?
COME TO THINK OF IT, WHAT HAVE YOU BEEN DOING IN HERE?
OH, THIS?
YEAH, I ASKED IKKŪ-SEMPAI AND SANTA TO HELP ME.
WE'RE COLLECTING INFORMATION ABOUT GRANDPA'S ACCOMPLISHMENTS.
WHAT ...?
SEEING THAT RECORDING MADE IT VERY CLEAR TO ME
JUST HOW AWESOME HE WAS.
I MEAN, WE ALL KNOW HE'S POWERFUL, BUT WHAT MADE HIM REALLY AWESOME WAS THAT HE WENT AROUND DOING ALL KINDS OF STUFF THAT REALLY SAVED THE WORLD.

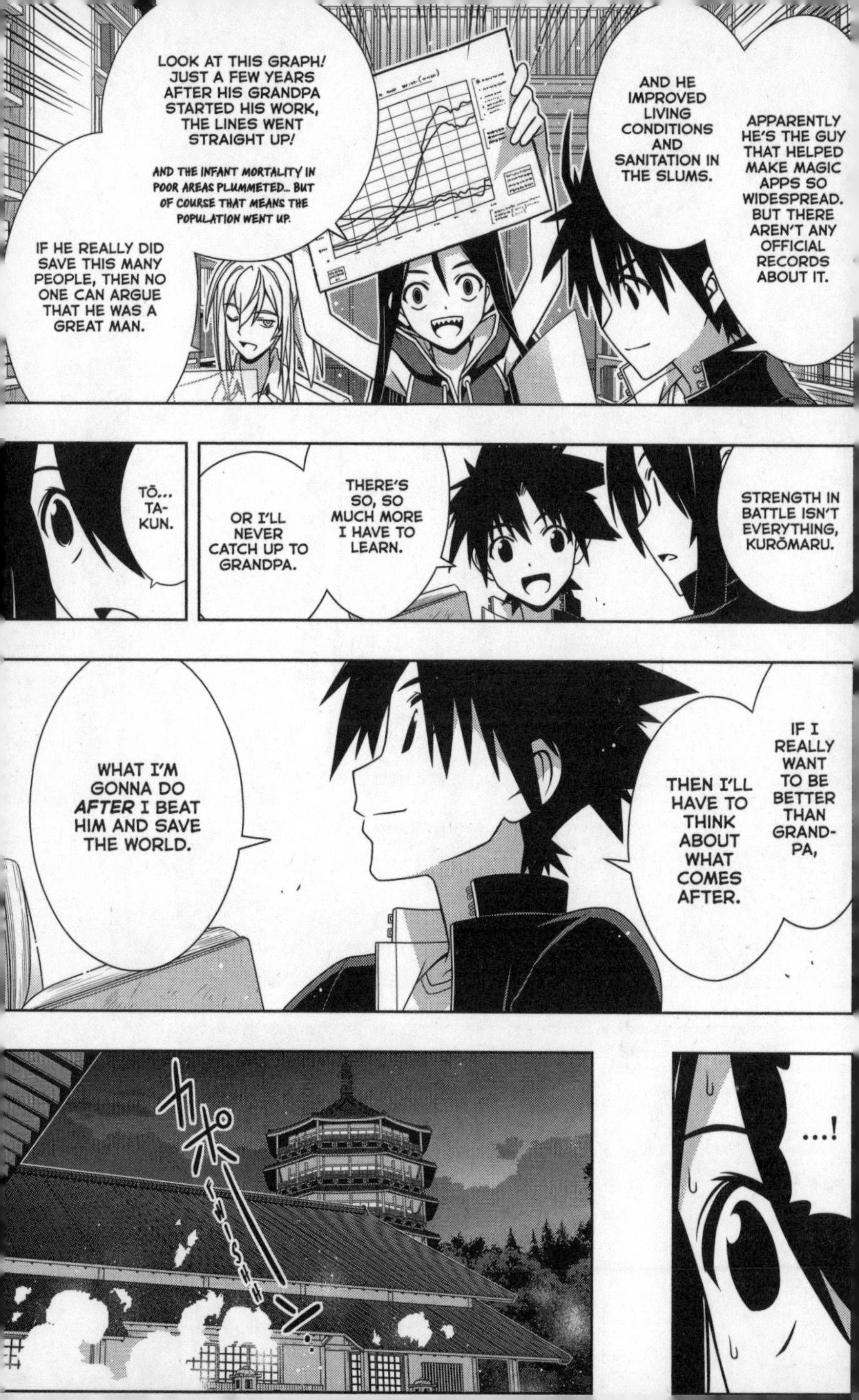
APPARENTLY HE'S THE GUY THAT HELPED MAKE MAGIC APPS SO WIDESPREAD. BUT THERE AREN'T ANY OFFICIAL RECORDS ABOUT IT.
AND HE IMPROVED LIVING CONDITIONS AND SANITATION IN THE SLUMS.
LOOK AT THIS GRAPH! JUST A FEW YEARS AFTER HIS GRANDPA STARTED HIS WORK, THE LINES WENT STRAIGHT UP!
AND THE INFANT MORTALITY IN POOR AREAS PLUMMETED... BUT OF COURSE THAT MEANS THE POPULATION WENT UP.
IF HE REALLY DID SAVE THIS MANY PEOPLE, THEN NO ONE CAN ARGUE THAT HE WAS A GREAT MAN.
STRENGTH IN BATTLE ISN'T EVERYTHING, KURŌMARU.
THERE'S SO, SO MUCH MORE I HAVE TO LEARN.
OR I'LL NEVER CATCH UP TO GRANDPA.
TŌ... TA-KUN.
IF I REALLY WANT TO BE BETTER THAN GRAND-PA,
THEN I'LL HAVE TO THINK ABOUT WHAT COMES AFTER.
WHAT I'M GONNA DO *AFTER* I BEAT HIM AND SAVE THE WORLD.
...!
WISHH

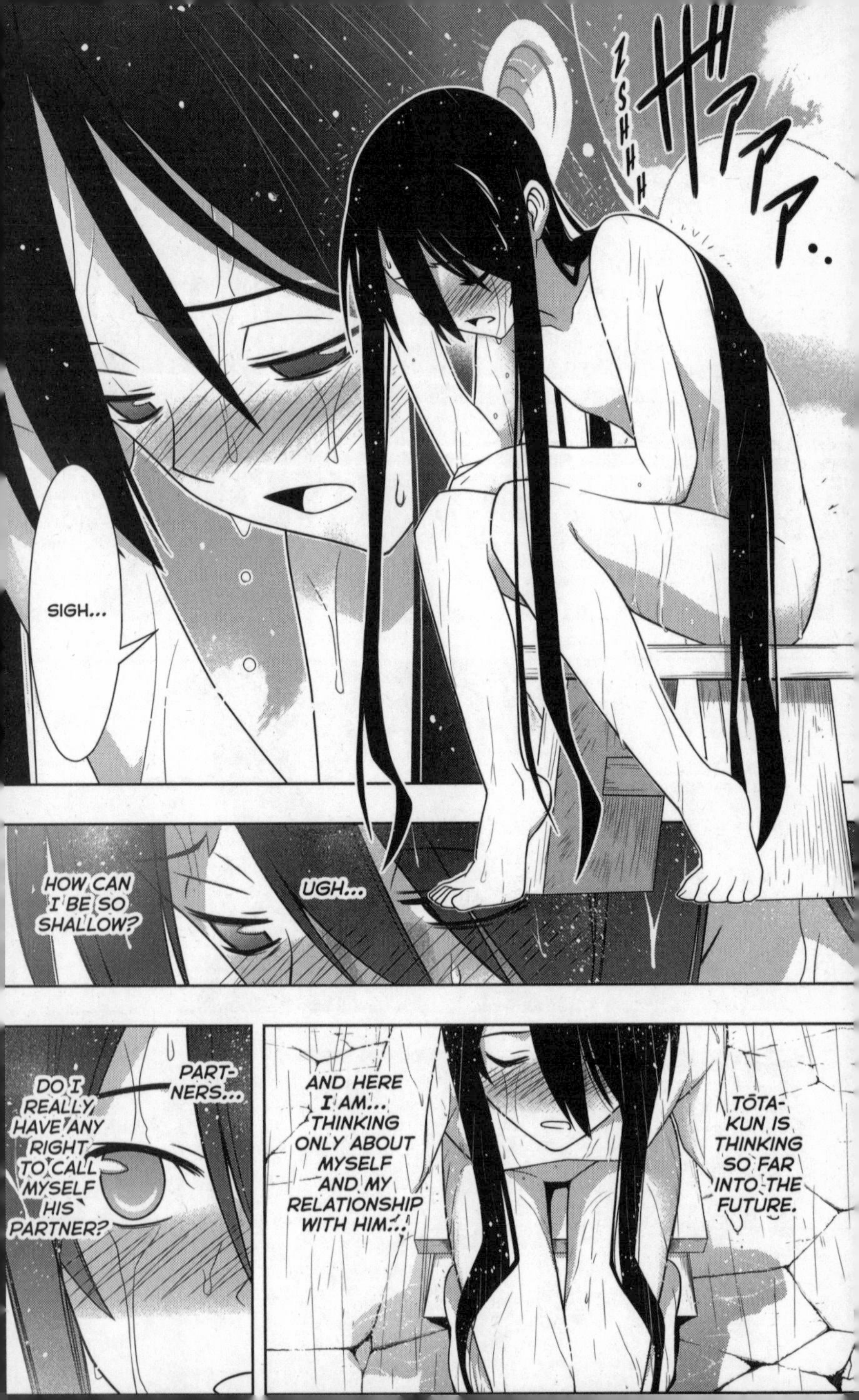
ZSHHHH
ザァァァ..
SIGH...
UGH...
HOW CAN I BE SO SHALLOW?
TŌTA-KUN IS THINKING SO FAR INTO THE FUTURE.
AND HERE I AM... THINKING ONLY ABOUT MYSELF AND MY RELATIONSHIP WITH HIM...
PARTNERS...
DO I REALLY HAVE ANY RIGHT TO CALL MYSELF HIS PARTNER?

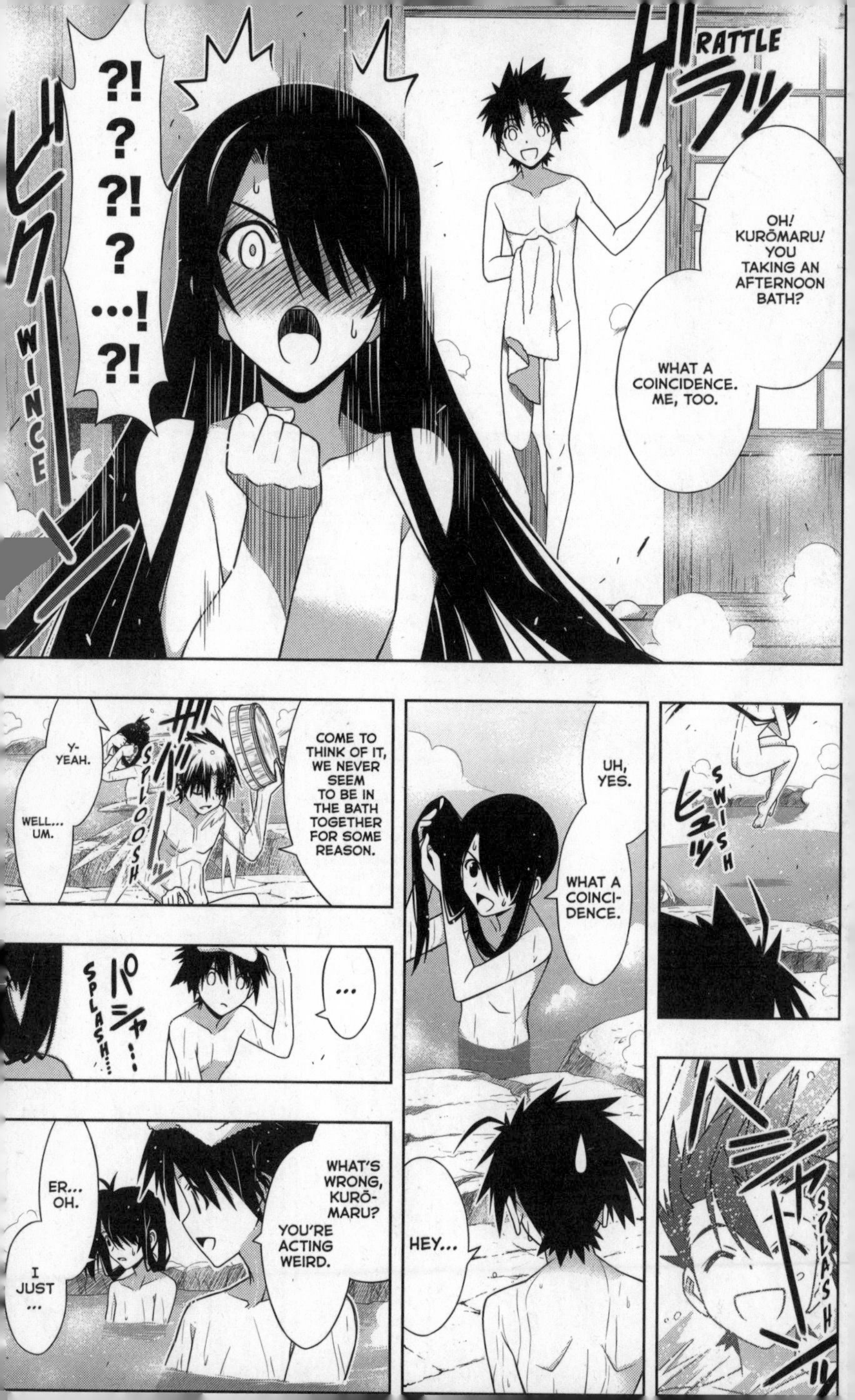
RATTLE
OH! KURŌMARU! YOU TAKING AN AFTERNOON BATH?
WHAT A COINCIDENCE. ME, TOO.
?! ? ?! ? ...! ?!
WINCE
SWISH
SPLASH
UH, YES.
WHAT A COINCIDENCE.
HEY...
COME TO THINK OF IT, WE NEVER SEEM TO BE IN THE BATH TOGETHER FOR SOME REASON.
SPLOOSH
Y-YEAH.
WELL... UM.
...
SPLASH...
WHAT'S WRONG, KURŌMARU? YOU'RE ACTING WEIRD.
ER... OH.
I JUST ...

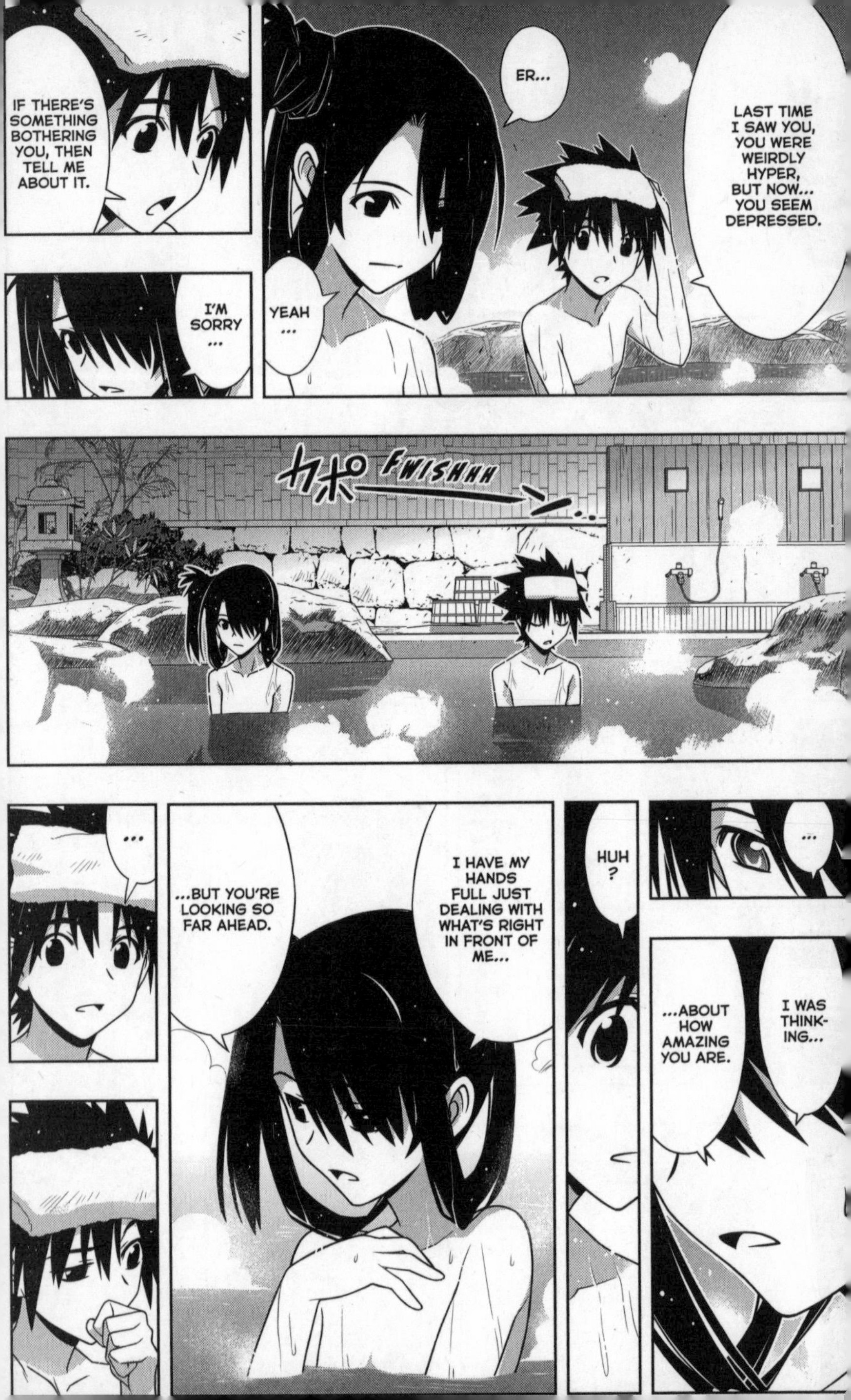
LAST TIME I SAW YOU, YOU WERE WEIRDLY HYPER, BUT NOW... YOU SEEM DEPRESSED.
ER...
YEAH...
IF THERE'S SOMETHING BOTHERING YOU, THEN TELL ME ABOUT IT.
I'M SORRY...
カポ
FWISHHH
...
I WAS THINKING...
...ABOUT HOW AMAZING YOU ARE.
HUH?
I HAVE MY HANDS FULL JUST DEALING WITH WHAT'S RIGHT IN FRONT OF ME...
...BUT YOU'RE LOOKING SO FAR AHEAD.
...

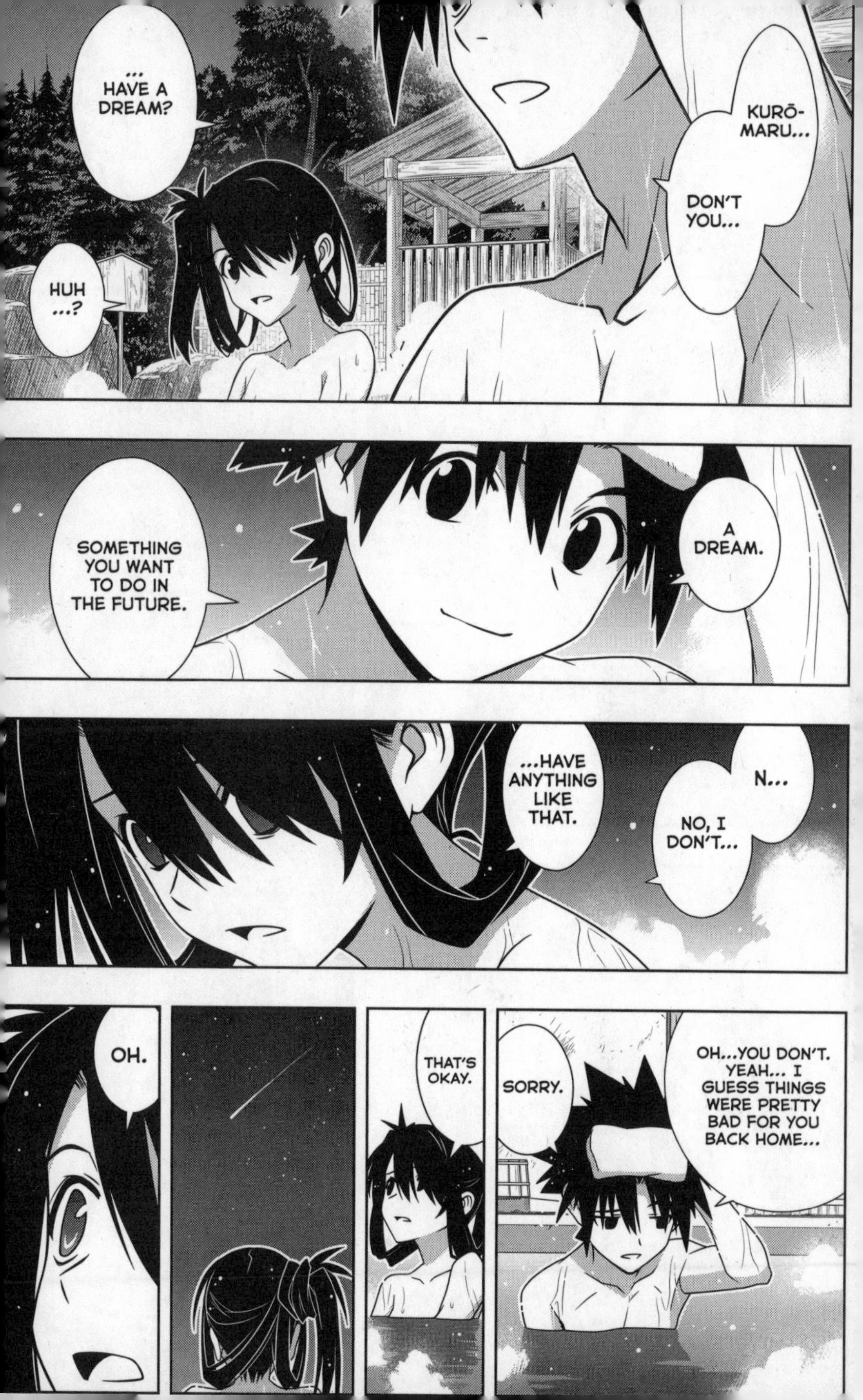
KURŌ-MARU...
DON'T YOU...
... HAVE A DREAM?
HUH ...?
A DREAM.
SOMETHING YOU WANT TO DO IN THE FUTURE.
N...
NO, I DON'T...
...HAVE ANYTHING LIKE THAT.
OH...YOU DON'T. YEAH... I GUESS THINGS WERE PRETTY BAD FOR YOU BACK HOME...
SORRY.
THAT'S OKAY.
OH.

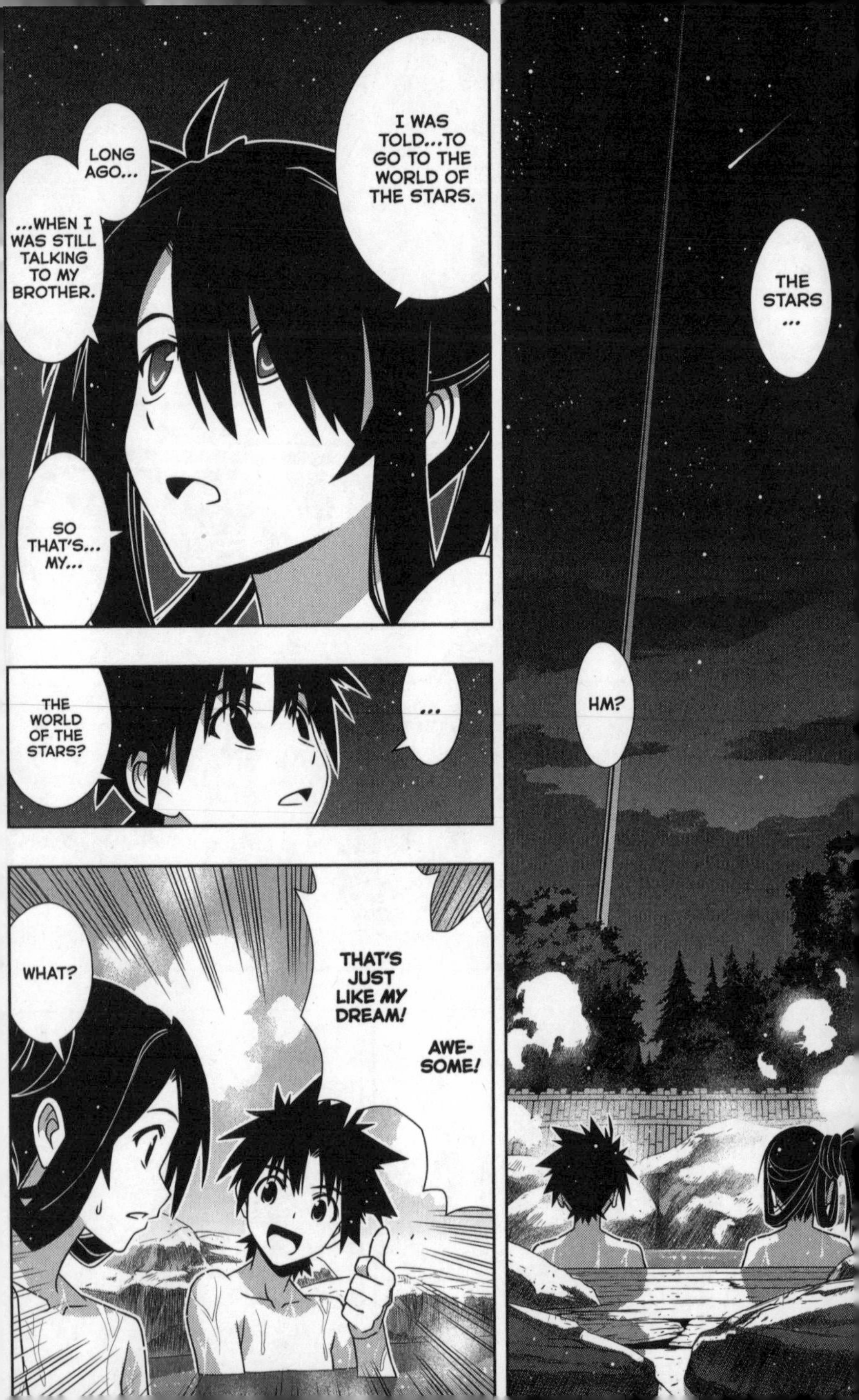
THE STARS...
HM?
I WAS TOLD...TO GO TO THE WORLD OF THE STARS.
LONG AGO...
...WHEN I WAS STILL TALKING TO MY BROTHER.
SO THAT'S... MY...
...
THE WORLD OF THE STARS?
THAT'S JUST LIKE *MY* DREAM!
AWE-SOME!
WHAT?

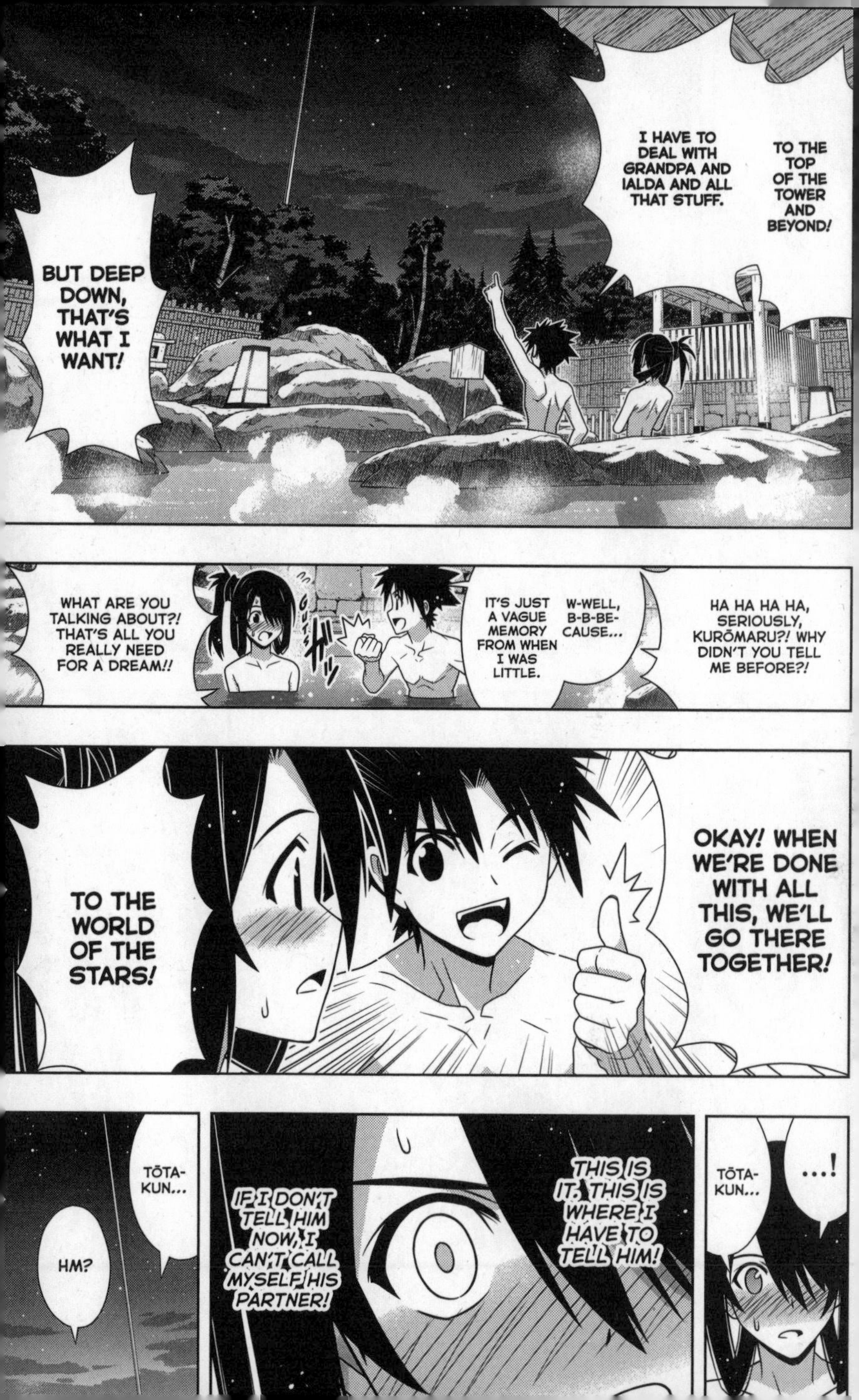
TO THE TOP OF THE TOWER AND BEYOND!
I HAVE TO DEAL WITH GRANDPA AND IALDA AND ALL THAT STUFF.
BUT DEEP DOWN, THAT'S WHAT I WANT!
HA HA HA HA, SERIOUSLY, KURŌMARU?! WHY DIDN'T YOU TELL ME BEFORE?!
W-WELL, B-B-BE-CAUSE...
IT'S JUST A VAGUE MEMORY FROM WHEN I WAS LITTLE.
WHAT ARE YOU TALKING ABOUT?! THAT'S ALL YOU REALLY NEED FOR A DREAM!!
OKAY! WHEN WE'RE DONE WITH ALL THIS, WE'LL GO THERE TOGETHER!
TO THE WORLD OF THE STARS!
...!
TŌTA-KUN...
THIS IS IT. THIS IS WHERE I HAVE TO TELL HIM!
IF I DON'T TELL HIM NOW, I CAN'T CALL MYSELF HIS PARTNER!
TŌTA-KUN...
HM?

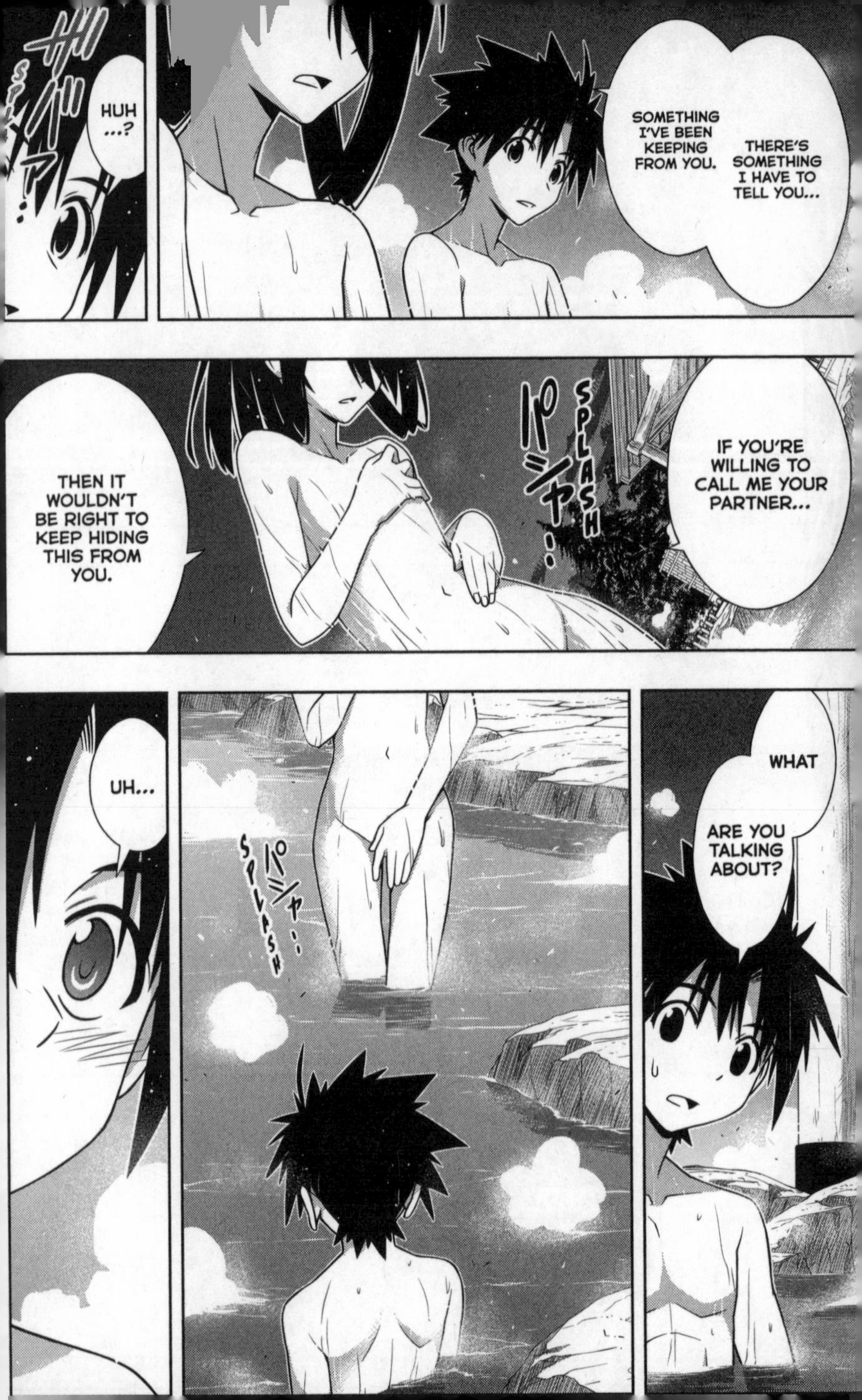
THERE'S SOMETHING I HAVE TO TELL YOU...
SOMETHING I'VE BEEN KEEPING FROM YOU.
HUH ...?
IF YOU'RE WILLING TO CALL ME YOUR PARTNER...
SPLASH
THEN IT WOULDN'T BE RIGHT TO KEEP HIDING THIS FROM YOU.
WHAT ARE YOU TALKING ABOUT?
SPLASH
UH...

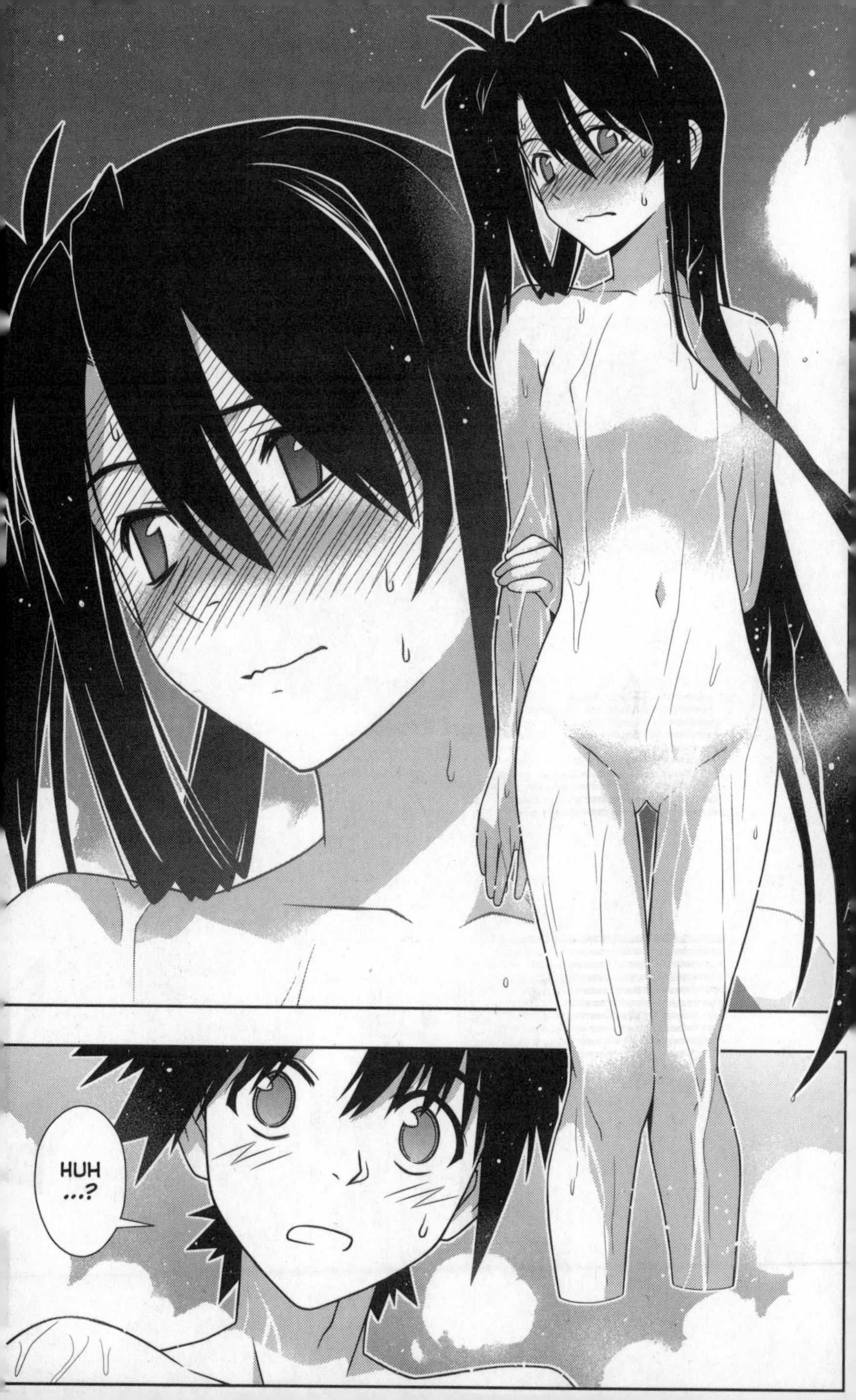
HUH ...?

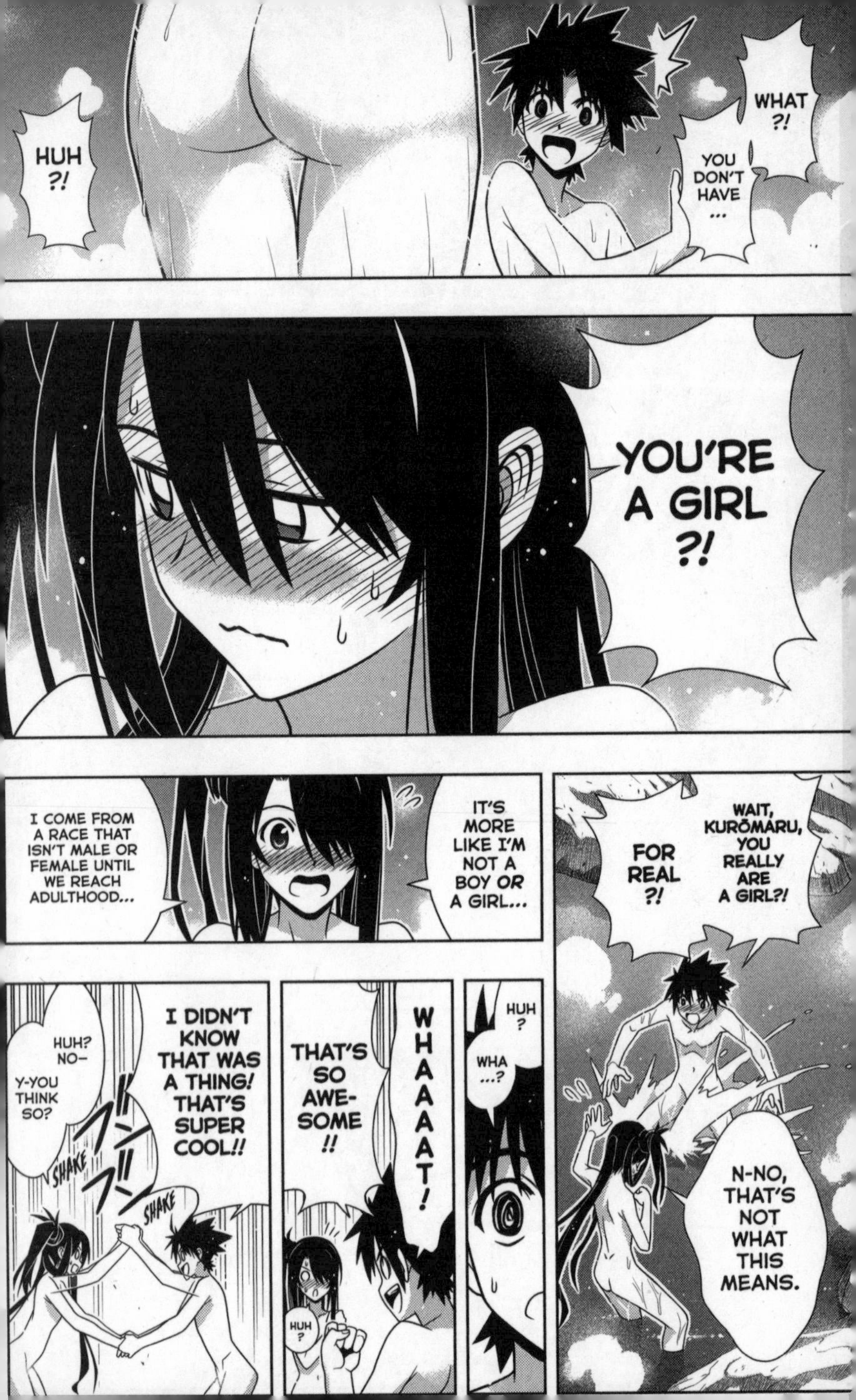
WHAT ?!
YOU DON'T HAVE ...
HUH ?!
YOU'RE A GIRL ?!
WAIT, KURŌMARU, YOU REALLY ARE A GIRL?!
FOR REAL ?!
N-NO, THAT'S NOT WHAT THIS MEANS.
IT'S MORE LIKE I'M NOT A BOY *OR* A GIRL...
I COME FROM A RACE THAT ISN'T MALE OR FEMALE UNTIL WE REACH ADULTHOOD...
HUH ?
WHA ...?
WHAAAAAT!
THAT'S SO AWE-SOME !!
HUH ?
I DIDN'T KNOW THAT WAS A THING! THAT'S SUPER COOL!!
SHAKE
SHAKE
HUH? NO—
Y-YOU THINK SO?

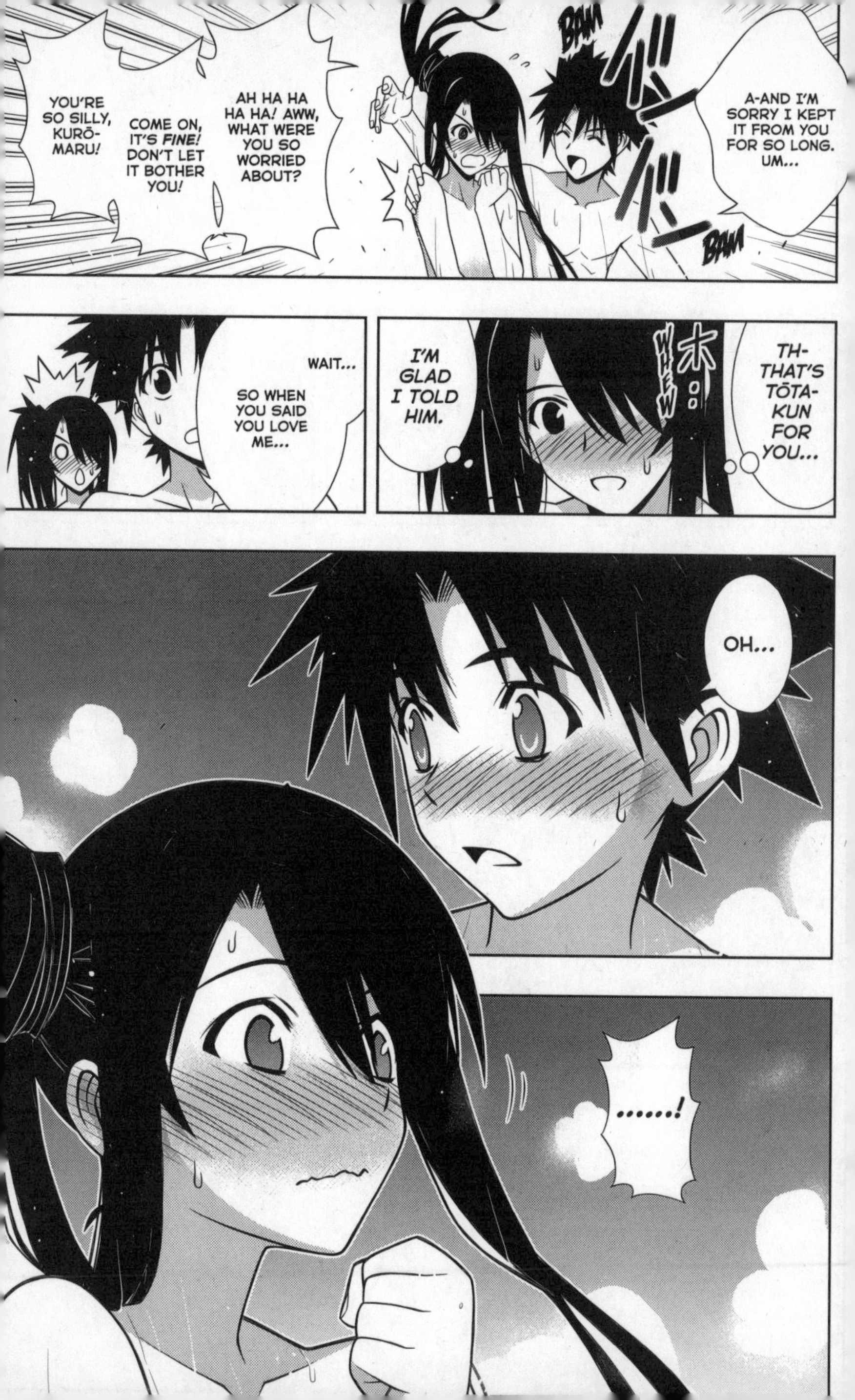
BAM
A-AND I'M SORRY I KEPT IT FROM YOU FOR SO LONG. UM...
BAM
AH HA HA HA HA! AWW, WHAT WERE YOU SO WORRIED ABOUT?
COME ON, IT'S *FINE!* DON'T LET IT BOTHER YOU!
YOU'RE SO SILLY, KURŌ-MARU!
*TH-THAT'S TŌTA-KUN FOR YOU...*
WHEW
*I'M GLAD I TOLD HIM.*
WAIT...
SO WHEN YOU SAID YOU LOVE ME...
OH...
......!

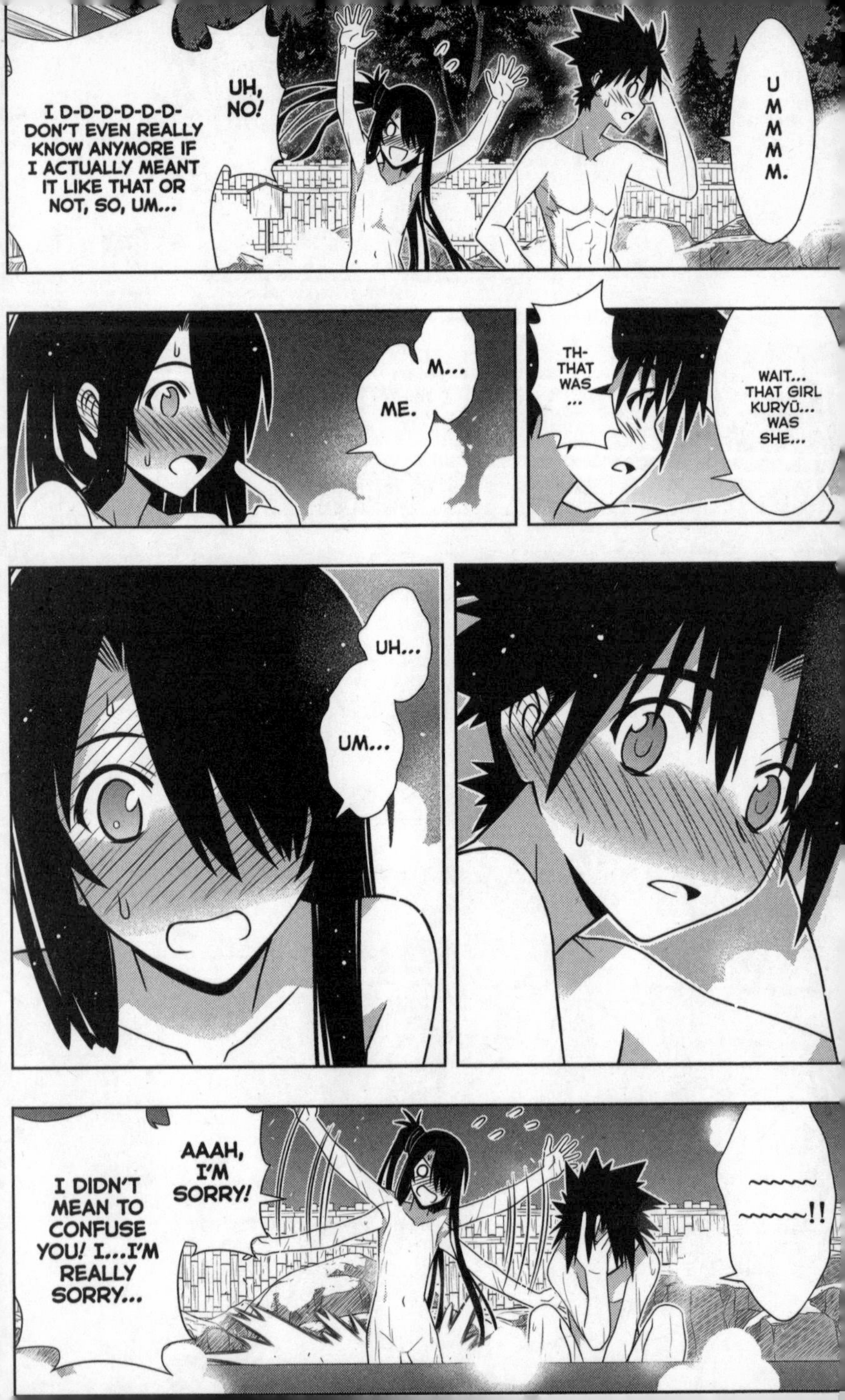
UMMMMM.
UH, NO!
I D-D-D-D-D-D-DON'T EVEN REALLY KNOW ANYMORE IF I ACTUALLY MEANT IT LIKE THAT OR NOT, SO, UM...
WAIT... THAT GIRL KURYŪ... WAS SHE...
TH-THAT WAS...
M... ME.
UH... UM...
~~~~~ ~~~~~!!
AAAH, I'M SORRY!
I DIDN'T MEAN TO CONFUSE YOU! I...I'M REALLY SORRY...
~~~~~

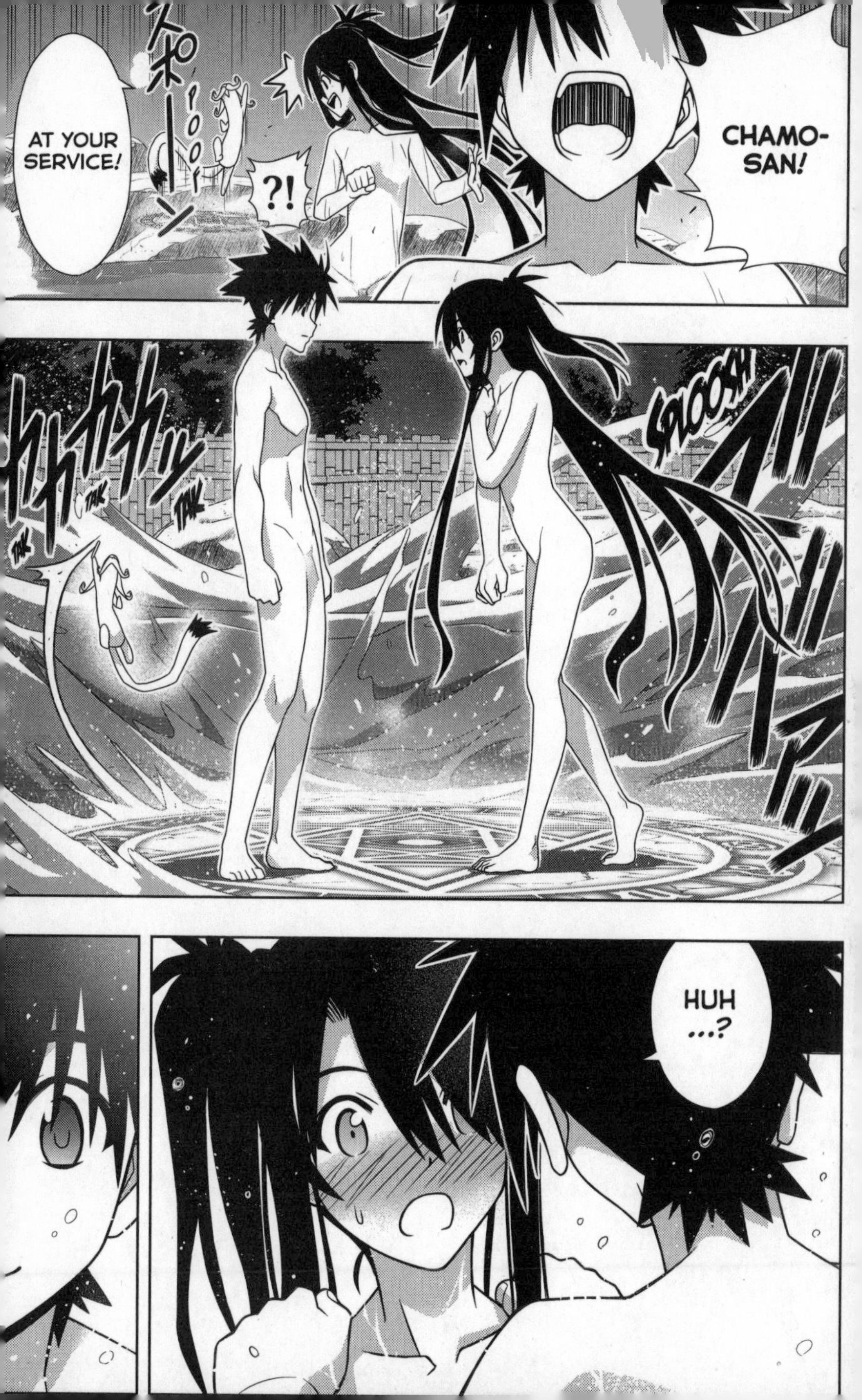
CHAMO-SAN!
AT YOUR SERVICE!
?!
SPLOOSH
TAK
TAK
TAK
TAK
HUH ...?

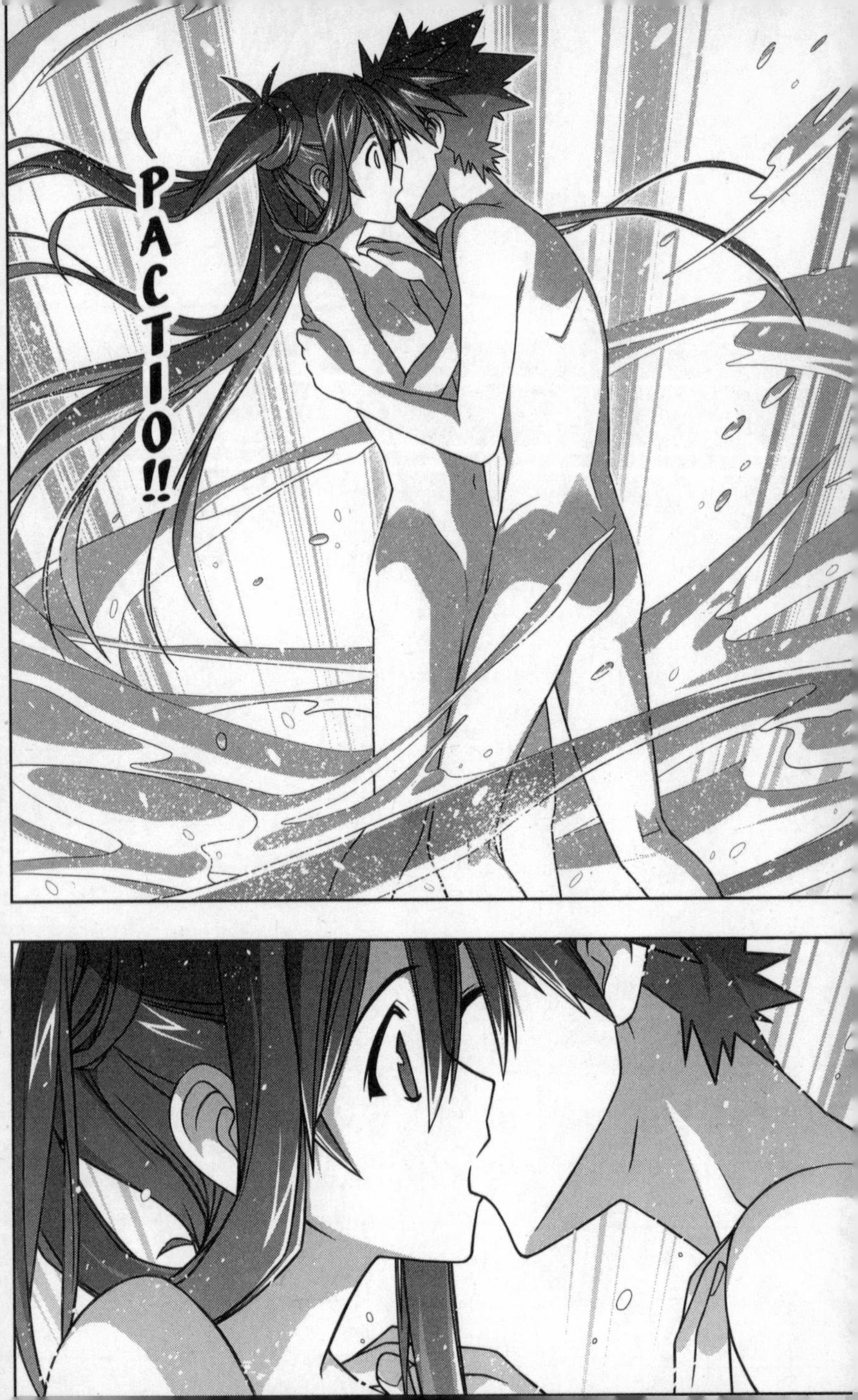
PACTIO!!

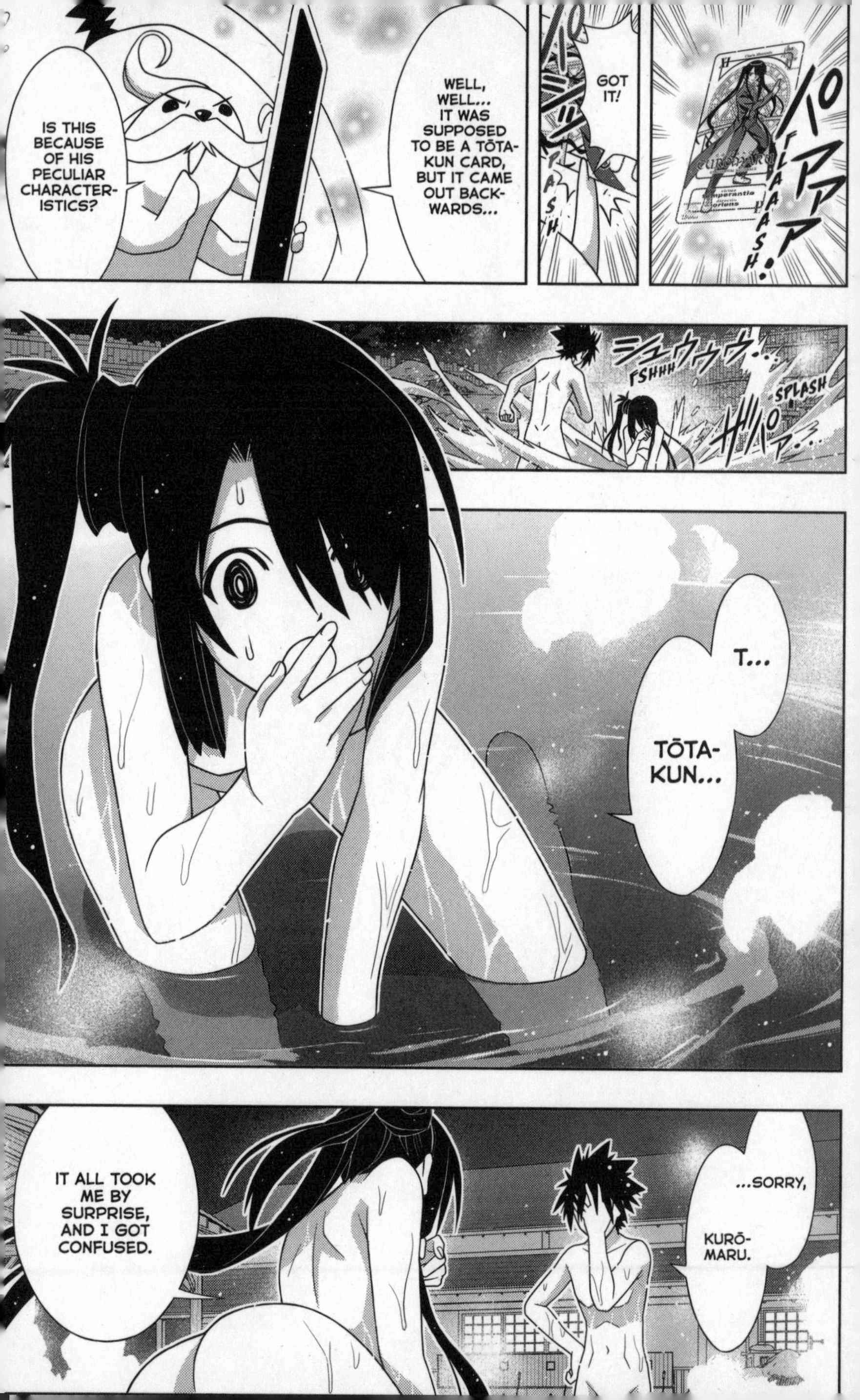
FLAAASH!
GOT IT!
FLASH
WELL, WELL... IT WAS SUPPOSED TO BE A TŌTA-KUN CARD, BUT IT CAME OUT BACKWARDS...
IS THIS BECAUSE OF HIS PECULIAR CHARACTER-ISTICS?
FSHHH
SPLASH
T...
TŌTA-KUN...
...SORRY, KURŌMARU.
IT ALL TOOK ME BY SURPRISE, AND I GOT CONFUSED.

YOU'RE MY PARTNER!

IT DOESN'T MATTER IF YOU'RE A BOY OR A GIRL!

...

YEAH.

YOU'RE MY PARTNER!

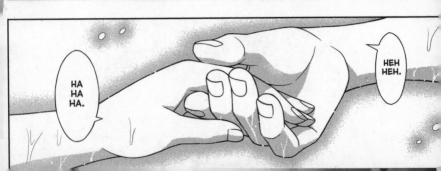

HA HA HA.

HEH HEH.

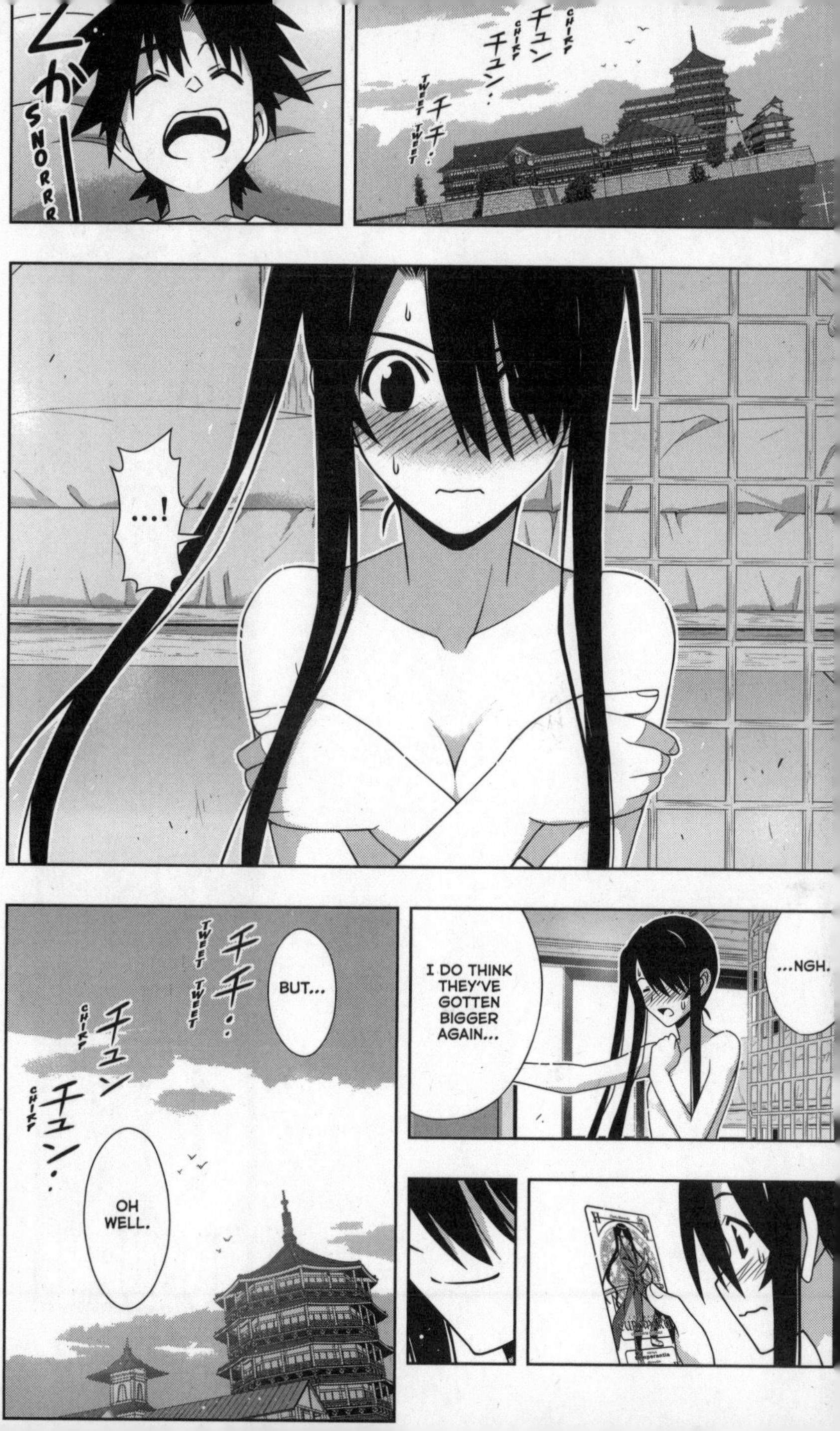
CHIRP CHIRP
チュンチュン…
TWEET TWEET
チチ…
ぐが
SNORRR
…!
…NGH.
I DO THINK THEY'VE GOTTEN BIGGER AGAIN…
TWEET TWEET
チチ…
BUT…
CHIRP CHIRP
チュンチュン…
OH WELL.

UQ HOLDER!

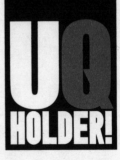

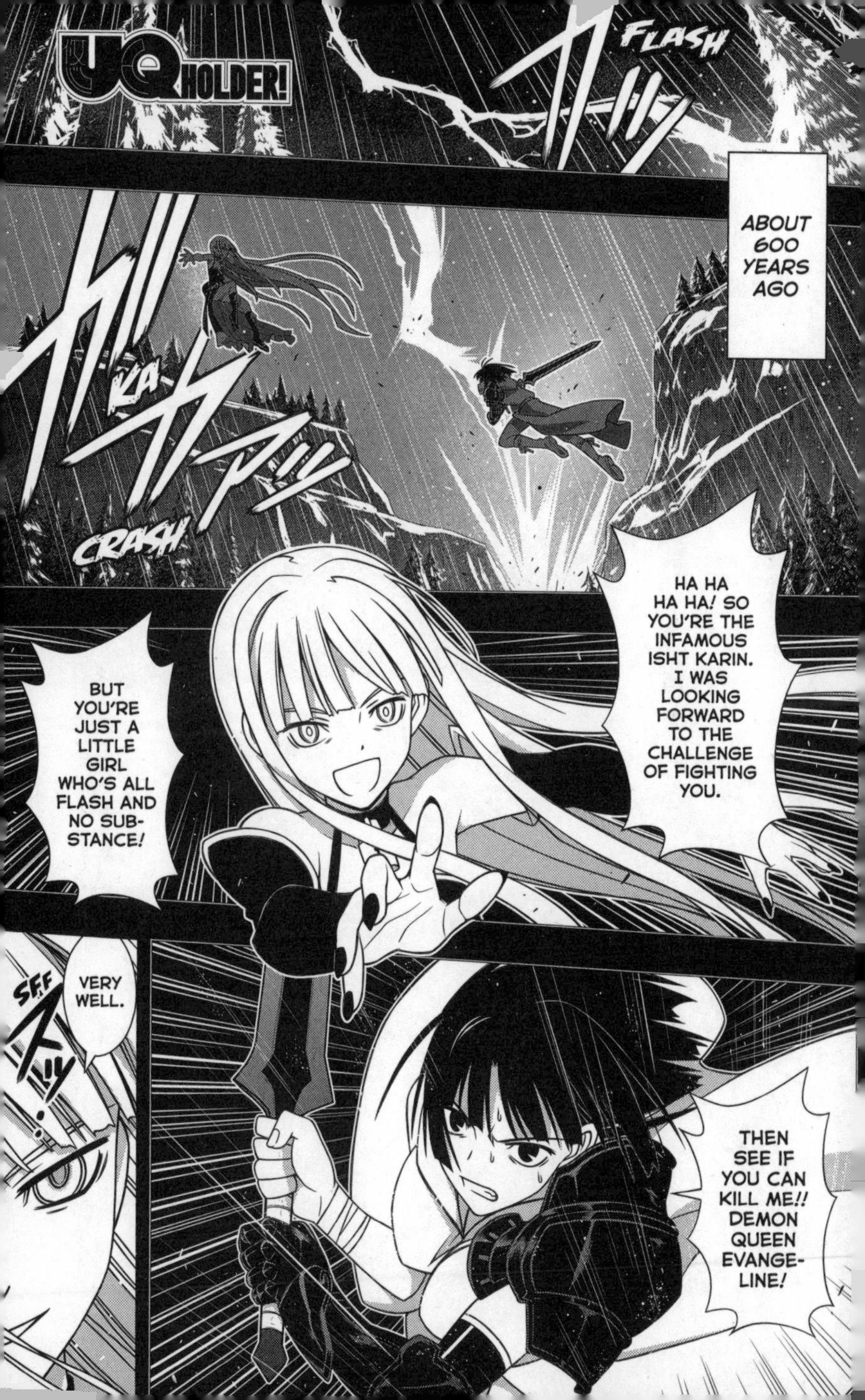
UQ HOLDER!
FLASH
ABOUT 600 YEARS AGO
KA
CRASH
HA HA HA HA! SO YOU'RE THE INFAMOUS ISHT KARIN. I WAS LOOKING FORWARD TO THE CHALLENGE OF FIGHTING YOU.
BUT YOU'RE JUST A LITTLE GIRL WHO'S ALL FLASH AND NO SUBSTANCE!
THEN SEE IF YOU CAN KILL ME!! DEMON QUEEN EVANGELINE!
VERY WELL.
SFF

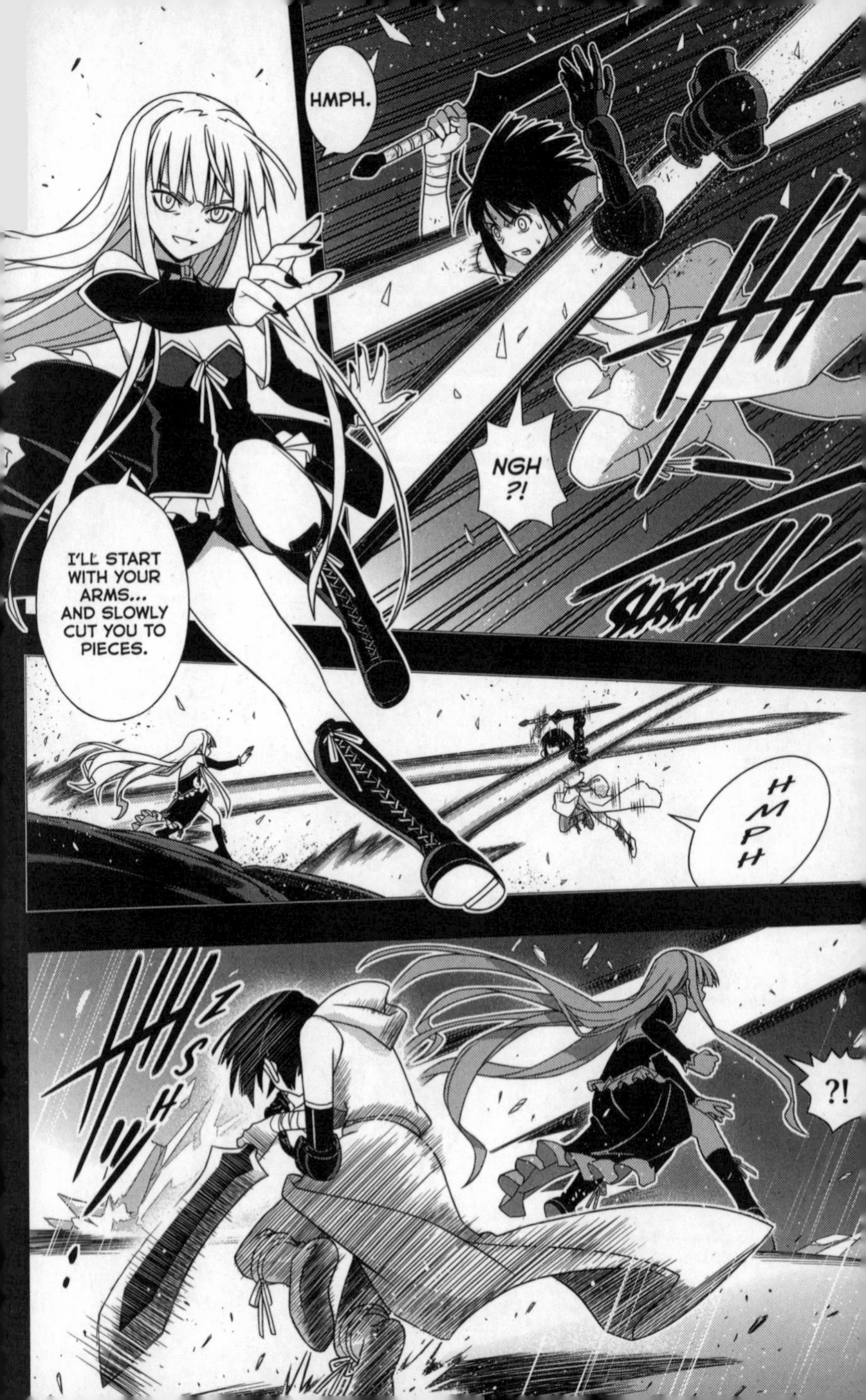
HMPH.
NGH ?!
SLASH
I'LL START WITH YOUR ARMS... AND SLOWLY CUT YOU TO PIECES.
HMPH
?!
ZSH

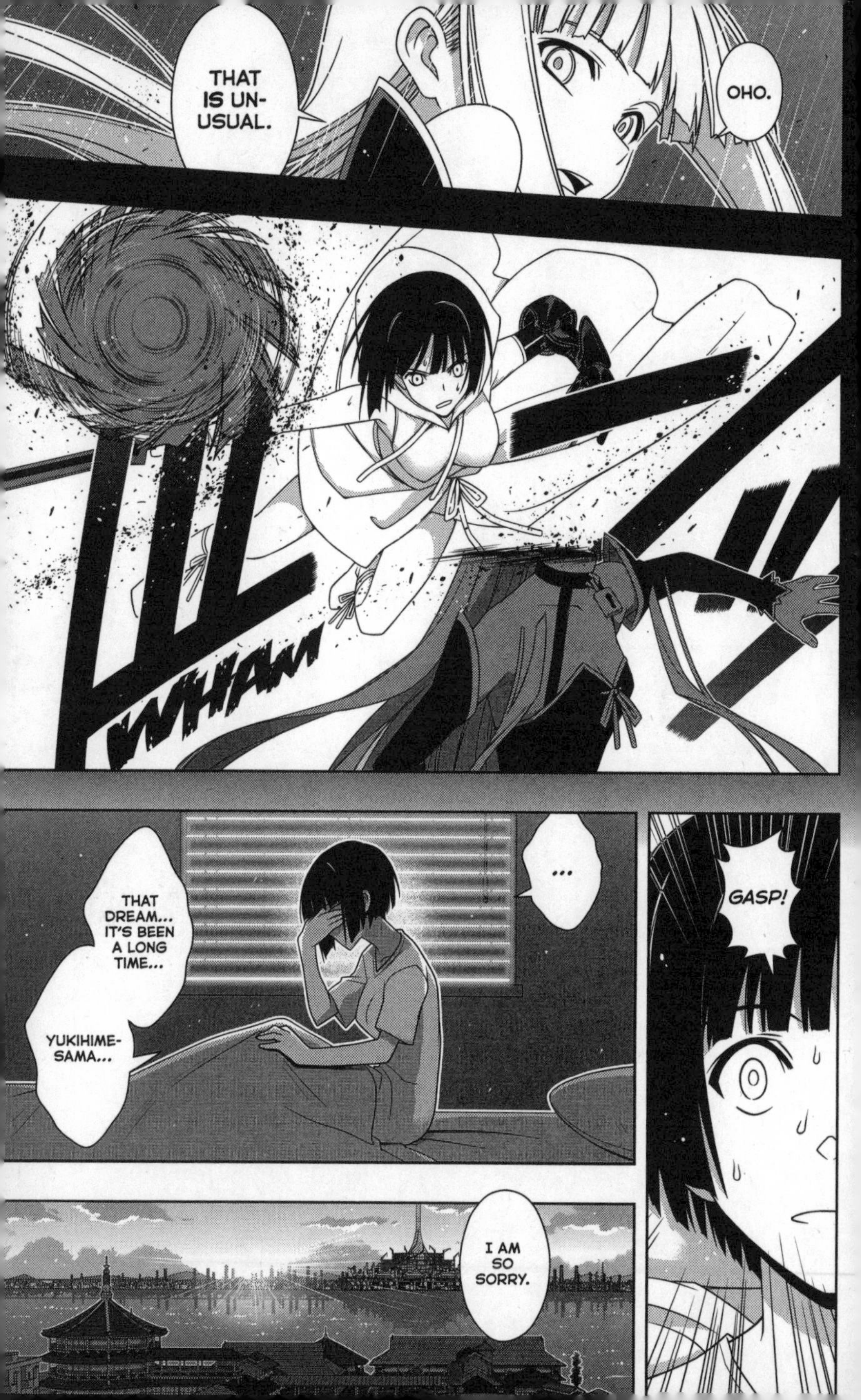
OHO.
THAT IS UN-USUAL.
WHAM
GASP!
...
THAT DREAM... IT'S BEEN A LONG TIME...
YUKIHIME-SAMA...
I AM SO SORRY.

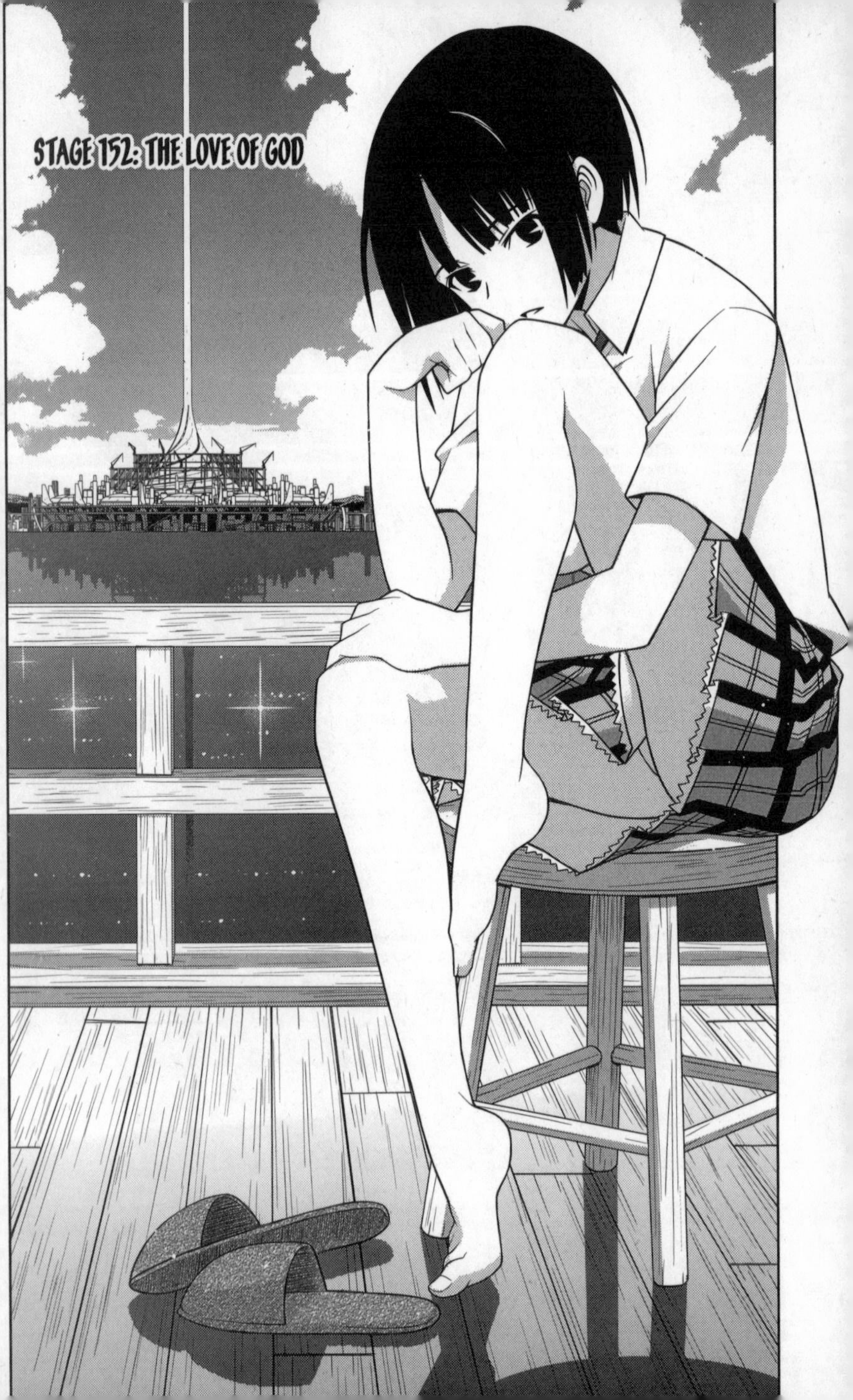
STAGE 152: THE LOVE OF GOD

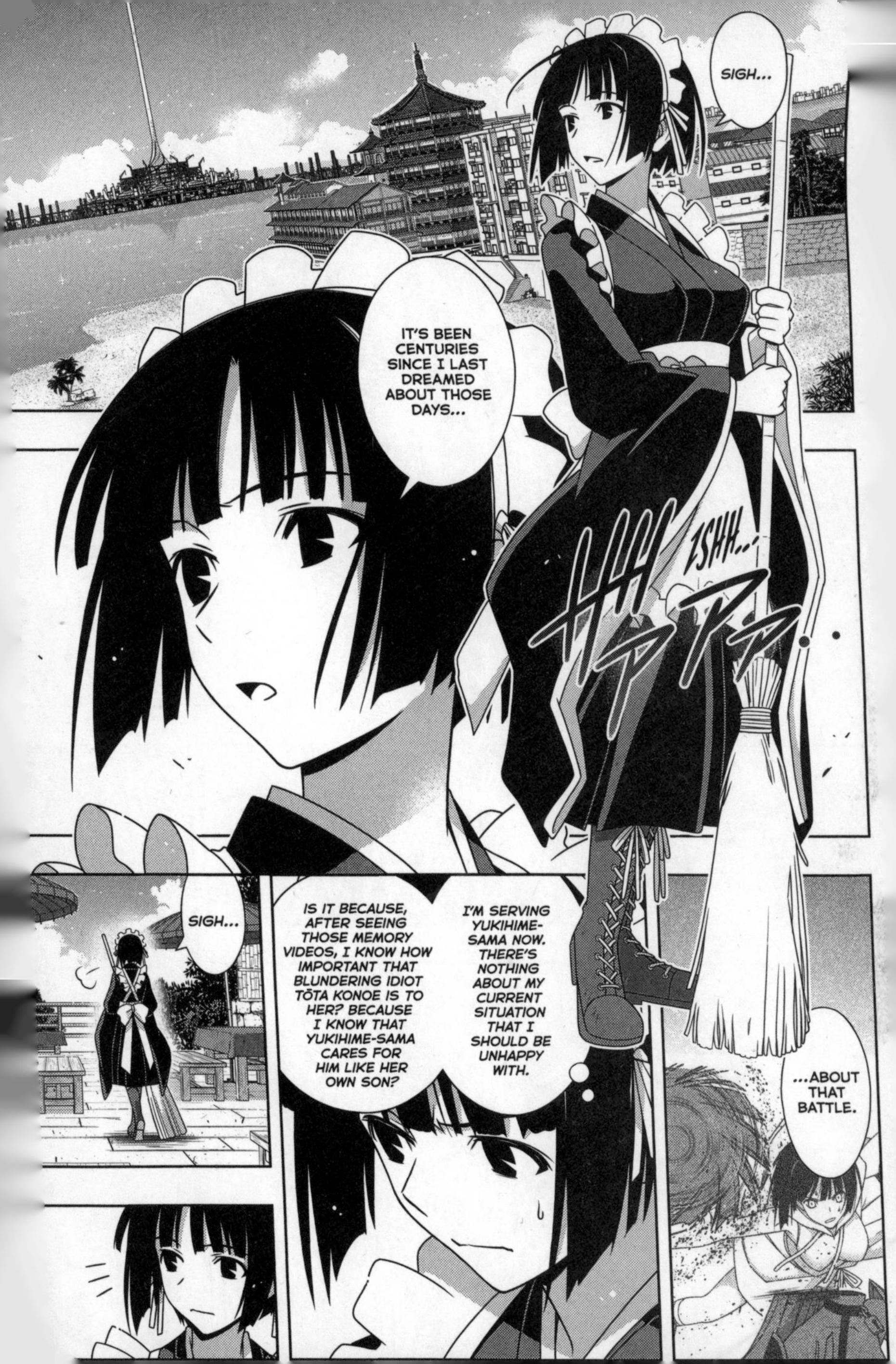
SIGH...
IT'S BEEN CENTURIES SINCE I LAST DREAMED ABOUT THOSE DAYS...
ZSHH...
...ABOUT THAT BATTLE.
I'M SERVING YUKIHIME-SAMA NOW. THERE'S NOTHING ABOUT MY CURRENT SITUATION THAT I SHOULD BE UNHAPPY WITH.
IS IT BECAUSE, AFTER SEEING THOSE MEMORY VIDEOS, I KNOW HOW IMPORTANT THAT BLUNDERING IDIOT TŌTA KONOE IS TO HER? BECAUSE I KNOW THAT YUKIHIME-SAMA CARES FOR HIM LIKE HER OWN SON?
SIGH...

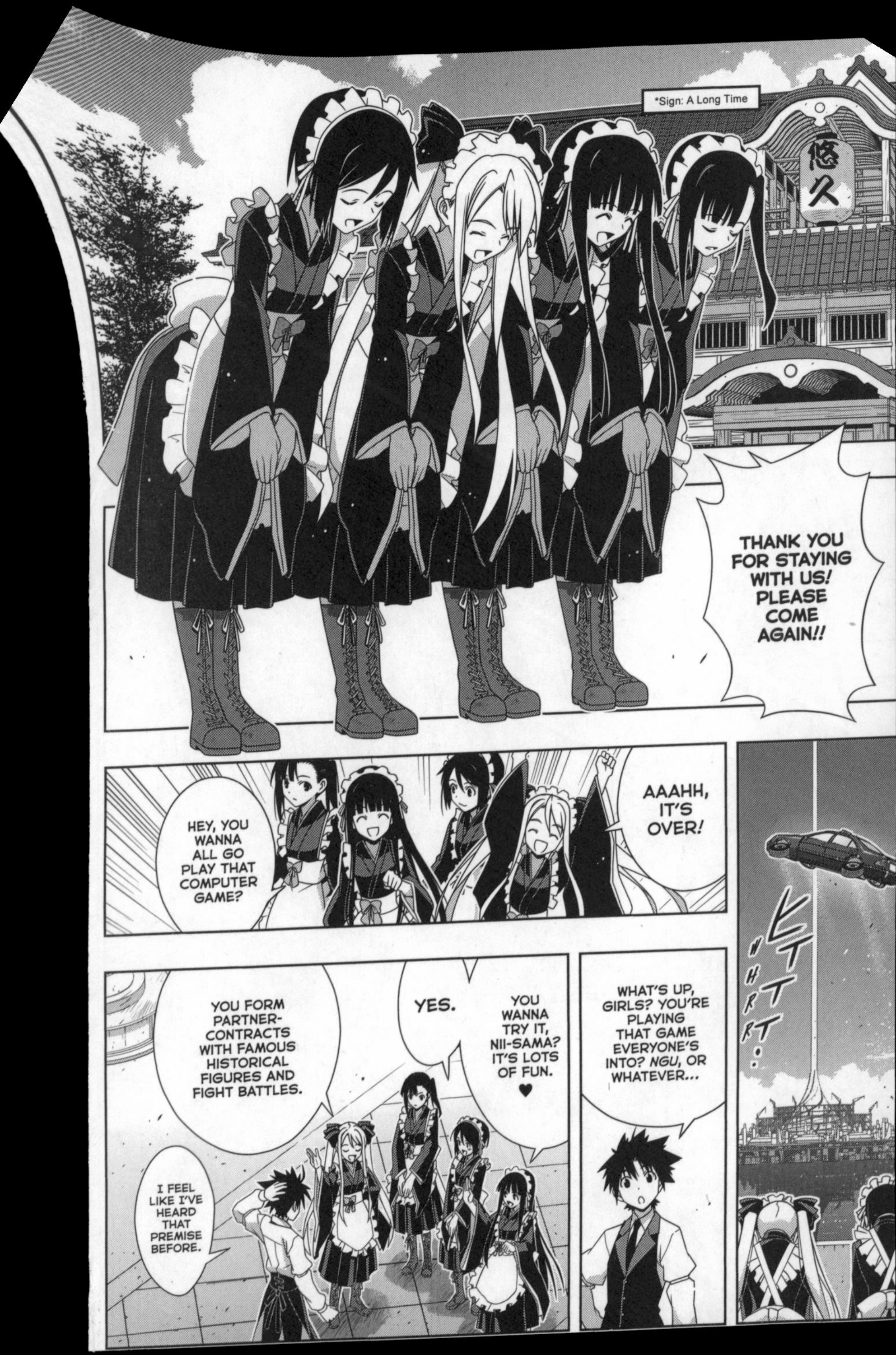
*Sign: A Long Time
悠久
THANK YOU FOR STAYING WITH US! PLEASE COME AGAIN!!
WHRRT..
AAAHH, IT'S OVER!
HEY, YOU WANNA ALL GO PLAY THAT COMPUTER GAME?
WHAT'S UP, GIRLS? YOU'RE PLAYING THAT GAME EVERYONE'S INTO? NGU, OR WHATEVER...
YOU WANNA TRY IT, NII-SAMA? IT'S LOTS OF FUN. ♥
YES.
YOU FORM PARTNER-CONTRACTS WITH FAMOUS HISTORICAL FIGURES AND FIGHT BATTLES.
I FEEL LIKE I'VE HEARD THAT PREMISE BEFORE.

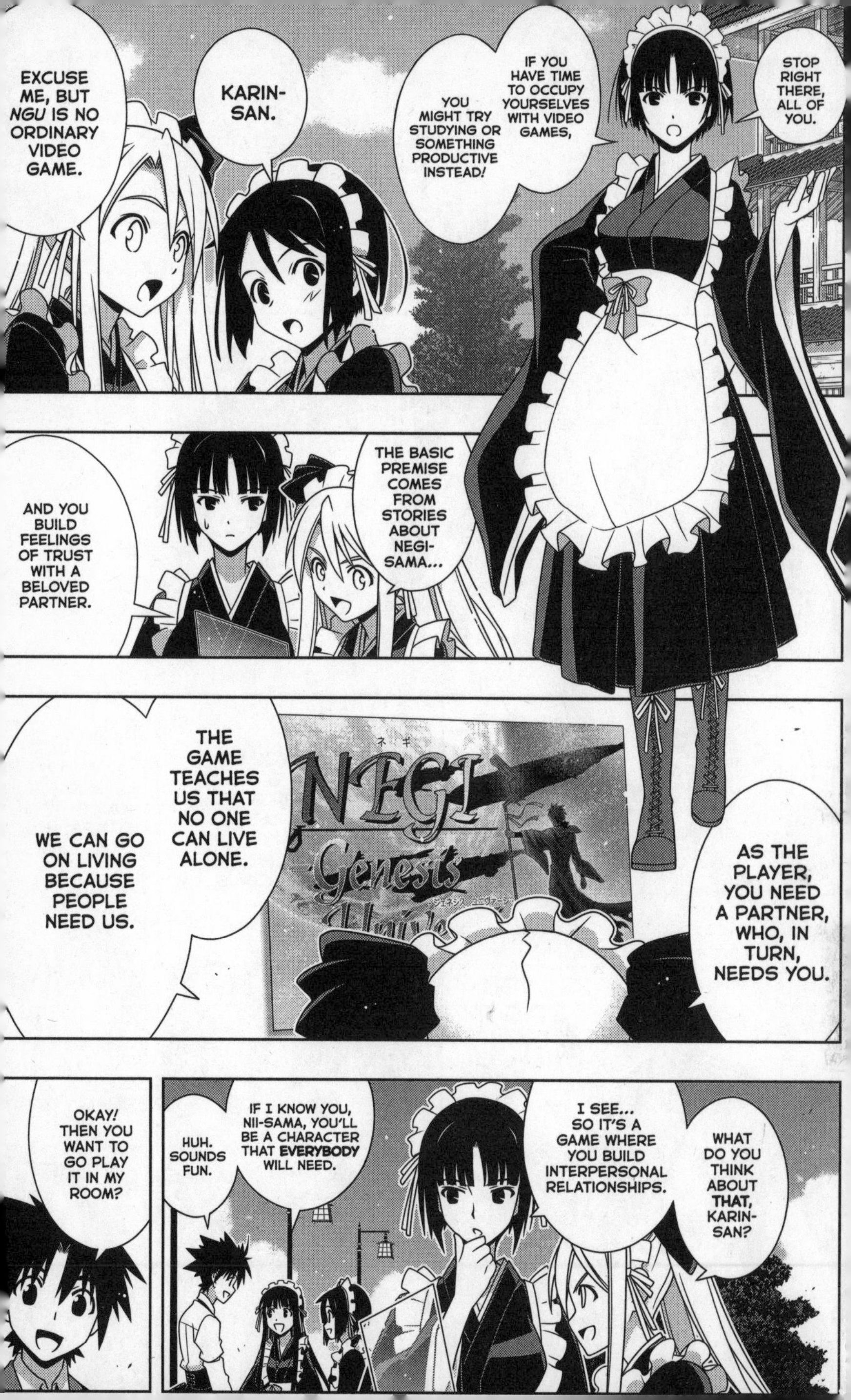
STOP RIGHT THERE, ALL OF YOU.
IF YOU HAVE TIME TO OCCUPY YOURSELVES WITH VIDEO GAMES,
YOU MIGHT TRY STUDYING OR SOMETHING PRODUCTIVE INSTEAD!
KARIN-SAN.
EXCUSE ME, BUT *NGU* IS NO ORDINARY VIDEO GAME.
THE BASIC PREMISE COMES FROM STORIES ABOUT NEGI-SAMA...
AND YOU BUILD FEELINGS OF TRUST WITH A BELOVED PARTNER.
AS THE PLAYER, YOU NEED A PARTNER, WHO, IN TURN, NEEDS YOU.
NEGI
Genesis
THE GAME TEACHES US THAT NO ONE CAN LIVE ALONE.
WE CAN GO ON LIVING BECAUSE PEOPLE NEED US.
WHAT DO YOU THINK ABOUT **THAT**, KARIN-SAN?
I SEE... SO IT'S A GAME WHERE YOU BUILD INTERPERSONAL RELATIONSHIPS.
IF I KNOW YOU, NII-SAMA, YOU'LL BE A CHARACTER THAT **EVERYBODY** WILL NEED.
HUH. SOUNDS FUN.
OKAY! THEN YOU WANT TO GO PLAY IT IN MY ROOM?

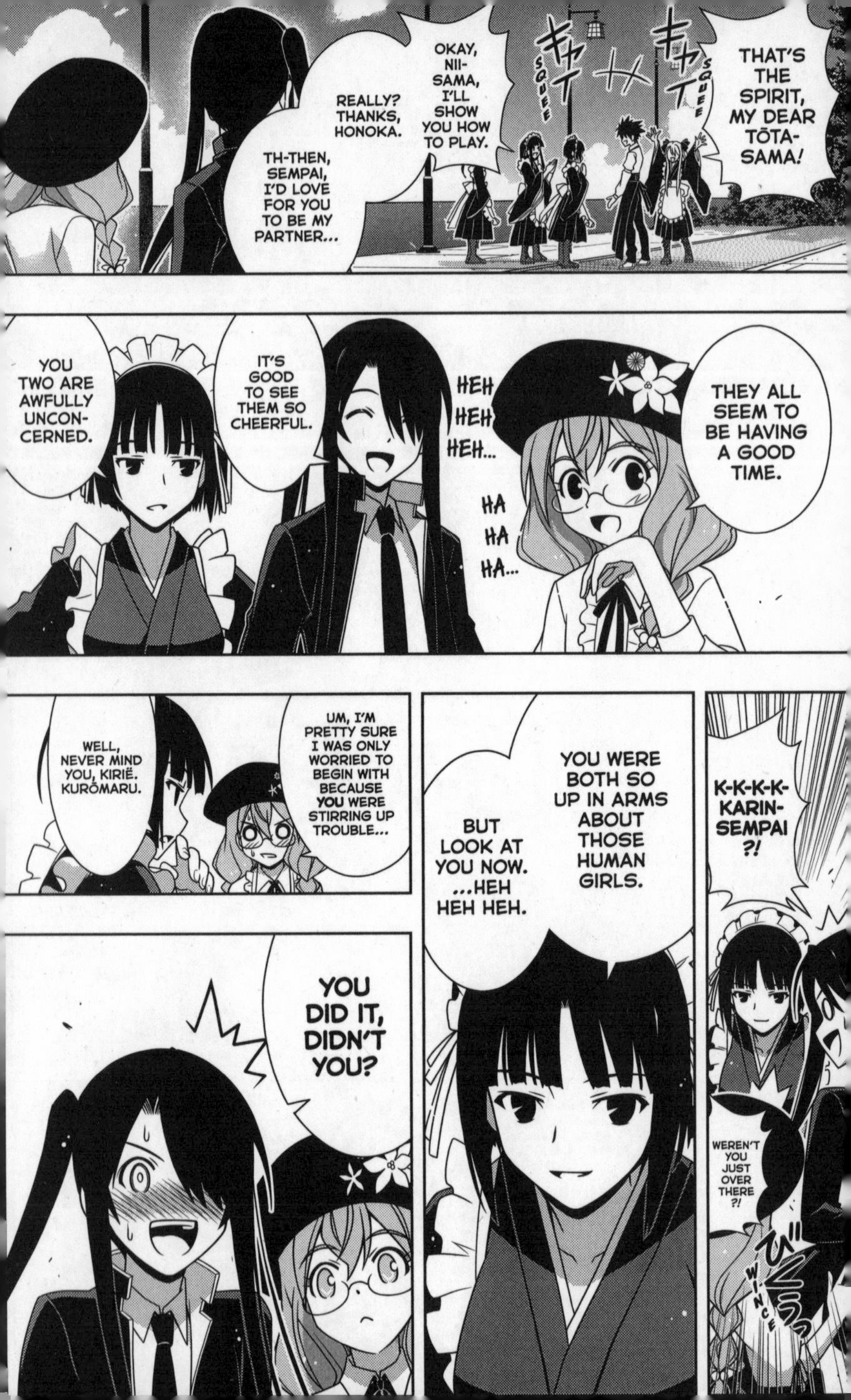
THAT'S THE SPIRIT, MY DEAR TŌTA-SAMA!
キャ
SQUEE
キャ
SQUEE
OKAY, NII-SAMA, I'LL SHOW YOU HOW TO PLAY.
REALLY? THANKS, HONOKA.
TH-THEN, SEMPAI, I'D LOVE FOR YOU TO BE MY PARTNER...
THEY ALL SEEM TO BE HAVING A GOOD TIME.
HA HA HA...
HEH HEH HEH...
IT'S GOOD TO SEE THEM SO CHEERFUL.
YOU TWO ARE AWFULLY UNCONCERNED.
K-K-K-K-KARIN-SEMPAI?!
WEREN'T YOU JUST OVER THERE?!
WINCE
YOU WERE BOTH SO UP IN ARMS ABOUT THOSE HUMAN GIRLS.
BUT LOOK AT YOU NOW. ...HEH HEH HEH.
UM, I'M PRETTY SURE I WAS ONLY WORRIED TO BEGIN WITH BECAUSE YOU WERE STIRRING UP TROUBLE...
WELL, NEVER MIND YOU, KIRIË. KURŌMARU.
YOU DID IT, DIDN'T YOU?

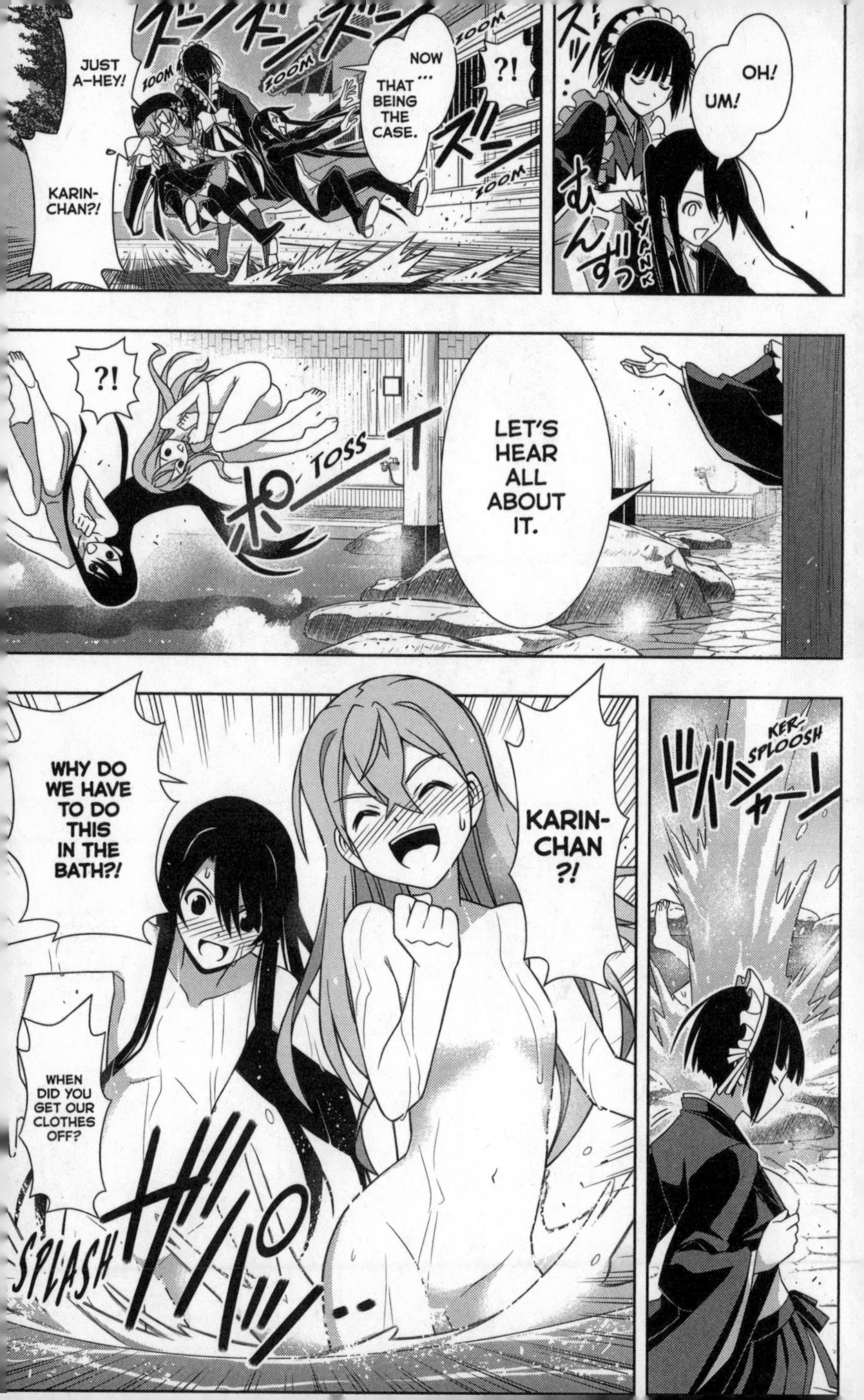
OH!
UM!
YANK
NOW... THAT BEING THE CASE.
?!
ZOOM
ZOOM
ZOOM
ZOOM
JUST A—HEY!
KARIN-CHAN?!
LET'S HEAR ALL ABOUT IT.
TOSS
?!
KER-SPLOOSH
KARIN-CHAN?!
WHY DO WE HAVE TO DO THIS IN THE BATH?!
WHEN DID YOU GET OUR CLOTHES OFF?
SPLASH

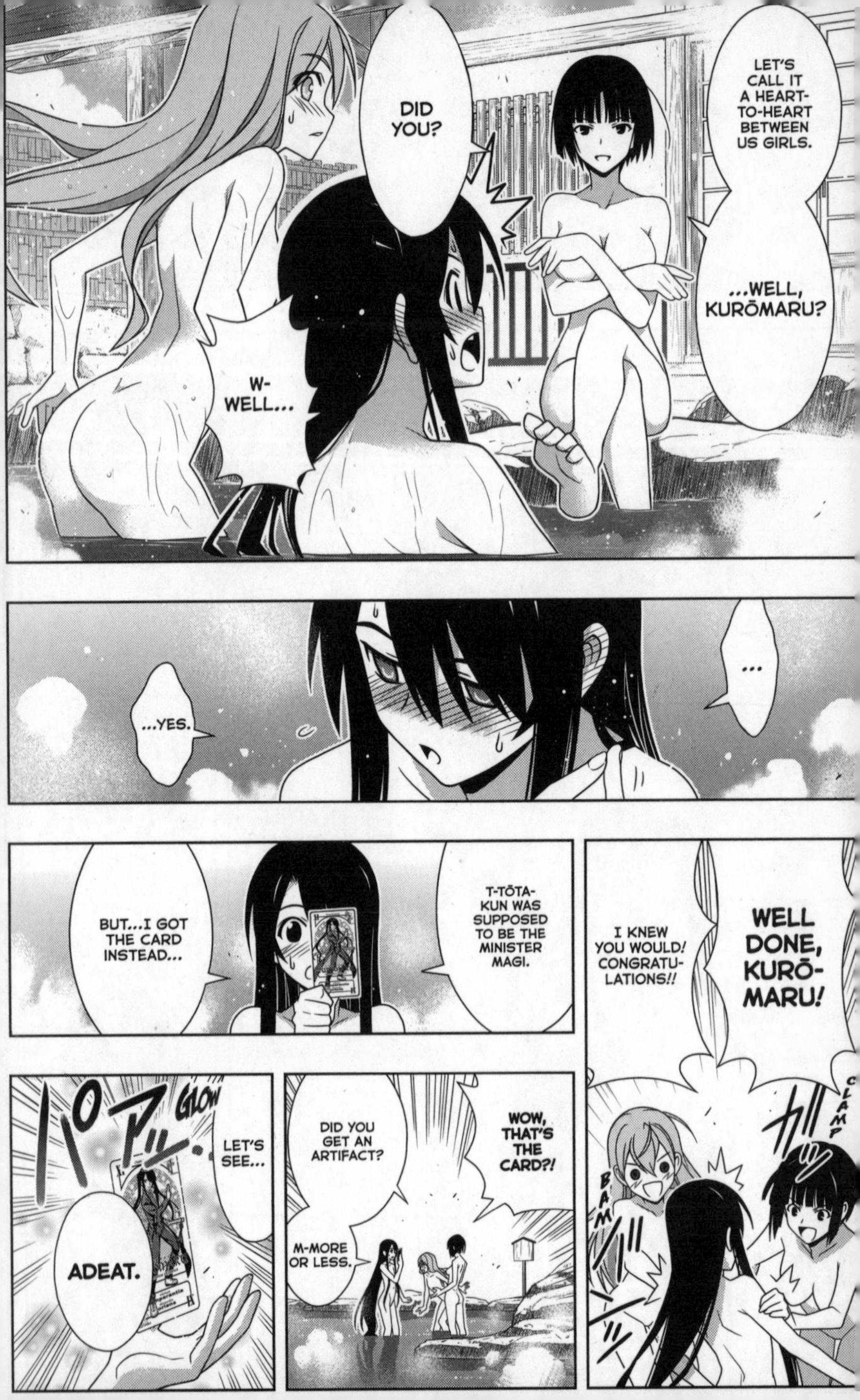
LET'S CALL IT A HEART-TO-HEART BETWEEN US GIRLS.
...WELL, KURŌMARU?
DID YOU?
W-WELL...
...
...YES.
WELL DONE, KURŌMARU!
I KNEW YOU WOULD! CONGRATULATIONS!!
CLAMP
BAM
T-TŌTA-KUN WAS SUPPOSED TO BE THE MINISTER MAGI.
BUT...I GOT THE CARD INSTEAD...
WOW, THAT'S THE CARD?!
DID YOU GET AN ARTIFACT?
M-MORE OR LESS.
GLOW
LET'S SEE...
ADEAT.

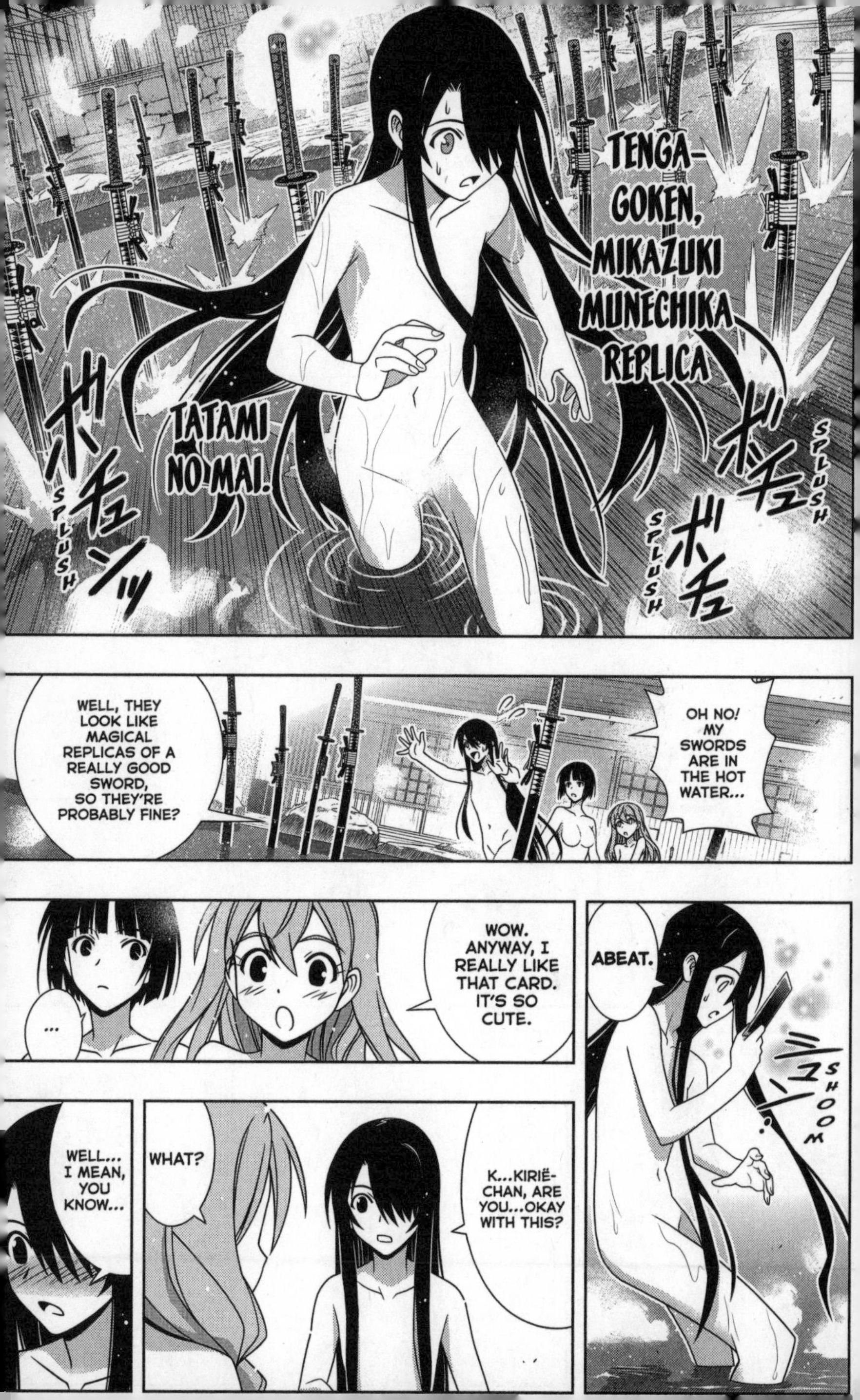
TENGA-GOKEN, MIKAZUKI MUNECHIKA REPLICA
ボチュ
SPLUSH
ボチュ
SPLUSH
TATAMI NO MAI!
ボチュンッ
SPLUSH
OH NO! MY SWORDS ARE IN THE HOT WATER...
WELL, THEY LOOK LIKE MAGICAL REPLICAS OF A REALLY GOOD SWORD, SO THEY'RE PROBABLY FINE?
ABEAT.
SHOOM
WOW. ANYWAY, I REALLY LIKE THAT CARD. IT'S SO CUTE.
...
K...KIRIË-CHAN, ARE YOU...OKAY WITH THIS?
WHAT?
WELL... I MEAN, YOU KNOW...

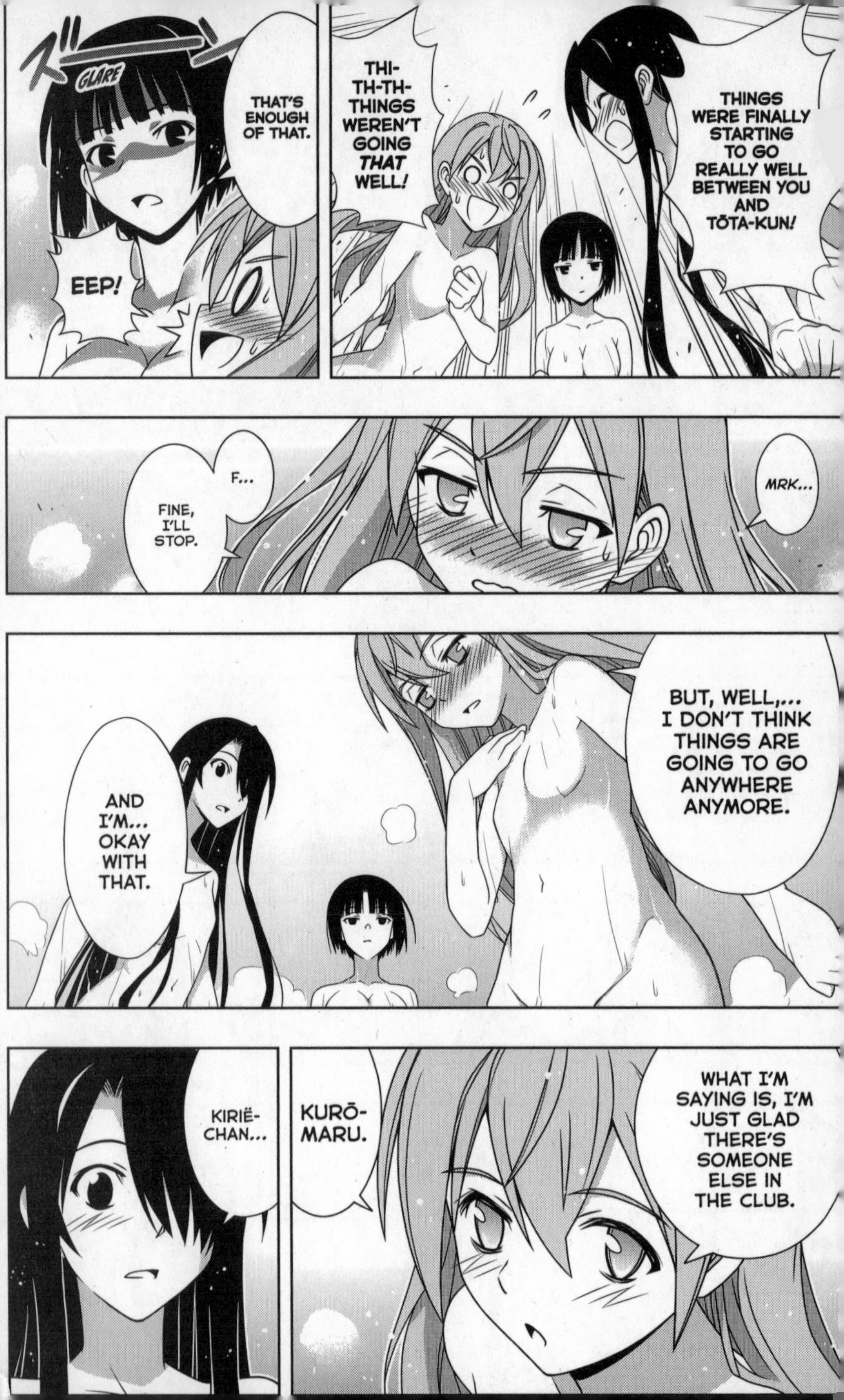
THINGS WERE FINALLY STARTING TO GO REALLY WELL BETWEEN YOU AND TŌTA-KUN!
THI-TH-TH-THINGS WEREN'T GOING *THAT* WELL!
GLARE
THAT'S ENOUGH OF THAT.
EEP!
MRK...
F...
FINE, I'LL STOP.
BUT, WELL,... I DON'T THINK THINGS ARE GOING TO GO ANYWHERE ANYMORE.
AND I'M... OKAY WITH THAT.
WHAT I'M SAYING IS, I'M JUST GLAD THERE'S SOMEONE ELSE IN THE CLUB.
KURŌ-MARU.
KIRIĒ-CHAN...

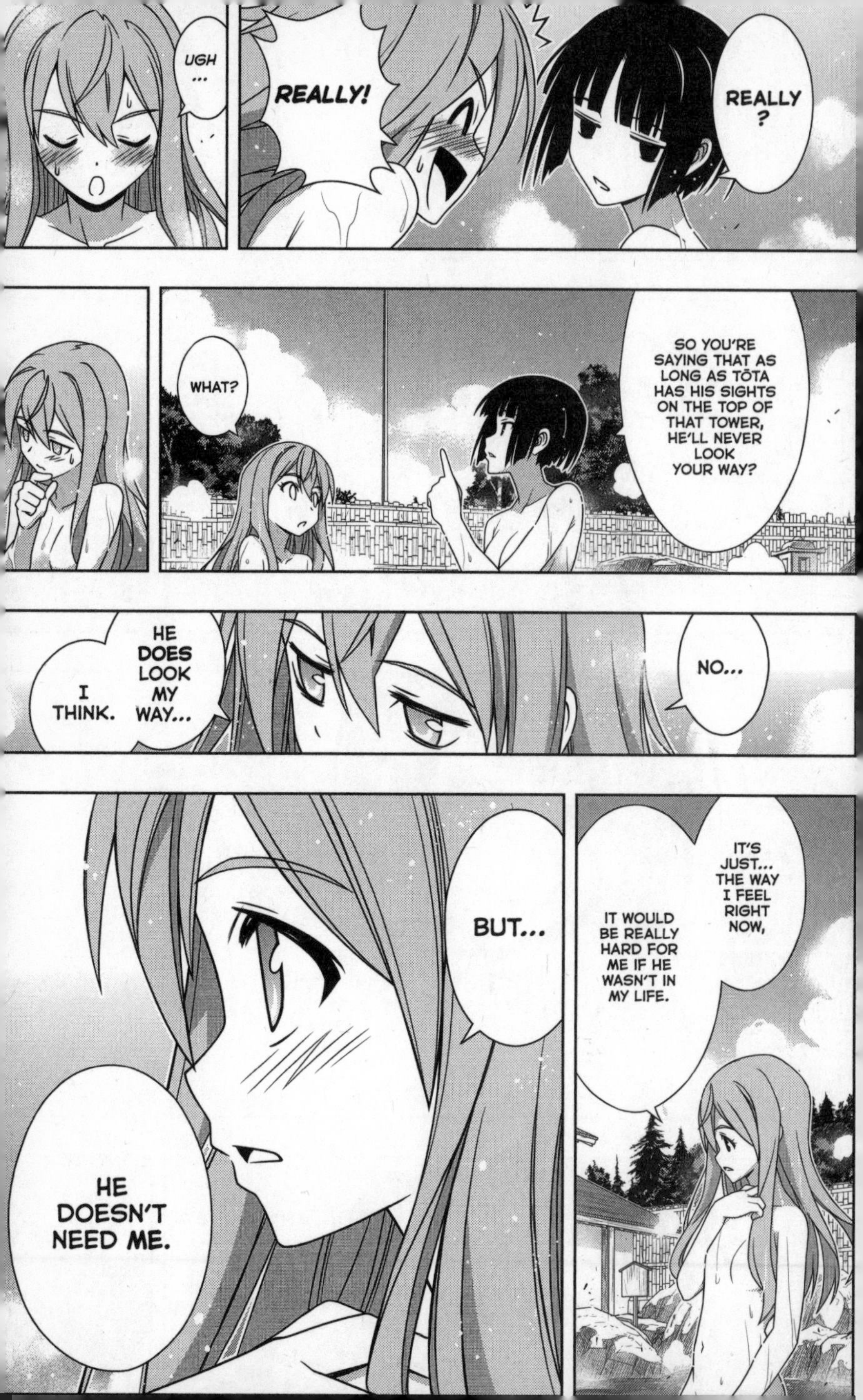
REALLY?
REALLY!
UGH ...
SO YOU'RE SAYING THAT AS LONG AS TŌTA HAS HIS SIGHTS ON THE TOP OF THAT TOWER, HE'LL NEVER LOOK YOUR WAY?
WHAT?
NO...
HE DOES LOOK MY WAY... I THINK.
IT'S JUST... THE WAY I FEEL RIGHT NOW,
IT WOULD BE REALLY HARD FOR ME IF HE WASN'T IN MY LIFE.
BUT...
HE DOESN'T NEED ME.

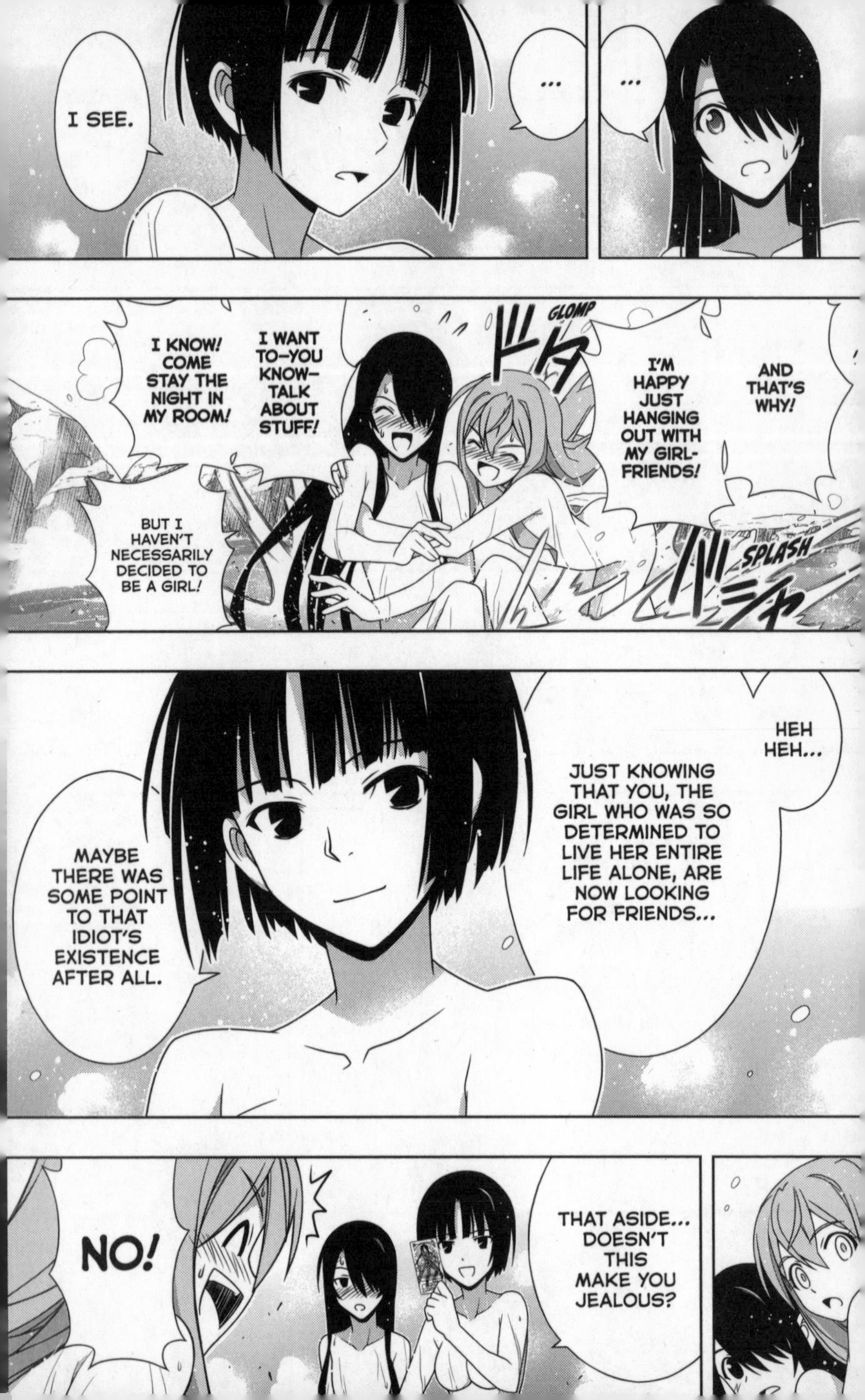
...
...
I SEE.
AND THAT'S WHY!
I'M HAPPY JUST HANGING OUT WITH MY GIRL-FRIENDS!
GLOMP
ドタ
I WANT TO—YOU KNOW—TALK ABOUT STUFF!
I KNOW! COME STAY THE NIGHT IN MY ROOM!
SPLASH
バシャ
BUT I HAVEN'T NECESSARILY DECIDED TO BE A GIRL!
HEH HEH...
JUST KNOWING THAT YOU, THE GIRL WHO WAS SO DETERMINED TO LIVE HER ENTIRE LIFE ALONE, ARE NOW LOOKING FOR FRIENDS...
MAYBE THERE WAS SOME POINT TO THAT IDIOT'S EXISTENCE AFTER ALL.
THAT ASIDE... DOESN'T THIS MAKE YOU JEALOUS?
NO!

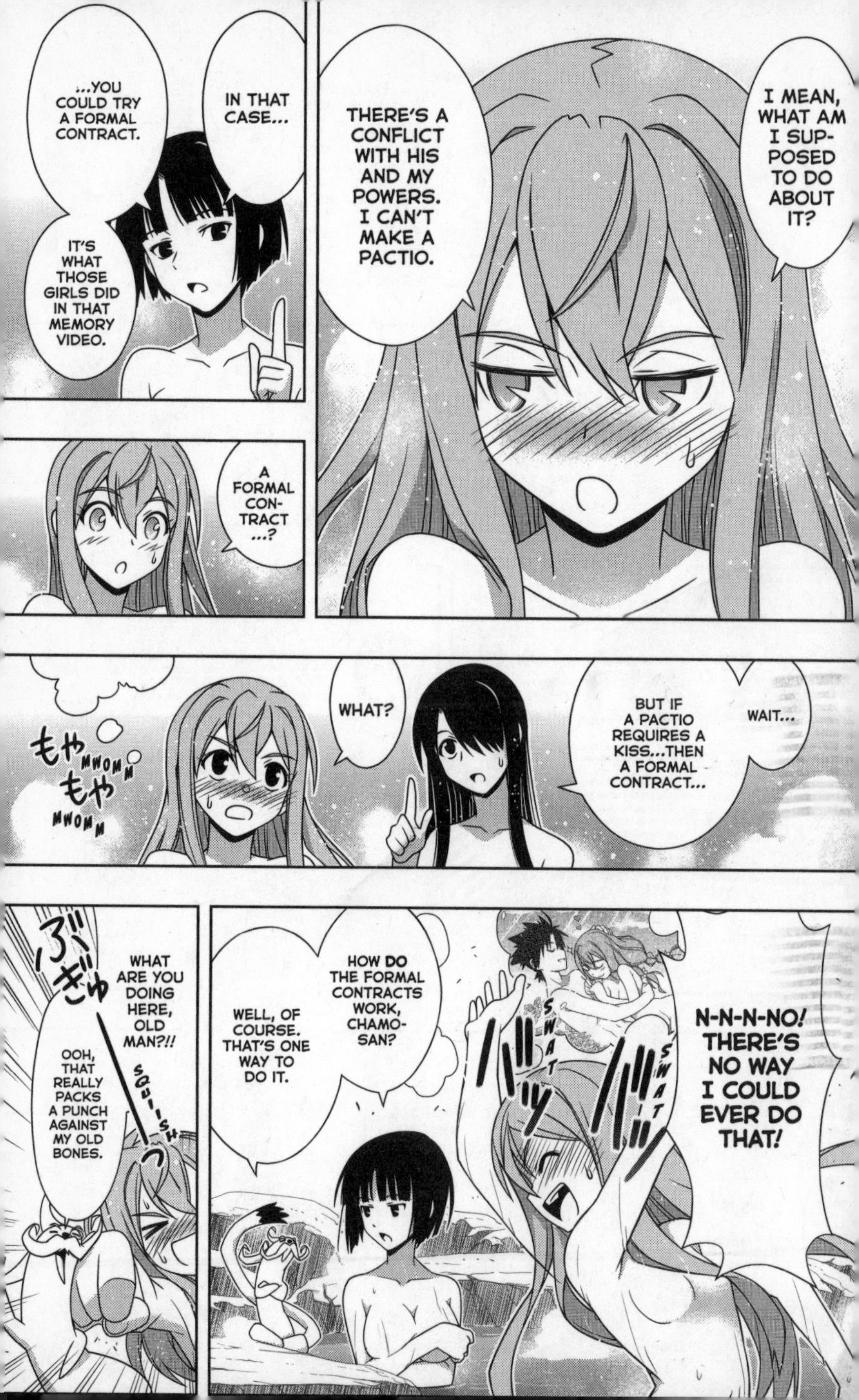
I MEAN, WHAT AM I SUP-POSED TO DO ABOUT IT?
THERE'S A CONFLICT WITH HIS AND MY POWERS. I CAN'T MAKE A PACTIO.
IN THAT CASE...
...YOU COULD TRY A FORMAL CONTRACT.
IT'S WHAT THOSE GIRLS DID IN THAT MEMORY VIDEO.
A FORMAL CON-TRACT...?
WAIT...
BUT IF A PACTIO REQUIRES A KISS...THEN A FORMAL CONTRACT...
WHAT?
もや MWOMM
もや MWOMM
N-N-N-NO! THERE'S NO WAY I COULD EVER DO THAT!
SWAT
SWAT
HOW DO THE FORMAL CONTRACTS WORK, CHAMO-SAN?
WELL, OF COURSE. THAT'S ONE WAY TO DO IT.
ぶぎゅ
SQUISH
WHAT ARE YOU DOING HERE, OLD MAN?!!
OOH, THAT REALLY PACKS A PUNCH AGAINST MY OLD BONES.

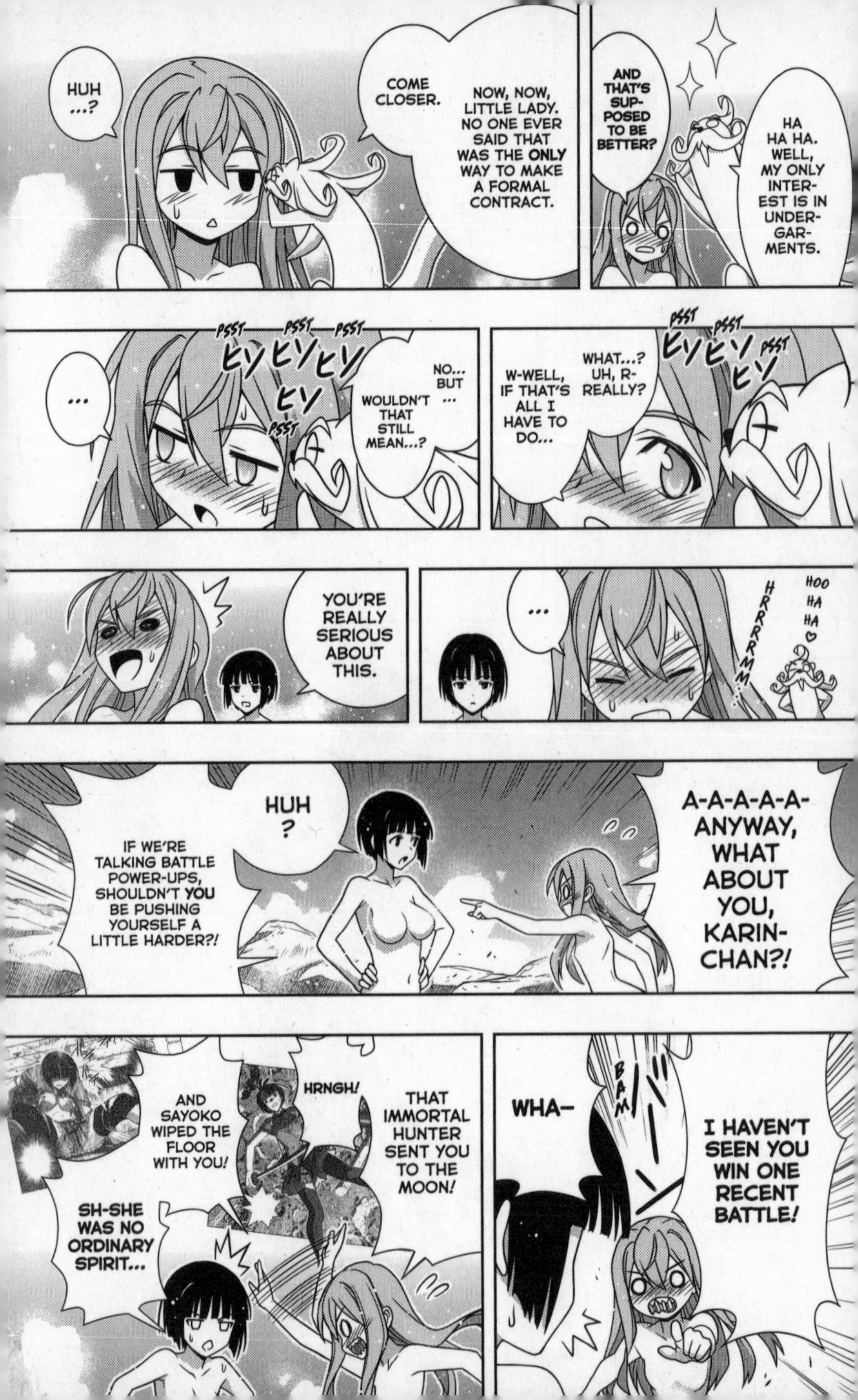
HA HA HA. WELL, MY ONLY INTER-EST IS IN UNDER-GAR-MENTS.
AND THAT'S SUP-POSED TO BE BETTER?
NOW, NOW, LITTLE LADY. NO ONE EVER SAID THAT WAS THE ONLY WAY TO MAKE A FORMAL CONTRACT.
COME CLOSER.
HUH ...?
PSST PSST PSST
ヒソヒソヒソ
WHAT...? UH, R-REALLY?
W-WELL, IF THAT'S ALL I HAVE TO DO...
PSST PSST PSST
ヒソヒソヒソ
ヒソ
PSST
NO... BUT ...
WOULDN'T THAT STILL MEAN...?
...
HOO HA HA ♡
HRRRRMM...
...
YOU'RE REALLY SERIOUS ABOUT THIS.
A-A-A-A-A-ANYWAY, WHAT ABOUT YOU, KARIN-CHAN?!
HUH ?
IF WE'RE TALKING BATTLE POWER-UPS, SHOULDN'T YOU BE PUSHING YOURSELF A LITTLE HARDER?!
I HAVEN'T SEEN YOU WIN ONE RECENT BATTLE!
BAM
WHA-
THAT IMMORTAL HUNTER SENT YOU TO THE MOON!
HRNGH!
AND SAYOKO WIPED THE FLOOR WITH YOU!
SH-SHE WAS NO ORDINARY SPIRIT...

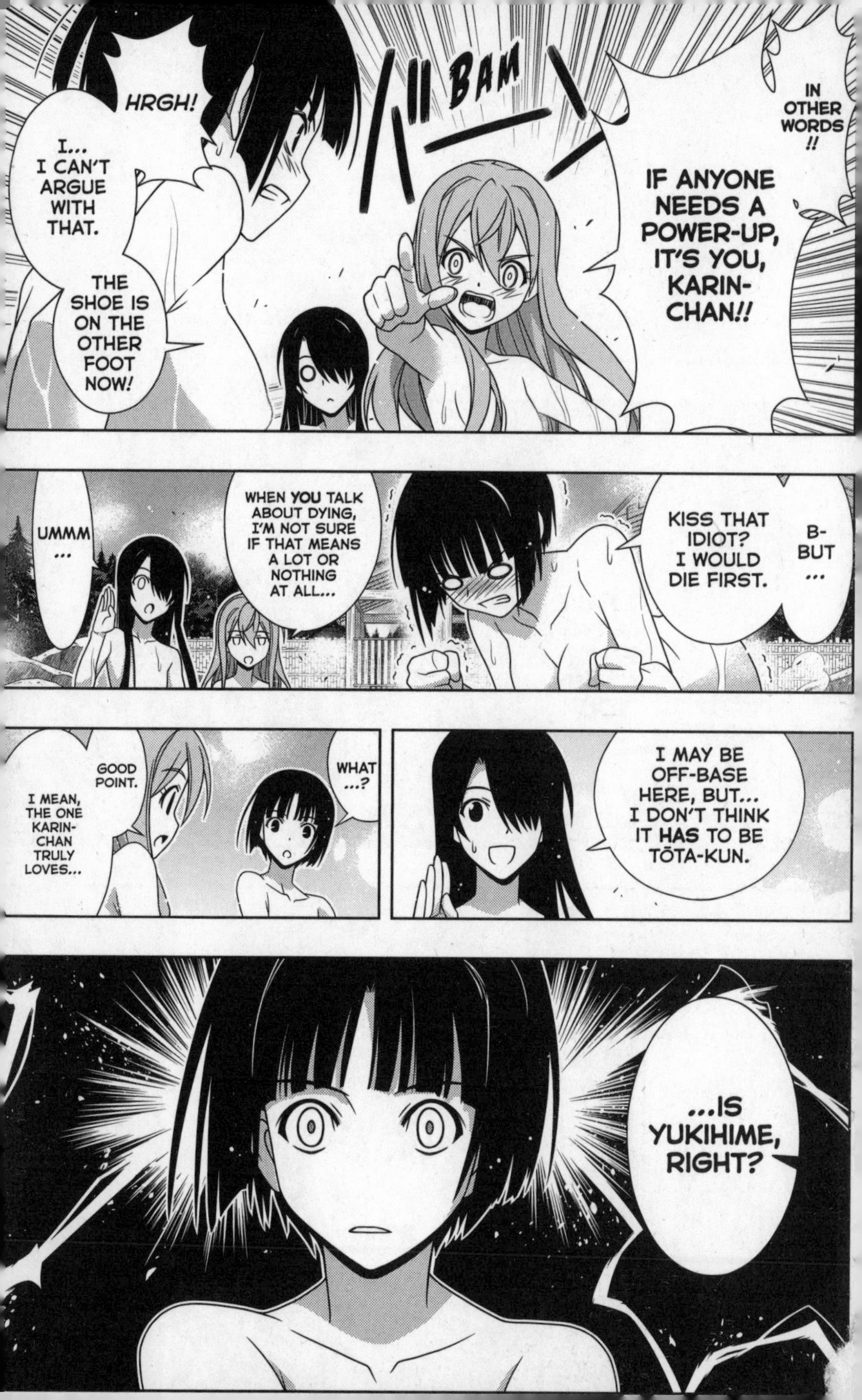
IN OTHER WORDS!!
IF ANYONE NEEDS A POWER-UP, IT'S YOU, KARIN-CHAN!!
BAM
HRGH!
I... I CAN'T ARGUE WITH THAT.
THE SHOE IS ON THE OTHER FOOT NOW!
B-BUT...
KISS THAT IDIOT? I WOULD DIE FIRST.
WHEN YOU TALK ABOUT DYING, I'M NOT SURE IF THAT MEANS A LOT OR NOTHING AT ALL...
UMMM...
I MAY BE OFF-BASE HERE, BUT... I DON'T THINK IT HAS TO BE TŌTA-KUN.
WHAT...?
GOOD POINT.
I MEAN, THE ONE KARIN-CHAN TRULY LOVES...
...IS YUKIHIME, RIGHT?

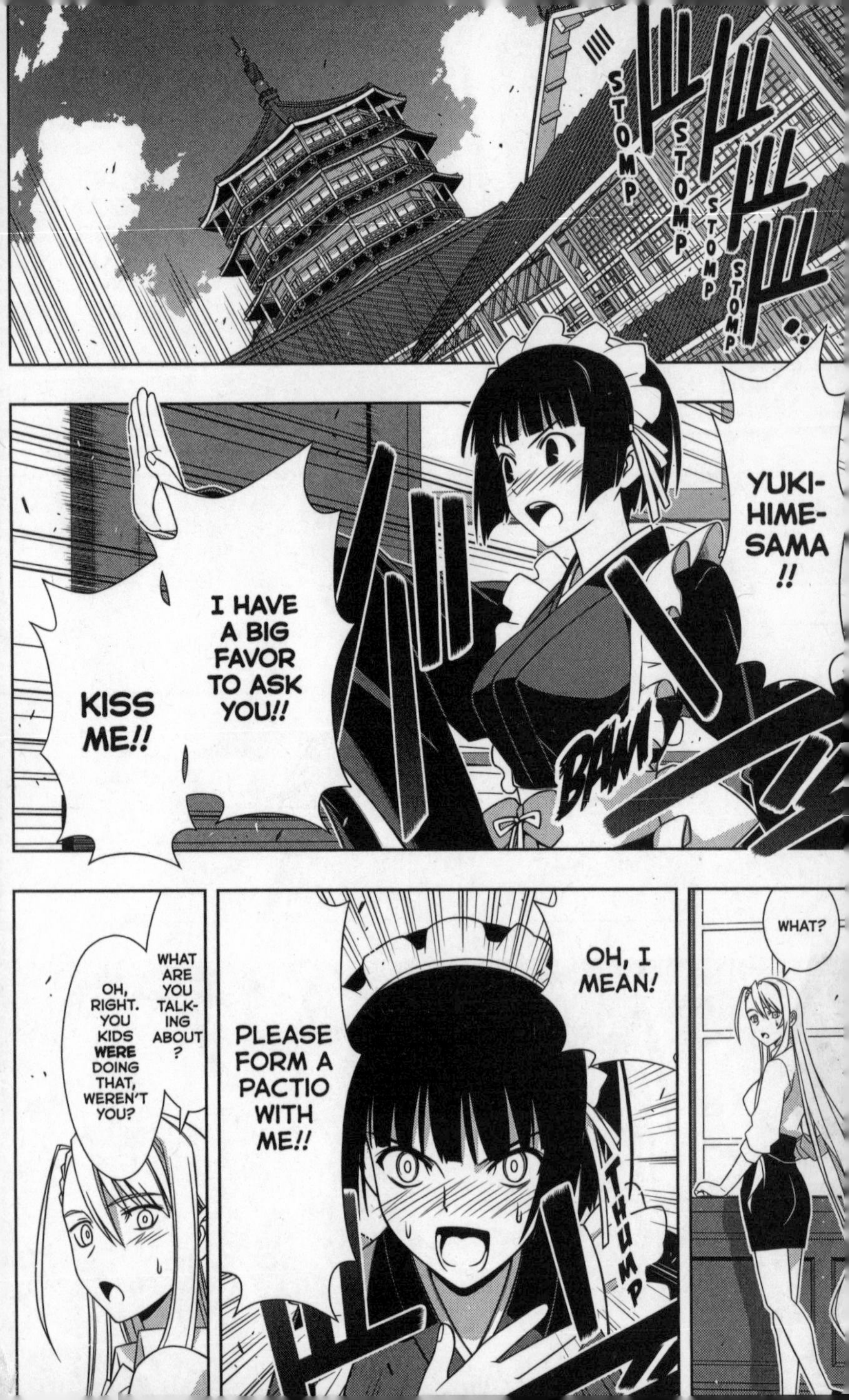
STOMP
STOMP
STOMP
STOMP
YUKI-HIME-SAMA!!
I HAVE A BIG FAVOR TO ASK YOU!!
KISS ME!!
BAM
WHAT?
OH, I MEAN!
PLEASE FORM A PACTIO WITH ME!!
THUMP
WHAT ARE YOU TALKING ABOUT?
OH, RIGHT. YOU KIDS WERE DOING THAT, WEREN'T YOU?

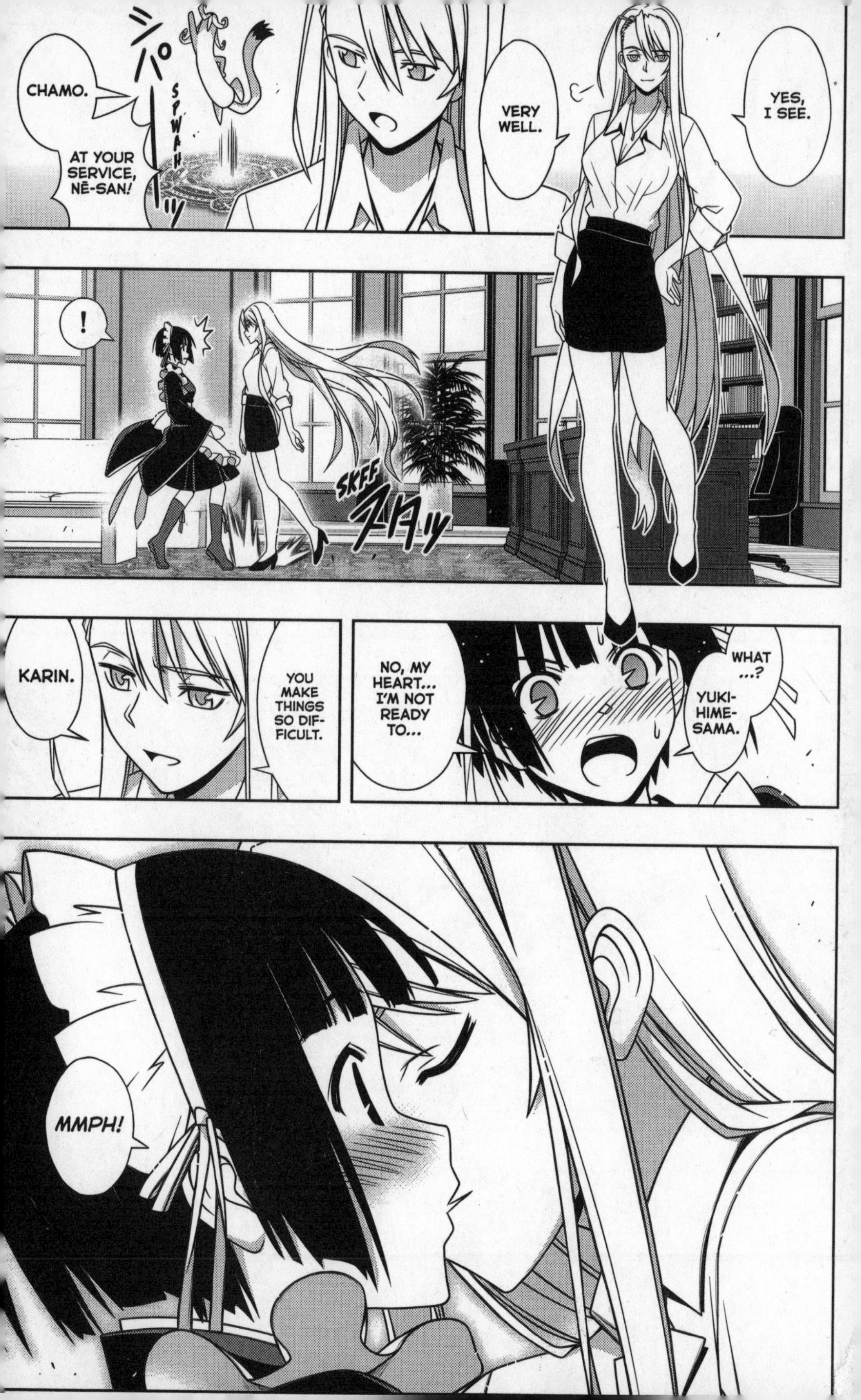
YES, I SEE.
VERY WELL.
CHAMO.
SPWAH
AT YOUR SERVICE, NĒ-SAN!
!
SKFF
WHAT ...?
YUKI-HIME-SAMA.
NO, MY HEART... I'M NOT READY TO...
YOU MAKE THINGS SO DIF-FICULT.
KARIN.
MMPH!

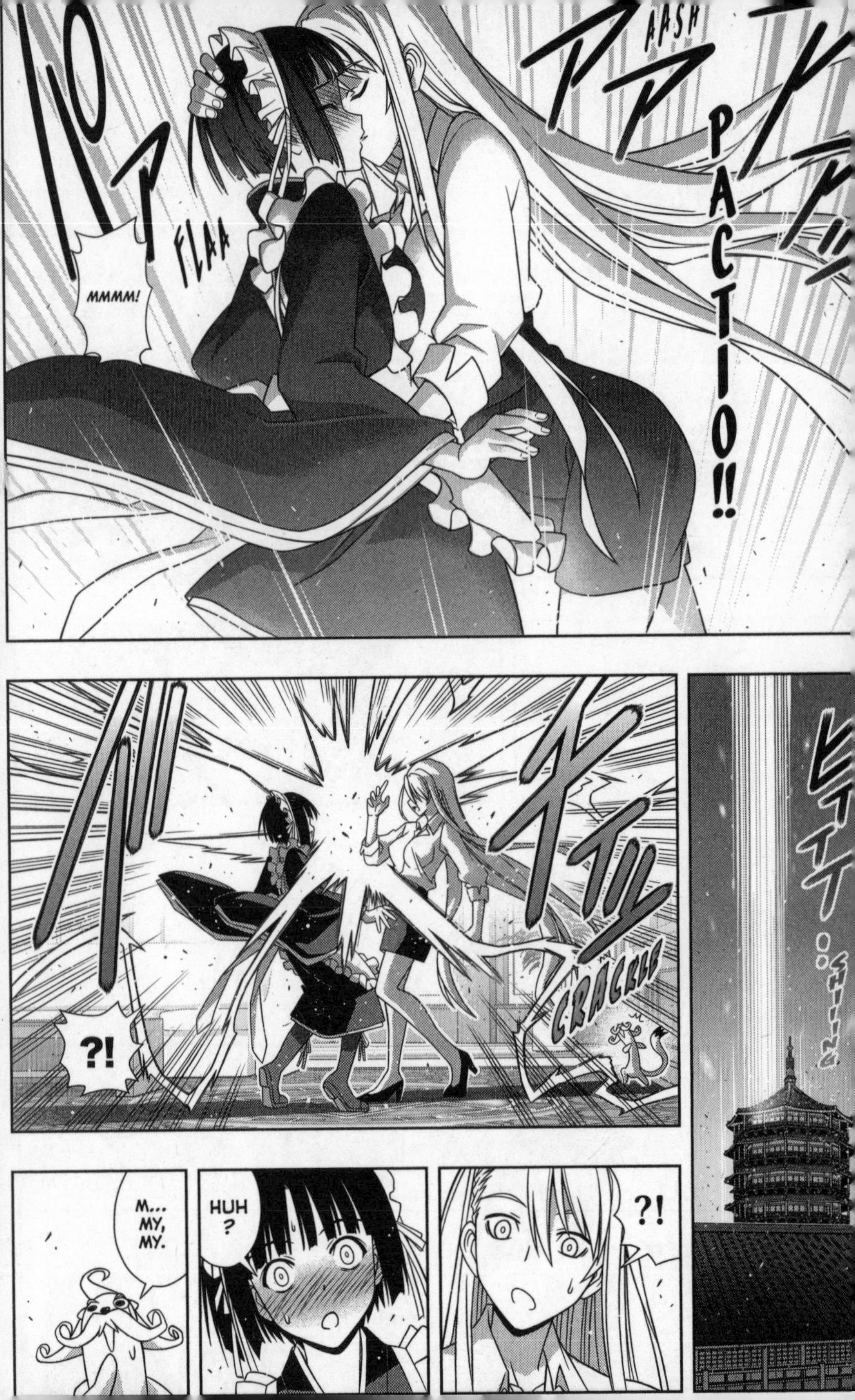
AASH
PACTIO!!
FLAA
MMMM!
SHIIING
CRACKLE
?!
?!
HUH ?
M... MY, MY.

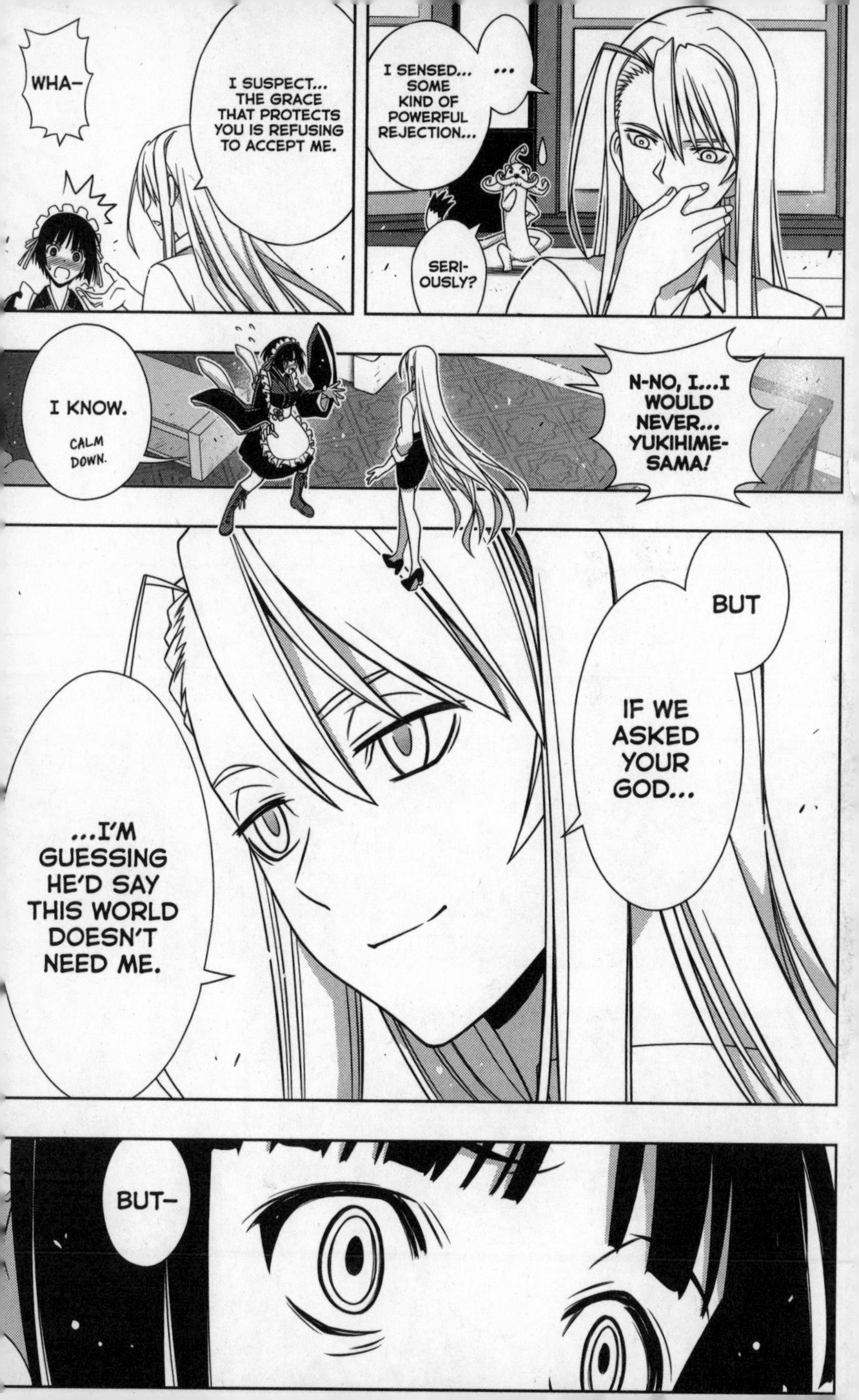
I SENSED... SOME KIND OF POWERFUL REJECTION...
...
SERI-OUSLY?
I SUSPECT... THE GRACE THAT PROTECTS YOU IS REFUSING TO ACCEPT ME.
WHA-
N-NO, I...I WOULD NEVER... YUKIHIME-SAMA!
I KNOW.
CALM DOWN.
BUT
IF WE ASKED YOUR GOD...
...I'M GUESSING HE'D SAY THIS WORLD DOESN'T NEED ME.
BUT-

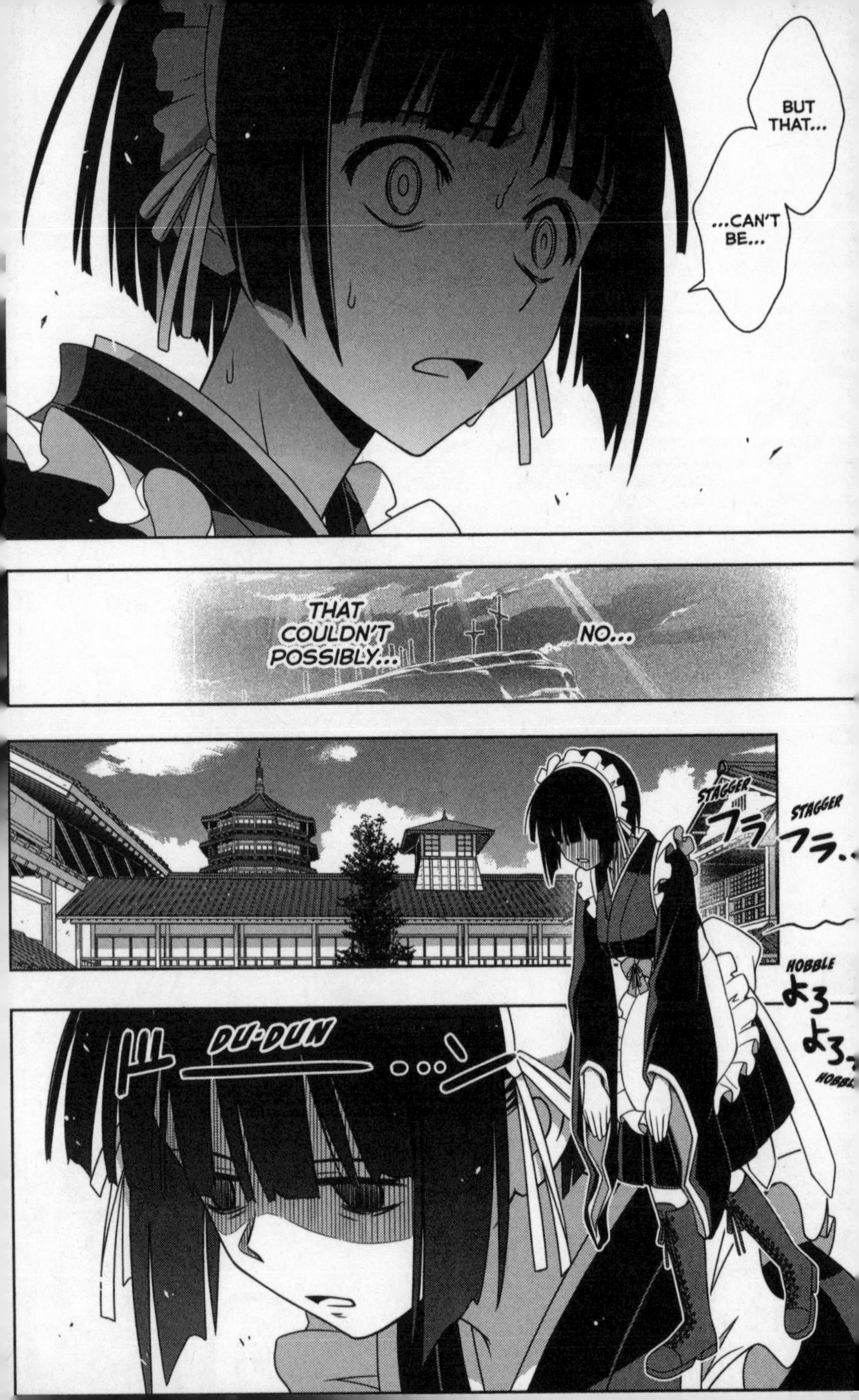
BUT THAT...
...CAN'T BE...
NO...
THAT COULDN'T POSSIBLY...
STAGGER
フラ
STAGGER
フラ..
HOBBLE
よろ
よろ..
HOBBLE
ドン
DU-DUN
——...!

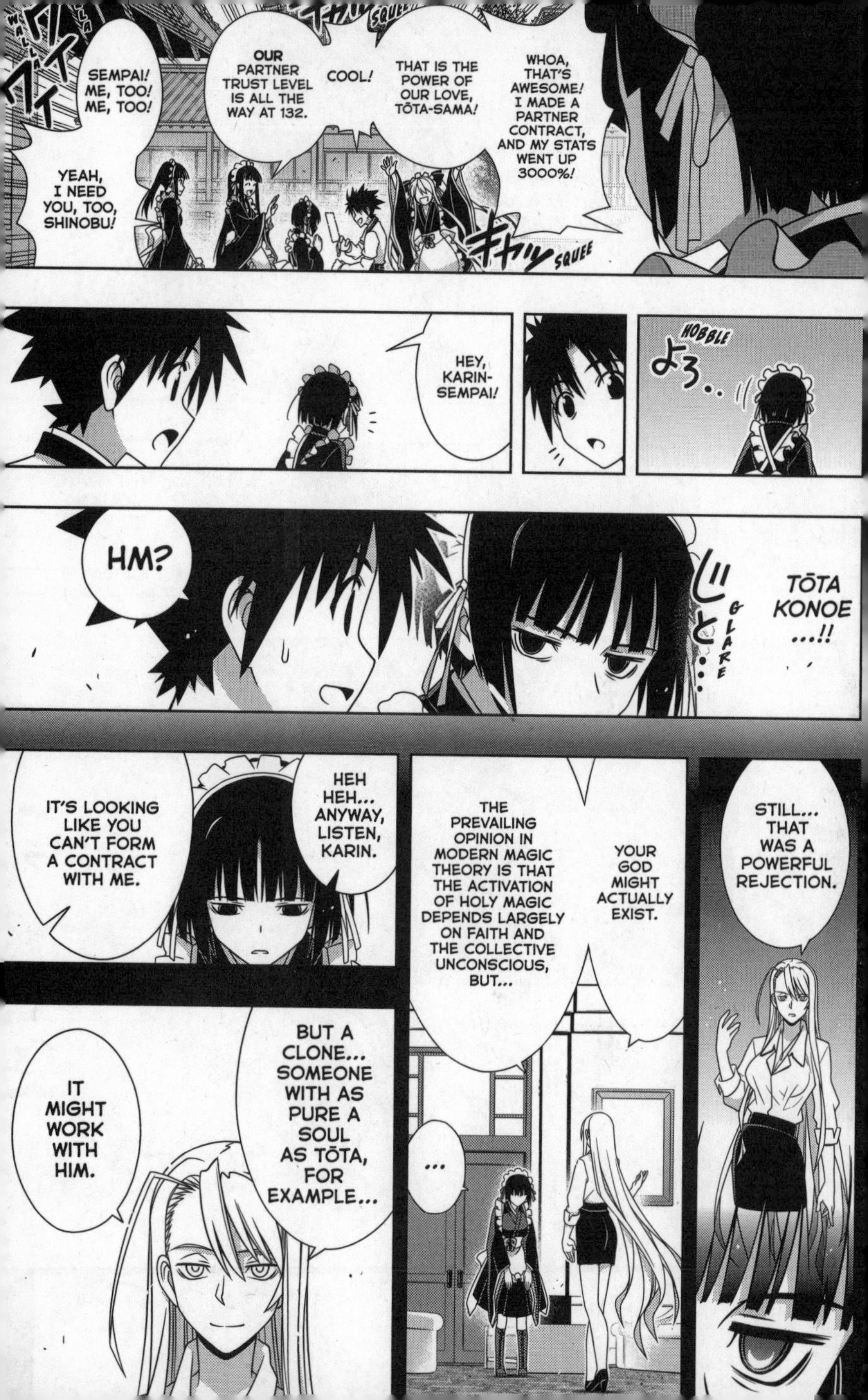
WHOA, THAT'S AWESOME! I MADE A PARTNER CONTRACT, AND MY STATS WENT UP 3000%!
キャッ SQUEE
THAT IS THE POWER OF OUR LOVE, TŌTA-SAMA!
COOL!
OUR PARTNER TRUST LEVEL IS ALL THE WAY AT 132.
SQUEE
SEMPAI! ME, TOO! ME, TOO!
WALLA
YEAH, I NEED YOU, TOO, SHINOBU!
よろ.. HOBBLE
HEY, KARIN-SEMPAI!
TŌTA KONOE ...!!
GLARE
HM?
STILL... THAT WAS A POWERFUL REJECTION.
YOUR GOD MIGHT ACTUALLY EXIST.
THE PREVAILING OPINION IN MODERN MAGIC THEORY IS THAT THE ACTIVATION OF HOLY MAGIC DEPENDS LARGELY ON FAITH AND THE COLLECTIVE UNCONSCIOUS, BUT...
...
HEH HEH... ANYWAY, LISTEN, KARIN.
IT'S LOOKING LIKE YOU CAN'T FORM A CONTRACT WITH ME.
BUT A CLONE... SOMEONE WITH AS PURE A SOUL AS TŌTA, FOR EXAMPLE...
IT MIGHT WORK WITH HIM.

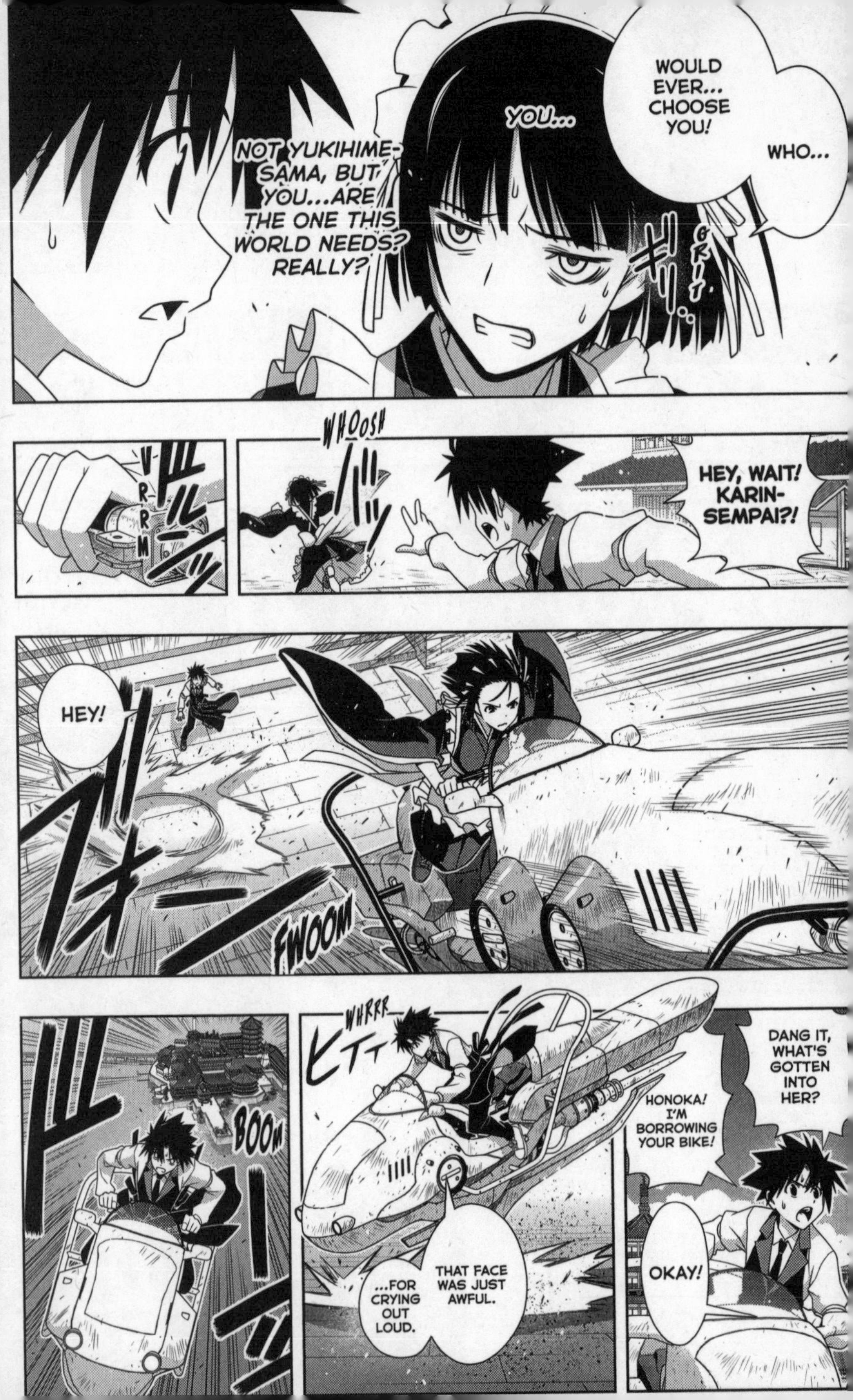
WHO...
WOULD EVER... CHOOSE YOU!
YOU...
GRIT
NOT YUKIHIME-SAMA, BUT YOU...ARE THE ONE THIS WORLD NEEDS? REALLY?
WHOOSH
HEY, WAIT! KARIN-SEMPAI?!
V-R-R-M
FWOOM
HEY!
DANG IT, WHAT'S GOTTEN INTO HER?
HONOKA! I'M BORROWING YOUR BIKE!
OKAY!
WHRRR
THAT FACE WAS JUST AWFUL.
...FOR CRYING OUT LOUD.
BOOM

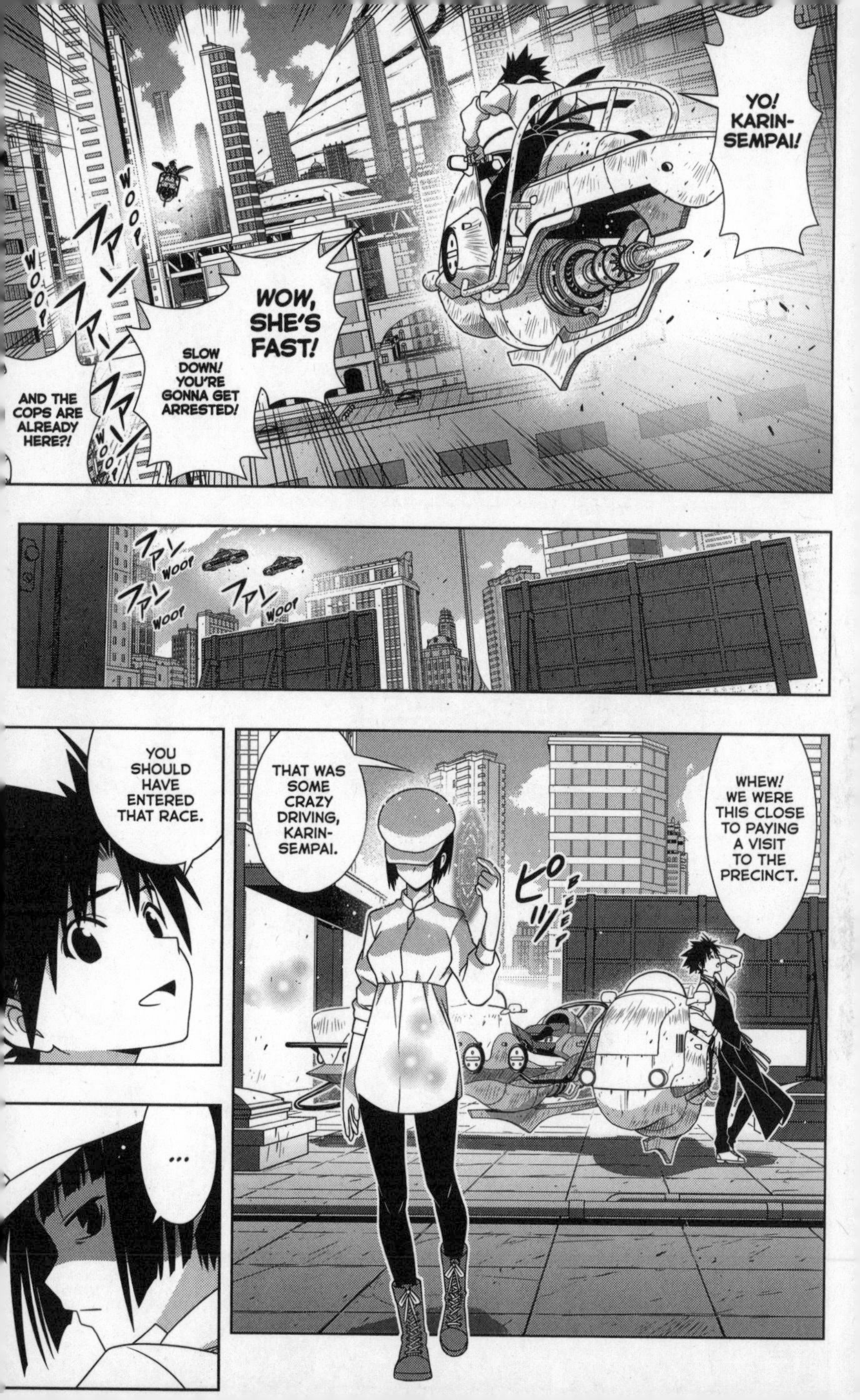
YO! KARIN-SEMPAI!
WOW, SHE'S FAST!
WOOP WOOP
SLOW DOWN! YOU'RE GONNA GET ARRESTED!
WOOP
AND THE COPS ARE ALREADY HERE?!
WOOP WOOP WOOP
WHEW! WE WERE THIS CLOSE TO PAYING A VISIT TO THE PRECINCT.
BEEP
THAT WAS SOME CRAZY DRIVING, KARIN-SEMPAI.
YOU SHOULD HAVE ENTERED THAT RACE.
...

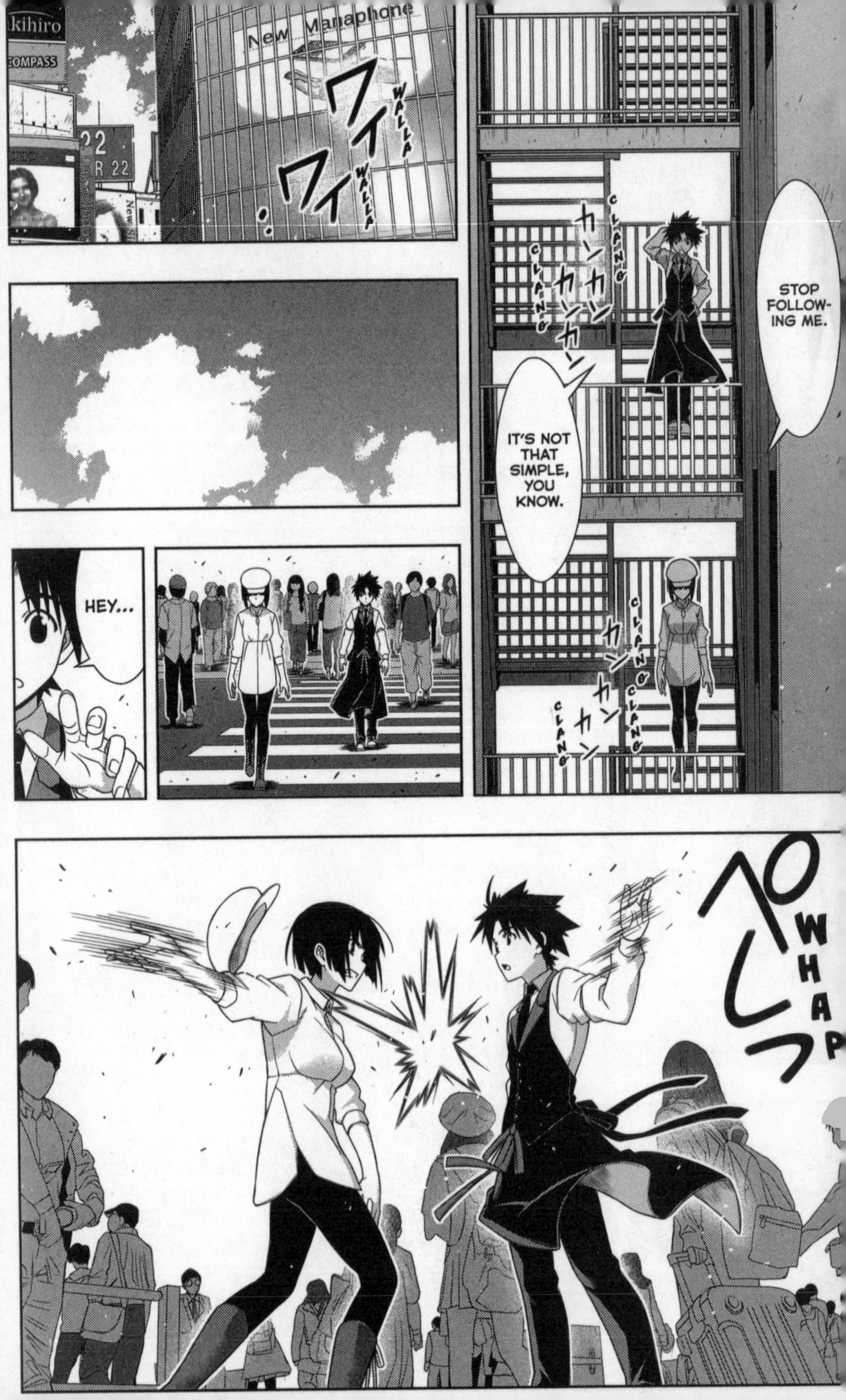
STOP FOLLOWING-ING ME.
CLANG CLANG
IT'S NOT THAT SIMPLE, YOU KNOW.
CLANG CLANG CLANG
New Manaphone
kihiro
COMPASS
WALLA WALLA
HEY...
WHAP

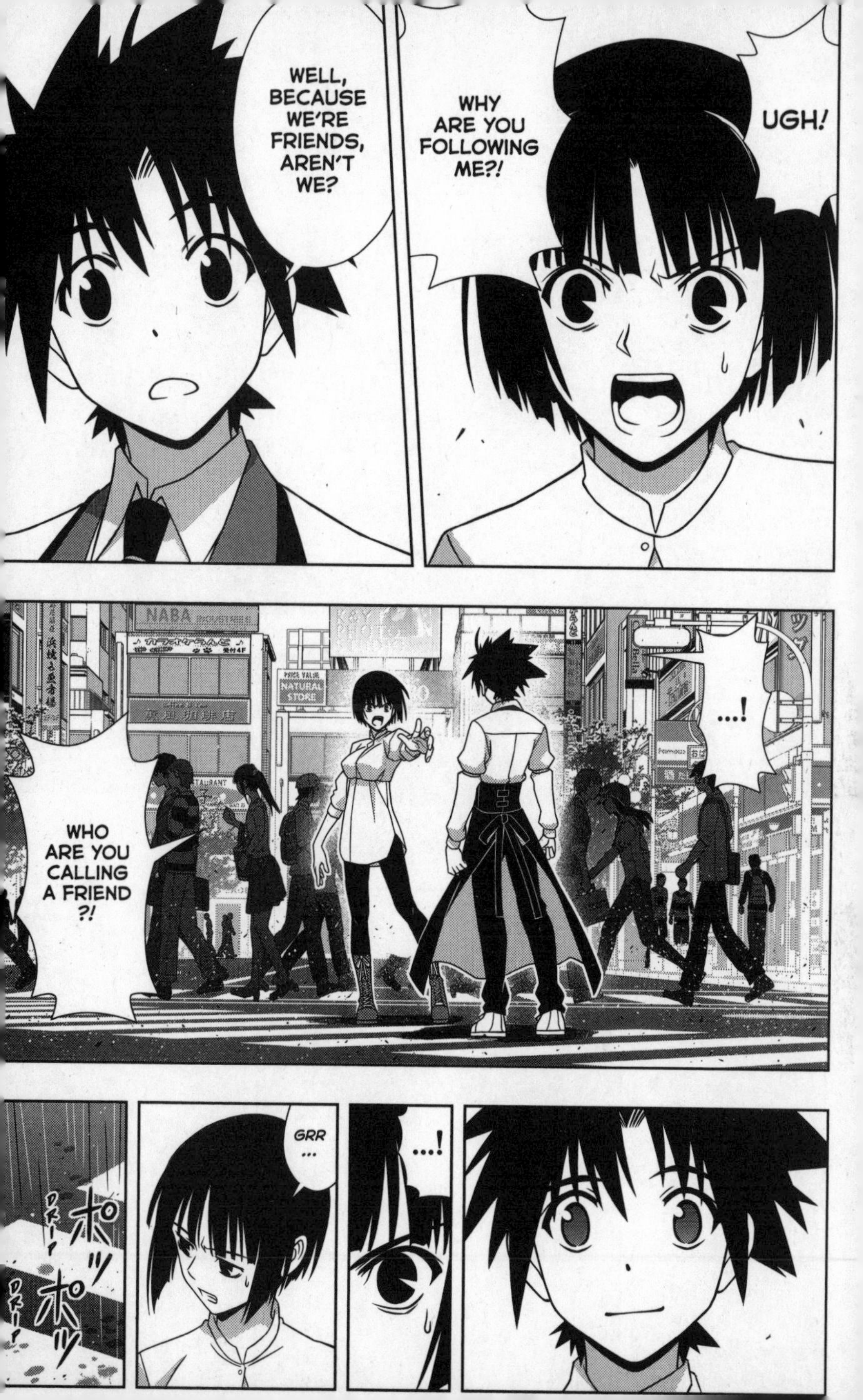
UGH!
WHY ARE YOU FOLLOWING ME?!
WELL, BECAUSE WE'RE FRIENDS, AREN'T WE?
...!
WHO ARE YOU CALLING A FRIEND ?!
NABA
PRICE VALUE
NATURAL STORE
...!
GRR ...
ポツ
DRIP
ポツ
DRIP

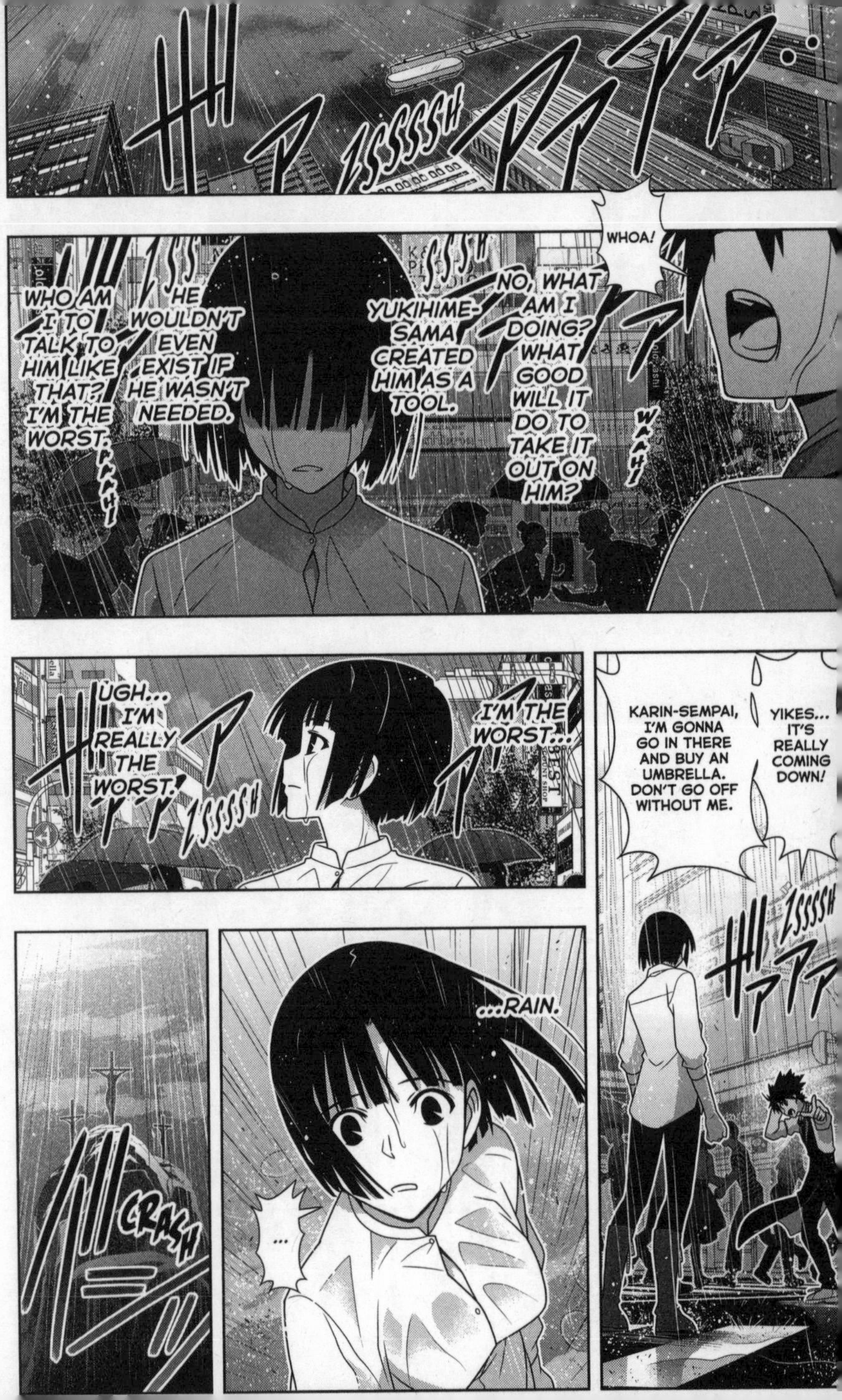
ZSSSSH
WHOA!
NO, WHAT AM I DOING? WHAT GOOD WILL IT DO TO TAKE IT OUT ON HIM?
WAAH!
YUKIHIME-SAMA CREATED HIM AS A TOOL.
SSSH
HE WOULDN'T EVEN EXIST IF HE WASN'T NEEDED.
WHO AM I TO TALK TO HIM LIKE THAT? I'M THE WORST.
PAAH!
YIKES... IT'S REALLY COMING DOWN!
KARIN-SEMPAI, I'M GONNA GO IN THERE AND BUY AN UMBRELLA. DON'T GO OFF WITHOUT ME.
ZSSSSH
I'M THE WORST...
ZSSSSH
UGH... I'M REALLY THE WORST.
...RAIN.
...
CRASH

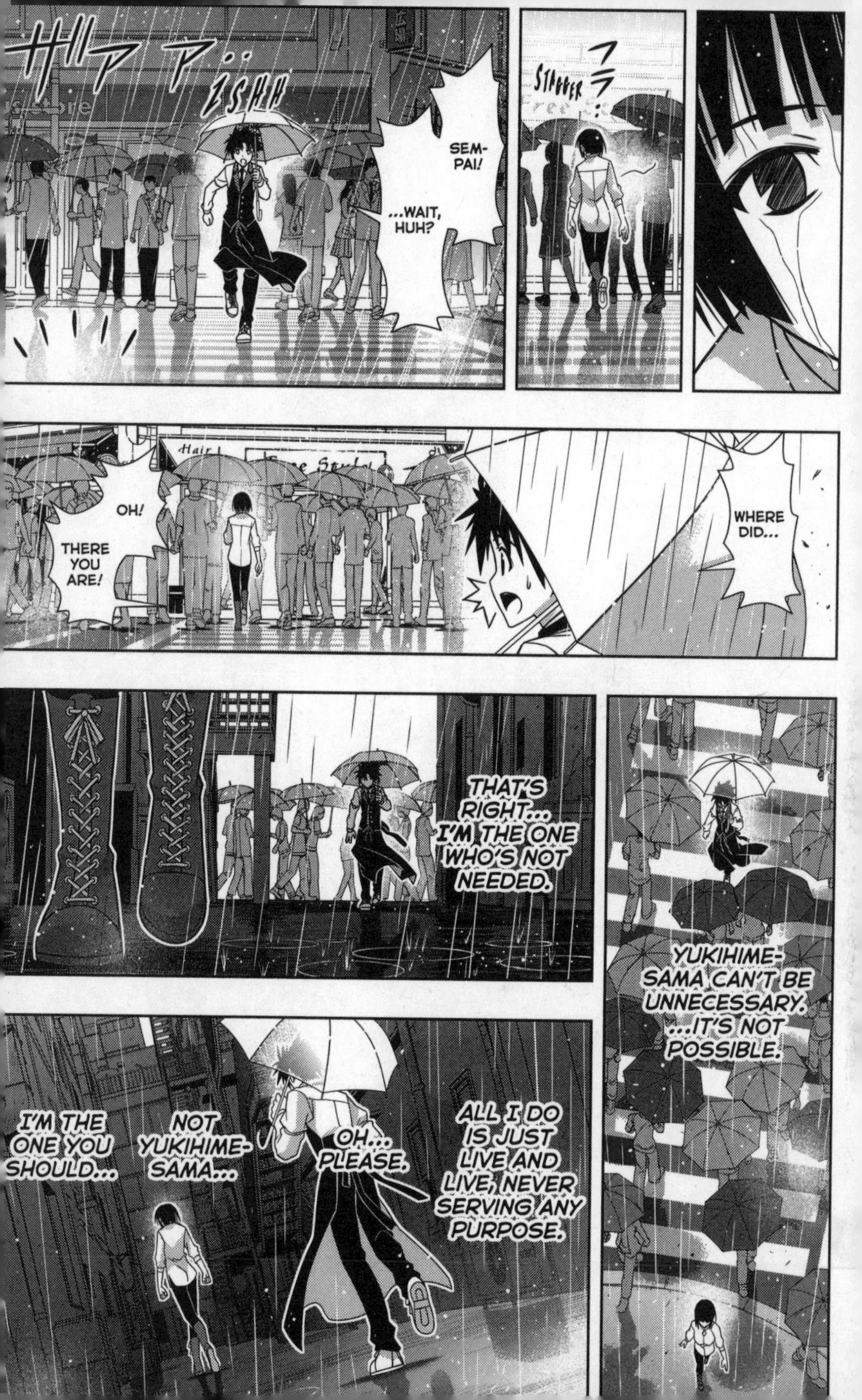
STAGGER
フラ
SEM-PAI!
...WAIT, HUH?
ザァァ...
ZSHHH
WHERE DID...
OH!
THERE YOU ARE!
YUKIHIME-SAMA CAN'T BE UNNECESSARY. ...IT'S NOT POSSIBLE.
THAT'S RIGHT... I'M THE ONE WHO'S NOT NEEDED.
ALL I DO IS JUST LIVE AND LIVE, NEVER SERVING ANY PURPOSE.
OH... PLEASE.
NOT YUKIHIME-SAMA...
I'M THE ONE YOU SHOULD...

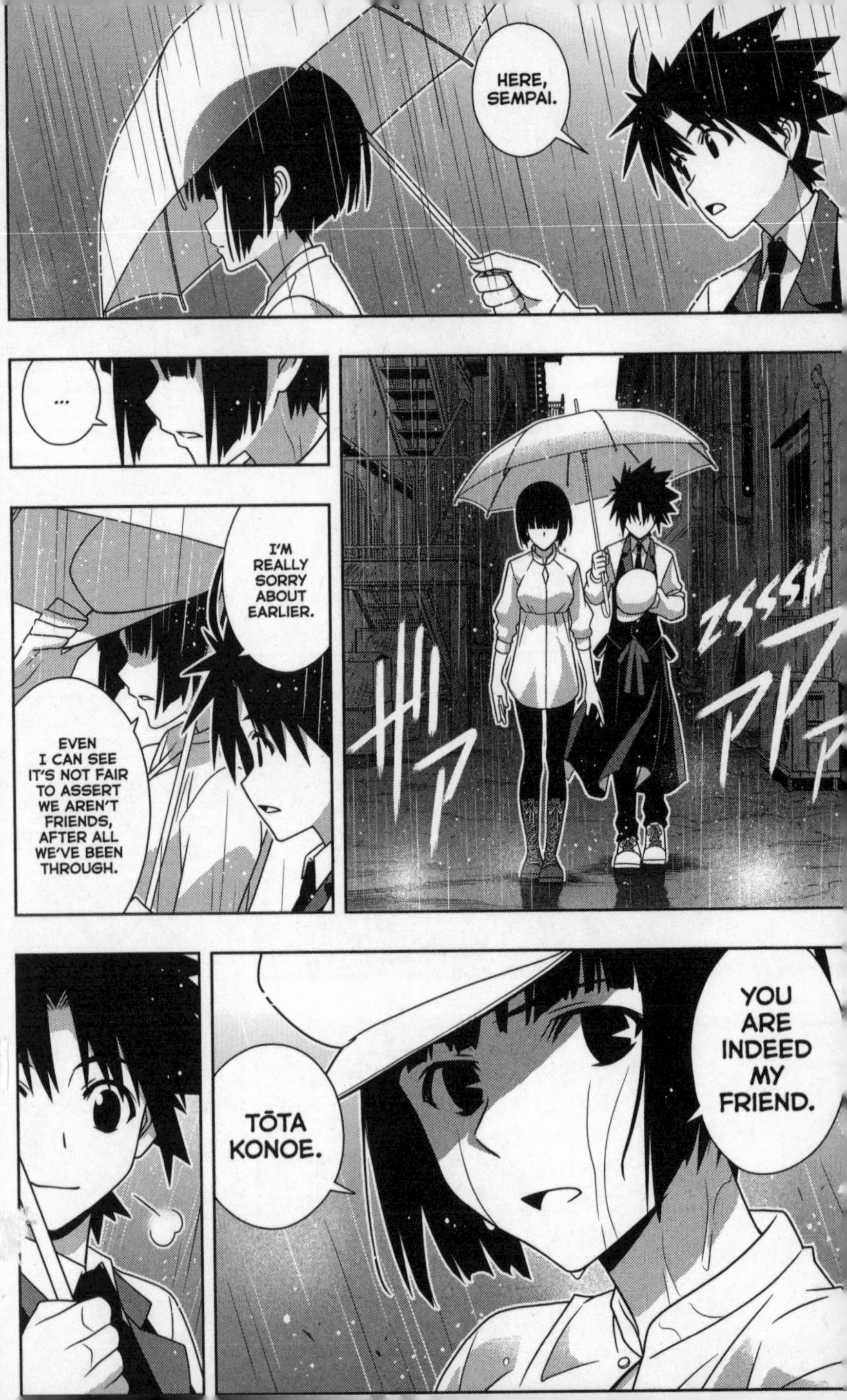
HERE, SEMPAI.
ZSSSH
...
I'M REALLY SORRY ABOUT EARLIER.
EVEN I CAN SEE IT'S NOT FAIR TO ASSERT WE AREN'T FRIENDS, AFTER ALL WE'VE BEEN THROUGH.
YOU ARE INDEED MY FRIEND.
TŌTA KONOE.

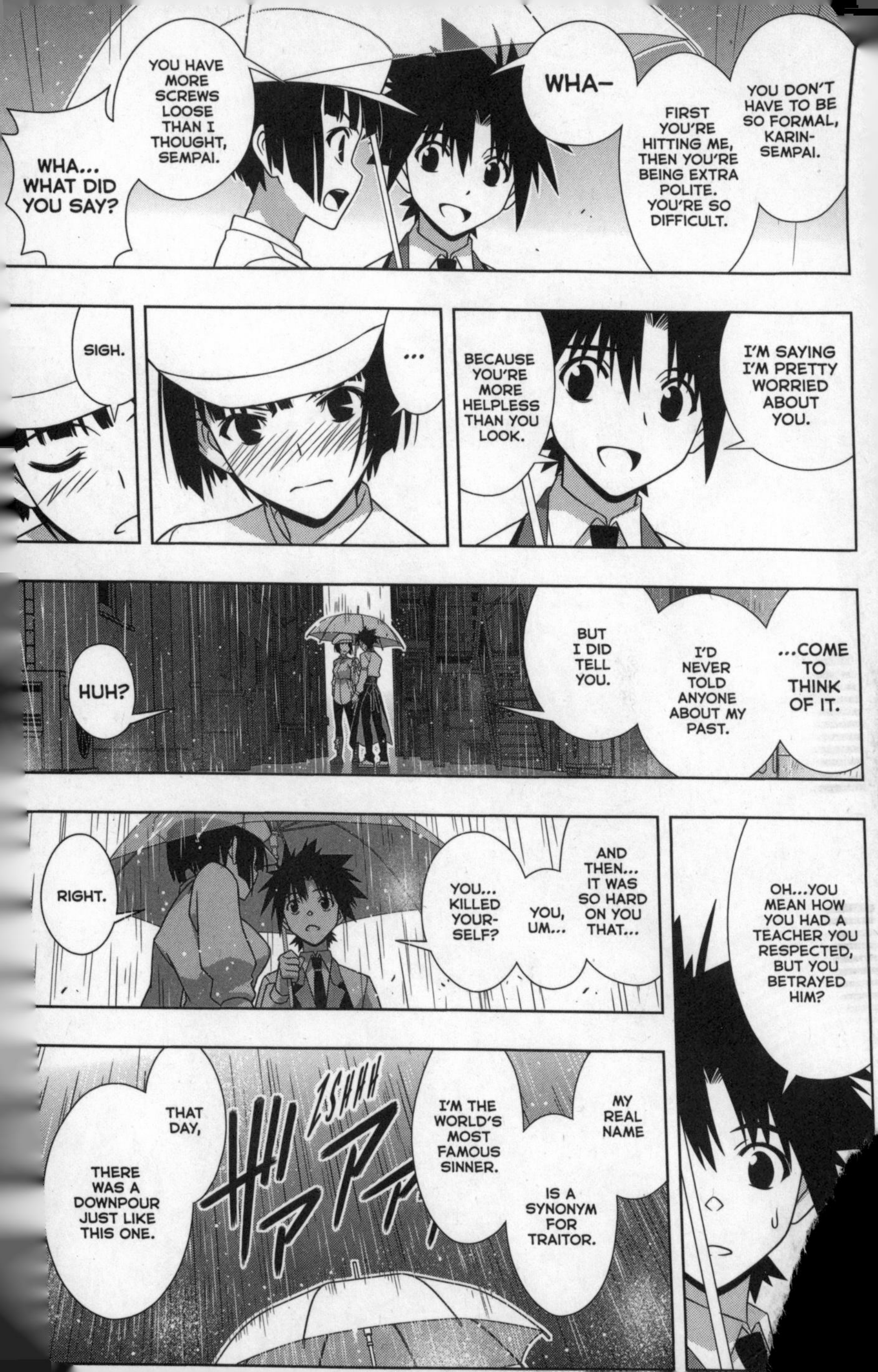
YOU DON'T HAVE TO BE SO FORMAL, KARIN-SEMPAI.
FIRST YOU'RE HITTING ME, THEN YOU'RE BEING EXTRA POLITE. YOU'RE SO DIFFICULT.
WHA–
YOU HAVE MORE SCREWS LOOSE THAN I THOUGHT, SEMPAI.
WHA... WHAT DID YOU SAY?
I'M SAYING I'M PRETTY WORRIED ABOUT YOU.
BECAUSE YOU'RE MORE HELPLESS THAN YOU LOOK.
...
SIGH.
...COME TO THINK OF IT.
I'D NEVER TOLD ANYONE ABOUT MY PAST.
BUT I DID TELL YOU.
HUH?
OH...YOU MEAN HOW YOU HAD A TEACHER YOU RESPECTED, BUT YOU BETRAYED HIM?
AND THEN... IT WAS SO HARD ON YOU THAT...
YOU, UM...
YOU... KILLED YOURSELF?
RIGHT.
MY REAL NAME
IS A SYNONYM FOR TRAITOR.
I'M THE WORLD'S MOST FAMOUS SINNER.
ZSHHH
THAT DAY,
THERE WAS A DOWNPOUR JUST LIKE THIS ONE.

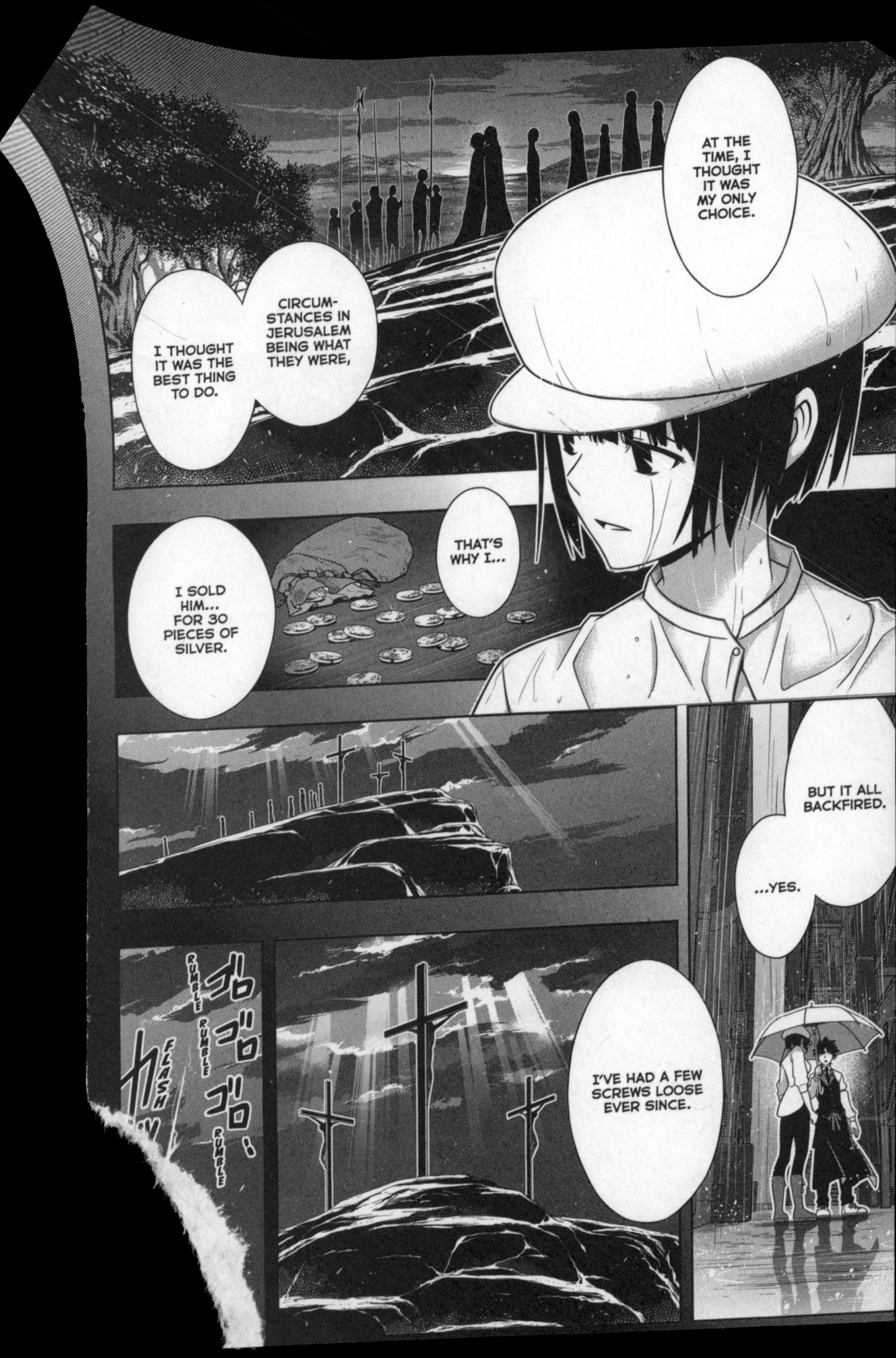
AT THE TIME, I THOUGHT IT WAS MY ONLY CHOICE.
CIRCUM- STANCES IN JERUSALEM BEING WHAT THEY WERE,
I THOUGHT IT WAS THE BEST THING TO DO.
THAT'S WHY I...
I SOLD HIM... FOR 30 PIECES OF SILVER.
BUT IT ALL BACKFIRED.
...YES.
I'VE HAD A FEW SCREWS LOOSE EVER SINCE.
ゴロゴロゴロ
RUMBLE RUMBLE RUMBLE
カッ
FLASH

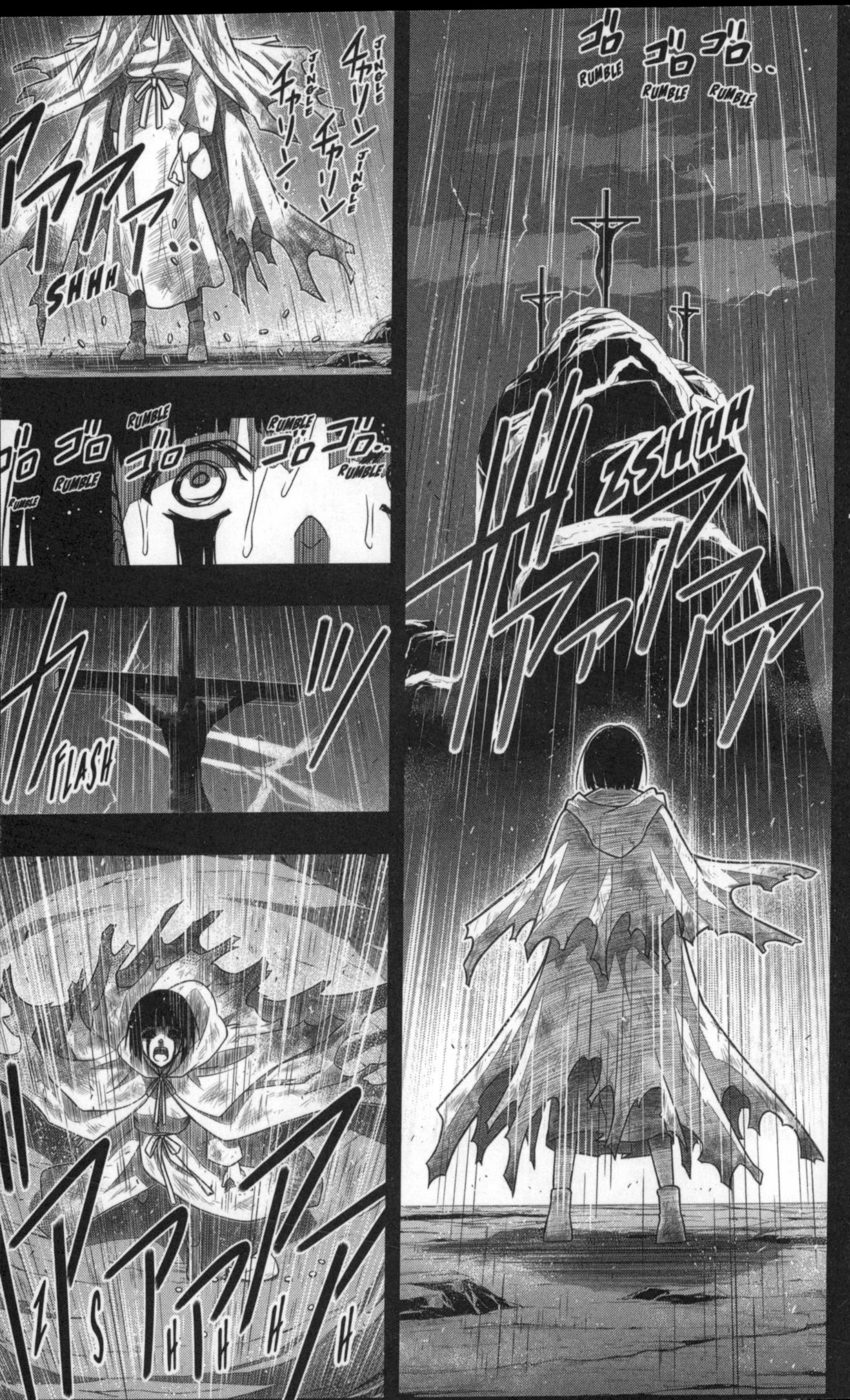
ゴロ ゴロ ゴロ..
RUMBLE RUMBLE RUMBLE
ザァァァァ
ZSHHH
チャリーン チャリーン..
JINGLE JINGLE
ファァァ..
SHHH
ゴロ ゴロ ゴロ ゴロ ゴロ..
RUMBLE RUMBLE RUMBLE RUMBLE RUMBLE
カッ
FLASH
ザァァァァ
ZSHHHH

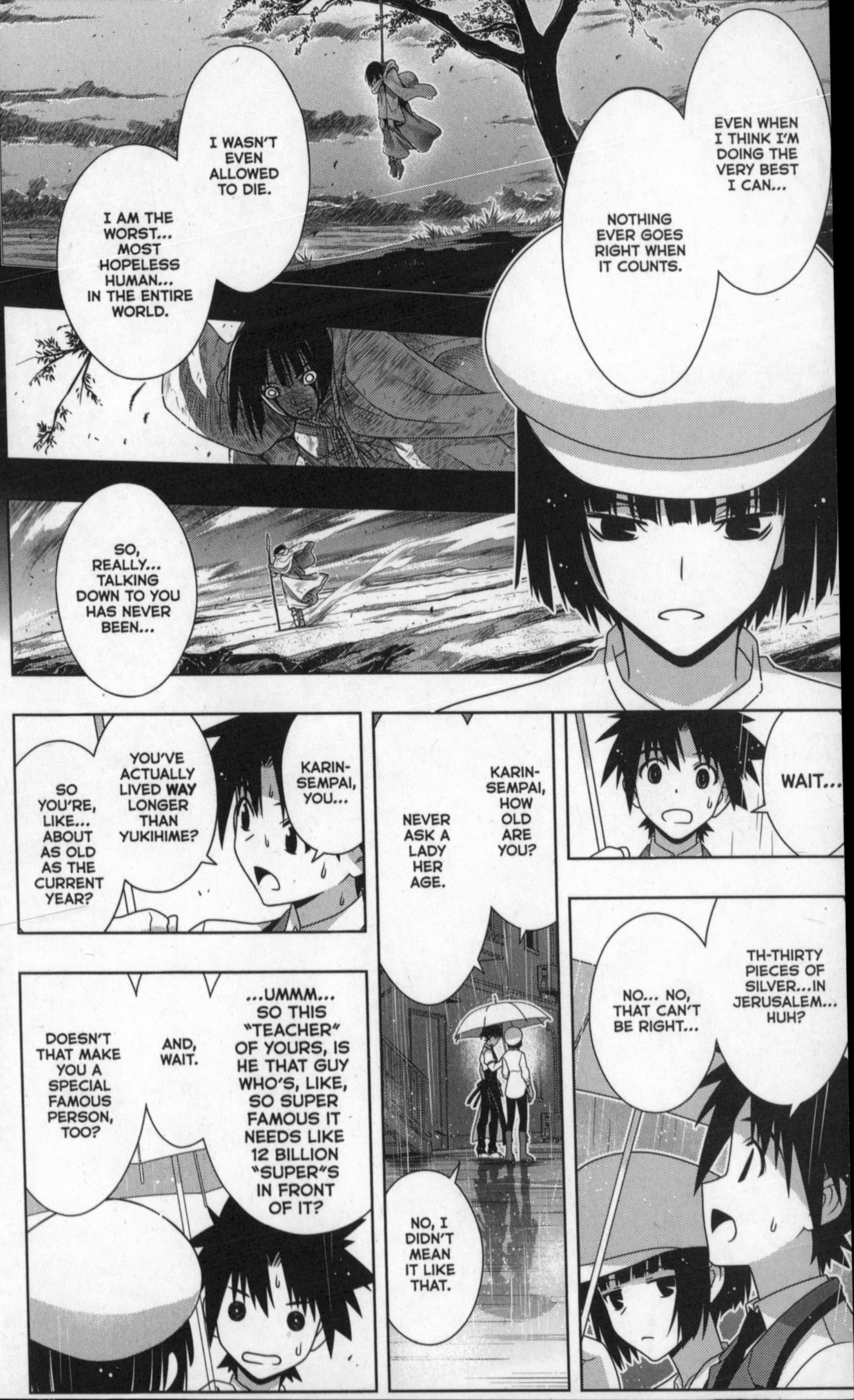
EVEN WHEN I THINK I'M DOING THE VERY BEST I CAN...
NOTHING EVER GOES RIGHT WHEN IT COUNTS.
I WASN'T EVEN ALLOWED TO DIE.
I AM THE WORST... MOST HOPELESS HUMAN... IN THE ENTIRE WORLD.
SO, REALLY... TALKING DOWN TO YOU HAS NEVER BEEN...
WAIT...
KARIN-SEMPAI, HOW OLD ARE YOU?
NEVER ASK A LADY HER AGE.
KARIN-SEMPAI, YOU...
YOU'VE ACTUALLY LIVED WAY LONGER THAN YUKIHIME?
SO YOU'RE, LIKE... ABOUT AS OLD AS THE CURRENT YEAR?
TH-THIRTY PIECES OF SILVER...IN JERUSALEM... HUH?
NO... NO, THAT CAN'T BE RIGHT...
NO, I DIDN'T MEAN IT LIKE THAT.
...UMMM... SO THIS "TEACHER" OF YOURS, IS HE THAT GUY WHO'S, LIKE, SO SUPER FAMOUS IT NEEDS LIKE 12 BILLION "SUPER"S IN FRONT OF IT?
AND, WAIT.
DOESN'T THAT MAKE YOU A SPECIAL FAMOUS PERSON, TOO?

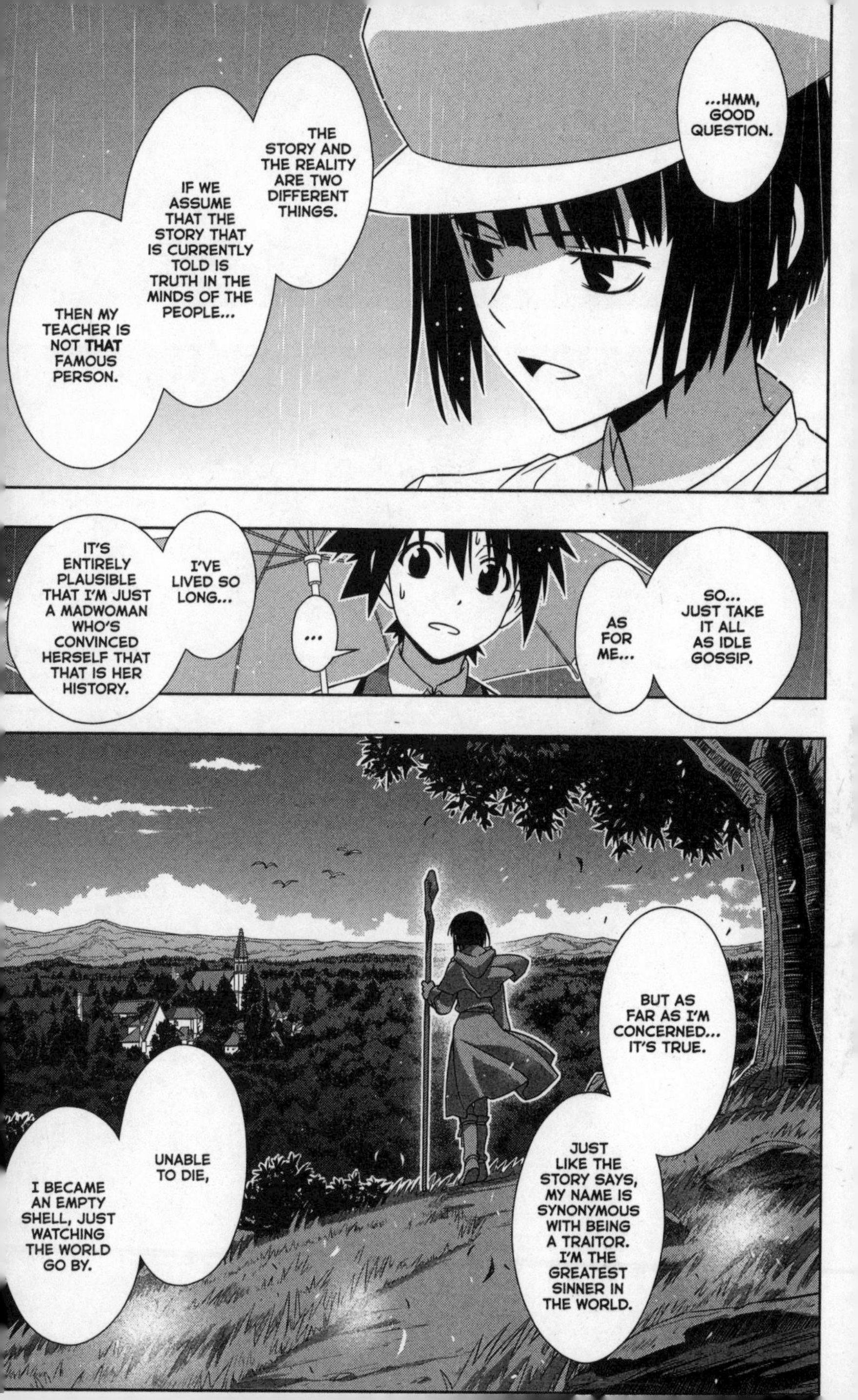
...HMM, GOOD QUESTION.
THE STORY AND THE REALITY ARE TWO DIFFERENT THINGS.
IF WE ASSUME THAT THE STORY THAT IS CURRENTLY TOLD IS TRUTH IN THE MINDS OF THE PEOPLE...
THEN MY TEACHER IS NOT **THAT** FAMOUS PERSON.
SO... JUST TAKE IT ALL AS IDLE GOSSIP.
AS FOR ME...
...
I'VE LIVED SO LONG...
IT'S ENTIRELY PLAUSIBLE THAT I'M JUST A MADWOMAN WHO'S CONVINCED HERSELF THAT THAT IS HER HISTORY.
BUT AS FAR AS I'M CONCERNED... IT'S TRUE.
JUST LIKE THE STORY SAYS, MY NAME IS SYNONYMOUS WITH BEING A TRAITOR. I'M THE GREATEST SINNER IN THE WORLD.
UNABLE TO DIE,
I BECAME AN EMPTY SHELL, JUST WATCHING THE WORLD GO BY.

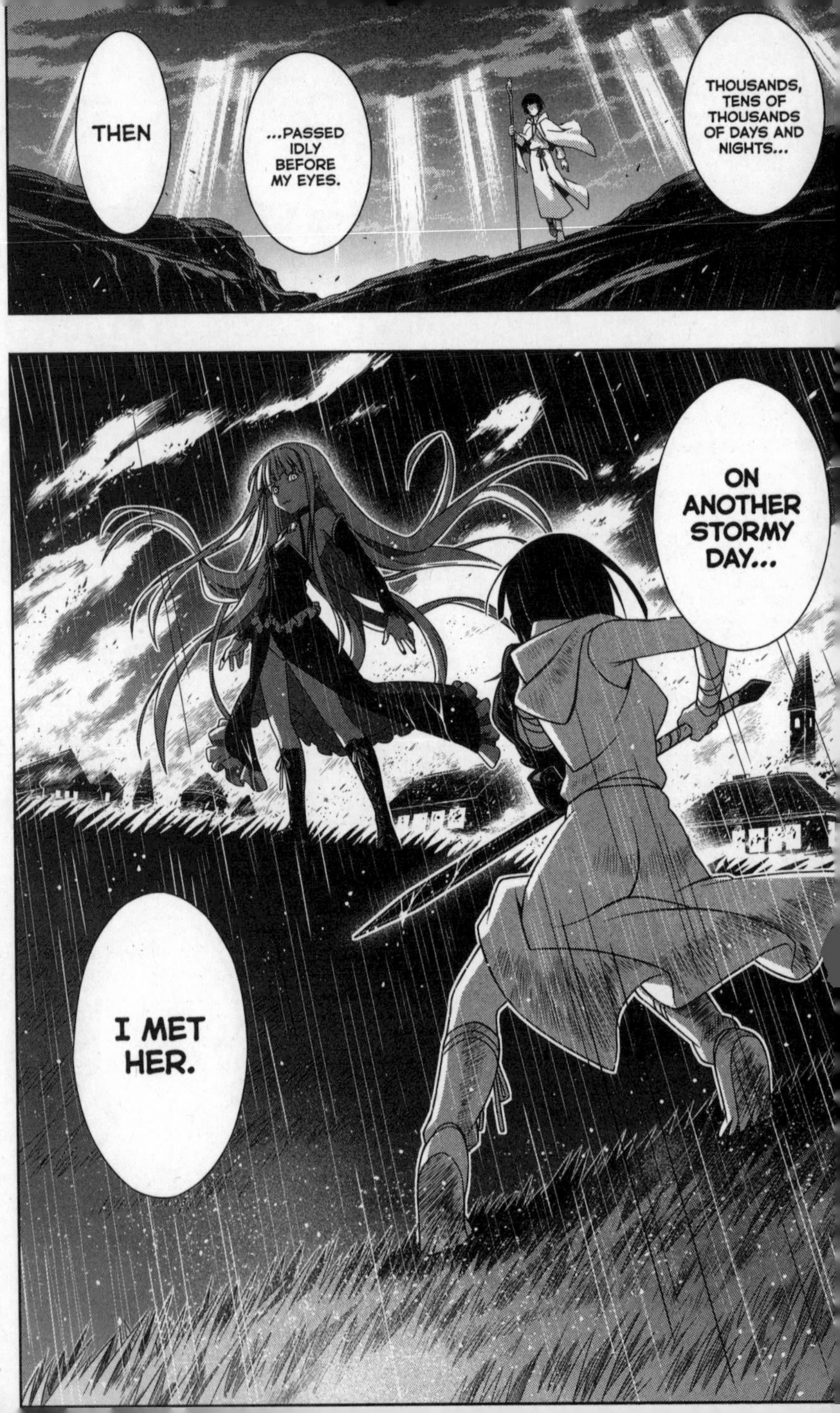
THOUSANDS, TENS OF THOUSANDS OF DAYS AND NIGHTS...
...PASSED IDLY BEFORE MY EYES.
THEN
ON ANOTHER STORMY DAY...
I MET HER.

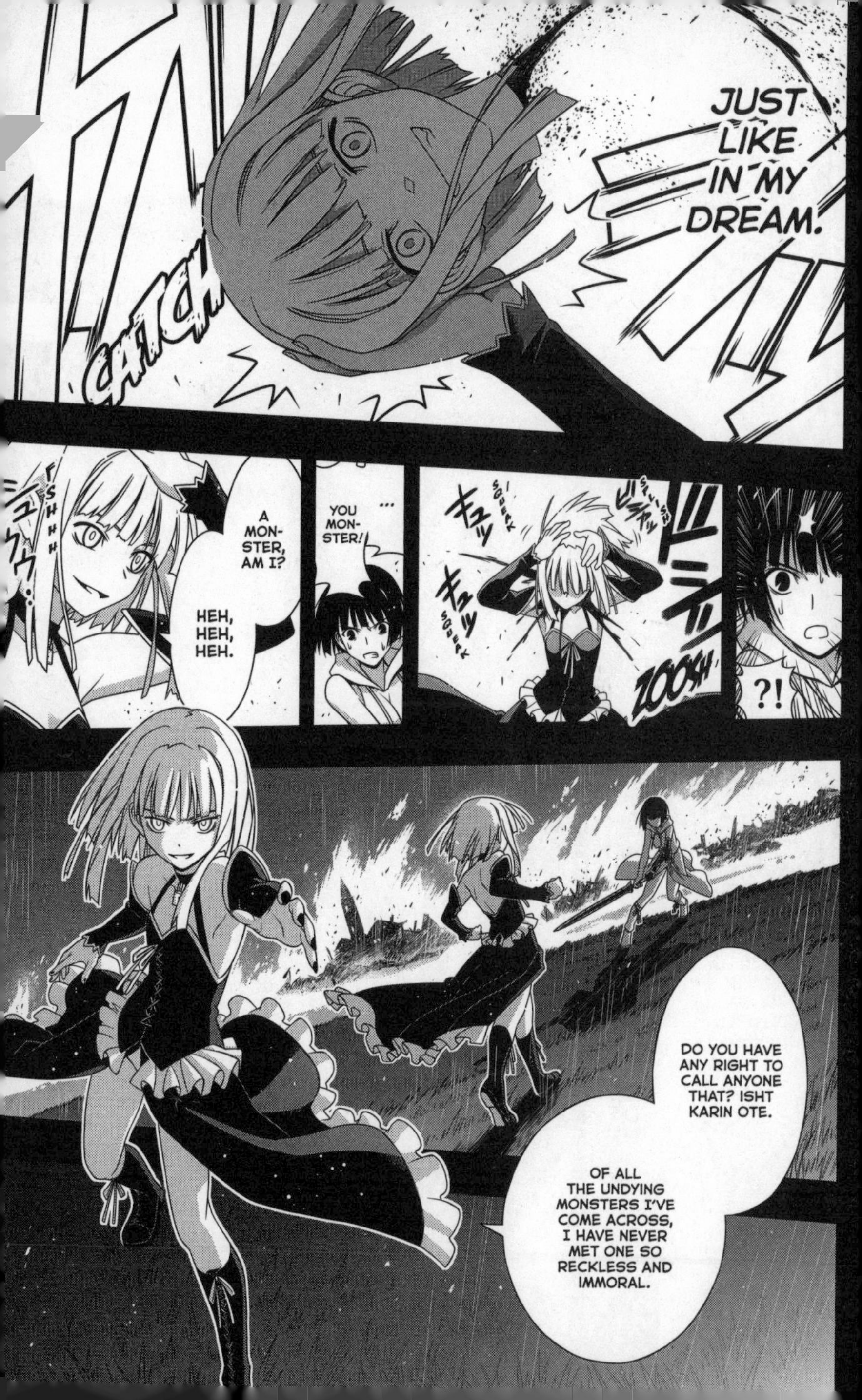
JUST LIKE IN MY DREAM.
CATCH
?!
ZOOSH
SWISH
SQUEAK
SQUEAK
...
YOU MONSTER!
A MONSTER, AM I?
HEH, HEH, HEH.
FSHHH
DO YOU HAVE ANY RIGHT TO CALL ANYONE THAT? ISHT KARIN OTE.
OF ALL THE UNDYING MONSTERS I'VE COME ACROSS, I HAVE NEVER MET ONE SO RECKLESS AND IMMORAL.

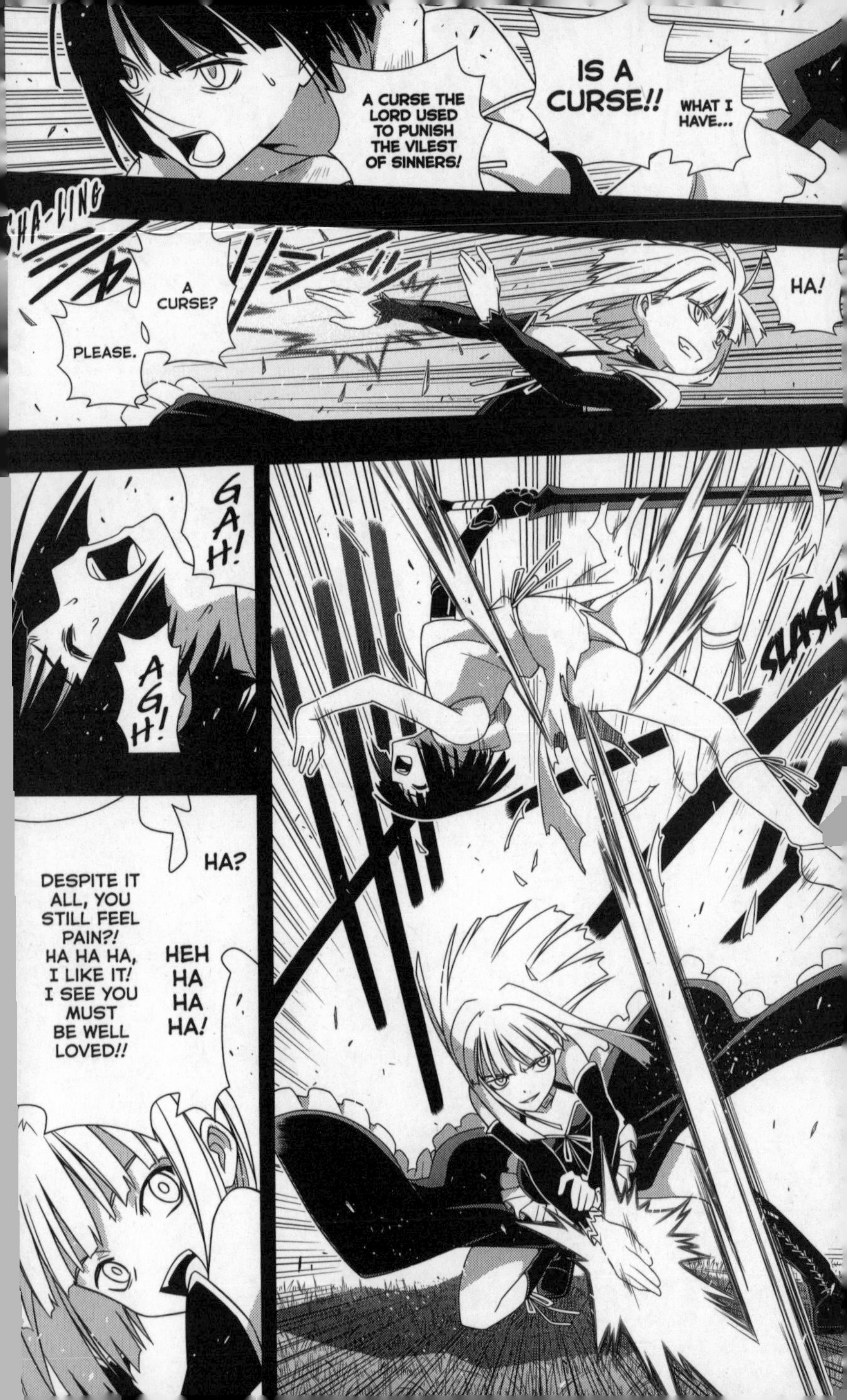
WHAT I HAVE...
IS A CURSE!!
A CURSE THE LORD USED TO PUNISH THE VILEST OF SINNERS!
HA!
A CURSE?
PLEASE.
SHA-LING
SLASH
GAH!
AGH!
HA?
HEH HA HA HA!
DESPITE IT ALL, YOU STILL FEEL PAIN?! HA HA HA, I LIKE IT! I SEE YOU MUST BE WELL LOVED!!

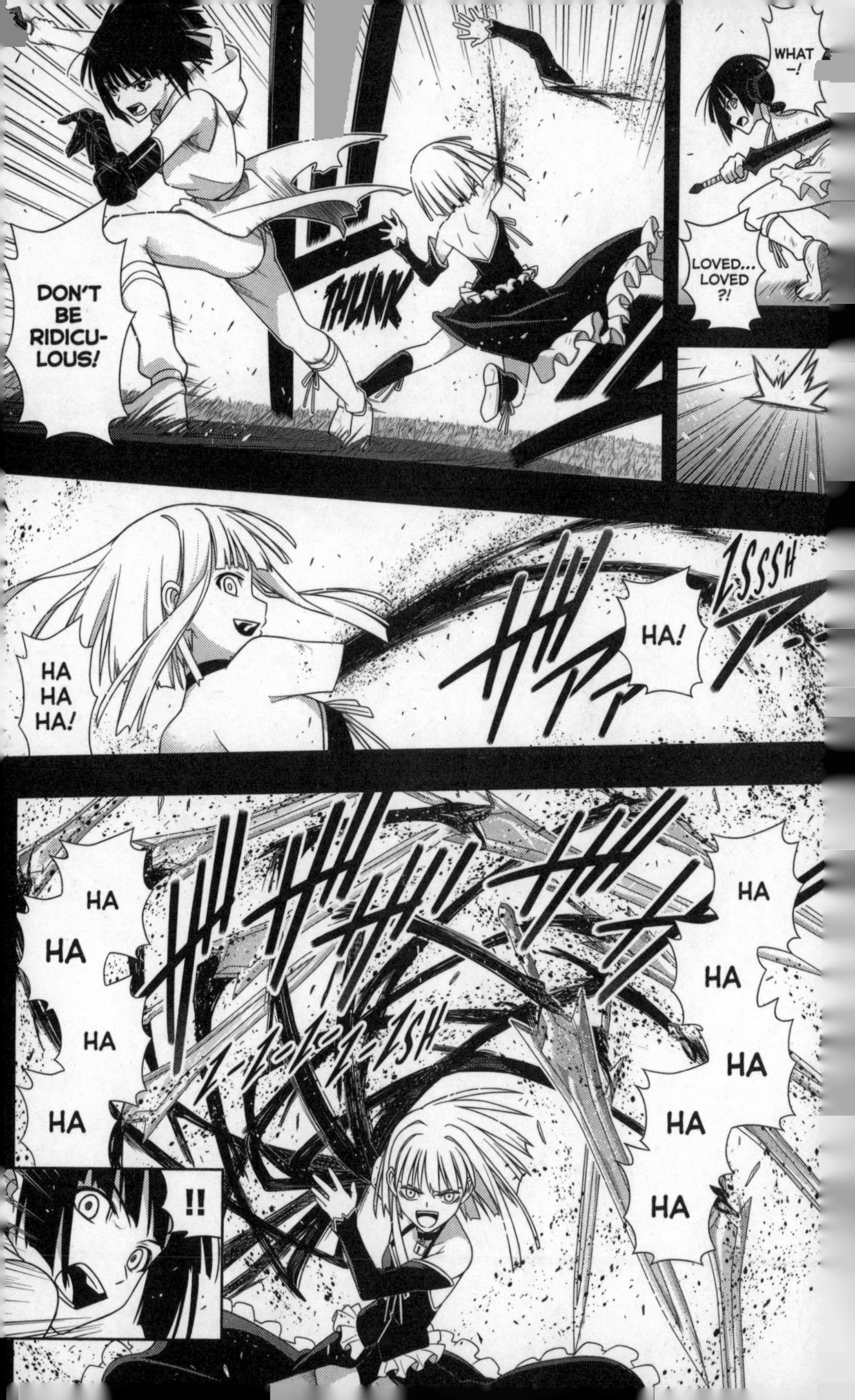
WHAT –!
LOVED... LOVED ?!
THUNK
DON'T BE RIDICU-LOUS!
ZSSSH
HA!
HA HA HA!
HA HA HA HA HA
HA HA HA HA
!!

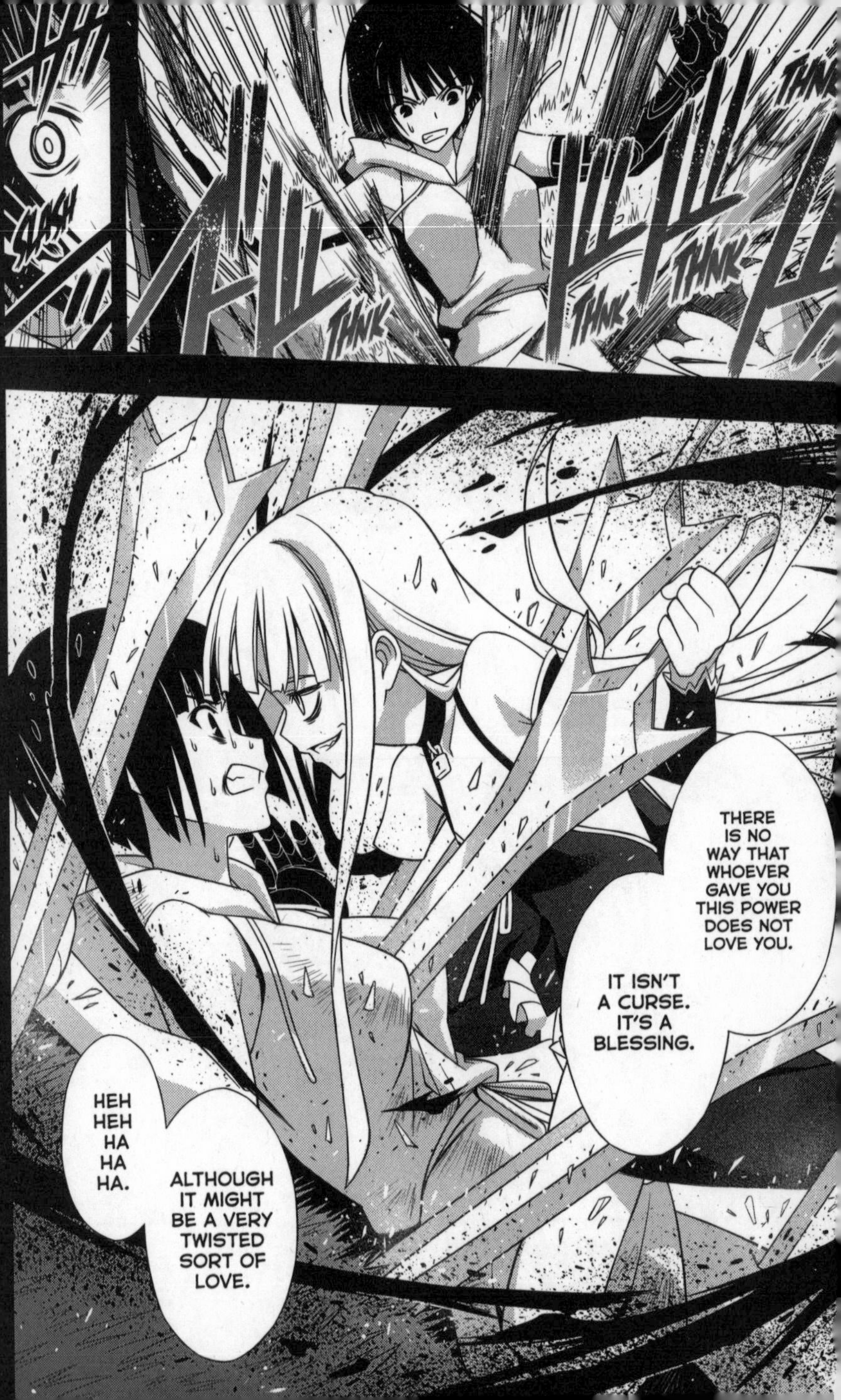
THNK
THNK
THNK
THNK
THNK
THERE IS NO WAY THAT WHOEVER GAVE YOU THIS POWER DOES NOT LOVE YOU.
IT ISN'T A CURSE. IT'S A BLESSING.
HEH HEH HA HA HA.
ALTHOUGH IT MIGHT BE A VERY TWISTED SORT OF LOVE.

悠久 HOLDER!

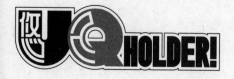

# UQ HOLDER!

STAFF

Ken Akamatsu

Takashi Takemoto

Kenichi Nakamura

Keiichi Yamashita

Yuri Sasaki

Madoka Akanuma


Thanks to Ran Ayanaga

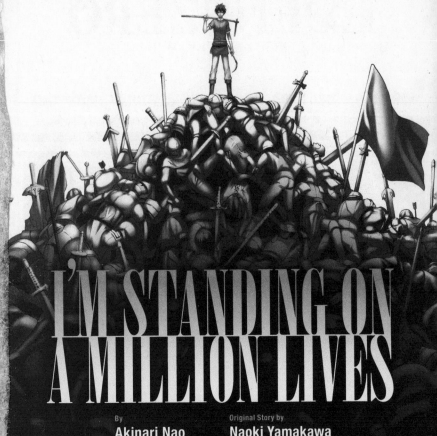

# I'M STANDING ON A MILLION LIVES

By
**Akinari Nao**

Original Story by
**Naoki Yamakawa**

**A dark and sexy body-horror action manga perfect for fans of *Prison School* and *High School of the Dead*!**

Shuichi Kagaya is a smart kid, and most smart kids his age would be thinking about college. Shuichi is also a monster, and he's smart enough to know that monsters don't go to college. But after he uses his monstrous form to save his classmate Claire Aoki, it doesn't matter what his plans for the future were, because he's not the one making the decisions anymore. Now that the seductive, sadistic Claire knows Shuichi's secret, she's got her own ideas about what a monster is good for—because he's not the first monster she's met...

**KC**
**KODANSHA COMICS**

# GLEIPNIR

Gleipnir © Sun Takeda/Kodansha Ltd.

**"You and me together...we would be unstoppable."**